Hildebrand's Travel Guide

MEXICO

Publisher
K+G, KARTO+GRAFIK Verlagsges. mbH

Schönberger Weg 15–17
6000 Frankfurt/Main 90
First Edition 1986
Printed in West Germany
ISBN 3-88989-060-1

Distributed in the English Market by
Roger Lascelles, Cartographic and Travel Publisher,
47 York Road, Brentford, Middlesex TW8 0QP
ISBN 0-903909-47-2

Distributed in USA by
Hippocrene Books,
171 Madison Avenue/New York/N.Y. 10016
ISBN 0-87052-226-4

Authors
Matthias von Debschitz, Dr. Wolf-Günter Thieme,
Werner Schmidt, Rudolf Wicker, Dr. Gerhard Beese,
Hans-Horst Skupy, Ortrun Egelkraut, Dr. Elisabeth Siefer,
Robert Valerio

Edited by
Bernadette Boyle, Ellen Knutson

Photo Credits
Matthias von Debschitz, Frank Deinhard, Hans Patzelt,
Dr. Wolf-Günter Thieme, Klaus Wolff

Illustrations
Eckart Müller, Peter Rank, Manfred Rup

Maps
K+G, KARTO+GRAFIK Verlagsgesellschaft mbH

Translation
Jacqueline Baroncini

Lithography
Haußmann Repro, 6100 Darmstadt

Type Setting
LibroSatz, 6239 Kriftel

Printed by
Schmitt+Läufer, 6300 Gießen

Contents

1

2

Holiday Inn
MIL 973
FELICIDADES
Agua Mineral
Peñafiel
EL MEJOR TEHUACAN
SAUZA
GRAN RESERVA
7 SANMARCOS
Calanda

3
DE BELLAS ARTES

4

BN
HN
UNIVERSIDAD NACIONAL D MEXICO
PLUS
PTOLOMEO
COPERNICO

5

6

7

8

9

10

11

12

13

14

15

16

17

18

19

20

22

23

24

25

26

27

28

29

30

31

33

34

35

36

38

39

42

40

41

43

44

45

46

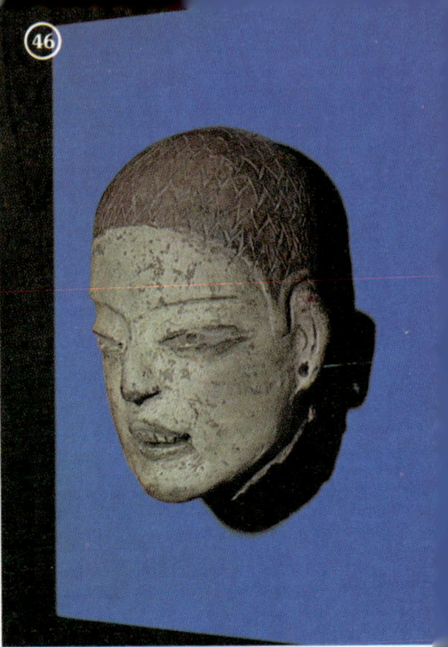

47

48

49

50

51

53

Captions

1. View of the colonial city of Guanajuato; in the middle stands the Jesuit church.

2. Entrance to the Insurgentes metro station at the intersection of Insurgentes and Chapultepec – one of Mexico City's busiest intersections. Chapultepec Castle is visible in the distance.

3. Palacio de Bellas Artes (Palace of Fine Arts), Mexico City's opera house and concert hall. Located in the city centre, this white marble building completed in 1934 is the home of the famous Ballet Folklórico de Mexico.

4. The library of the Universidad Nacional de Mexico. The façade, the work of the artist and architect Juan O'Gorman, is covered completely with stone mosaics.

5. Pilgrims gathered before the cathedral of Our Lady of Guadelupe. On the hill in the background stands the sanctuary of Tepeyac.

6. Hustle and bustle at the famous market of Toluca, the capital of the state of Mexico.

7. and 8. Maya women of Yucatán in traditional dress.

9. The face of this "Veracruzano" displays typical mestizo features.

10. A peddlar of "antiques" in Teotihuacán.

11. A seller at the fish market in Mazatlán.

12. Dancer in festive Spanish dress at a performance in Guadalajara.

13. One of the flower-adorned tourist boats which plies the canals of Xochimilco, Mexico City.

14. Mariachi band in Xochimilco.

15. The "Danza de las Plumas" (Dance of the Feathers) performed by the Ballet Folklórico at the Palacio de Bellas Artes.

16. Children outside a typical Maya hut in Yucatán.

17. Village street in Yucatán.

18. A farmer and his children outside their home in Veracruz.

19. Woman at a market in the Mexican Plateau displaying a typical way of carrying heavy loads.

20. The richly-decorated cupola of the "Rosario" (Chapel of the Rosary) of the monastery church of Santo Domingo in Puebla.

21. Children at a nuptial mass in Puebla.

22. The reconstructed façade of the Pyramid of the Sun at Teotihuacán.

23. Chichén Itzá, Yucatán: "El Castillo", the temple of Kukulkan, as seen from the Temple of the Warriors. Maya-Toltec, 11th century A. D.

24. Chichén Itzá, Yucatán: The Temple of the Warriors and its surrounding pillars. Maya-Toltec, 11th century A. D.

25. Chichén Itzá, Yucatán: The interior of the Temple of the Warriors. In the foreground, the Chacmool; behind it, the Snake Pillars. Maya-Toltec, 11th century A. D.

26. Oaxaca: The Observatory at Monte Albán. In the background, the North Platform. Zapotecan, up to the 12th century A. D.

27. Uxmal, Yucatán: The ceremonial buildings of the city. In the centre, the House of the Turtles; to the left, the Quadrangle of the Nuns; and to the right, the Temple of the Magician. Maya, 7th–9th centuries A. D.

28. Palenque, Chiapas: View from the north acropolis. To the left, the palace with the observatory tower; to the right, the Temple of the Cross. Classic Maya, 7th–9th centuries A. D.

29. El Tajín, Veracruz: The main ceremonial square. To the right is the Pyramid of the Niches. Totonac, 11th–14th centuries A. D.

30. Cholula, Puebla: The Great Pyramid overgrown with vegetation and crowned by the church of Santa Maria de los Remedios. 6th–16th centuries A. D.

31. Tulum, Quintana Roo: The temple platform "El Castillo" overlooking the Caribbean Sea. Cocom Maya, 15th–16th centuries A. D.

32. Tula, Hidalgo: The platform of the Temple of Tlahuitzcalpantecutli, the Morning Star God. Toltec, 9th–10th centuries A. D.

33. Tula, Hidalgo: The atlantes, colossal statues of Toltec eagle warriors, atop the Temple of the Morning Star God. 9th–10th centuries A. D.

34. Villahermosa, La Venta Park (an open-air museum), Tabasco: A "cabeza", a gigantic stone Olmec head found on the Gulf coast. Circa 6th–4th centuries B. C.

35. Villahermosa, La Venta Park (an open-air museum), Tabasco: Figure with a shaved head holding an offering. Olmec, circa 6th–4th centuries B. C.

36. Museum of Anthropology, Mexico City: The Calendar Stone with the face of the sun god Tonatiuh at its centre (see chapter "The Aztec Calendar", p. 239–241). Aztec, 15th century A. D.

37. Museum of Anthropology, Mexico City: Head of a huge clay idol from the Valley of Mexico. Pre-Classic culture, circa 4th century B. C.

38. Palenque Museum, Chiapas: Glyphs carved out of gypsum plaster. Classic Maya, 8th century A. D.

39. Museum of Anthropology, Mexico City: Carved stela from Yaxchilan, Chiapas depicting a seated kazik (tribal chief). Classic Maya, 8th century A. D.

40. Museum of Anthropology, Mexico City: Clay figure of a priest or a god wearing a necklace of maize kernels. Huaxtec, from the state of Veracruz.

41. Museum of Anthropology, Mexico City: Clay figure of a kazik or a priest dressed in a richly decorated garment and wearing fine jewels. Mixtec, 14th–15th centuries A. D.

42. Museum of Anthropology, Mexico City: The "Rey de Kabáh", a larger-than-life limestone head of the God of Maize with a mustache, tatoos and a crown of maize. Architectonic sculpture from Kabáh, Yucatán. Classic Maya, 7th–8th centuries A. D.

43. Museum of Anthropology, Mexico City: Votive clay figures belonging to the so-called Jaina group. Gulf coast of Campeche, Classic Maya, 7th–8th centuries A. D.

44. Museum of Anthropology, Mexico City: Large figure of a seated god found in Oaxaca. Zapotecan grave statue, 8th–10th centuries A. D.

45. Museum of Anthropology, Mexico City: Large clay earth mother figure from the Valley of Mexico. Pre-Classic culture, circa 1st–2nd centuries A. D.

46. Museum of Anthropology, Mexico City: Head of a votive terracotta statue from Tlatilco, Mexico. Late Formative, circa 2nd–1st centuries B. C.

47. Museum of Anthropology, Mexico City: Clay vessel in the shape of an acrobat deposited in a grave in Tlatilco. Valley of Mexico, Late Formative period, 3rd–1st centuries B. C.

48. Museum of Anthropology, Mexico City: "Tlalocan", Paradise of the Rain God Tlaloc. Reproduction of a mural from Tepantitlán. Classic Teotihuacán, circa 6th century A. D.

49. Museum of Anthropology, Mexico City: Stone votive mask covered with jadestone mosaics. Classic Teotihuacán; circa 6th century A. D.

50. Museum of Anthropology, Mexico City: Monumental statue of the water goddess Chalchiutlicue made of volcanic tufa. Early Classic Teotihuacán, circa 5th century A. D.

51. National Palace, Mexico City: Detail of a mural by Diego Rivera showing the Tlatelolco market with the market arbiter in the middle and the city of Tenochtitlán in the background.

52. Highland landscape with saguaro cacti and maguey agaves.

53. The rugged landscape of the Barranca del Cobre (Copper Canyon) in Chihuahua (see chapter "Chihuahua-Pacifico", p. 263–265).

54. The beach at Puerto Vallarta, Jalisco. This popular resort on the Pacific Ocean lies within easy reach of Guadalajara, the second-largest city in the country.

55. The beach promenade of Puerto Vallarta.

First Encounters

Spellbound, I watched Martha as she manoeuvred her car through the pandemonium of the capital city's traffic. Mexico City, probably the world's largest metropolis by now, is confusing. Broad streets flanked by walls of multi-storey buildings alternate with charming colonial districts. Elevated highways intersect spacious palm-fringed avenues. Baroque churches, monuments, and parks and gardens dot a cityscape which goes on and on as far as the eye can see – and scattered throughout are cars, cars and more cars. This chaos of vehicles may seem inextricable to the uninitiated, but Martha, all the while chatting merrily and gesticulating with her expressive hands, negotiated it with such ease that I could only sit and stare in amazement. In no time at all, we were in the Zona Rosa, Mexico City's fashionable restaurant and shopping district.

A boy flagged us into a large parking lot. "Yes, go ahead and wash it", Martha said in reply to the question the boy in the cashier's booth mumbled as he handed her a parking stub. As this exchange was going on, another car pulled in just inches away from us. "They live off tips", she said. "What do you feel like eating?"

Martha was my first "blind date" in Mexico. One day, a friend of mine handed me the telephone receiver and said, "This is Martha. She speaks good English and loves Europe. Why don't you say a few words to her?" Without hesitating, Martha agreed to go out to dinner with me. She was helpful, friendly and full of life – and she was an excellent guide. Like all Mexicans, she loved her country and got carried away when she talked about it. This kind of patriotism is contagious – even the foreigner finds himself smitten, his enthusiasm aroused.

We went to one of Mexico City's big, popular restaurants. First, we were led to the bar where we could study the leather-bound menu over an aperitif. It was early afternoon, every table was taken. Here, in the restaurants of the Zona Rosa, the business community meets for lunch… and often stays until evening! The high society comes here to see and be seen as well.

Young couples approached us with arms opened wide to embrace my companion. A peck on the cheek for the ladies – everyone seemed to know everyone else. I mumbled my pleased-to-meet-you's ("mucho gusto") and immediately found myself being drawn into conversations from all sides. Once again, I was struck by the air of spontaneous cordiality that filled the room. Invitations rained upon me from left and right. "Come see us at our house in Acapulco this weekend!" "We're throwing a party at our hacienda this Friday, are you two coming?" At first, I thought these people were just being polite – after all, who was I to be invited? But no, they were all sincere. It was only natural that their friendship with Martha would extend to me, a stranger. Besides, Mexicans are, quite simply, very sociable people.

By the time our maitre d' led us to our table, the food we had ordered was ready, and we were served immediately. We began with a delicious "sopa de elote" or cream of maize soup. In a corner of the restaurant, a five-man band played traditional melodies from Veracruz; the lovely strains of the harp could be heard above all the rest. It was obvious that my initiation into Mexican life was being effected in the most pleasant way possible – and where else in the world could a newcomer get a taste of the best so soon? Sitting there, I could feel the fascination of Mexico take hold of me – a fascination which has yet to let me go.

(v. Debschitz)

Esta es su casa

It began in a rather complicated way. Martha had spent five minutes on the telephone tracing the route for me on the map, but later, in my hired car and with the map spread open on my lap, I found myself becoming confused by the Indian names on the street signs: Chilpandingo, Citlatépetl, Cacahuamilpa – they all looked the same to me.

I had set out early to get where I was going so as not to disappoint my Mexican hosts – I knew there was one thing in particular that was expected of me as a German, and that was punctuality!

Not that it would ever induce them to be punctual themselves! No, the hostess in hair curlers and a dressing gown only wants the satisfaction of seeing that the German guest invited for 8:30 pm actually arrives at 8:30 pm. Fine, but then he'll have to wait – with a drink in his hand, of course – until the other guests arrive and the party can begin… and that won't be for another hour or so.

When in Mexico, it never hurts to be as European as one is. With this in mind, I picked up a big bouquet of roses for the lady of the house at one of the fabulous flower markets of Mexico City. It was incredible: an armful of the most magnificent roses costs about as much as a spray of violets does at home. "I'll take five dozen, if you please."

Sweltering in my coat and tie (I was properly dressed for this visit), I drove up and down the Colonia Condesa district in a hopeless search for one little street. Finally, I spotted a post office, or rather, a stand out in the open where letters are postmarked, telegrammes taken down and packages piled up. Ignoring the queues, which were made up mostly of "muchachas", housemaids, sporting aprons and primly plaited hair, I went right up to a window. "Disculpame, señor", I said, trying to get the attention of the master of the rubber stamp. Without a word, he indicated the far end of the queue. In Mexico, one waits one's turn –

and that's exactly what I did before finally making my enquiry about the location of that elusive street. At this point, I was already 20 minutes late.

When I reached the small colonial house with the large wooden door, I could feel the beads of sweat rising on my forehead. How embarrassing to be so late, especially considering that I knew my hosts only from the telephone. I pressed the doorbell. From inside, I heard a muffled "quien?" (who?). The housemaid didn't open the heavy, colonial door, however, until I had explained exactly who I was. She led me into a huge living room which actually looked more like a reception hall. From the outside, the house didn't look half this big. Antiques were strategically placed throughout the room and the Papal blessings hung framed on a pillar – a souvenir of a European holiday. Even though Mexico has officially broken with Rome, the Mexican people still regard the Pope as the highest religious authority.

"Bienvenido. Esta es su casa!" That simple sentence spoken by my host contained all the warmth inherent in the Mexican character. It translates as "This is your house" or "Look upon my home as your home". The spontaneous hospitality of the Mexicans is proverbial; for them, a stranger is a friend first. A welcome like this dispels the atmosphere of formality in a matter of minutes. I studied my host's open, intelligent face – a face upon which the Indian elements of the Mexican race were finely chiselled. He noticed how exhausted I was. "You're a little early, young man. My daughter is still out shopping, but she'll be back in no time."

(v. Debschitz)

The Clash

In the market you see an Indian woman wearing a woven shawl, striped red and orange. But... don't red and orange clash? Well, yes, they do. So do green and turquoise, gold and plastic, concrete and bamboo. Mexico, like most Latin American countries, is known as a "country of contrasts". Contrasts in scenery and climate; also social contrasts, riches and poverty... More than contrasts, they are clashes, centuries old, derived from the great original clash of Cortez and Moctezuma. This historic confrontation has political, economic and social consequences today, the Mexican identity being a result of it and the subsequent clashes it engendered. The casual visitor to Mexico cannot help noticing these clashes: he will be shocked by the sight of hovels alongside skyscrapers or amused by horses and carts in the same street as Chevrolets, but in his short stay he can hardly hope to resolve or understand these oppositions. He could well spend the first fortnight grasping the fact that what he is seeing is real.

Since the visitor can do nothing about the negative political aspects of the clash, he might as well concentrate on its lighter side: the way it marks what is typically Mexican in colours, textures and materials – its aesthetic dimension. Take, for instance, this woman with her red and orange shawl. Round her neck she has a string of gaudy, obviously plastic beads, and in her ears, a pair of huge, antique, 24-carat gold earrings. How can she "stoop" to wearing plastic beads when she possesses jewels like the ones in her ears, which are clearly not only historic heirlooms but also worth a bomb?

In Europe, in the U. S., gold and plastic are always separated. The one is expensive, the other cheap, the one is decorative, the other functional: both are laden with conflicting social and aesthetic connotations. Before the Spanish came, however, the Mexican Indians attached no particular importance to gold. Where Old World kings fought over precious metals, the Aztecs fought over flowers!

Here is another clash sure to make the Western visitor queasy: a fruit bowl containing fresh ripe mangoes and, alongside these exotic delights, shiny plastic grapes. They are not even a good imitation. But in Mexico, there is no great sensitivity to the discrepancy between "natural" and "artificial". While Europeans are desperately trying to "get back to the earth", obsessed with the "real thing", Latin Americans are still far too close to the earth and to nature to feel any desire to "get back" to it. Most of them have never got away from it in the first place! They will serve you real coffee, picked off the bush in the backyard, in a paper cup without flinching.

Trivial as it seems, this clash can be a subtle source of disappointment for the traveller, who generally wants to see the authentic thing, the pure thing. He is dismayed when the "native" he has finally tracked down emerges out of the forest with a Japanese digital watch on his wrist. He wants everybody to speak some Indian language. He wants virgin beaches. Inside he instinctively concentrates on the exquisite Indian ceramic pots, the woven straw mats, desperately ignoring the polythene bags and PVC pipes in a vain effort to make real the vision he has travelled thousands of miles to see.

He does this, no doubt, because he is a Westerner, a native of a culture severed from its roots, its myths and its crafts by the Industrial Revolution. Perhaps by coming to Mexico he is unconsciously looking for his own distant past, his lost "authenticity". And Mexico refuses to give him this: the earthenware and Tupperware lie side by side on the table, slowly, insidiously filling him with a vague disillusionment he feels but cannot formulate.

The best advice to him might be to accept Mexico as it is. Give up your nostalgia for rustic furniture, for an imaginary paradise of wood and stone. Don't try to overlook the clash, just realize that part of Mexico's attraction lies in its paradoxes,

its mixing of impossibles. Although the clash may be a problem, it is also an art form. Who else but a Mexican, for instance, could come up with avocado flavoured ice cream? Visitors who sample this unique treat in the market at Oaxaca will find consolation for paradise lost!

(Valerio)

The Mexicans: An Attempt at Definition

There is a well-known story told in Mexico, the punch line of which makes the Mexicans chuckle with delight in spite of themselves: When God created the world, he distributed all the great and important things evenly throughout its many lands. One land in particular, however, seemed to be favoured above all the rest: he endowed it with wonderful beaches and seas full of fish, all the natural resources imaginable and a particularly pleasant climate. "Isn't it unfair to favour one land so much over all the others?" cried the angels. To this God replied, "Wait and see whom I have chosen to populate this land – the Mexicans!"

The inferiority complex of the Mexican people – especially vis-à-vis their big neighbour to the north – can hardly be characterized in a better way. The successors to great cultures – albeit cultures which had passed their prime by the time the Spanish conquistadores arrived – and the descendants of adventurers and fortune hunters from old Europe merged together over the course of almost five centuries to form a race of people which, while embracing and preserving both cultures, rejects them at the same time.

Despite their own great achievements – making it possible for Mexico to advance from a mere supplier of raw materials to a burgeoning industrial nation in a matter of a few decades – the Mexicans are still slaves to that which is foreign. They are proud of their country – but still think the grass is greener outside its borders. Their own achievements never seem to stand the test of comparison with the accomplishments of other countries; indeed, these are blindly admired with hardly a thought to the unique circumstances which bring such accomplishments about. Because of this, it's easy to get the wrong impression about how the Mexican views his own people.

The Mexican enjoys complaining about his country – its leaders and especially its politicians, economic abuses, and the mentality of his countrymen. But the foreigner should beware of joining in on these lamentations, for this could cause a great deal of irritation. Mexicans are, namely, ardent nationalists. They may foul their own nest a little, but a foreigner who follows suit is hardly appreciated – and rightly so! After all, can a non-Mexican ever get to know the country well enough to even begin to comprehend its complexity let alone to think he has the answers to its problems?

Despite 500 years of shared history, the Mexican Indian and the Southern European have never managed to merge together into a single racial entity – their inherent differences are just too extreme. Instead, they form two distinct ethnic and cultural elements within the Mexican population today. An inhabitant of Mexico's tropical rainforest and a technocrat in a Mexico City boardroom may live worlds apart, but they are both Mexicans. This raises the question: Does there exist such a thing as a "typical" Mexican?

With some six million Indians – a good eight percent of the total population – Mexico has the largest Indian population in the world. As many as 1.1 million of these people do not speak Spanish, but instead speak one of the over fifty Indian languages. Obviously, among the Indians themselves there are vast cultural differences: the primitive, pagan, inbred and consequently degenerate Lacandon Indians of the jungles of Chiapas can hardly be compared to the intelligent and educated Mixe of the jungles of the Oaxacan highlands. One of the latter was even elected president in 1858: Benito Juárez was a pureblood Zapoteca and probably the greatest statesman Mexico has ever known.

Another extreme is typified by the brilliant, multilingual, cosmopolitan industrialist or politician with a Harvard education and money in the bank – lots of it. He may also have Indian blood in his veins – even if only a few drops. Despite revolution, the devaluation of the peso and the weighty national debt, wealthy Mexican families have the means to support an opulent lifestyle that would impress an Arab oil sheik. A sort of social net exists in their circles which prevents any of their number from falling below a certain standard of living or losing more than a certain amount of influence. Not merely a few hundred, but more like a few tens of thousands of families make up the rich and powerful elite in Mexico. The six-year presidential term (and the fact that the incumbent may not seek re-election) is certainly to their advantage as it gives everyone a chance to enjoy the lucrative benefits of an appointment to a federal office. Influence and connections come with such a post, and these translate into good business and increased profits for the office holder. The strategy is to somehow manage to always be on the winning side. Even so, those who find themselves out in the cold for six years (as a result for having actively supported the wrong candidate) need not despair, for their time will come with the next change of government.

And there wouldn't be much point in damning the rich as parasites: anyone chased out of office today will likely be replaced by an even less desirable appointee tomorrow. All the revolutions in the world have shown this to be true – and the Mexican Revolution of 1910–1917 was unfortunately no exception.

(v. Debschitz)

Rockets, Ribbons and Turkeys

The nuptial mass is over in the church of Santa María in Zaachila, a town of some 20,000 inhabitants with no cinemas, no amusement arcades, only half a dozen 2-storey buildings and one asphalt road. It is just 10 a.m., but here in the south the sun is already high. There are almost no shadows, and the white façade of the church looks even whiter, even more like icing. The newly married couple emerges and is greeted with handfuls of rice and a childlike chant of "Beso! Beso! Beso!" (Kiss! Kiss! Kiss!). They comply. The man is short, dark and thin; the woman, short, dark and fat. What will happen when, at the house of the groom, the chant changes to "Que la cargue! Que la cargue!" and he is obliged to carry her over the threshold? Isn't she, perhaps, just a little too heavy? Then again, maybe he has been practising. The bride is not wearing white but a very pale shade of orange... a discreet but clear indication to all that she is not quite a virgin. For this reason, the wedding will last a mere 3 or 4 days, instead of the usual 6 or 7.

Outside the church there is no waiting limousine. Everyone will proceed to the godfather's house "walking half the way, and the other half on foot", as the Mexicans say. The couple cannot disappear into a car, but must parade through the main square and along the main avenue (alright, the *only* avenue!). Weddings here are public spectacles – which is as it should be where there are no cinemas! And the colourful procession lasts all day.

Behind the couple come their relatives and guests; in front of them are two distinct groups of musicians and – at the head of the procession – the coheteros, rocket-throwers, with home-made catherine wheels and rockets on bamboo sticks which they nonchalantly light with cigarettes and toss over their shoulders in a vaguely upward direction. The rockets arch into the deep blue sky, crack it, and fall back down as charred sticks, spiralling ashes sending small curls of yellow smoke through the air. The sharp crack reaches every quarter of town, announcing to all that the procession is underway.

The first group of musicians, the brass band, comes after the coheteros. The old men with rusty saxophones play marches that get more and more out of tune as they pass round the mescal, a local liquor similar to tequila which they pour from a Coca-Cola bottle into bamboo cups. Then comes the estudiantina, as its name implies a group of students. They are sober, in tune, play mandolins, accordions, and tambourines, and sing love songs. Their flamboyant black capes adorned with long, scarlet, blue and yellow ribbons contrast with the earth-coloured ponchos and sandals worn by members of the brass band.

The procession enters the wide dirt yard of the godfather's house.

While the two musical groups entertain in turn, some 150 guests are seated at long wooden tables and given bread and chocolate served in earthenware bowls and spiced with cinnamon, almonds and walnuts. After a couple of hours of eating, drinking and dancing, "breakfast" is over and the procession resumes. This time it is going from the godfather's house to that of the groom, accompanied by girls bearing baskets of fruit and sweets on their heads. At the threshold comes the second chant: "Que la cargue!" The skinny groom flexes his muscles, heaves, staggers and deposits the woman of his dreams about a metre and a half inside the house. Here there are more long wooden tables and bowls of chocolate, as well as vast amounts of food which can be eaten on the spot or taken away in plastic bags handed out by the hosts: to refuse the repast is unthinkable. There is also espuma, a drink made from maize and white cacao whipped into a foam, served in painted gourds and slurped up with a wooden spatula. "Foam" is only for special occasions: to make it, ordinary cacao beans must be buried in the earth in clay pots for a whole year until they lose their colour and turn to dust. At the groom's house the estudiantina disbands, and the brass band alternates with a tropical combo. The afternoon is wearing on and the mescal is not wearing off, and eventually it is time to start dancing under the grapefruit trees. At 5 o'clock the procession returns to the house of the godfather: by this time the brass band is flagrantly disobeying every known harmonic law, but no one is remotely bothered...

It is on this third leg of the day-long procession that the high point of a wedding in Zaachila is reached and the turkey "comes into play". The dance of the "guajolote", a native American species of turkey that was a symbol of prosperity in pre-Hispanic times, is preserved in Zaachila and other small towns in the area, such as Tlacolula. It is performed for the married couple by a man, a woman, and a turkey – although the last is a somewhat reluctant participant. The woman holds the turkey by the wings and dances around the man, trying – more or less earnestly, depending on her mood – to thrust its beak into the man's face. The man defends himself with a clay jug of black chilli sauce and a basket of tortillas. Circling each other, they move along the street in front of the bridal pair. Every so often the bird, the jug and the basket change hands and another couple takes up the dance, drawing curious children out of houses of tin, kicking up dust, making mangy dogs cower against adobe walls. At the godfather's house the dance ends, the clay jug is broken and the chilli sauce spills onto the dust, a symbol of the fertility wished on the bride and groom. Unfortunately, the dance of the turkey has been known to end, after many glasses of mescal, in bloodshed and blindness. And since the whole procession is a public spectacle, anyone – including "innocent" tourists who have been hiding behind their cameras – could, at any moment, find themselves armed only with a jug and a basket in a mortal struggle with a turkey. So if you come across this custom, watch out!

The fiesta continues in both the godfather's and the groom's houses for some three days. On the first day there is eating, drinking, dancing and the procession described; on the second, drinking and dancing; and on the third just drinking. The fourth day of the celebration is reserved for lying perfectly still in whatever position you happen to land in. To remain standing at the end of a wedding would be a terrible insult to all concerned! *(Valerio)*

Ahorita

"The bill, please!" The waiter, his round Indian eyes fixed on some point in the distance, replies, "Ahorita, señor." "Ahora" is the Spanish word meaning "right now", "at once" or – when children are being called – "on the double". "Ahorita" is the Mexican way of saying "right away". Of course, the waiter will not return with the bill for another five minutes or so, for nothing happens right away in Mexico.

Much speculation has gone on about the concept of time expressed by the word "mañana", which to a Mexican can mean tomorrow, or next year, or even never. "Ahorita" is, as it were, the smaller unit of time into which "mañana" is divided. Everything in its own sweet time!

The amiability of the Mexicans, especially of those of Indian ancestry who live in the cities, can turn into impassiveness at the slightest sign of pressure. With "ahorita", a Mexican signals his willingness to comply with a request as soon as possible – in other words, at his convenience. But woe be it if the request is expressed as a command – this is considered tactless and rude and only results in a longer wait: "Ahorita, señor, vengo en segida" – I'll be right there.

Mexicans react sensitively to force. Neither the man in the street nor the petty official nor even the lowly employee behind a desk will let himself be intimidated by a raised voice or a display of impatience. If he detects a tone of arrogance or feels he is being pressured, he can become as stubborn as a "mulo" – a mule. And if all this fuss over a mere triviality – what, after all, could be so important to a tourist? – is carried too far, his eyes will start glistening with resentment. It could be you've made him uneasy (maybe you'll report him to the boss), but you're not going to get what you want any faster that way. Foreigners are well advised to avoid an overbearing attitude. You will get what you want much faster if you ask for it with as much politeness as your command of the language – and sign language, of course – allow. Then you can expect to hear, "ahorita, señor", and the wait can begin… .

(v. Debschitz)

Motorist's Misery

Mexico City's greatest enemy is the overwhelming build-up of traffic on its streets and highways. If you ever find yourself behind the wheel of a car here, and you want to get from one point on the map to another, be prepared to experience how an otherwise affable and engaging capital can suddenly turn nasty and mean. In a city with as high a population as this one, it's only natural that a few hundred thousand others will want to get from the same point of departure to the same destination at exactly the same time as you!

Everyone is out to get ahead – in the fastest way possible! There is one handicap, however: with only a few yards between each red light, engine gunning is virtually out of the question – but heaven forbid that another driver reach the next intersection first!

According to unofficial but very believable figures, there are 7 million motor vehicles registered in Mexico City. Two-thirds of these may look like they should have been sent to the car cemetery years ago, but in Mexico City, cars never die – skilful mechanics keep even the most ancient jalopies alive and running indefinitely. Admirers of Detroit's 1950's models will get their money's worth here. But the car that can be seen most often on Mexico City's streets is that odd, unassuming German original, the VW Beetle – made in Mexico, of course!

Those who would like to undertake their voyage of discovery through Mexico City by hired car should be prepared to spend a few interesting hours behind the wheel. During rush hour, which lasts from about 7 o'clock in the morning until 10 o'clock at night, ring roads like the Anillo Periférico Poniente (an "Oriente", that is, an eastern ring road, it has been in the planning for years) serve better as parking lots. In other words, everything comes to a standstill. Everyone knows this but no one wants to accept it. Horns are honked incessantly in an attempt to break the impasse. After about ten minutes, relief is usually in sight: the traffic starts rolling forward... but, after about ten yards of ground is covered, it all comes to a halt again.

Some years ago, Mexico City's fathers, who despite motorized escorts with flashing red lights often get stuck in traffic themselves, came up with a means of combatting vehicular congestion. Avenues along which one could formerly "sightsee" at a top speed of 5 m. p. h. were turned into veritable one-way raceways called "ejes viales". At the same time, however, someone came up with the bright idea of reserving one lane for oncoming traffic. Buses and emegency vehicles coming from the opposite direction make driving on the "ejes" similar to driving on an obstacle course. Parking is not allowed; stopping is hardly possible and heaven forbid you should have a breakdown, for this could turn these expressways back into the "parking lots" they once were.

Strong nerves and a cool and level head are what is needed to survive the traffic in Mexico City. In addition, these attributes will come in handy if you want to take advantage of one of Mexico's supreme rules of the road: the one who's ahead is the one who's right. In practice this means that, at intersections, motorists will try their best to squeeze ahead by forcing their way between cars jammed in the cross traffic. Try it sometime yourself – it's fun and it keeps you in shape!

Mexicans may have a generous attitude towards distance when travelling the wide open spaces of their country, but in congested traffic every inch counts. It may be a comfort to the tourist to know, however, that an unmistakeable cry of despair from behind the wheel will soften the heart of even the most hardened Mexican motorist. You may then find yourself crossing a busy boulevard unhindered – an act which would otherwise get you banished for life.

This might seem like a draconian form of punishment, but the consequences of lesser offences are not quite so harsh. Policemen are only human – and they suffer like the rest of us as a result of exhaust fumes. Just because a policeman would rather use his whistle to keep the traffic rolling than to round up traffic violators is no reason to accuse him of a lack of the proper sense of duty. His zealous desire to serve will become quite evident when he has to apprehend an offender on an inconsequential side street. His face will light up with delight – all the exhaust fumes have finally paid off! Because his superior will also want his share of the payoff, you shouldn't be too tightfisted when it comes to haggling over the amount. Besides, he could lose his patience, pull out his pad and present you with a real "multa" (traffic ticket) – and that would cost you even more.

The rule to heed when on Mexico City's streets is: be on your guard. Don't take a green light at face value – it could be mistaken for a red one by a car coming from the left or the right. Especially at night, there are a lot of young drivers on the road who are out to show their "novias" (girlfriends) that nothing can stop them. Don't trust the blinkers on the car ahead of you – it could be that the driver's signalled swerve to the right is only preparation for a sharp turn to the left. Be wary of cars which don't seem to brake at intersections – it could be that their brake lights simply don't work and you might find yourself involved in a rear-end collision.

An important rule of the road to take to heart is: watch what the driver in front of you is doing and don't worry about what's going on behind you. Thanks to the many who follow this rule, surprisingly few accidents occur in Mexico City.

(v. Debschitz)

Chihuahua al Pacífico

The alarm clock wakes us at an ungodly hour. Half asleep, we collect our luggage and stumble down to the lobby to join the others in our group. It's still dark outside. With stomachs growling, we peer into the hotel restaurant to see if there's anything for breakfast. Pedro, by his own account 14 years young (but he looks even younger), has assured us that despite the early hour – it's 6 am – we'll be able to get something to eat before setting off on the "most beautiful train trip in the world", the thrilling 665 km (413 miles) from Los Mochis on the Golfo de California, over the Sierra Madre Occidental, up to an elevation of 2,500 m (8,200 feet) and then down to the city of Chihuahua.

From out of nowhere, "bolillos" (rolls) and "huevos mexicanos" (scrambled eggs garnished with an abundance of onions, chillis and tomatoes) appear on our tables. Pedro has roused the kitchen personnel.

Amazing, the little fellow. With his few words of English, he exudes authority. The evening before, he welcomed us to this small hotel, assigned us our rooms, helped us with our luggage and then sent us out – he insisted we see the sights of his hometown, Los Mochis. It was useless to argue, so we formed small groups and trotted out in all directions. We even succeeded in finding the market he had described to us – aromatic and attractive. I took the opportunity to pick up a bottle of tequila for the trip.

Pedro also advised us against taking the taxi to Topolobampo – too far, too expensive, and besides, it would get dark soon. Too bad – I was looking forward to seeing this little fishing village again and revisiting the hotel where I once stayed. Its restaurant is shaped like a ship; looking at it from the street, you can imagine it to be a galleon picked out of the sea and placed on the rocks by a giant hand. Sitting on the terrace once, I saw fins ploughing through the lovely sand-bordered bay in front of me. "Tiburones (sharks)?" I asked anxiously, for I'd already put my swimming trunks on. No, I was assured, it was only a school of playful dolphins – and where dolphins play, sharks stay away.

Our group starts coming to life. With the help of the houseboy Pedro has loaded our gear onto a small truck and now he herds us onto a bus with air conditioning kept in operation by a roaring diesel engine. The sun beats down on it as we wait in front of the hotel. Today is going to be a real scorcher!

Los Mochis' station is located on the outskirts of the city. Here, we get our first glimpse of the train which will be our home for the next eight hours, the train which bears its itinerary in big letters on its Pullman cars: "Chihuahua al Pacífico" – from the highland plains of central Mexico to the blue waters of the Pacific. We shall follow the route in the opposite direction.

Pedro eagerly helps us get our bags into the overhead luggage nets. It's about time to express our thanks to the little fellow, so I slip a rolled-up bill into his hand. "No, señor, por que?" he asks. "Don't you want a tip?" "Not yet, señor," he says as he gives me a hand with my lounge chair. I can't seem to get the mechanism to work, but he deftly turns the chair around 180 ° to face the direction the train will be travelling in.

Departure. The seats are a bit spongy, but otherwise quite comfortable, and I've noticed that the car behind ours displays the word "comedor", which tells me we won't starve. Indians wearing wide belts of tooled leather and cowboy boots with pointed toes push their way through the car. The sombreros on their heads are standard – they are just as essential here as an umbrella is in London.

Slowly, we roll out of the city and on toward the distant mountains. The tracks are surrounded by thorny bush. There is a road running parallel to the tracks, but it soon meanders off and disappears as we head uphill. You can't get very far with a car around here: there's only one way to get to Tarahumara country, and that is via these tracks.

The air conditioner hums above our heads. The sky outside is a pale blue and the sun is already high above the horizon – it's amazing how fast it rises here. In the evening, it falls just as quickly – you can follow its movements with your eyes. Here, on the Tropic of Cancer, twilight comes and goes in a matter of minutes. For now, however, we have the entire day ahead of us. We sit back and enjoy the pleasant rhythm of the train as it rolls over the sleepers. It's still a long way to the Tarahumaras.

With theatrical flair, a man enters our parlour car. He holds his sombrero tightly aginst his chest. His swarthy face is full of concentration. He scrutinizes us. In a sonorous voice, he begins delivering a eulogy on the president who inaugurated the Chihuahua al Pacífico Railroad in 1961: Adolfo López Mateos. In the most eloquent terms, he praises the vision and perseverance of the man who carried through this momentous project: the completion of a railway link between the highlands and the coast. Throughout his discourse, our chronicler paces up and down the aisle, turning abruptly at each end so we won't miss a single word of what he has to proclaim. With gesticulations worthy of a Shakespearean actor, he adds spark to descriptions of the nearly insurmountable obstacles which hampered the completion of the project. I translate for the others as best I can.

Actually, the railway was first talked about in 1850 as a means of transporting copper from the Barranca del Cobre (Copper Canyon) to port for shipment. At that time, the Frenchman Pasquier de Dourmartin was given the concession to build a railway from Chihuahua to the Pacific, but couldn't find a suitable financier for the project. Then, in 1897, concessions were given to Enrique C. Creel and Alfred A. Splendove and construction began the following year. The first section, between Chihuahua and Miñaca, was completed in 1900.

In the meantime, our friend has become noticeably hoarse. He does, after all, have to talk above the noise of the train and the giggles of the passengers.

The Kansas City, Mexico and Oriental Railroad, a private company, carried out the construction of two sections between the years 1902 and 1912: a section in the highlands extending the existing railway to the town of Creel, and one on the Pacific coast from Topolobampo to San Pedro. The revolution put a halt to the project: the most difficult 180 km (122 miles) through the Sierra Madre remained incomplete for the time being.

It wasn't until 1952 that the project was taken up again, this time by the Mexican government. In one of the greatest engineering feats ever accomplished – comparable only to the new Trans-Siberian Railway, the Baikal-Amur-Magistrale – tracks were laid through the rugged and forbidding terrain of the sierra: thousands of feet of rock were drilled, dozens of valleys were crossed, niches were blasted out of steep cliffs and innumerable rivers were spanned. A total of 89 tunnels and 39 bridges were constructed. But what can cold statistics say about this amazing achievement... the successful completion of a railway line through one of the most inhospitable terrains in the world?

Exhausted, the orator passes his hat around. We give generously. At the next stop, he gets off. The train is his workplace: if you don't have a job, create one for yourself – that's the Mexican way!

Clouds of diesel fumes close in on me as I stand outside on the platform of the last car. It gets worse whenever we pass through a tunnel, but the closeness to this giants' playground, this ever-changing, up-and-down scenery of cliffs and gorges makes up for my burning eyes. As we enter a curve, I notice an opening in the mountain wall ahead of us and far above. Soon we are rumbling over a viaduct and I realize that the tracks lead up there. In a few minutes, our train will disappear into that opening. No, I'm wrong. We enter the mountain down here and exit above. Then the tracks continue upward like a spiral only to disappear into another tunnel.

Pedro suddenly appears on the platform with two cans of soda. "Refresco, señor?" "How did you get here? I thought you were in the hotel in Los Mochis." Pedro tells me that he spends his summer holidays on the train, training as it were to become a steward. He's not doing this to supplement his allowance –

no, he accompanies groups on their journey from the Pacific to the highlands and back again in order to contribute to the support of his family. The other members of the train personnel appreciate him for his helpfulness and are only too glad to entrust the care of foreign tourists to him. He does, after all, speak a little English, which unfortunately cannot be said of our two official, uniformed hostesses.

The bridges which speed by under my feet have no guardrails. Between the sleepers, I can see hundreds of feet into the abyss. I get dizzy as I look through the viewfinder of my camera. The railway cars chug through gashes in the cliff wall, so close that it almost touches us. Suddenly – so unexpectedly that I hardly know which way to turn – the first canyon appears; its red-blue walls slope down in terraces and disappear into nothingness.

Friendly Indian children wave to us from railway cars we pass as we roll along. They live here. Papa is one of the many railwaymen whose job it is to keep the tracks in good working order. He has his work cut out for him, for the spirits of the barranca have not yet learned to accept this man-made path which slices through their realm. Rockslides are a common occurrence. A not-so-common occurence, however, is the punctual arrival of a train, as they are constantly being shunted. Freight trains piled high with logs battle with the scheduled passenger trains for space on the single-track railway until they can get to the next siding.

Hours have gone by. Despite the odour of diesel fuel, I can smell the pine trees which are scattered about this magnificent mountain landscape. Finally, we are 2,500 m (8,200 feet) above sea level – we've made it! The plateau is virtually flat. The train comes to a halt. The sign at the station reads "Divisadero Barranca". Everyone gets off. An Indian market awaits us on the platform – Tarahumara women have set out their handicrafts on small stools about them. It all looks very nice, but as we shall be spending the night here there will be time tomorrow to pick up Tarahumara costume dolls, woodcarvings, baskets and other souvenirs before the next train leaves for Creel. We gather up our belongings and walk 50 metres to the point where the ground under our feet abruptly comes to an end. On the edge of this precipice stands the rustic hotel of the two Sandoval sisters – our lodgings for the night.

The sun adds golden highlights to the reddish and blue-grey tones of the canyon wall, plunging steeply downward for hundreds of metres. This giant hole in the earth's crust extends clear to the horizon.
A rockfall blocks our view of the canyon floor, so we can only imagine the Urique River – which, over the course of millions of years, created this masterpiece of nature – some 1,700 m (5,000 feet) below us. This is the climax of our journey – and we are at a loss for words!

(v. Debschitz)

Rose Petals or CO_2

There is a 50% chance that upon your arrival in Mexico one of the first things you see will be a gigantic red and white Coca-Cola advertisement. If not, it will likely be a gigantic red, white and blue advertisement for Pepsi. In either case, those on their first trip to Latin America will probably be dismayed. Just as they will be dismayed when, after tramping thro' the jungle for days, they peer through the dense undergrowth and make out, stuck on the side of a bamboo shack, the same sign – smaller and rustier, perhaps, but unmistakable.

Travellers need not despair. The real Latin America is out there! The influence of the West is deceptive: it is certainly ubiquitous, but it is also superficial, especially in the provinces. Despite the influx of fizzy drinks there is still an immense variety of exotic beverages to be savoured, any one of them delicious enough to make you renounce those glucose-and-carbon-dioxide concoctions for all time!

How about a tall cool glass of chilacayota? Made from mashed up pumpkin-like calabashes, it is sweetened with molasses and spiced with cinnamon and shreds of lemon peel. It is served with chunks of fresh pineapple and lumps of nicuatole made from maize, the Indian answer to jelly. The week before Easter, to celebrate "La Samaritana", chilled chilacayota is served complete with lemon peel, pineapple chunks, and a sprinkling of fresh rose petals!

The ancient Mexicans were magicians not only with tastes but with textures. Try tejate, made from boiled maize sweetened with chocolate; to this is added pizle, ground seeds of the mamey fruit. They do not affect the flavour, but produce a yeasty froth on the surface of the pale brown liquid.

A less subtle, simply refreshing drink is horchata de coco, a mixture of condensed milk, ground rice and coconut milk.

If your mouth is burning up from some particularly hot chilli dish, do NOT reach for a glass of water, which takes off the sting as long as you are swallowing it, then makes you feel worse by spreading the chilli all the way down your throat! Instead, ask for atole – thick, smooth, and a good substitute for milk as a lining for the stomach and the mouth. It has very little flavour of its own, but is the best antidote to the excess of flavour in many Mexican dishes.

Less elaborate than chilacayota or tejate but more widely available are the aguas or diluted fruit juices. The vast variety of fruit in Mexico is transformed into an endless array of drinks: pineapple, tamarind, lime... . Very typical are tuna, the fruit of a cactus (barbary fig), and jamaica, a red flower. Absolutely not to be missed is the agua made from guanábana, a large fruit which looks like a hunk of crocodile on the outside and is white, fibrous and delicately aromatic inside. Guanábana is THE tropical fruit par excellence. However, if all these exotic flavours make you sick or you can't get over your fear of microbes, rest assured, you can revert to something fizzy and familiar. Just remember those gigantic signs you saw while driving away from the airport!

(Valerio)

Night of the Dead

The Mexicans' view of death – so different from our own – stems from the legacy of their Indian ancestors. To a Mexican, death is a natural part of life... and life is something he is intimately acquainted with. His deep religiousness – and who is to say how much of that is attributable to Catholicism and how much is deeply rooted in traditional beliefs? – prevents him from harbouring false notions about death. Death signifies the end of life, but not the end of existence. This means that one's loved ones remain in one's midst even after the end of their earthly life. For the Indians, in particular, death is nothing to be fearful of: it is merely a transformation from one form of being into another. Life is likened to a flower which slowly opens and then closes again. Flowers have great significance in Mexico – that's why you see more floral decorations on the "Día de los Muertos", the Day of the Dead, than on any other day of the year.

All Saints' and All Souls' Days, November 1st and 2nd, are the days of "happy death" in Mexico. The children get all kinds of sweets to nibble on, all created by Mexico's confectioners in a variety of macabre forms: sugar skeletons, marzipan skulls and chocolate coffins. Street vendors sell "pan de muertos": bread baked in the shape of a bone and covered with icing, and the plastics industry produces its own line of morbid symbols in fluorescent colours especially for the occasion. While children are busy scaring each other with plastic skeletons in the twilit streets, their mothers are busy cooking for the souls of their dearly departed. Deceased relatives who left the family an inheritance get their favourite dishes cooked for them on this day.

Bearing flowers, mountains of fruit and trays of food, the Mexicans form processions to the cemeteries where they will commune with the souls of departed family members in the night between All Saints' and All Souls'. In the countryside, you can see paths of flowers leading from the cemeteries to the villages, marking the roads for the souls of children which might otherwise lose their way. The cemeteries themselves are ablaze with the light from thousands of candles, and churchbells peal loudly, inviting the souls to partake of their meal. What the "ánimas" (the souls) don't eat, is eaten by their living relatives – with true mortal gusto!

I asked a Mexican friend of mine – a man who had studied in Europe and who certainly could have been considered a cosmopolitan type – what he thought of this custom. "Of course I expect my children to visit me on the "Día de los Muertos'", he declared energetically. "I also expect them to bring me something good to eat. After all," he continued, "who can say that I won't really eat it?" No Mexican would care to remain in eternity forever without proper nourishment.

The Night of the Dead is known as "Animecha Ketzitakua" by the Tarasco Indians of the central Mexican state of Michoacán, whose capital, Morelia, lies a good five hours by car from Mexico City. The religious observances here are ushered in with a duck hunt on the banks of romantic Lake Pátzcuaro, the lake which contains Mexico's richest store of fish. In the early morning hours of October 31st, the hunters slip soundlessly into the marshes in their canoes and, with harpoons poised, await the break of day. The ducks are felled in flight or on the water by whizzing spears and transformed into delicious dishes to be offered to the dead as refreshment. On this day, no fishing is done in the waters of the lake – the returning drowned could get tangled in the nets.

The main observances take place on the pyramid-shaped rock island of Janitzio in the centre of Lake Pátzcuaro. In the eerie glow of candlelight reflecting off the headstones, women and children dressed in the finery of their local costumes pile up delicacies before the graves of deceased family members: roast pickled duck in bowls draped with fine cloths, "pan de muertos", fruit and flowers. Concentration can be seen on the finely chiselled faces of the women as they crouch near the graves in their Sunday best, their heads wrapped in shawls. Will the monotonous bells of the small cemetery chapel coax the souls of their loved ones to the grand fiesta? And if so, when will they come? or are they already here among the living once again? At about 1 am, songs ring out and prayers asking for the repose of the souls of the dead are dispatched to the heavens. The Night of the Dead has been observed this way for centuries – maybe even for thousands of years – but while church bells call the souls to supper today, 400 years ago it was the drums of the shamans.

On this night, thousands of people bearing thousands of candles line the banks of the lake, making it look as though it were encircled by an opal-studded ring. Prayers are spoken here as well. The few tourists present are hardly noticed – as long as their camera flashes don't interfere with the lines of communication between the living and the dead. Hotels and inns are booked solid for this occasion, so make reservations well in advance. If you want to understand Mexico a little better, look first into the eyes of the Tarasco women on the Night of the Dead!

(v. Debschitz)

Charros

When Hernán Cortés and his tiny army waded onto Mexican soil in 1519, they brought along something which filled the Indians with both awe and fear: 16 large animals whose backs seemed to have been fused together with the bodies of these strange soldiers. It has even been conjectured that the Indians were more intimidated by these "fighting machines" than they were by the fire and smoke spitting weapons the fair-skinned conquerors carried. The horse was unknown to indigenous Americans, and during the first decades of Spanish domination, it remained taboo for them: if an Indian were to mount a horse, he would, in his own eyes, be elevating himself to the social level of the Spanish conquerors.

In the course of time, however, this reticence gave way to deep attachment. Today it is the Mexicans who seem to be one with their trusty steeds – indeed, the Mexican horseman is culturally and historically just as charismatic a figure as the cowboy of the Old West. For anyone who has seen the elegance and power of a "charro" in the saddle, the equestrian feats of Hollywood's celluloid heros quickly pale.

Thanks to the horse, the vast tracts of land in the north of Mexico could be put to use. Spanish landowners employed "vaqueros" (cattle herdsmen): from horseback they drove, tended and guarded herds numbering thousands of head of cattle. These Mexican buckaroos were the forerunners of the North American cowboys – the ones who came to fame when the American southwest, once a part of the Mexican Republic, fell to the United States.

In Mexico today, equestrianism is a sport of the leisure classes. The title "Caballero" is a form of address literally meaning "horseman". Actually it means far more than that: it is horseman, knight and gentleman all wrapped up in one. A charro is a horseman who has mastered the techniques of the former hacienda cowboys and who rides with the same power and skill. Practically every Sunday, those who can afford it test their skill at colourful and daring "charreadas" or rodeos, which take place in Mexico's larger cities.

Greeted by the enthusiastic shouts of the crowd, the charros and charras parade into the ring in their costly costumes. The short, dark jackets, tight-fitting, silver-buttoned trousers and richly decorated, wide-brimmed sombreros date from Colonial times. At a breathtaking gallop, the charros rush around the "ruedo" (the ring) behind a runaway calf which must be brought to the ground from the saddle with a single sharp tug on the tail. At full speed, they ride alongside an unsaddled bronco, then spring onto its back with only its mane to hold on to. This test of skill is aptly called the "paso de la muerte", a name which hints at the mortal risk involved in its execution. Bull riding is another skill displayed by the charros, who also work wonders with the "reato" or lasso. "Florear" (to decorate with flowers) is the verb used to describe the fancy rope work performed with one and sometimes two lassos.

Some 20,000 charros are organized into approximately 300 clubs throughout Mexico. The membership of these clubs includes politicians, business leaders and other prominent public figures. The charreada may be a gentleman's sport, but it is hardly conceivable without the presence of Mexico's "china poblana", the cavaliers' female counterparts who lend pageantry and style to these meets as they ride smartly in their side-saddles, dressed in their colourful crinoline costumes.

The best known charreadas in Mexico City are those held almost every Sunday at 10 am at the Rancho del Charro on Avenida Ejército Nacional near Chapultepec Park. It is said that to know Mexico, you have to have experienced the incomparable atmosphere of a charreada at least once – an atmosphere evoked by the leathery smell of the harnesses and saddles, the horses damp with sweat and by the macho riders themselves – the daring charros mexicanos.

(v. Debschitz)

Moctezuma's Revenge

When your stomach starts growling at you and you feel the first twinges of pain in your lower abdominal tract, you'll know you've got it: the dreaded Moctezuma's revenge. The Aztec ruler, who in 1519 was so easily duped by a handful of Spaniards because he mistook their leader for the returning god Quetzalcóatl, has been avenging himself on foreign visitors ever since. Many find themselves suffering the blows of his terrible scourge after only a few days' sojourn in his former realm. "The runs", a bane to travellers the world over, strikes with particular vengeance in Mexico, which is why it is known as "the Aztec gallop" by people in the travel business there. Mexicans simply call it "turista".

The medical profession is quite sure about the causes of "turista": intestinal bacteria, normally beneficial to the functioning of that vital area, suddenly run rampant as a result of a change of surroundings. They multiply at an explosive rate and bring on the intestinal cramps and nausea so typical of the illness. Start with the high altitude (Mexico City lies some 2,300 m/7,500 ft above sea level), add some hot, spicy food and perhaps a tequila or two too many and the bacteria burst into activity. Stress is another contributing factor: days spent climbing pyramids, nights that go on and on and, of course, the endless stream of new impressions naturally take their toll on the organism.

Take some good advice: avoid stress in the first few days. Give your body the opportunity to accustom itself to the high altitudes. Keep in mind that at 2,300 m every machine – and this includes the human body – performs at only 75 per cent of its normal capacity as a result of the low oxygen level. Take it easy, keep away from very hot foods and avoid heavy meals after 10 pm (which is, unfortunately, when Mexicans normally eat supper).

Europeans who live in Mexico swear by tequila: a shot of "añejo" (aged tequila) before every meal will keep those sinister bacteria from causing mischief. But please note that the success of this preventive is dependent upon the dosage: too much alcohol weakens the body's defence mechanisms. Be careful with drinking water and watch out for ice cubes in your drinks as they can also contain disease-producing bacteria.

May Asclepius' disciples forgive me for offering medical advice (but, who knows, they may even say I'm right): don't wait until Moctezuma's revenge strikes. Before you leave home ask your chemist for a compound containing Saccharomyces cerevisiae (brewer's yeast), a fungus which will – simply put – occupy every vacant space in the intestines, thus leaving no room for virulent bacteria to multiply and cause harm. With the aid of this medication, even my small daughter remained free of "turista" throughout a stay of several weeks in Mexico. This prophylactic treatment, which should be started a few days before departure (one dose of bacteria with every meal), is known as an "antibiotic therapy". Practitioners of natural medicine affirm that it does not disturb the symbiosis between the human body and the bacteria occurring in the intestines.

If "turista" has struck, you won't necessarily have to confine yourself to your room; but do make sure there is a "baño" (toilet) handy wherever you go. To avoid spending precious holiday time in misery, forget whatever you've brought along in your medicine kit and pick up a prescription-free antibiotic at a local "farmacia" (chemist's). I have fond memories of Kaomycin – it may throw the entire intestinal environment out of balance for weeks (it contains penicillin), but it kills the bacteria and puts you back on your feet in a matter of a day. Caution! it tastes like it looks – pink. Yuk!

(v. Debschitz)

Who's Afraid of Moctezuma?

It is a well-known and unfortunate fact that very few North Americans or Europeans visiting Mexico for the first time escape the dreaded "Moctezuma's Revenge" – to give it its more poetical name. As a result, large numbers of visitors make the tragic mistake of avoiding typical Mexican food altogether. In a country where Indian languages are fast disappearing and Indian music was long ago nigh-buried under the influx of European, Afro-Caribbean and, later, North American influences, it is in the food that the Indian past is most faithfully preserved. Despite the arrival of rice from the east and spaghetti from the west, the staple pre-Hispanic ingredients of maize, beans, chillis, squashes, cinnamon and a vast array of herbs, still form the basis of the popular diet today. Most tourists are probably not aware that there are not two or three different kinds of chillis, but dozens, each with its own distinctive flavour. These, along with the endless variety of herbs, ground seeds, and even flowers used in Mexican cuisine, make it one of the richest – if not exactly the safest – in the world. Connoisseurs have placed Mexico among the top three or four nations for its cuisine, in the ranks of France, China and India. The variety of food within the republic is such that natives of Mexico city are frequently just as surprised by what they find in the provinces as are foreigners. In the south there is a saying: "If it moves, it's food". In different places crickets, snakes, lizards, monkeys, iguanas, tortoises – that is, almost anything that jumps, swings or slithers – are served up. If it's true that "you are what you eat", then the Mexicans ought to be pretty strange people!

Visitors who put up with a little initial stomach trouble will be handsomely rewarded in the end. Their palates will be delighted and their minds will be enlarged.

Specific dishes which should not be missed are the moles (sauces made from a variety of different chillis, herbs, nuts and, sometimes, chocolate) of Puebla and Oaxaca; and the camarones al mojo de ajo (large prawns fried in garlic and lemon juice) of the coasts, especially Veracruz. The richness and subtlety of flavour of the moles, in particular, make them comparable only to the curries of India, and make a few extra microbes well worth bearing!

(Valerio)

Lord, Look Down Upon Your People . . .

The Beginnings When considering the cultural history of Mexico and Central America, one should bear the following fact in mind: the two continents of the western hemisphere exhibit a peculiarity which sets them apart from other regions of the world – human development in an anthropological sense did not take place here. Traces of early hominids, such as those unearthed in Africa, Europe and Asia, have never been found in either of the Americas – there simply was no "Homo americanus". Evidence of other primate forms, which has always been found where there are traces of early man, is also lacking.

It can thus be said that the New World has always been a land of immigrants. The first inhabitants of the Americas were of the same species as modern man, that is, Homo sapiens. They came from Asia, not in one great wave of migration, but as smaller groups in search of edible game. It is still impossible to determine over which period of time these migrations took place, but they may have begun about 40,000 years ago, during the last ice age. At that time the Bering Strait was not a body of water, but a land bridge between the Asian and American continents. The first Americans were a people of primarily Mongoloid stock who came out of the vast expanses of northern and eastern Asia.

This was by no means a homogeneous group, however. The Mongoloid race includes a wide range of physical types, and these people were culturally diverse as well. This is especially evident in the languages which developed. Many of these are still available for research, and by studying them experts are able to differentiate between various cultural backgrounds. It is interesting to note that no skeletal discoveries dating back to the early migrations have ever been made. Remains of human bones have been found in Brazil and Nicaragua, but scientists have not yet been able to date them conclusively. "Tepexpan Man", found in the Valley of Mexico, cannot be much more than 15,000 years old. The oldest known American artefacts date from the same period: spear points and flint tools discovered near Clovis, Texas and Folsom, New Mexico.

Advanced cultures evolved in only three areas of North and South America: in the region which now comprises the American Southwest (the states of New Mexico, Arizona and southern Colorado); in the central Andes (Peru, Bolivia and Colombia); and in Mesoamerica, which in cultural-historical terms comprises central and southern Mexico and Guatemala. In these three regions, social and economic conditions provided an ideal setting for the development of advanced civilizations. The factors necessary for such a development include a relatively high concentration of people (relative to the environment and its resources), the establishment of permanent settlements, and the development of a well-functioning agricultural system to provide sufficient food for the population. At the same time, agricultural production must yield enough surplus to free portions of the work force for other tasks. This paves the way for the construction of representational structures such as temples, palaces and monumental burial sites. These prerequisites were met in the three above-mentioned regions at different times.

Another prerequisite is an efficient leadership and administrative apparatus which is in a position to organize labour and distribute economic goods. This is not necessarily a democratic regime, but is often an hereditary autocracy or priestly hierarchy authorized by divine right. In the case of ancient Mexico it can be said that the local hierarchies, the so-called theocratic systems, appeared before the centralized imperial systems.

From the time of his arrival in Mesoamerica, man had a long way to go before reaching the cultural level manifested by the architectural remains which can be admired throughout the region today. Museums contain hunting weapons and grinding tools made of stone which were fashioned by an early Stone Age culture dating from about 10 000 B. C. At this time, man had not yet cultivated maize or other crops demanding an organized system of agriculture. "Tepexpan Man", who would seem by all indications to have died during a mammoth hunt, dates from this epoch.

In the next phase, which lasted until approximately 2000 B. C., man developed agriculture: maize, squash, chilli, papayas and avocados were systematically cultivated. Towards the close of this phase, the first pottery appeared in central Mexico (Tehuacán).

This chronology based exclusively on archaeological findings is, of course, broad and undifferentiated. There are obviously no written or authentic sources which could supply us with more exact clues. According to this outline the next phase, the Pre-Classic or Formative, begins in about 2500 B. C. This phase is characterized by intensive farming: maize, beans, cotton and tobacco were planted.

The Pre-Classic phase also saw the development of religious rites: innumerable clay figurines – fertility symbols – served votive purposes. The "earth mother" cult was responsible for erecting the first temple platform piled high with sacred objects. A typical example of such is the Cuicuilco Complex on the outskirts of Mexico City. The Formative phase also marked the beginning of monumental architecture in central and southern Mexico. Traces of structures which date back to this period can be found on the Yucatán Peninsula (levels I–IV of Dzibilchaltun near Mérida), in Oaxaca (phases I and II of Monte Albán), and in the Central Plateau (the first two stages of Teotihuacán).

Above all, the Formative phase is identified with the civilization of the Olmecs, recognized as the earliest advanced civilization in Mexico and the one which sparked the development of the Classic cultures which were to follow. Traces of Olmec or La Venta culture (also known by the name of one of its most important sites) have been found in the Gulf coast states, Veracruz and Tabasco.

This culture was first thought to have been limited to this one region, but as more and more of its remains were discovered the general consensus had to be revised. At almost every site where careful and thorough archaeological research was carried out, traces of Olmec influence were unearthed. It is now known that the Olmec civilization was a universal one which extended from central Mexico to southern El Salvador.

Olmec civilization reached its peak in about 500 B. C., but its beginnings can be traced back to the second millenium B. C. The period known as late Olmec overlapped in time with the early Classic period of Mesoamerican civilization.

The most important sites of Olmec (La Venta) civilization

The Classic Period

Around the year A. D. 200, the culture designated by Mexico scholars as "Classic" began to emerge from the foundations laid by the Olmecs of the Pre-Classic period. This was the age that brought forth those manifestations of ancient Mexican culture that are most apparent to the visitor (the earliest levels of the great ruins of the Central Plateau and the Maya region date from the first millenium A. D.). The transition from one cultural horizon to another did not occur over a set period of time as chronological tables may suggest. Rather, it was a process which began at different times in different cultural zones and lasted for different lengths of time as well.

The most magnificent structures on the Central Plateau – the pyramids at Teotihuacán, which have been reconstructed and are open to view – were built during the Classic period. El Tajin, the site of the famous Pyramid of the Niches, and the pyramid at Cholula, the largest structure of its kind in Mexico, also date back to this era. In northern Veracruz, the Huaxtec and Panuco cultures were blossoming, as were the Colima, Nayarit and Jalisco cultures on the Pacific coast. The Classic period also saw the rise of Monte Albán in Oaxaca, the ceremonial centre of the Zapotecs. Moreover, it witnessed the phenomenon of the Maya, whose civilization has excited the imagination of specialists and non-specialists alike up to the present day and can certainly be counted among the most important civilizations mankind has produced.

Teotihuacán: The Place where Men become Gods

In Mexico's Central Plateau, not 50 km (31 miles) from Mexico City, lies Teotihuacán, popularly known as "The Pyramids" to visitors from north of the border. This is quite an apt designation, as the site's most visible and imposing structures are two temple platforms known as the Pyramids of the Sun and Moon. Although it is now known with certainty that these temples had nothing to do with any solar or lunar cult, these names, coined at one time, have never been replaced.

In truth, nothing is known about this immense complex nor about the civilization which created it. Archaeological research and interpretation have provided us with the little we know: written sources simply do not exist. Evidence of the influence this culture wielded can be found throughout Mexico. Furthermore, ceramic objects which originated in this central Mexican state have been unearthed as far away as Tikal in Guatemala. Buildings and stelae obviously created under the influence of Teotihuacán have also been found in Tikal, as well as in other Maya cities. At the same time, traces of Maya culture have been found in those levels of central Mexican ruins which date from the Teotihuacán era – proof that the two most important Classic civilizations were aware of each other's existence.

Clear evidence of cultural exchange can be found in the ruins of Xochicalco near Cuernavaca in the central highland state of Morelos. Here, in the middle of the first millenium A. D., a ceremonial centre arose which was obviously an amalgamation of cultures. The structures themselves were built in the style of Teotihuacán, but their embellishments are clearly Maya. There is a ball court here as well – a Maya invention. Archaeological findings show that the ceremonial ball game was unknown in Teotihuacán – or rather, it was not practised there. The people of Teotihuacán certainly knew of its existence – they just never made it a part of their own cult practices.

As a crossroads between the advanced cultures of the highlands and lowlands, Xochicalco is significant in other respects as well. This centre boasted an observatory, something which is not known to have existed in Teotihuacán, and its people seemed to have been familiar with an unusual game which employed word and number glyphs.

The name "Teotihuacán" – Nahuatl for "the place where men become gods" – shows what strange notions the Aztecs had about the place. While they were familiar with it, they could not place it historically. They did have some knowledge of the Toltecs, their kinsmen and predecessors in the Central Plateau, but otherwise they knew nothing concrete about former cultures and times. Hence, sites like Teotihuacán took on mystic significance for them.

The Spaniards were shown large fossilized bones, thought by the Aztecs to be the remains of a giant human – one of the race of giants which had supposedly built Teotihuacán. In the Aztecs' cosmogony, the place was connected with the creation of one of four earlier eras – an era which predated the historic, i. e. Toltec, era. The Aztecs believed that Teotihuacán was the burial site of kings and warriors who had lived and died in this prehistoric age; thus they called the city's main avenue "The Street of the Dead". "Calle de los Muertos" is the name by which it is still known today.

As the Aztecs knew very little about the former inhabitants of this legendary city, the Spaniards in turn heard only vague rumours and reports. It was said, for example, that in historic times dialects called "Popolca" and "Chuchon" were spoken in the region of Tacuba, Teotihuacán and Texcoco. It has since been shown that these dialects – which are clearly remnants of an ancient tongue that was in no way related to the language of the Toltecs and Aztecs – are spoken today in southern Puebla and Oaxaca.

The excavation of Teotihuacán began in the early 1900s with the unearthing of the Street of the Dead and the Pyramid of the Sun by the archaeologist Leopoldo Batres. Due to the drastic methods used in those days, errors were made which subsequently led to the formation of many misconceptions, some of which live on to the present day. The six archaeological digs which have been carried out since that time, however, have succeeded in correcting the majority of the earlier blunders. The most recent excavation and reconstruction project has shed new light on the so-called Street of the Dead, which was not a street at all, but a series of connected plazas, each with a dance platform or "altar" at its centre, and each separated from the others by high stairways. This detail – the plazas and sunken patios surrounded by stairways – is one of the main features of Teotihuacán architecture. The Ciudadela (citadel), an imposing ceremonial courtyard containing a temple pyramid buried under numerous superstructures, is one of the most remarkable examples of this architectural style.

Excavations carried out on this pyramid have brought to light the most spectacular pictorial relics of Classic Teotihuacán culture: mural paintings on the temple platform which had been walled-in during the subsequent (Post-Classic) period.

Representations of the "Plumed Serpent" and Rain God decorate the steps of the pyramid in alternating patterns. Shells and water symbols serve to clarify the connection between the two motifs: this temple was dedicated to the cult of the god of rain and vegetation, later called "Tlaloc" by the Aztecs. He was symbolized by the Plumed Serpent or "Quetzalcoátl", which was to take on new life in the Aztec era as the symbol of another god. Hence the origins of the religious traditions and iconography which were to be adopted and adapted by the Nahua peoples.

Another important Aztec concept which can clearly be traced back to Teotihuacán is that of "Tlalocan", the Home of the Rain God. In the village of Tepantitla, situated on the outskirts of the immense Teotihuacán excavation site, a mural was discovered in an excavated building complex in 1942. The mural was seriously damaged, but experts have been able to reconstruct and interpret it. A copy of the reconstruction is on view in the Teotihuacán room of the Anthropological Museum in Mexico City. In the upper half of the mural, the Rain God rises out of the sea; above his head is a quetzal bird with outstretched wings. From his hands, life-giving water drips onto the earth. On either side of this figure, priests praying and offering sacrifices can be seen. Below these figures, an animated scene depicting people playing and singing in "paradise" makes up the lower half of the mural. Situated somewhat apart from them is a weeping figure with stylized speech balloons coming from his mouth – he is begging entry into paradise!

The Home of the Rain God apparently represented the concept of a paradisiacal afterworld in the Teotihuacán era – a concept which later became part of the cultures of the Nahua peoples. The Aztecs, however, divided their afterworld into nine parts, to which the deceased were sent according to social class, mode of death and the gravity of sins committed in life. The vivid and appealing mural at Tepantitla is the only picture we have of this vision of paradise.

The giant Pyramid of the Sun is certainly one of the most awesome specimens of Mesoamerican architecture which still exists today. The second-largest structure in the Americas (after the Cholula pyramid) is 63 m (207 ft) high, measures approximately 225 m (738 ft) around the base, and has a volume of over one million cubic metres (35 million cubic feet). Architectonic studies have shown that the Pyramid of the Sun was not the result of a process of enlarging upon a smaller core, but was built in its entirety all at once. Tunnels bored through the axis of the pyramid in 1935 turned up no evidence of an earlier structure.

Around about the 10th or 11th centuries A. D., Teotihuacán, the most magnificent of the classic civilizations, collapsed. Its end was basically not a violent one; rather, it seems to have just declined and fallen, although signs of fire suggest that its ultimate demise was hastened by force. Such incidences of violence marked the arrival of the Nahua peoples and the dawn of a new, completely different cultural phase in Mexico.

The Maya:
The Arrogance of Power

While our knowledge of the other great cultural phenomenon of the Classic period – the phenomenon of the Maya – is not extensive, we do know more about it than we know about Teotihuacán. These two cultures flourished at the same time, but they were destined to meet different fates. Teotihuacán, which originated in the central Mexican plateau, was overshadowed by subsequent civilizations and forgotten by its people. The civilization of the Maya, on the other hand, sprang up in the lowlands and rainforests of the south, and while its great temple cities were eventually swallowed up by the jungle, thus disappearing, the Maya people still exist today as an ethnic entity. The two civilizations did have one fundamental characteristic in common: they were both theocratic cultures, i. e. their governments were politically decentralized, divinely-ordered hierarchies of priests who were, at the same time, scientists and scholars.

The Classic phase – the golden age of Maya civilization – came to an end throughout the entire Maya region around the year A. D. 900. When the Spaniards under the command of Montejo showed up in southern Mexico, they found nothing more than the miserable vestiges of a culture which, while having its roots in Classic Maya, was the product of a process of degeneration and assimilation. In the village of Mani they encountered a princely family which traced its descent back to the Maya; and in Tayasal on Lake Petén Itzá in Guatemala, they came upon a thriving Maya city whose people offered them bitter resistance. As is the case with Teotihuacán, the opportunities for building a store of knowledge about the Maya are limited, and what we do know is the result of painstaking archaeological research. An important source of information on Late-Maya culture

Principal sites of Maya civilization
0
100 km
0
50 miles
Gulf of Mexico
Caribbean Sea
Pacific Ocean
Isla de Cozumel
Dzibilchaltun
Chichén Itza
Merida
Mayapán
Cobà
Yucatan
Tulum
Uxmal
Kabah
Jaina
Labna
Sayil
Campeche
Edzna
Quintana Roo
Chetumal
Campeche
Xpujil
Kohunlich
Rio Bec
Hondo
MEXICO
San Pedro
Belize
Tabasco
Uaxactún
Belmopan
Tikal
Palenque
BELIZE
Tayasal
Lago Petén Itzá
Usumacinta
Ococingo
Yaxchilan
Bonampak
Chiapas
Lacantún
Quen Santo
Chama
Chixoy
Chajcar
Quirigua
Cobán
Panzamalá
Ulúa
GUATEMALA
Copán
Motagua
Quetzaltenango
HONDURAS
Kaminaljuyú
Antiqua
Guatemala
Cozumalhupa
EL SALVADOR

does exist, however: Bishop Diego de Landa's (1524–1579) "Relación de las cosas de Yucatán" which contains insights into traditional customs and religious concepts and practices.

It was not until the 19th century, when the American explorer John Lloyd Stephens and the artist Frederick Catherwood published their "Incidents of Travel in Central America, Chiapas and Yucatán" (1841), that this culture became a focal point of scientific and general interest. Catherwood's illustrations conveyed to an awestruck public an image of palace and temple ruins hidden under a blanket of jungle vegetation, a vision of cities lost in the impenetrable tangle of the Central American rainforest.

In those early days of research, most interpretations of Maya culture were based upon romantic or fanciful notions, but since then, Maya studies have come into their own as a full-fledged branch of science which is in a position to provide us with an accurate enough picture of the rise and fall of this civilization. Modern scholars are aided by the Maya themselves, a people who developed an exact system of mathematics and recorded astronomic calculations and dates with almost religious zeal. Their number system and calendar have now been deciphered and their dates matched to our own, but their system of writing remains a mystery – although most proper and place names can now be read.

While extensive excavations have been and are being carried out, it must be said that most digs of the past were of a superficial and unscientific nature, undertaken mainly for the purpose of clearing, reconstructing and preparing sites for access to tourists. The best example of this kind of misguided archaeological activity can be found at Uxmal in the state of Yucatán. From these mistakes, however, many lessons have been learned. Current digs, such as the mammoth project in Yaxchilán on the Usumacinta River, are everything that serious, scientific archaeological explorations should be.

What is currently known about the Maya can be outlined as follows:

A centralized political entity which could be designated a "Maya state" or a "Maya empire" never existed. For the entire period during which Maya civilization flourished, the region was divided up into numerous (the exact number is not known) locally-governed city-states. Some of these existed peaceably side by side, while others were in a state of constant strife. As a rule, the Maya sites of today are not ruins of cities, but of temple districts which served as ceremonial centres for large, politically diverse areas in which the people shared uniform religious beliefs.

The priests' authority was not founded upon political power, but on religious power, or rather, upon the scientific knowledge with which they enriched their community.

These priest-scholars made many advances in the fields of astronomy, weather forecasting and in determining when to plant and harvest crops. It has been suggested that in these temple complexes a sort of "Olympian truce" was observed – in other words, that the priests did not involve themselves with everyday political affairs nor with the settling of conflicts and disputes. The degree of influence they had over the Kaziks, the secular rulers, is not known.

Geographically, the Maya region can be divided into three zones, each of which displays a distinctive architectural and artistic style.

The North Zone comprises the states of Yucatán, Quintana Roo and the eastern part of the state of Campeche. Its most important archaeological sites are: Dzibilchaltún (near Mérida), Chichén Itzá, Izamal, Mayapan, Uxmal, Labná, Sayil and Kabáh, Kohunlich and the Rio Bec region.

The Central Zone encompasses Tabasco, the southwestern part of Campeche, the northern part of Chiapas and, last but definitely not least, the Petén in Guatemala. The Petén is bordered to the north by the Chenes region, to the west by the Usumacinta River, to the east by Belize and to the south by the Guatemalan departments of Izabal and Alta Verapaz. The most important archaeological sites here are Tikal, Uaxactún, the Sayaxché region, Bonampak, Yaxchilán, Piedras Negras, Palenque, Toniná and Comalcalco.

The South Zone includes the southern part of Chiapas, the Guatemalan highlands, the departments of Izabal and Alta Verapaz, western Honduras and El Salvador. The most important archaeological sites are Zaculeu, Kaminaljuyu, Chincultic, Chamá, Alta Verapaz, Quirigua and Copán.

It is difficult to tell just how many Maya sites exist. In recent years, infrared satellite photographs have aided in the discovery of countless new ones, showing how densely built up the area encompassing the Mexican states of Yucatán, Quintana Roo and Campeche, the Guatemalan Petén and the territory of Belize must have been during the Classic period.

The earliest architectural traces of the Maya date from the close of the Pre-Classic period around A. D. 150. Archaeological findings point to the Central Zone (and in particular, Tikal and Uaxactún) as the cradle of Maya civilization, but excavations conducted by Tulane University have uncovered levels at Dzibilchaltún which are just as ancient as those of the Central Zone sites. One may also assume that architectural activity began in the North Zone during this early period as well.

The fourth century A. D. heralded the actual start of the Classic phase, which was characterized by a surge in population, an increase in the number of urban centres and an increase in the volume of construction carried out in those centres. Findings show that from the seventh century onward, buildings went up at a rapid pace; in fact, almost all remnants of Maya culture visible today date back to the years A. D. 650–900, the golden age of the Classic period. Around the year A. D. 900, this flourishing culture came to a sudden end – a fact which has puzzled Maya scholars up to the present day. It is commonly believed that a disaster of some kind must have been involved – for seldom in history has a civilization collapsed so quickly and so completely.

According to a theory advanced by J. E. S. Thompson – the theory which scholars today consider the most plausible – the downfall of Maya civilization resulted from the degeneration of its ruling class. The clergy and nobility, scholars contend, had become so despotic and exploitive as to cause the people to rise up in a kind of peasants' revolt against them.

A wealth of evidence exists to back up this theory. During the Post-Classic period, the volume of construction as well as the size and number of buildings erected took on monumental proportions. This obviously demanded an equally monumental effort on the part of the labour force. As the temples and palaces grew in size and number, so too did the legions of the "unproductive" – the administrators and priests for whose needs others had to provide. And we know from existent Maya burial sites – the opulence of which bespeaks the effort expended in fitting them out – that the daily needs of these nobles and priests were not satisfied by mere bread alone.

In short, a relationship of this nature can only function as long as the upper echelon continues to produce scientific, intellectual or spiritual achievements which are beneficial to the community. It is clear that toward the end of the ninth century, this was no longer the case. Chances are that the people, who had come to expect practical guidance and useful results, grew tired of their parasitic leaders and either expelled or simply abandoned them. This notion is supported by the existence in Tikal and other places of stelae displaying signs of vandalism – the faces of the Kaziks depicted on them have been scratched out. This could hardly have been the work of grave plunderers or of fanatic Christians. It must have been the work of the Maya themselves – a way of doing damage to the memory of leaders who had fallen from favour. We know how thorough the Maya must have been in ridding themselves of their elite, for, as a result of this extreme action, an entire culture came to an end.

The Maya-Toltecs in Yucatán

The Toltec ruler Ceacatl Topiltztin, also known as Quetzalcoátl, left Tula with a group of his people and, so the legend goes, travelled "eastward over the sea". Traces of Toltec influence found in Yucatán temple cities show that this legend has a historic foundation. In connection with the first Toltec invasion recorded in the annals of Yucatán history, the name "Kukulcan" – the Maya rendering of Quetzalcoátl – appears.

The arrival of the Toltecs must have taken place shortly after the collapse of the Classic Maya civilization around the year A. D. 900. The militaristic invaders took advantage of the power vacuum in the south to stage their attack and seize territory.

An interesting fact is that the Toltecs, who had the entire area under military control, passed up Uxmal, Labná, Sayil and Kabáh in order to set up their capital at Chichén Itzá and to establish Izamal as their main ceremonial centre. These two cities had played only subordinate roles in Classic times. Of course, that may have been the reason why they were chosen: as lesser cities, they did not have a strong, established body of traditions of their own. Under the Toltecs, Chichén Itzá, in particular, underwent a glorious transformation and the entire Yucatán region experienced a second cultural blossoming.

Chichén Itzá has been carefully reconstructed in recent times and is now one of the greatest tourist attractions on the Yucatán Peninsula. Within the Temple of the Warriors and "El Castillo", the temple of Kukulkan, are smaller structures dating from the first Toltec invasion. In the twelfth century, these were covered over with the larger, more awesome structures now visible.

The Toltec invaders were strikingly tolerant towards the native Maya population: instead of forcing their own religious concepts upon them, they let them retain their belief in the ancient gods of maize and vegetation. The innovative, astral-based religion of the Nahua peoples remained the preserve of the military and political leaders set up by the Toltec conquerors. The co-existence of two distinct religious ideologies is manifested in that blend of structural and decorative styles which is the hallmark of Maya-Toltec architecture. While the temples of Chichén Itzá are practically copies of the Temple of the Morning Star at Tula, they are embellished with the traditional motifs found in Maya friezes and reliefs. Most prevalent of all motifs is the mask of the rain god Chac: the monstrously distorted face of a half-man-half-beast with a sweeping trunk-like snout – a symbol of rain.

This blending process was not only limited to religion and architecture; it soon made itself felt in the ethnic make-up of the people as well. Almost from the onset, the conquerors mingled with the indigenous Maya, thus setting the stage for the growth and development of a "mixed" civilization. This process of integration continued up to the arrival of the Spanish. We know from artefacts and bones dredged up from the bottom of the "Cenote Sagrado" or Sacred Well (a deep circular sinkhole with a pool at the bottom) that the water gods who resided there were worshipped continuously from Pre-Classic times to the 16th century.

The wealth of legends and lore handed down from the Late Maya-Toltec or Cocom phase has much to tell us about life and customs one thousand years ago. It is chronicled, for instance, that the last great pilgrimage to Chichén Itzá took place in 1536. Prince Tutul Xiu, who led the pilgrimage, was reportedly murdered along with his followers by Prince Nachi Cocom, the lord of the region of Chichén Itzá. From this it may be concluded that pilgrims had access to ceremonial centres in enemy territory – thus supporting the theory that an "Olympian truce" was observed in these places. It is also reported that, under these circumstances, Nachi Cocom's heinous crime provoked general outrage.

Around the year 1200, the Cocom took possession of Chichén Itzá, thereby ushering in the end of the era of Toltec rule. They moved the capital to Mayapan, where it remained until around 1450. City planning and construction in this late phase were very distinctive: temple complexes of the kind found in the old ceremonial centres were no longer built. While temples certainly existed, secular buildings housing complexes and the like predominated. Elements such as fortified walls and enormous casemates in which war material was stored and troops put up appeared for the first time. These impressive defence works can be seen today in Mayapan and in the coastal town of Tulum in Quintana Roo.

With the trend towards concentrating the population in fortified cities came a decline in architectural refinement. Raw blocks of stone piled up and stuck together with thick layers of plaster replaced the carefully hewn limestone used in earlier constructions. Embellishments were no longer carved in relief, but merely cut into the plaster. Furthermore, the Mayas didn't know much about statics, so they tried to make up for their ignorance by concentrating on voluminousness. This tendency to overcompensate was especially pronounced in the Cocom phase: the warped walls of many buildings display a crudeness of style and construction which is virtually unrivalled.

Typical examples of Late Maya architecture can be found in Tulum, a town on the Caribbean familiar to us through early Spanish chronicles.

In 1511, a lifeboat carrying the crew of a Spanish ship which had gone aground on a sand bar off the island of Jamaica, went ashore on the eastern coast of the Yucatán Peninsula. Some of the men were sacrified to the gods; others became slaves of Kinich, the lord of Zama (the present-day Tulum). In 1518, the explorer Grijalva sailed past Tulum. He was to describe the sight in euphoric terms, comparing the city with Seville. One year later, one of the shipwrecked Spanish crewmen joined up with Cortés. This man, who had lived among the Maya – or rather, the Cocom – in Tulum for eight years, became Cortés' first interpreter, a function he fulfilled until the arrival of the legendary Doña Marina.

This man was the only European interpreter we know of. We certainly could have learned a great deal from this witness to the final phase of ancient Indian culture, but sadly, he left no records.

"City of Beans" and "Place of Food" – The Zapotecs and Mixtecs of the Valley of Oaxaca

Following the fall of Tenochtitlán and the collapse of the Aztec empire – when the conquistadores began sorting through and dividing up the spoils – Captain-General Hernán Cortés named himself "Marqués del Valle", Marquis of the Valley. The valley in question was the fertile Valley of Oaxaca, known for its physical beauty, its mild, temperate climate and its high productivity. The newly-created marquis, however, had a difficult time taking possession of his domain. Not wanting anything at all to do with Catholicism and European culture, the Zapotec subjects of His Most Catholic Majesty fought bitterly against the Spanish, successfully resisting bondage and massacre.

The Aztecs, too, had had their difficulties with the Zapotecs when they ranged out to Oaxaca during their campaigns of conquest in the late 15th century. The purpose of their invasion was to secure free access to the port on the Isthmus of Tehuantepec from which their merchant ships sailed the Pacific coast down to Peru. Of foremost importance, however, was the route to Soconusco, the source of that coveted import, cocoa. The exact location of this far-off province has never been determined, but it is thought to be somewhere in southwestern Guatemala or in Nicaragua. The Aztecs eventually managed to bully the Zapotecs into granting them unhindered passage through their territory and the right to set up garrisons in Oaxaca and Tehuantepec, but they never managed to conquer or control the area in any way. The great importance the Aztecs attached to Tehuantepec is illustrated by the fact that Moctezuma II, an able and energetic soldier in his youth, was sent there while still a prince to command the garrison and represent Aztec interests.

The Spaniards did not fare much better: while they did gain control of the valley and the route to Tehuantepec, they never did vanquish the Highland Zapotecs and the Chinantepecs. These peoples, whose home was in the inaccessible highlands, were feared because of their giant lances, described by Spanish chroniclers as being 7.6 metres (25 feet) long.

Zapotec civilization was of the ancient theocratic kind. While this level of cultural development disappeared without trace in the central highlands after being eclipsed by the culture of the Post-Classic Nahua peoples, it continued thriving and developing in the Valley of Oaxaca well into historic times. Thus it is possible for us to draw general conclusions about the nature of other theocratic civilizations, such as Teotihuacán, Cholula and Xochicalco.

In his report on events which occurred during the conquest of Mexico – set down in 1674 – the Spanish monk Francisco de Burgoa tells us much about the Zapotecs and their system of government. De Burgoa writes that after the fall of Tenochtitlán, the Spaniards initially left the Zapotecs alone despite the fact that they were allies of the Aztecs. Finally, in 1563, the last Zapotec king, Cocijo-pij, was indicted and subsequently deposed – an act which amounted to a flagrant travesty of justice. According to de Burgoa's report, the Zapotec king was the Aztec ruler's equal, and the

Distribution of the Mixteca-Puebla Style

alliance between the two dissimilar states was consolidated through politically-motivated marriages. Most importantly, the monk's report tells us something about the inner workings of Zapotec government. We learn, for instance, that the king was by no means an absolute monarch like the Aztec ruler, but that he had a number of councillors at his side (not under him). Furthermore, he shared power and rank with a high priest, whom he had to approach with deference and respect and whose instructions he was obliged to follow.

It is obvious that the office of the "uija-tao", the Zapotecs' "pope", was the older institution in Zapotec society. This authentic and fully-functioning relict of a theocratic culture reflected the nature and workings of other ancient highland cultures. The "uija-tao" resided in a palace in Mitla, now restored and open to the public.

A distinctive feature of Zapotec theocracy was its pantheon of gods. Like those of the Maya, Zapotec gods were similar to the gods of Teotihuacán and totally unlike the deities worshipped by the Toltecs and Aztecs. At the head of the pantheon was the rain god Cocijo, also known as Pitao, "Great One". His name was incorporated into the names of most Zapotec kings. The rain god appeared in four different forms, corresponding to the four cardinal points. This god stood at the centre of the Zapotec calendar. In contrast, the sun god (an astral god) was at the centre of the Aztec calendar.

The Zapotecs were – and are – concentrated mainly in the almost subtropic and extremely fertile Valley of Oaxaca. The names of the cities testify to the productivity of this area: Etla, "City of Beans", and Loouanna, "Place of Food". While Loouanna is a pure Zapotec name, the majority of Zapotec place names have come down to us in their Aztec (Nahuatl) form. The old capital Zaachila-yoo ("Place of Rule") for instance, is known to us by its Aztec name, Teotzapotlan. Even the name "Zapotec" – actually "Tzapotec" – is an Aztec word derived from the zapote fruit, a typical crop of the region.

While their commercial centres were located in the valley, the Zapotecs' oldest and holiest place was situated high atop a plateau – Monte Albán. With the exception of a small "palace" attached to the nearby observatory and used as a residence for priests, all building compounds and structures here were obviously built for ceremonial purposes. Monte Albán was never a defended city.

The oldest traces of settlement and artistic activity which have been identified in the Valley of Oaxaca date from the period known as Monte Albán I, which ran from approximately 700 to 300 B. C. and saw the first cult monuments decorated in detailed relief. The best known representative of early Monte Albán architecture is the Courtyard of the Dancers, so named because of its series of reliefs depicting crippled or dwarf-like figures in strangely contorted poses. These reliefs – which show marked Olmec influence – are of a style known as Olmecoid. Recent excavations conducted by the Instituto Nacional de Antropologia y Historia under Ignacio Bernal have unearthed traces of the Olmecs in other important Zapotec cities as well. In addition to Teotitlán del Valle, Macuilxochitl and Daintzu, other sites with Olmec horizons are certain to be discovered as the digging goes on.

The "Dancers" are accompanied by glyphs of the sort typical to Zapotec culture, but because there is no proof that such glyphs were in use during Monte Albán I, it must be assumed that they were added at a later date. A Zapotec calendar and system of writing did not appear until Monte Albán III, which extended over the second half of the first millenium A. D. In the culture of Monte Albán, this was the Classic phase – the time when architecture and the cult behind it reached their pinnacles. All buildings were reconstructed, covered over or built anew. The Monte Albán we see today is the product of this phase.

During Monte Albán IV, the site lost its significance as a cult centre and was abandoned. We do not know if this happened suddenly or in successive stages, only that the "holy mountain" retained its significance as a burial site for persons of rank. This was a time of cultural change in the valley as well as on Monte Albán, as evidenced by the ceramic burial offerings found there.

While early Zapotec pottery was simple in form and decorated only with scratched-out designs, later pottery was fashioned in more elaborate shapes. In this period, the simple, walled-in burial chambers of early Monte Albán gave way to cruciform crypts of the kind also found in Mitla and Zaachila. These profound changes came about as a result of the infiltration of the Mixtecs, a people related to the Zapotecs. The Mixtecs came to the Valley of Oaxaca from the Gulf of Tehuantepec and eventually overshadowed their kinsmen ethnically and culturally.

Over two hundred graves have been found in Monte Albán thus far – most of them on the plateau's southern flank. Virtually all of them, when found, had already been ransacked and plundered by treasure hunters and grave robbers. Very little remains: some pottery, some of the magnificent idols and effigy vessels, some bones. The early "excavators" were primarily interested in precious metals and if "Tomb No. 7" – discovered intact in 1932 – is typical, there can be no doubt that they made quite a catch. The discovery of Tomb No. 7 caused a sensation in the world of Mexican archaeology equal to that caused in the world of Egyptology by the discovery of the tomb of Tutankhamen ten years before. Plunderers had not found this underground crypt as they had been digging in the wrong place. The Mixtec prince buried here was surrounded by about 500 funerary objects, each more precious and beautiful than the one before. Today, these objects are on exhibit in the museum inside the Monastery Santo Domingo in Oaxaca – one of the main attractions for visitors to that city.

An interesting discovery was made during the investigation of this and other Monte Albán tombs. While almost all the large crypts date from earlier Zapotec periods, they had obviously been cleared of their furnishings by the Mixtecs, who had then fitted them out in their own way. To interpret this as an act of hostility would be a gross mistake: these peoples were just too closely related. Furthermore, their religious beliefs were similar, if not identical.

This close kinship is clearly portrayed in the Mixtec painted manuscripts or codices, among the most beautiful examples of Mexican art which have been handed down to us. Some of these, most notably the Borgia Codex, give us insight into the religious beliefs, the gods and the concepts of the afterworld which were current in this civilization.

The Zapotecs exist today as an ethnic entity with the corresponding

sense of ethnic pride. The more than one hundred thousand Mexicans who call themselves "Zapoteca" are proud not only of "their" Benito Juárez, but also of an almost two-thousand-year-old cultural tradition which the Spaniards may have managed to bend but never did manage to break!

The Nahua Peoples: Morning Star and Human Sacrifice

For the historic Mexicans – i. e. the Aztecs – their predecessors, the inhabitants of Tollan, were a people shrouded in myth and mystery. The Nahuatl word "tolteca", which conveyed an attitude of respect, meant "artist, scientist" – an indication that while the Aztecs had an idea of the cultural achievements of their ancestors, those achievements had taken on a legendary aura for them. The Aztecs integrated the Toltecs into their mythical conception of history by identifying them as the founders of human civilization, the first people to inhabit the world of the fifth sun, the era in which the Aztecs themselves lived.

About seven centuries passed between the fall of the Classic civilizations of the central highlands and the rise of the Aztec empire – seven centuries which, in the highlands, were marked by the presence of the Toltecs and Chichimecs. In all probability, the advancing Toltecs had something to do with the fall of Teotihuacán. They settled in the plateau of Hidalgo and established their capital, Tollan (Tula), there. What is interesting about the Toltecs are not those aspects of their culture which they adopted from past cultures (pottery, the ball court, certain architectural details), but the innovations they brought with them which gave expression to their utter uniqueness.

Toltec social organization was based on a rigid hierarchy strictly aligned to the priest-king at the head of the state. His power rested upon two socially prominent castes, those of the eagle and jaguar knights. These have been aptly compared to the Knights Templar – a fraternal order whose function lay in ritual observances and in warfare. The Nahua peoples with their militaristic ideology stood in marked contrast to the earlier theocracies which, as far as we know, were relatively peace-loving and certainly did not wage wars of conquest. The religious beliefs of the Toltecs were also different: their central deity was the Morning Star God, called Tlahuitzcalpantecutli or "Lord in the House of Dawn". In addition, Quetzalcoátl played a central role. This god in the guise of a plumed-serpent was adopted from Teotihuacán but given new substance by the Toltecs. According to Aztec legend, Quetzalcoátl was repugnant-looking: his face was hairy and his features coarse. For this reason, he lived as a recluse in his palace, surrounded by riches more grand than any ever amassed before.

It must be mentioned that, in Aztec legend, Toltec wealth, prosperity and grandeur took on fabulous proportions. For them, the mythical

Toltecs were the exact opposites of the Chichimecs.

The Toltec phase ended with the fall of their empire around A. D. 1200. What followed was the formation of Chichimec kingdoms, some of them mere city-states, some of them with control over larger areas. These states situated around Lake Texcoco were the ones the Mexica (or the Aztecs, as we call them) encountered when they arrived in the 14th century. Like the Toltecs and Chichimecs before them, the Mexica were a nomadic tribe of hunters who, upon their arrival, came under the influence of the old cultures, learned from them, and quickly developed their own unique civilization.

Fortunately for us, a number of codices from the Chichimec realm (later the heartland of the Mexica empire) still exist. Miraculously, the archives of the city of Texcoco were spared from the destructiveness of the Spaniards. In one of these manuscripts a certain Ixtlilxóchitl, himself a member of the royal house of Texcoco, recounts the history of the Chichimec people. He writes that they came out of the north, led by a legendary king by the name of Xolotl. They acquired the trappings of culture when they came into contact with the Toltecs who, after the downfall of their kingdom, had settled in Colhuacán and other cities around the lake. Here we clearly see that the Toltecs took on the role of teachers to the less-civilized Chichimecs. Our chronicler tells of a dynasty founded by Xolotl and describes how the Chichimecs gained control over the entire Valley of Mexico. Ixtlilxóchitl's history does not portray the Chichimecs politically as a tribal alliance or a "nation", but as a multitude of tribes – much like the Gauls and Teutons of Caesar's time. These peoples had similar cultural traits (or a similar lack thereof) and a common language. Some lived in enmity with one another, and others, in harmony. The most important power factors which the events of the 13th century brought to the fore were the Tepanec city-state of Azcapotzalco and the dynasty of Texcoco. The latter, which is also known as the dynasty of Colhuacán, spawned such famous rulers as the great Nezahualcoyotl.

Of course, the existing centres of power sought continuously to integrate other tribes into their realms. This was probably necessary as a means of preventing inbreeding and preserving the typical Chichimec "bellicose spirit". The archives show that the ruler of Texcoco carried the honorary title of "Lord of the Chichimecs" ("chichimecatl tecutli").

Encounters between city-dwellers and their less-civilized kinsmen generally took a violent course – as was the case when the Tepanecs had to send troops to assist the lord of Colhuacán in averting the attacks of an agressive, predatory band which had settled near the lake on a hill called Chapultepec (Hill of the Locust). The Aztecs had arrived! Historians place this event at the end of the 13th century. Eventually, this band of ruffians was forced to acknowledge the supremacy of Colhuacán, but they continued provoking trouble and finally had to be expelled. The Mexica retreated to an island in the lake where there was nothing but "reeds and water", as an Aztec chronicler piteously remarked. This island was to become the foundation for the great city of Tenochtitlán and of present-day Mexico City: the seeds of the Aztec empire had been planted!

(Thieme)

Eagle and Serpent: The Aztec State

According to chronological data supplied by their own historians, the Aztecs (or Mexica) arrived at Chapultepec in 1256 and were expelled from there by the Tepanecs and the princes of Colhuacán shortly before the end of the 13th century. Furthermore, the Aztecs report that in the course of this punitive action their leader was killed and their population decimated; the survivors were reduced to fleeing to a number of miserable islands in Lake Texcoco. No one knows exactly how the wretched fishing settlement they established there could have evolved into the great city of Tenochtitlán in so short a time: within a hundred years, it had become the centre of an empire that dominated the entire central plateau.

Recent findings show that the founding of the Aztec capital of Tenochtitlán did not actually take place until around 1370. It is also known that a settlement had already existed on the islands – Tlatelolco, later a district, or better, a suburb of Tenochtitlán. The residents of Tlatelolco had even begun building up the banks of earth which made possible the later expansion of the Aztec city.

The name "Tenochtitlán" is probably of pre-Aztec origin and means "Place of Tenoch", Tenoch most likely being the name of a prince or ruler of some kind. Following their arrival, the Aztecs had to find a way to connect this name to themselves and their history. Tradition has it that priests went out to look for a sign from their tribal god, Huitzilopochtli, telling them where to establish their city. When they reached the appointed place, the god let his will be known: an eagle devouring a snake sat perched on a nopal cactus which was growing out of a rock. This positive sign offered the Aztecs a suitable etymology for the word "Tenochtitlán": in Nahuatl, the nopal cactus is "nochtli" and rock is "tetl". Hence, Tenochtitlán could mean "the place where the cactus grows from the rock". Later, this mythical scene was immortalized in the crest of the City of Tenochtitlán. Today, it is also incorporated in the emblem of the Republic of Mexico.

In a matter of only a few decades, the Aztecs managed to bring the region surrounding Lake Texcoco as well as the entire central plateau under their control. Their centralized system of government, their "unspent" aggressivity and a probable population explosion were all factors which contributed to their rapid rise.

With the reign of their fourth king, Itzcoatl (1425–1437), Aztec history emerges from the shrouds of legend. It is said that this king had all the old codices burned because they were "full of lies". Then, having wiped out all written traces of the past, he manipulated history to his own liking. His successor, Moctezuma I (actually Moctecuhzoma; "Moctezuma" is a Spanish corruption) was the great conqueror: the territory he brought under Aztec control corresponded roughly in size to the realm the Spaniards were to encounter seventy years later. After eliminating the last of the petty principalities in the Valley of Mexico he turned toward the south, sweeping through Oaxaca and down to the Gulf of Tehuantepec. Axayacatl – "Water Face" – vigourously pursued a similar policy of conquest, subduing Tlatelolco once and for all and conquering the Valley of Toluca.

During the reign of Axayacatl's brother and successor, Tizoc, the great stone cylinder depicting fifteen tributary princes was raised in the main plaza of Tenochtitlán. This monument is now one of the main attractions of the Aztec Room in the Museum of Mexico City. Tizoc also commissioned the reconstruction of the Great Temple dedicated to the gods Huitzilopochtli and Tlaloc, an undertaking which was eventually completed during the reign of Ahuitzotl (1486–1502). The latter, whose name means "Water Creature", conquered Colima, Acapulco and other regions on the Pacific, and strengthened the Aztec's position in the port city of Tehuantepec. Ahuitzotl is also credited with having launched a large-scale military expedition into the cocoa-growing district of Soconusco which yielded a rich haul of booty.

Finally, under his regime the Huaxtec regions on the Gulf coast were "pacified" and annexed. This great ruler died young: he drowned in a disastrous flood that ravaged the entire city of Tenochtitlán. But the Aztec empire he left behind was the one that Hernán Cortés and his band of adventurers discovered and conquered bit by bit following their arrival in Veracruz in 1519.

Moctezuma and Cortés: Two Worlds Collide

The confrontation between the Spaniards and Aztecs and the point in time when it occurred were both preordained – neither of the parties involved could have done anything to alter their fate. Neither of them knew the first thing about the other: they had nothing in common, no basis for mutual understanding, no knowledge of the other's mentality or cultural background. Under these circumstances, neither of the two may be blamed or criticized: Moctezuma and Cortés both behaved in accordance with their own individual histories. The story of how two dissimilar worlds collided – the history of the conquest and its main participants – has been told time and time again, mostly from the point of view of the Europeans.

Cortés' letters to the Spanish king and Bernal Diaz de Castillo's "Memoirs" tell one side of the story – and this side is well known. The Aztec version, however, has only recently become the subject of

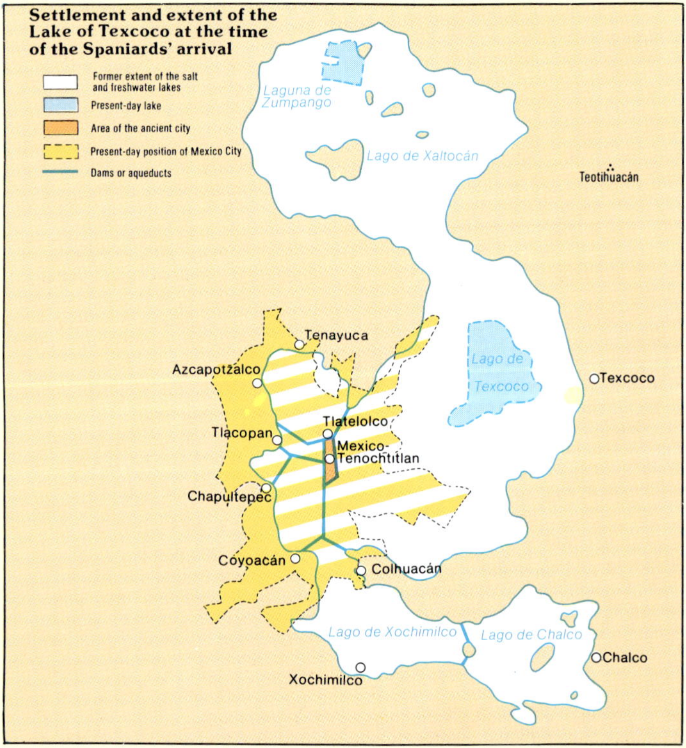

research and investigation. Thanks to the Spanish friars who came with the conquistadores to spread the Christian faith, we have a wealth of information about the Aztecs, their history and their way of life. Some of these missionaries, notably Bernardino de Sahagún and Diego de Durán, tried to save what they could: they collected ancient documents, wrote down tales and legends, learned Nahuatl, taught the Indians Spanish and taught them to write Nahuatl as well, using the Latin alphabet. In this way, the Spanish friars compiled volumes of memoirs and historical records which report on events during the short amount of time between the arrival of the Spaniards and the downfall of the Aztec civilization.

The Aztec "empire" encountered by the Spaniards was certainly not a consolidated political organization: it was not supported by a uniform ideology or culture; its people shared no sense of solidarity. It came into being through wars of conquest and was held together – albeit loosely – by military force. The conquered peoples were forced not only to pay tribute to the Aztecs in Tenochtitlán, but to give up their status as independent states. Obviously, they had reason enough to resent their Aztec lords and to try any means possible to free themselves from foreign domination.

In the years prior to the conquest, Aztec supremacy found itself resting on unsteady ground. The monarch, who was lord of the Aztec people and head of the government, the priesthood and the military, was virtually incapacitated. Moctezuma II, who in his youth had been an able and energetic officer, took to brooding as he got older. He surrounded himself with augurs, soothsayers and astrologers who informed him of ill omens and prophesied the return of the great god Quetzalcoátl. He was burdened by anxiety and a pessimistic nature, and convinced of the inevitability of fate. Of course, the Spaniards who stepped onto Mexican soil on Good Friday of the year 1519 had no notion of Moctezuma's emotional state. They were obsessed with the expectation (based on earlier reports) of finding gold and coming away with enough spoils to ensure them all personal wealth.

Upon landing, the Spaniards first came into contact with the Huaxtecs of Cempoala. These people received them with a mixture of curiosity and caution, but also with a great deal of hospitality. The leaders of the neighbouring Tlaxcaltecs quickly realized that with the support of these strangers they could shake off the yoke of Aztec subjugation. The Tlaxcaltecs and others got their wish – but what a price they had to pay!

It did not take long before the Aztec authorities in Tenochtitlán heard of the goings-on in the east – of the remarkable strangers who had come from the sea on "floating mountains", as the Indians called their ships. Moctezuma sent out emissaries laden with gifts to welcome the "gods". Tradition has it that they spoke the following words of greeting: "May it please the Lord to hear us! Your representative Moctezuma has sent us to pay you homage. He has your city of Mexico in his care!"

The Spaniards were reticent at first, and took their time to study the situation. The nature of Aztec rule, however, soon became clear to them. After having had the opportunity to observe the arrogance of the tax collectors and the hostility the subjugated peoples harboured for Tenochtitlán, they began working out a plan of action, taking into account the political realities. Exiled chiefs, deposed princes, and politicians stripped of their offices soon joined up with the Spaniards, offering them their invaluable services.

One such person was Ixtlilxochitl, whom the Aztecs had driven out of Texcoco. In the Valley of Chalco region, the Spaniards were offered not only porters and food supplies, but auxilliary troops as well. One of the most important sources of help that the Spaniards had at their disposal was the Indian woman Doña Marina, or Malinche, who joined up with Cortés in Tabasco. Once the wife of an independent Kazik, she had been sold into slavery and was full of hatred for the Aztecs. Besides Nahuatl, she spoke Maya and was thus able to communicate with Gerónimo de Aguilar, who had lived for years in Tulum as prisoner of the Maya. Doña Marina quickly learned Spanish, and thereafter served Cortés not only as interpreter, but as a keen and loyal advisor as well. Her contribution to the success of the Mexican conquest can hardly be overstated: she knew the land, its political set-up, its rulers and their vulnerable spots.

Moctezuma and his officers and ministers were not in the least surprised by the appearance of the Spaniards in Veracruz. The Aztec ruler had had the movements of Spanish ships in the Gulf of Mexico monitored for some time: he had also been aware of the presence of Spaniards on the Yucatán coast in 1517/18. Chances are that he was at some point presented with illustrated manuscripts which gave him an idea of the strange appearance of the intruders and of the unusual "deer" they had with them. The Aztec emissaries sent to Veracruz were accompanied by draughtsmen who portrayed everything they saw. The Spaniards' cats, dogs and, of course, their horses seemed to intrigue them the most.

Moctezuma can hardly be blamed for treating the Spaniards as guests. Only when their hostile intentions became apparent did his incapacity to take charge become a critical problem. One thing the Aztecs did not know about at this time, in any case, was European weaponry: harquebuses and cannons must have struck them with sheer terror when they first saw them in action. The impending disaster became inevitable when Cortés made the decision to press forward to Tenochtitlán. By this time a faction of nobles, who recognized the Spaniards as the enemy, had already rallied behind Moctezuma's nephew Cuauhtémoc. The massacre of the people of Cholula provided them with all the evidence they needed of the Spaniards so-called "peaceful intentions". Moctezuma vacillated. The events of the following months clearly show that he had already begun isolating himself midway through the year 1519 and that his councillors and officers only reluctantly supported him.

On November 3, 1519 the Spaniards reached the mountain pass overlooking Mexico City and were met by an Aztec delegation led by Tzihuacpopoca. The gold leaf and feather banners presented to them were wrongly taken to be tokens of greeting. In fact, they were meant as a threat: such banners were customarily carried by prisoners on their way to the sacrificial altar. Once in the city – no military action of any kind had been taken to prevent them from entering – they were treated as guests, albeit with some misgivings. They took up quarters in Moctezuma's palace, a structure easy to fortify and defend. Moctezuma himself stayed with them, although hardly of his own free will: he was more their prisoner than their guest. All this happened shortly before the Aztec celebration of "Toxcatl", an important annual religious observance.

The atmosphere in Tenochtitlán seems to have been very tense on the eve of this celebration. Mutual mistrust prevailed and a feeling of imminent confrontation filled the air. During this decisive phase, Cortés had to return to Veracruz to face troops sent out by the governor of Cuba, Velásquez, with orders to bring him back. His own troops were left in Moctezuma's palace under Alvarado's command. All sources are in agreement about the further course of events: shortly after the celebration began, the Spaniards sealed off all entrances to the temple precinct and massacred the dancers and priests, all of whom were clearly unarmed and defenceless. Obviously, the Spaniards alone were to blame for this senseless bloodshed.

From that moment on, it was all-out war. The Indians took up arms under Cuauhtémoc's command and laid siege to the palace where Moctezuma, now bound and shackled, was openly being held prisoner. They soon realized, however, that their arms were powerless against the well-entrenched Spaniards, so they staged a more effective form of assault: they waited until the palace stores of food and water ran out. Under these conditions, the Spaniards could not hold their position for long.

On the gloomy, wet night of June 30th 1520, they and their Tlaxcalan allies left the stronghold. At first they managed to remain unseen, but when they reached the third causeway they were spotted by the Aztecs and pursued by them in their boats. At the cost of half their men, the Spaniards eventually managed to reach the mainland and allied territory. This went down in history as the "Noche Triste" or Sad Night. What happened next is well known. Cortés had been successful in recruiting troops from among those sent out to arrest him, and with regrouped forces he attacked Tenochtitlán and conquered it within a year. Cuauhtémoc was taken prisoner and murdered; Moctezuma's son, Chimalpopoca, fell in battle. Moctezuma himself was spared having to witness the fall of the Aztec empire as he had been killed by a stone thrown at him during the siege of his palace.

While there can be no doubt that the Spaniards would have attacked the Aztec empire sooner or later and that – thanks to their superior weaponry – they would have been victorious in any event, it is also clear that Cortés did not want to stage his attack at the time he did and under the given strategic circumstances. The senseless massacre of the dancers in the temple precinct which ultimately led to the death of half his comrades seems to have been the result of a loss of nerve on Alvarado's part. In the story of the conquest Moctezuma hardly plays a role. While he indeed became Alvarado's prisoner toward the end, he had become a prisoner of himself long before that. Wrapped in gloom, full of indecision and torn by imaginary fears, he lived in a fantasy world of which the Spaniards had no notion. They were appalled by the practice of human sacrifice, so central to Aztec cult ritual, and believed it was the work of the Antichrist himself. It is not hard to imagine how they felt as they watched their captured comrades being butchered by priests at the top of temple pyramids. How could they have known that, to the Aztecs, death on the sacrificial altar was the greatest honour that could be given a warrior: he would then become an attendant of the Sun God and be granted entry into the highest level of the Aztecs' paradise.

In the worlds which separated the culture of Old Spain from the realities of the New World were the many reasons why the Aztecs and Spaniards could not meet, but only collide. *(Thieme)*

The Aztec State at the time of the Spaniards' arrival
0 100 km
0 50 miles
Gulf of Mexico
Bahia de Campeche
Pacific
Ocean
Golfo de Tehuantepec
Huaxtecs
Chichimecs
Tarascos
Totonacs
Zapotecs
Maya
Tuxpan
Querétaro
R. Panuco
R. Grande
Tula
Teotihuacán
Patzcuaro See
Tzintzuntzan
Tlacopan
Texcoco
Mexico-Tenochtitlan
Region of Tlaxcala
Tlaxcala
Zempoala
Veracruz
Cholula
Satellite reg. Teotitlan del Camino
R. Balsas
Region of Yopetzinco
Acapulco
Oaxaca
Mixtec region of
Tututepec
R. Atoyac
Tehuantepec
R. Coatzacoalco
Way to Soconusco
Tuxtla Gutiérrez
R. Grijalva
San Pedro
Tribute district of Soconusco

Important Archaeological Sites

For advanced students of pre-Hispanic Mexican history, the Indian names of temple sites and archaeological zones conjure up clear images of what is to be found there. Novices, however, quickly find themselves "in over their heads" when it comes to locating places with cumbersome names like Cacaxtla or Tajin, Xochicalco or Tepoztlan on the map and then matching them up with the corresponding pre-Columbian culture. Mexico's many archaeological sites are widely scattered throughout its vast territory.

The following pages contain a list of the principal archaeological sites, their locations, corresponding cultures and main attractions. It must be mentioned, though, that this list is in no way complete – if it were, it would go beyond the limits of this and any other travel guide. On the Yucatán Peninsula alone, 300 important Maya sites have been identified; and throughout Mexico, there are some 20,000 (!) pre-Columbian ruins still waiting to be excavated and studied.

Travellers to Mexico who are interested in visiting archaeological sites should set aside three days for those in the vicinity of Mexico City: one full day should be set aside for Teotihuacán, and at least a half-day for Tula. An additional day is needed for Cholula and Cacaxtla. Tepoztlán and Xochicalco can also be taken in on a day's excursion.

Excavation sites	Indian culture	Of special interest	Nearest town	Region	Climate
Bonampak	Maya	Coloured murals	Villahermosa	Guatemalan border	tropical hot and humid
Casas Grandes	Hohokam/ Toltec	Platforms, ball courts	Ciudad Juárez	U. S. border	cold in winter hot in summer
Cacaxtla	Totonac Maya	Coloured murals	Puebla	2 hrs east of Mexico City	temperate
Chichén Itza	Maya/ Toltec	Temple of Kukulkan, Temple of Warriors, Observatory	Mérida	Yucatán Peninsula	hot and sunny
Cobá	Maya	7-tiered Pyramid	Mérida	Caribbean Coast Yucatán Peninsula	hot and sunny
Cholula	Olmec – Toltec	Tepanapa Pyramid (largest in America)	Puebla	1½ hrs east of Mexico City	temperate
Edzna	Maya	Temple of the Five Stories	Campeche	Gulf coast Yucatán Peninsula	hot and sunny
Kabáh	Maya	Codz-Pop, Palace of Geometric Decoration	Mérida	Northern Yucatán Peninsula	hot and sunny
Kohunlich	Maya	Pyramid of the Masks	Chetumal	Belize border	hot and humid
Labná	Maya	Mirador Pyramid, Arch of Labná	Mérida	Northern Yucatán Peninsula	hot and sunny
La Quemada/ Chicomoztoc	Toltec	Citadel, palace, temple	Zacatecas	Northeast of Guadalajara	temperate
La Venta	Olmec	Gigantic stone heads	Villahermosa	Gulf coast	hot and humid
Mayapán	Maya	Post-Classic architecture	Mérida	Western Yucatan Peninsula	hot and sunny

Mitla	Zapotecs/ Mixtecs	Geometric stone mosaics	Oaxaca	Valley of Oaxaca	temperate/warm
Monte Alban	Zapotecs/ Mixtecs	Courtyard of the Dancers, Tombs	Oaxaca	Valley of Oaxaca	temperate/warm
Palenque	Maya	Temple of Inscriptions Tomb of High Priest	Villahermosa	Gulf region	tropical, hot, humid
Sayil	Maya	Palace	Mérida	Northern Yucatán Peninsula	hot and sunny
El Tajin	Totonacs	Pyramid of Niches	Poza Rica	s. w. Gulf region	hot
Teotihuacán	Teotihuacans	Pyramid of the Sun Pyramid of the Moon	Mexico City	Central Highlands	temperate
Tepoztlán	Aztecs	Pyramid of the Pulque God Tepozteco	Cuernavaca	1½ hrs. south of Mexico City	temperate – warm
Tula	Toltecs	Temple, atlantes (Toltec warriors)	Mexico City	Central Highlands	temperate
Tulum	Maya	El Castillo, Temple of the Frescos	Mérida/ Cancun	Caribbean coast Yucatán Peninsula	hot and sunny
Uxmal	Maya	Palace of Governors, Pyramid of the Magician	Mérida	Northern Yucatán Peninsula	hot and sunny
Xel-ha	Maya	Temple at the Lagune	Mérida/ Chetumal	Caribbean coast Yucatán Peninsula	hot and sunny
Xochicalco	Teotihuacan/ Maya influence	Temple of Quetzalcoátl (Plumed Serpent)	Cuernavaca	2 hrs. south of Mexico City	temperate – warm
Yagul	Zapotecs/ Mixtecs	Palace of the Six Patios	Oaxaca	Valley of Oaxaca	temperate – warm
Zaachila	Zapotecs/ Mixtecs	Tombs	Oaxaca	Valley of Oaxaca	temperate – warm

Revolution...

The typical caricature of a Mexican shows a man in a wide-brimmed sombrero seated on a mule and holding a pistol in each hand. Nothing could be further removed from reality than this ridiculous image of a classic, indefatigable rebel. When the topic "revolution" comes up in Mexico, the lament most often heard is "We're sick to death of it". But exactly which of the many "revolutions" is being discussed at any one moment is hard to tell. In ninety out of a hundred cases, it is neither the war of independence against the Spaniards nor Benito Juarez' liberal reform programme: rather, the revolution of 1910 and the traumatic events of that time seem to have entrenched themselves most firmly in the hearts and minds of the Mexicans. There are still many people alive today who can remember that quarter century of murder and war.

From the "insurgentes" to freedom...

The name "the insurgentes" was coined by the Spanish authorities. They meant it depreciatively, of course, but it soon became a title of honour and was later given to the longest street in Mexico, the Avenida Insurgentes. The first and most eminent "insurgent" was Miguel Hidalgo y Costilla (1753–1811). In his youth, he was a gifted Jesuit student and member of many debating clubs. At this time, the Jesuits were actively involved in spreading the spirit of the Enlightenment in Mexico – much to the displeasure of the Spanish crown. Impressed by the American and French revolutions, the members of scholarly circles soon transformed their societies into revolutionary cells. Human rights and liberation from the Spanish yoke were the central ideas of the day.

Hidalgo became a priest – more for the sake of a career than out of any sense of calling. He left the pastoral work to his fellow priests and devoted himself to politics and agricultural experiments. His personal life was far from being directed by priestly ideals and vows. He accepted the leadership of the conspiratory groups which had formed in many of Mexico's cities. Before they were able to mount an attack, however, the Spaniards learned of their existence and they were thus forced to act hastily.

On September 16th 1810, the war of independence against Spain began with the "Grito de Dolores", Hidalgo's famous cry ("grito") for insurrection from the bell tower of the church of Dolores. The bell he tolled now stands as a memorial above the central portal of the National Palace in Mexico City. This first, premature revolt against the colonialists came to an end after seven short months. Hidalgo was executed in Chihuahua on July 30th 1811.

Ideas, of course, cannot be put to death. The fight for freedom went on until 1821 when the Spaniards were finally driven out of Mexico.

But for the newly-independent land, the road to freedom was to be a long and hard one. Although the country was indeed independent, it had an emperor at its helm – a native one, but an emperor all the same. General Augustín Iturbide put himself on the Mexican throne as Augustín I in 1822: in 1823, however, he was deposed by republican generals and declared an outlaw by congressional decree. He fled abroad, but was captured and executed upon attempting to return to Mexico one year later.

The political conditions in Mexico following the departure of the Spaniards can only be described as chaotic. A power vacuum had been left behind and the young republic did not have a political structure strong enough to bear the weight of independence. Under the presidency of Guadelupe Victoria (1824–1834) the federal republic was created. Unfortunately, it functioned better on paper than in reality. During the turbulent years between 1821 and 1861, there were no fewer than 58 governments, none of which was capable of controlling the entire country. Interestingly enough, only two of them lasted out their entire term; 56 came to a premature end through coups d'état. The reasons for this chaos are obvious: none of the groups which made up Mexico's class society was strong enough to wield power on its own, and a basis for a functioning democracy was simply non-existent. Furthermore, the different groups each had their own interests to look after and none of them intended to answer to a central authority. The landed gentry, the army and the clergy constantly plotted and schemed against one another and built up regional spheres of influence for themselves in order to bypass the authority of the central government.

The social question was an ever more volatile one. The great mass of people were impoverished smallholders, exploited farm hands and uprooted Indians. Social injustice became more and more apparent; finally, a seemingly-infinite number of problems were crying out for drastic solutions.

Continued foreign intervention contributed to the land's political instability. One of the most illustrious and fascinating personalities of this era was General Antonio Lopez de Santa Ana. His rise to the presidency occurred partly thanks to legal elections and partly thanks to coups d'état. Now seen by some as a hero and by others as a traitor, he held the fate of Mexico in his hands for several decades. He became the key figure in Mexico's fateful confrontation with the United States which began as a territorial skirmish in the north and ended up as all-out war.

The northern Mexican states of Texas, New Mexico, Arizona and California were sparsely populated, trackless, desolate areas which no-one in the capital city paid any attention to. But some time after Mexico allowed North American pioneers to settle in Texas, the capital city was forced to take notice. As their numbers grew, Mexico imposed restrictions; hostile encounters between the settlers and the token Mexican forces increased. General Santa Ana led his army on a punitive expedition to Texas and was victorious at the Alamo. At San Jacinto, however, the Texans, uttering the battle cry "Remember the Alamo!" defeated Santa Ana, took him prisoner and forced him to recognize Texan independence.

That was only the beginning. In 1845, Texas joined the United States and the U. S.-Mexican War broke out.

Mexico's defeat in this war turned into a national disaster. With the loss of all its territory north of the Rio Grande, the country was demoralized and humiliated. Santa Ana was driven into exile in 1855. As so often happens, however, these difficult times brought the Mexicans together as a people and strengthened their sense of a national identity. Intellectuals and Federalists united to create Mexico's first constitution in 1857 – a constitution which did away with special privileges for the military and the clergy. The church, the country's largest owner of land and capital, resisted bitterly, even going so far as to threaten any and all who swore allegiance to this constitution with excommunication. With the aid of the church, the Conservatives overthrew the government and the president was forced to flee. These events precipitated the rise of Benito Juárez and his pupil, Porfirio Díaz.

Benito Juárez was – and this point is emphasized with pride in Mexico today – a pureblood Indian, that is, a Zapotec from the state of Oaxaca. As a boy, he was singled out by his teachers for the priesthood, but his future was to take a different course. Juárez, who did not learn Spanish until he was thirteen, became a lawyer, took on high posts in the administration of the state of Oaxaca and eventually became governor. In the 1850's, he occupied high federal posts in Mexico City and was appointed head of the Supreme Court. In accordance with the constitution, he was therefore first in line for the presidency should the president be unable to carry out the functions of his office. This occurred in 1858, and Benito Juárez was named president of Mexico.

As a proponent of reform laws and initiator of the new, liberal constitution, Juárez was not exactly a candidate after the hearts of the Conservatives, the military or the clergy. They overthrew the government and Juárez was forced to flee. The shabby black coach which took him zig-zagging across the country became a symbol of Mexican patriotism. From his northern retreat, he was able to organize the resistance (with the aid of the United States) and a lengthy civil war broke out which went down in Mexican history as the War of the Reform. In 1861,

Spanish Colonial Policy in Mexico

Following the discovery of the New World by Columbus (who was convinced he had reached India), the two naval powers of Spain and Portugal began a fierce battle over territorial rights and spheres of influence. A treaty effected by the Spanish Pope Alexander VI in 1494 set the line of demarcation between the two colonial empires at 370 miles west of the Cape Verde Islands. It was not until 1513, when Florida was discovered and Balboa reached the Pacific Ocean, that the explorers realized that they had discovered a "new world" and not an easterly route to India. Some time passed before the arrival of Hernán Cortés and the other conquistadores. It is clear that their coming had nothing to do with humanistic ambitions, but that they operated solely out of a desire for profits. They were drawn by their greed for silver and gold and the prospect of exploiting the natural resources of these faraway lands.

A bona fide desire to spread the "true faith" may have moved the one or the other to come to the Americas, but more often than not the crucifix and the Bible were, at best, pretexts used to cloak economic interests. The Aztec empire quickly fell and the Spaniards soon found themselves faced with the question of how to administer this vast new territory. This had not been a problem during the conquistadores' lifetimes. Officers and troops, by virtue of their superior might, had taken pos-

after three years of fighting, Juárez entered the capital city victorious and took up his office as president.

But the shattered country was not to find peace for a long time to come. Its economy was in a shambles and the government was forced to declare a two-year moratorium on the payment of foreign-debt interest. Because of the role they had played in the civil war, the papal nuncio and the Spanish envoy were expelled from the country. These events caused alarm in Europe: Spain, France and Great Britain sent an expeditionary force to Mexico with orders to occupy a number of key centres as security for their financial claims.

And that was not all. With the intention of turning Mexico into a vassal of France, Napoleon III dispatched troops which managed to take Mexico City despite the bitter resistance of the Mexican people. The romantic and apolitical Archduke Maximilian of Austria accepted the imperial throne of Mexico, thereby sealing his fate as one of history's most tragic figures. Well-meaning and loyal, he truly believed he could bring peace and happiness to session of land and divided it among themselves, considering everything they found there – people, plants and domestic animals – to be their personal property. Strictly speaking, these men had been mutineers, for they had advanced westward against the orders of Velasquez. Their success seems to have mitigated the seriousness of their breach of authority, however, and all had quickly been forgotten and forgiven. The king had appointed Cortés governor and bestowed upon him the title of captain-general. But before too long it became clear that the new continent would be of untold economic importance for Spain. The crown recognized the necessity of creating order out of its administrative chaos – if only to secure itself a suitable portion of the spoils.

The Pope declared ex cathedra that the native Indians were human beings and not animals, and the crown thereby forbade both forced labour and slavery. Unfortunately, both pronouncements were virtually ignored in the colonies, save by a few idealistic monks who opposed the dissoluteness about them. More and more Europeans – people with nothing to lose – came to the New World to seek their fortunes. In 1535, the conquered lands were declared a viceroyalty. With the appointment of a viceroy who ruled as the direct representative of the crown, a central authority with control over the numerous governors was created. In addition to the viceroy, who embodied the highest judicial authority in the land, a type of court of appeal existed: the "audiencias" were charged with appointing officials and handling Indian affairs. *(Thieme)*

the Mexican people. What he completely disregarded, however, was his own anachronistic position and the hopelessly wide rift between his government and the people it was supposed to represent. The regime was supported by French troops and backed by the thin upper crust of Mexican society as well as by the clergy, who would have supported any regime that was not associated with the name of Benito Juárez.

Juárez had once again to retreat to the trackless northern reaches of the country, where he organized a guerilla war against the foreign usurpers. He was aided once more by the United States which was not interested in having a European satellite at its border.

The war against the foreign emperor pitted rag-tag, poorly armed troops of farmers and Indians against well-equipped professional soldiers from Europe. It became obvious that the ill-fated Maximilian had practically no support in Mexico when Napoleon III abandoned him in a change of strategy. Following the withdrawal of the French troops in 1867, the remainder of the imperial army soon found itself surrounded and had to capitulate. The emperor. who had refused to abandon "his" country, was taken prisoner in Querétaro and placed before a firing squad.

Juárez was left with the monumental task of mapping a secure future for his war-torn, devastated nation. It soon became apparent, however, that the great hero of the revolution was not so convincing in the role of president. His strong sense of justice and his personal integrity were certainly points in his favour, but he lacked the discipline that marks a good administrator.

He was twice re-elected president, finally losing support when his referendum on a measure to grant more power to the central government in Mexico City fell through. It may be said that his early death following a heart attack in 1872 saved Juárez from being judged by history as a dictator: his reputation as an irreproachable national hero lives on.

History is not so kind to his protégé and successor, Porfirio Díaz. The man who dominated Mexican history in the decades following Juárez' death had been his ardent pupil in Oaxaca. Later, he served as general in Juárez' army and commanded the southern division in the war against the foreign intruders. In 1870, he broke with his former mentor in opposition to his re-election after twelve years in office. Whether or not it can be called an irony of fate, this man was to go down in history as a dictator of the most sinister kind. His character was unlike that of the great Mexican national hero: he was robust, driving and practical, had a definite instinct for power and was cunning and unscrupulous.

On the other hand, Porfirio Díaz was an able president who brought peace to a troubled society, foreign capital to an ailing economy and industrialization to a purely agrarian nation. He also attempted to implement Benito Juárez' policy of land reform, but he failed – as Juárez had and as the presidents who followed him were to do. Disregarding the constitutional law prohibiting a president from serving more than two terms in office, he continued on as a dictator. After the turn of the century, though, the framework of his regime began showing signs of brittleness and the economic plight of the small farmers and farm workers became increasingly intolerable. In 1910, a revolution broke out against the Díaz regime which was to be the longest and bloodiest in Mexican history.

Age had not brought wisdom to the eighty-year-old dictator. In 1911, revolutionary forces forced him to resign, and in 1915, he died in exile in Paris. The heirs to the revolution of 1910, embodied in the PRI (Partido Revolucionario Institucional) still dominate the country today.

It is hard to pinpoint the reasons behind the rebellion against "porfirismo". Even today, a discussion of these among historians could easily turn into a heated argument. What is clear, however, is that a seemingly well-ordered and flourishing government was toppled by a force of diverse, unconnected opposition groups in a rather short period of time. Díaz' powerful administrative apparatus was a lumbering giant which lacked both the support of the people and that of the intellectual elite because of its undemocratic structure. The key figure on the intellectual front was Francisco I. Madero, who sought election to the presidency in 1910, thereby providing the spark which set off the revolution.

The actual force to be dealt with – the military force, that is – was provided by the Mexican people themselves. The "Army of the South" was a company of peon-guerillas under the command of the legendary Emiliano Zapata, a strong-willed and charismatic man of the people. Like his soldiers, Zapata was a landless farm labourer. While it can be said that this army was moved by a sense of patriotism, the situation in the north was quite different. The peasants' revolt in the states along the U. S. border was supported, organized and led by Pascual Orozco and Francisco "Pancho" Villa, two bandit "jefes" (chieftains) from Chihuahua in whom the revolution had planted the seeds of political consciousness, so to speak. What they had going for them was an army of resourceful veteran brigands who taught the farmers the tricks of their trade and drove the government forces from one ambush to the next and finally to defeat.

Their troops having taken Mexico City, Villa and Zapata share the presidential seat.

The government forces were not exactly one hundred percent behind their government, a fact which contributed to the rapid demise of the Díaz regime. These soldiers belonged to the same class of impoverished and exploited labourers as the rebels did and it is not hard to imagine where their sympathies lay. On more than one occasion, they deserted en masse or refused to raise arms against their brothers on the other side.

On May 25th 1911, Porfirio Díaz stepped down after 35 years of rule. Francisco Madero was inaugurated president on November 6th 1911. One would think that the goals of the revolution had thus been achieved; but not only did the fighting go on, it had, in fact, only just begun. It was virtually impossible to reconcile the interests and demands of the many victorious factions. Chaos, bloodshed and marauding continued to reign supreme.

In February of 1913, Madero was forced to resign; three days afterward, he was assassinated. General Victoriano Huerta assumed power, but he held it for just a little over a year. Over the next ten years, power changed hands constantly, the leading revolutionaries were killed (Zapata in 1919, Carranza in 1920, Pancho Villa in 1923) and rebellions, including the Yaqui uprising, broke out all over the countryside.

It was not until the presidency of Plutarco Elías Calles (1924–28) that a certain degree of political stability set in. In 1929 Calles founded the National Revolutionary Party, the forerunner of the Partido Revolucionario Institucional. During the presidency of Lázaro Cárdenas, Mexican politics underwent consolidation. Cárdenas was a liberal who advocated a moderate form of socialism. He nationalized the Mexican petroleum industry, ended the conflict with the Yaquis, and succeeded in strengthening the power of the federal government (to the disadvantage of regional interest groups and caudillos). During his administration, the Mexican nation acquired its present single-party political system with the PRI as caretaker of the revolution. According to official ideology, the revolution was thus "institutionalized". This may seem like a contradiction in terms, but what it actually means is that the party carries on the revolution in the name of the people.

Of course, this is no more than nebulous theory for the most part, but insofar as the party manages to consolidate a wide variety of interests, it can be said to function. All important groups within Mexican society are represented by factions within the party, and despite a few cracks and weak spots, the system has been operating satisfactorily up to now. After all, it has given this sorely tried nation almost a half century of peace and political stability. There is reason to hope that it will also eventually succeed in solving the country's economic problems (including the deficit in the balance of payments), in correcting its errors in development planning, and in getting a grip on the scourge of corruption. *(Thieme)*

Archaeological Research in Mexico

The Europeans' involvement with the cultures they encountered in the New World began quite soon after their arrival. Immediately following the Conquest, for example, a very exact map of Tenochtitlán, allegedly drawn up by Hernán Cortés himself, was sent to Carlos V in Spain. It is this very map upon which our present knowledge of the city's layout is based. Cortés' chronicler, Bernal Diáz, contributed a detailed description of the ruins of Teotihuacán. The notorious Bishop Diego de Landa wrote several voluminous treatises, the "Relaciones", in which he set down his view of things in the New World. All this documentation was, of course, biased and very subjective: it was in no way "adulterated" by what we now call scientific method.

True scientific interest in Mexico was the product of the Age of Enlightenment in Europe. Alexander von Humboldt, whose name stands as a symbol of his times, provided the crucial spark with an account of his travels in the New World undertaken in the late 1700s and early 1800s. Humboldt, however, had gathered inspiration for his studies from the work of Jesuit scholars before him. In 1767, these missionary-educators – Europeans and Mexicans alike – had been expelled from Mexico. In Italian exile, men like Clavijero, Maneiro, Sigüenza and de Alzate later published works which aroused the interest of scholars like Humboldt and "Mexico's first archaeologist", Meyer, and provided the incentive for their work.

Mexican studies were given a decisive push in the direction of an archaeological discipline by the travel documentation put together by John Lloyd Stephens, an American, and his genial illustrator, Catherwood. Published worldwide, the journals and the wealth of painstaking drawings accompanying them informed the public for the first time of the vast number of archaeological sites in Mexico, of Mayan cities languishing under jungle overgrowth and of the variety of architectural styles to be found. Like Humboldt before them, Stephens and Catherwood were only the most celebrated of the many who explored Mexico in the mid-19th century. Americans and Europeans alike began getting involved in this new field of activity: Sir Edward Taylor, Bandelier, Morgan, Radin and Alfred Koerber. Thus far, the phenomenon of ancient Indian cultures had been treated primarily from a theoretical and historical standpoint. Discoveries had been made accidentally and data gathered at random. Now men like Troncoso, Förstemann, Seler, Holmes and Maudsley began preparing and laying down the linguistic and archaeological fundaments of the new scientific discipline.

The first researcher who carried out systematic excavations and could thus be called an archaeologist by today's definition was Alfred Percival Maudsley. Beginning in Guatemala in 1881, he worked mainly in the Maya regions. The first large-scale dig was undertaken in Copán in Honduras by the archaeologists Gorden and Saville under the sponsorship of Harvard University's Peabody Institute. In Mexico, the first full-fledged excavations were carried out in Teotihuacán and Mitla between 1885 and 1910.

Archaeological activity is always dependent on the solving of logistics problems: the further away from the comforts of civilization an excavation site is, the more problems arise. Not until after the Mexican Revolution did it become possible to carry out excavations on a long-term and continuous basis. Another prerequisite is money: archaeological digs swallow up vast quantities of it and the question is, who can provide it all? Nowadays, it is usually the Mexican government, but foreign institutes and foundations also get involved.

After the Second World War, the United States became the foremost foreign sponsor of archaeological projects in Mexico, but European-sponsored projects are also in the works. Owing to the vast amount of archaeological sites and zones, only a limited number of excavations can take on the dimensions of large-scale projects: those being carried out by Ignacio Bernal in the Valley of Oaxaca and the Yaxchilan dig in southern Mexico fall into this category. In addition, archaeological digs of more limited scope are always being carried out: in Teotihuacán, for example, where the Street of the Dead was recently re-examined and subsequently presented in a new light; and in Cacaxtla in the state of Tlaxcala where the most extensive and well-preserved set of frescoes in Mexico were discovered just ten years ago.

Although he was not involved in any archaeological digs, special mention must be made of the German philologist, Eduard Seler, who rightfully deserves to be called the father of Mexican archaeology. He published the first grammars of the classical Indian languages; devoted himself to probing the ancient calendar system, the religious concepts and the pantheons of gods; and edited and interpreted the most important historical and mythological codices (hand-embellished manuscripts) still in existence, such as the Aubin, the Vatican B and the Borgia Codices. The work of this pioneering scholar forms one of the supports upon which our knowledge of ancient America rests.

(Thieme)

History at a Glance

ca. 13000–7000 B. C. Paleo-Indian phase Hunter-gatherers. Use of spear points, arrows, primitive stone tools, grinding stones.

ca. 7000–2000 B. C. Early agricultural phase Cultivation of crops such as maize, chilli, squash, cocoa, avocado, papaya.

Towards the close of this phase, the first appearance of pottery in the Maya heartland and in the central plateau (Tehuacán).

ca. 1500–900 B. C. Pre-Classic or Formative phase Extensive, systematic cultivation of crops; pottery with complicated designs; idols, first temples.

In the central plateau: Cuicuilco-Ticoman, Tlatilco, Teotihuacán I and II. On the Gulf coast: La Venta culture (Olmecs). Western Mexico: Mezcala, Chupicuaro, Nayarit, Jalisco. In the Late-Formative phase, Olmec influence throughout southern Mexico: Monte Albán I and II in Oaxaca, Dzibilchaltún I–IV in the Maya region.

ca. A. D. 200–900 Classic phase Temples and palaces; statues and relief sculpture; pronounced hierarchical social order.

In the central plateau: Classic Teotihuacán. On the Gulf coast: El Tajin. In western Mexico: Colima, Nayarit, Jalisco style. In the Maya region: Palenque, Yaxchilan, Bonampak, Uxmal, Kabáh, Labná, Sayil, Coba, Rio Bec region and others.

ca. A. D. 1000 The Maya-Toltecs in Yucatán.

A. D. 900–1300 Toltec dominance in the central plateau.

1325–1521 The Aztec empire.

1518 Juan de Grijalva explores the Gulf coast of Mexico.

1518 (November 18) Cortés leaves Cuba with 11 ships, 508 soldiers, 16 horses, 13 harquebuses and 10 cannons.

1519 (Good Friday) Cortés lands at the site of present-day Veracruz and founds the city.

1521 (August 13) Conquest of Tenochtitlán.

1528 Zumárraga becomes the first bishop of Mexico.

1529 Cortés is elevated in rank to captain-general.

1548–52 Deposits of silver found in Zacatecas and Real del Monte.

1566 Martin Cortés' attempted coup fails.

1571 The Inquisition comes to Mexico.

1572 The Jesuits come to Mexico.

1591 Mexico is declared a part of Spains' domain.

1602 Yanga slave uprising.

1621 The conflict between the church and the state comes to a head. The Vatican imposes a state of interdict on Mexico.

1767 The Jesuits are expelled from Spain and its colonies.

1810 (September 16) "Grito de Dolores": The insurgent leader, Father Hidalgo, issues a call for independence from Spain.

1811 Defeat of the "insurgentes" and execution of Hidalgo.

1813 Morelos establishes the first constituent congress.

1815 Morelos imprisoned and executed.

1822 May 18 Augustín Iturbide proclaimed emperor of Mexico.

1821 The Spanish withdraw and Mexico is declared a constitutional monarchy.

1823 Abdication and banishment of Iturbides.

1824–34 The early republic. First attempt at creating a functioning federal government.

1829 The Spanish attempt to reconquer Mexico fails.

1838–48 The caste war in Yucatán.

1839 Yucatán separates from Mexico.

1846–48 U. S.-Mexican War. Loss of the northern states.

1857 The reform laws and the constitution are promulgated.

1858 Benito Juárez becomes president.

1858–61 "War of the Reform" and agrarian revolts.

1861 French intervention.

1864–67 Reign of Maximilian as emperor of Mexico.

1867 (July 19) Maximilian executed by firing squad.

1867 Benito Juárez elected president.

1868 Caste war in Chiapas.

1872 (July 18) Death of Benito Juárez. Porfirio Díaz assumes the presidency.

1910 On November 20th the Serdan brothers fire the first shots of the Mexican Revolution.

1911 (May 25) Porfirio Díaz resigns the presidency and goes into exile.

1911–13 Presidency of Madero. He is murdered on February 22nd 1913, three days after his resignation.

1913–14 Huerta dictatorship.

1917 Promulgation of the Mexican constitution which is still in effect today.

1919 Murder of Emiliano Zapata.

1920 Murder of Venustiano Carranza.

1920–24 Presidency of Alvaro Obregón.

1923 Murder of Pancho Villa.

1924–1928 Presidency of Elías Calles. In 1929 he founds the National Revolutionary Party, the forerunner of the PRI (Partido Revolucionario Institucional).

1934–40 Presidency of Lázaro Cárdenas.

1938 Nationalization of Mexico's petroleum industry. Establishment of the state-run oil company, PEMEX.

1942 Mexico joins the Allies in the war against the Axis Powers.

1982 (December 1) Inauguration of President Miguel de la Madrid Hurtado.

(Thieme)

Mexico: Land of Geographic Diversity

Mexico lies between the United States and Central America. It has roughly the shape of a funnel linking the bulky landmass of Canada and the U. S. with the Central American isthmus (the southern extremity of the North American continent and land bridge between it and South America).

Mexico shares its approximately 3,119 km (1,938 mile) long northern border with the United States. In the south Mexico is bounded by Belize (formerly British Honduras) and Guatemala. In the east it is flanked by the Gulf of Mexico and the Caribbean Sea, and in the west, by the Gulf of California and the Pacific Ocean.

With a total length of 9,219 km (5,729 miles), Mexico's coastline is one of the longest in the world.

The peninsulas of Yucatán in the southeast and Baja (Lower) California in the west and northwest lie on each side of the wedge-shaped central plateau and are relatively isolated from the main lines of traffic.

European travellers to Mexico will find the country's dimensions enormous: Portugal, Spain, France, Italy, Belgium, Holland, Austria, Switzerland and Denmark could easily fit into the area it occupies. Distances are equally immense: there are 3,080 km (1,914 miles) between the northwestern tip of Baja California and the Guatemalan border; this corresponds to the distance from the northwestern tip of Ireland clear to the Bosphorus, the strait (in Turkey) where Europe ends and Asia begins.

The peninsula of Baja California, which, on the map, looks like a mere outgrowth of the state of California, actually measures a respectable 1,300 km (808 miles) in length. And even at the country's narrowest point the so-called Isthmus of Tehuantepec, the distance between the Gulf of Mexico and the Pacific Ocean is a good 217 km (135 miles).

In terms of latitudinal and longitudinal distance, the country is equally impressive. Eighteen parallels lie between its northernmost point at the Mexican-U. S. border (latitude 32° 42′ north) and its southernmost point at the River Suchiate (latitude 14° 30′ north) – the Rio Suchiate forms the border between Mexico and Guatemala. From its easternmost point on the northeast coast of the Yucatán Peninsula (longitude 86° 46′ west) to its westernmost point on the northwestern tip of Baja California (longitude 117° 7′ west), the country spans almost 30 meridians.

Mexico is essentially a mountainous land. At its core lies the central Mexican plateau, which, in the south reaches heights of around 2,000 m (6,500 ft), and in the north, of around 1,300 m (4,000 ft). The mountains which flank the plateau to the east, west and south tower up to heigths of between 3,000 and 4,000 m (9,800 and 13,000 ft). The highest peaks – some of which are still active volcanoes – have elevations of over 5,000 m (16,000 ft) and are capped with perpetual snow. The highest of these is Citlaltépetl, or Pico de Orizaba (in the state of Puebla), which rises to a height of 5,700 m (18,700 ft). East and west of the mountains, the land falls steeply to form two coastal plains of differing breadth.

The number given at the head of each section refers to the map on page 123.

1. Central Plateau (Altiplanicie Central)

The central Plateau, Mexico's heartland, covers an area of 300,000 sq. km (116,000 sq. miles) and has an average elevation of 2,000 m (6,500 ft) in the south and 1,300 m (4,000 ft) in the north.

In the north, the plateau gradually merges with the generally more level and uniform landscape of the northern plains (planicie septentrional), the direct extension of the central plateau. With a combined area of 750,000 sq. km (290,000 sq. miles) i. e. larger than that occupied by the state of Texas, these two adjoining geographic regions make up 38 percent of the country's total area.

The central plateau comprises the small states of Puebla, Tlaxcala, Hidalgo. Querétaro, Guanajuato, San Luís Potosí and Aguascalientes, the state of México, the Federal District (Distrito Federal, also known simply as Mexico City), and portions of the states of Michoacán and Jalisco.

2. Northern Plains (Planicie Septentrional)

The northern plains region, located directly to the north of the central plateau, includes the states of

Chihuahua, Coahuila, Durango, Zacatecas and Nuevo León.

In terms of topography, the northern plains differ considerably from the central plateau. They are characterized by two basic natural features: broad, flat basins or "bolsones", such as the Bolsón de Mapimi, and narrow mountain chains (seldom more than 15 km/9 miles across) which extend in an east-westerly direction and are criss-crossed by deep gullies and river valleys which cut serrate designs in their steep slopes.

The few rivers which drain this arid region carry water at only certain times of the year – but during wet periods, the amount of water they carry can be considerable! The water empties into the centre of the basins where it collects to form large lakes with no outlets. In this area of low annual precipitation and high year-round evaporation, only drought-resistant plants survive. The sparse vegetation consists mainly of fast-growing shrubs and thornbushes, cacti and other succulents.

Physiographically speaking, the northern plains are divided first and foremost into three river basins: in the north lies the basin of the Río Salado ("salted river") which lacks a drainage outlet; the eastern region is drained by the Pánuco-Moctezuma Rivers, and in the west lies the drainage area of the Santiago-Lerma

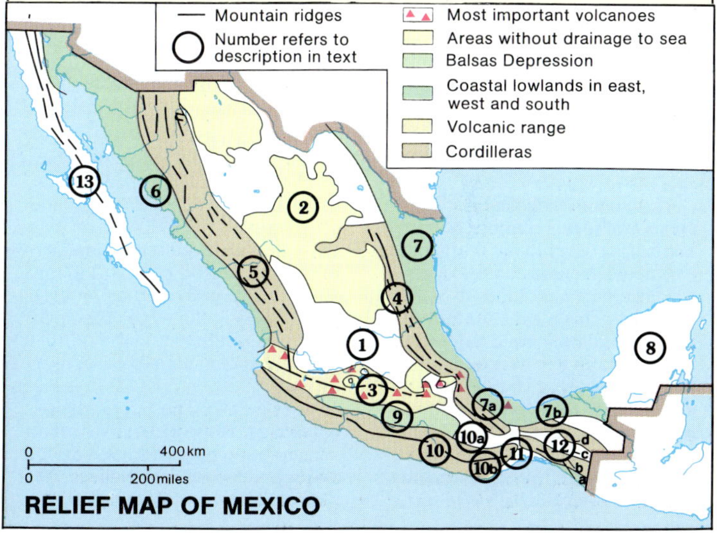

RELIEF MAP OF MEXICO

Rivers, which contains Mexico's largest lake, the Lago Chapala.

3. Transverse Volcanic Chain (Sierra Neovolcánica Transversal)

The 900 km (560-mile) long Sierra Neovolcánica Transversal, the only mountain range in the western hemisphere which runs in an east-westerly direction, spans Mexico from the Pacific to the Gulf coast and forms the southern boundary (at latitude 19° north) of the central plateau. This range contains the nation's highest peaks: Cofre de Perote (4,282 m/14,000 ft), Pico de Orizaba (at 5,700 m/18,700 ft, Mexico's highest mountain), La Malinche, and Ixtaccíhuatl ("white woman" or "sleeping woman", 5,286 m/17,300 ft) and Popocatépetl ("smoking mountain", 5,452 m/17,900 ft). As the name of the last mountain suggests, some of the highest peaks are active volcanoes. These mountains rise up into the "tierra helada", the cold, alpine zone and land of perpetual snow.

The Sierra Neovolcánica Transversal encloses a number of valleys and basins which have in the course of time been closed off by layers of solidified lava and deposits of volcanic ash. This means that there is no drainage outlet and that streams and rivers, unable to flow out to sea, form large bolson lakes. The most important of these basins and valleys are the Patzcuaro Basin in Michoacán (covering an area of 4,038 sq. km/1,560 sq. miles), the Valley of Toluca (which is in fact drained – by the Río Lerma), the Valley of Mexico (8,115 sq. km/3,130 sq. miles) and the so-called Eastern Basin, in which lie the cities of Puebla and Tlaxcala, the capitals of the states of the same name.

The Valley of Mexico (Cuenca del Valle de México), a fertile area first settled some 21,000 years ago, clearly forms the centre of this region. The vast lakes which once covered much of the valley have now disappeared due to artificial draining.

4. Eastern Sierra Madre (Sierra Madre Oriental)

The rugged range of the Sierra Madre Oriental forms the eastern boundary of the Valley of Mexico. It runs in an almost north-northwest-south-southeasterly direction through the states of Nuevo León, Tamaulipas, San Luís Potosí, Querétaro, Veracruz, Puebla and Hidalgo.

From the U. S. border to the Cofre de Perote, where it meets the Sierra Volcánica Transversal, it measures 1,200 km (745 miles) in length and is between 100 and 200 km (62 and 124 miles) wide. With an average elevation of 2,200 m (7,200 ft) this range forms no more than an elevated ridge along the edge of the plateau in the south, but in the north, it rises to impressive heights. Its highest peak (3,600 m/12,000 ft) is located near Saltillo. The Sierra Madre Oriental consists of chains of mountains running parallel to one another and separated by deep valleys. Altitudinal differences of up to 2,000 m

(6,500 ft) can be encountered within only a few miles.

The Sierra Madre Oriental contains several different vegetation zones; the transition between these zones can occur quite abruptly, again in the space of only a few miles. From east to west, tropical, moisture-loving vegetation gives way to drought-resistant plants which thrive in arid zones. The mountain slopes are covered with deciduous forests and thornbushes.

5. Western Sierra Madre (Sierra Madre Occidental)
The Sierra Madre Occidental forms the western boundary of the central plateau. The almost 1,400 km (870 mile) long and 130 km (80 mile) wide mountain range extends in a south-southeast to north-northwesterly direction parallel to the Gulf of California from the Río Santiago in the south to the U. S. border, where it connects with the mountains of New Mexico. The Occidental range cuts through the states of Sonora, Chihuahua, Durango, Zacatecas and touches Nayarit. It has an average elevation of 2,200 m (7,200 ft); its highest peaks (up to 3,600 m/12,000 ft) lie in the Sierra Tarahumara in the state of Chihuahua.

The Sierra Madre Occidental consists of a series of plateaux, primarily of volcanic rock, which, due to a recent upheaval, rise upward in the west and level out in the east. The sierra's descent to the Pacific coast is interrupted by numerous canyons of varying depths and widths, the most famous being the Copper Canyon or Barranca del Cobre.

The higher altitudes of the sierra support extensive coniferous forests.

6. Pacific (Northwest) Coast Plain
Between the Sierra Madre Occidental and the Gulf of California lies the northwest coastal plain. The plain begins in the desert state of Sonora (where it is at its widest – up to 280 km/170 miles wide) and continues south for 1,400 km (870 miles) until it meets the coastal spurs of the Sierra Madre Occidental (near the mouth of the Río Santiago) and comes to an abrupt end. As well as crossing the state of Sonora, the coastal plain stretches through the states of Sinaloa and Nayarit. It is not level throughout, but rather descends gradually from east to west. Its highest level is formed by the western slopes of the Sierra Madre. These give way to a hilly zone with elevations of between 50 and 500 m (160 and 1,600 ft) which supports only sparse drought-resistant vegetation (thorny plants in the south and desert vegetation in the north), and finally to a flat zone which is just 50 m (160 ft) above sea level and eventually slopes down to the Gulf of California.

Billions of gallons of water flow from the Sierra Madre every year and are carried by sixteen major rivers towards the Gulf of California. Along the coast these rivers have formed large fan deltas. Lagoons are also found along extensive stretches of the coastline.

7. Gulf Coast Plain

Mexico's eastern coast (along the Gulf of Mexico) can be divided into a number of low-lying areas. The largest of these, the Gulf coast plain, stretches from the U. S. border down to the state of Veracruz, where it continues as two smaller lowland regions – the river flats of the Rio Papaloapan (7a) and, in Tabasco, the alluvial plains of the Rio Rijalva and Rio Usumacinta (7b). The latter extend eastwards to join the limestone tableland of the Yucatán Peninsula.

The Gulf coast plain comprises parts of the states of Coahuila, Tamaulipas, Nuevo León, San Luís Potosí, Hidalgo and Veracruz. In the north, where it borders on a similar plain in the U. S., it is approximately 300 km (186 miles) wide. It extends for almost 1,100 km (680 miles) southwards, narrowing as it does so, until it measures only 75 km (47 miles) across.

The eastern slopes of the Sierra Madre Oriental form the highest reaches of the coastal plain. These give way to chains of low hills, to broad beaches and finally to a narrow belt of lagoons which border on the Gulf.

While the north is characterized by scrub vegetation, the south, blessed by abundant rainfall particularly during the summer months, possesses such rich vegetation that the entire region resembles a tropical garden. Coconut plantations, tropical fruit gardens and citrus plantations abound; banana trees provide shade for the coffee plants which grow on the slopes of the Sierra Madra.

In the south, the Gulf coast plain continues as the river flats of the Rio Papaloapan – a vast alluvial plain covering some 45,000 sq. km (17,370 sq. miles) and watered by the Papaloapan and other rivers.

East of the Papaloapan basin lies the basin of the Grijalva-Usumacinta river system. This flat alluvial plain extends over an area of approx. 60,000 sq. km (23,000 sq. miles), covering large portions of the states of Tabasco and Campeche and a small portion of Chiapas. The Grijalva-Usumacinta, the seventh-largest river system in the world in terms of volume of water carried yearly (134 billion cubic yards) continually deposits sediment on the plain. Due to its minimal incline and the even flow of water from the rivers which feed it, 25–30% of this "amphibious land" remains flooded all year round.

8. Yucatán Peninsula

The Yucatán Peninsula constitutes the easternmost portion of Mexico's territory. Bounded in the north and west by the Gulf of Mexico, and in the east by the Caribbean Sea, its total area of 180,000 sq. km (69,500 sq. miles) is divided up between Mexico (125,000 sq. km/48,250 sq. miles), Belize and Guatemala (the

Petén region). The Mexican portion of the Peninsula contains the states of Campeche (in the southwest), Yucatán (in the north) and the autonomous territory of Quintana Roo (in the east). The Yucatán Peninsula is a low tableland (maximum elevation 350 m/1,150 ft) formed by flat or only slightly layers of limestone, the porosity and solubility of which has made for the formation of caverns and sinkholes. Precipitation penetrates the surface quickly, preventing the formation of fixed bodies of water except in the immediate vicinity of the coast. Drainage occurs subterraneously through the extensive system of karst caverns.

9. Balsas Depression

Visitors to Mexico who travel from the capital city to the well-known coastal resort of Acapulco will cross the basin of the Rio Balsas (also known as the Balsas Depression), a tectonic trough through which the Balsas flows. With an area of 112,000 sq. km (43,200 sq. miles), the trough extends through parts of the states of Puebla, Morelos, México, Michoacán, Oaxaca, and makes up almost the entire state of Guerrero.

The Balsas River basin is shaped like an almost perfect right-angled triangle. It is bordered in the north by the Sierra Volcánica Transversal, in the east by the Oaxacan-Pueblan mountain range, and in the southwest by the Sierra Madre del Sur, which runs almost parallel to the Pacific coast. The surrounding mountains, which rise to heights of 2,000 m (6,500 ft) and more, plunge fairly abruptly into the central basin, which has an average elevation of only 1,000 m (3,300 ft). At its centre, it is only 500 m (1,600 ft) above sea level, and in the west, only 200 m (650 ft), which puts it in the "tierra caliente" climatic zone (see "Climate"). Only about six percent of the basin's total area is flat; the rest displays a marked and vivid relief. The uplands are arid and covered primarily with thorn bushes and cacti.

10. Southern Mexican Mountain Ranges

The Balsas Depression is flanked to the south and to the east by the two mountain ranges of southern Mexico: the many small chains which make up the Oaxacan-Pueblan mountain system, and the Sierra Madre del Sur (southern Sierra Madre).

10a. The Oaxacan-Pueblan Range

The Oaxacan-Pueblan system of mountains, which includes the smaller ranges of the Sierra de Tehuacán (limestone, arid) and the Sierra de Juárez, covers the entire state of Oaxaca and parts of the state of Puebla. It is 300 km (185 miles) in length, averages 75 km (46 miles) across, and connects the mountains of the Sierra Volcánica Transversal in the northwest to those of the Sierra Madre del Sur in the southeast. The mountains have an average elevation of 2,000 m (6,600 ft). The most densely populated portion of the range is the Valley of Oaxaca, which lies between 5,000 and 6,300

Mexico at a Glance

Name: Estados Unidos Mexicanos (United Mexican States)

Location: On the map, Mexico can be found between the 117th and the 87th west meridians and between the 33rd and the 15th north parallels. Geographically, it belongs to North America. From the northern tip of Baja California to the southeast corner of the state of Chiapas, the country spans 3,200 km (1,988 miles); its northern frontier, which stretches from the northern tip of Baja California to the mouth of the Rio Grande, is 2,100 km (1,305 miles) long.

With an area of 1,958,128 sq. km (761,605 square miles), Mexico is the third-largest country in Latin America (after Brazil and Argentina).

Form of Government: Mexico was first declared a republic in the year 1824. Its president and the members of its bicameral legislature (Congreso de la Unión) are elected by universal suffrage. The constitution dates from February 1917, but it has been amended many times since then.

Administrative Organization: Mexico is divided geographically into five regions and politically into 31 states – each with a governor and an elected assembly – plus the Federal District (Mexico City).

1. Northest Mexico: Baja California Norte, Baja California Sur, Nayarit, Sinaloa, Sonora. 2. North Mexico: Chihuahua, Coahuila, Durango, Nuevo León, San Luís Potosí, Tamaulipas, Zacatecas. 3. Central Mexico: Aguascalientes, the Federal District (Mexico City), Guanajuato, Hidalgo, Jalisco, México, Michoacán, Morelos, Puebla, Querétaro, Tlaxcala. 4. Gulf Coast Mexico: Campeche, Quintana Roo, Tabasco, Veracruz, Yucatán. 5. South Mexico: Chiapas, Colima, Guerrero, Oaxaca.

Government: The head of state and government is the President of the Republic, who serves a six-year term after which he may not be re-elected.

This office is currently held by Miguel de la Madrid Hurtado, who was elected in July 1982 and took office on December 1 of that year.

The nation's legislative body is the congress. It consists of a senate, whose 64 members are elected for six-year terms, and a chamber of deputies whose 400 elected members serve three-year terms.

Distribution of Seats in the Lower House:

PRI	– Partido Revolucionario Institucional	299 seats
PAN	– Partido Acción Nacional	55 seats
PSUM	– Partido Socialista Unido Mexicano	17 seats
PPS	– Partido Popular Socialista	11 seats

PST	– Partido Socialista de los Trabajadores	10 seats
PDM	– Partido Democrático Mexicano	8 seats

Population: According to census figures for 1980, Mexico then had a population of 67,382,581. Today, this figure is estimated to have increased to more than 75.5 million, making Mexico the second-most densely populated country in Latin America after Brazil. While this figure is by no means too high for a country of Mexico's size, demographic differences are causing problems of immense proportions. In the Valley of Mexico (with Mexico City at its centre), the population density stands at 350/sq. km; in Baja California, it is 3/sq. km, and in Quintana Roo, 4/sq. km.

Seventy-five percent of the Mexican population are mestizos (people of mixed Indian and European ancestry); Indians make up 8 percent and whites of mostly Spanish origin make up between 10 and 15 percent of the population. Some sources place the proportion of Indians at 29 percent, and that of mestizos at 55 percent. There are approximately 150,000 foreigners living in Mexico.

The number of pure-blood Indians, whites and creoles or "moriscos" (mulattos) seems to be decreasing, while the number of mestizos seems to be on the rise. Exact figures to back this trend are hardly obtainable due to the impossibility of determining the ratio of racial components in any one individual. Moreover, definitions as to what is white and what is Indian vary according to the individual and his own sense of ethnic affiliation.

Language: Mexico has the largest Spanish-speaking population in the world. Only 3.5 percent of the people speak an Indian language exclusively, and 8 percent are bilingual.

Indian languages, in particular Nahuatl, have contributed a wealth of words to Mexican Spanish. Evidence of these borrowings is stronger in the countryside than in the cities. Of the more than 200 native languages and dialects spoken at the time of the Conquest, only about 50 survive today, and most of these are spoken by only small numbers of the population.

Religion: The overwhelming majority of the Mexican people profess to be Roman Catholics, but in rural areas and among the urban Indian population affiliation with the Catholic Church often exists in name only. Many ancient religious concepts are still alive, having been absorbed into the faith taught by the Spanish priests. In many cases, Catholic ritual has merely provided new forms for the worship of old gods. This is especially evident in the Mexicans' extreme devotion to the Blessed Virgin Mary and to the saints. *(Thieme)* feet above sea level. The main centre in the valley is Oaxaca, capital of the state of the same name.

10b. Southern Sierra Madre (Sierra Madre del Sur)

The southern boundary of the Balsas Depression is formed by the Sierra Madre del Sur, a chain of mountains which runs parallel to the Pacific through the states of Colima, Michoacán, Guerrero and Oaxaca. It begins in the northwest, at the Bahia de Banderas (where the Gulf of California meets the Pacific Ocean) and ends in the southeast, in the lowland region at the Isthmus of Tehuantepec which spans Mexico from coast to coast.

The Sierra Madre del Sur is approximately 1,200 km (745 miles) long and between 80 and 120 km (50 and 75 miles) wide; it reaches heights of up to 3,000 m (10,000 ft). In the northwest, the range is composed of granodiorite, a plutonic rock (formed by solidification of molten lava) similar to granite; the portion running through the state of Michoacán is composed of sedimentary rock from the Lower Cretaceous period, and that running through Guerrero and Oaxaca is composed of Precambrian rock (i. e., of the earliest geological era), in particular, gneiss, with intrusions of plutonic rock. Almost the entire coastal flank of the mountain range drops abruptly to the sea – there are hardly any beaches. It is only in the vicinity of the rivers which flow down from the mountain heights that lowlands and narrow beaches are found. The Bays of Acapulco and Zihuatanejo-Ixtapa (a newly developed resort in northwestern Guerrero) were actually once river basins which, due to the rising level of the Pacific, are now permanently inundated. Just off the Mexican coast, running parallel to the steep western slopes of the almost trackless (only a few of Mexico's east-west lines of traffic cross it), little developed and sparsely populated Sierra Madre del Sur, is the Trinchera (trench) de México, an oceanic depression which reaches depths of up to 5,700 m (18,700 ft).

Between the highest elevations of the Sierra Madre and the deepest parts of the Mexican Trench there is a distance of only 80 km (50 miles), but within these 80 km lie differences in vertical distance of up to 9,000 m (30,000 ft)! Here, along a fault running parallel to the coast, a continental plate meets an oceanic plate creating a zone of high seismic activity such as that along the San Andreas fault in California where two plates grind against each other. The greatest number of earth tremors ("tremblores") and earthquakes of medium magnitude in Mexico are recorded here, along the stretch of coastline between Zihuatanejo in the northwest and Acapulco in the southeast. Really destructive earthquakes ("terremotos") are extremely rare.

While in the northwestern and central coastal regions thornbush steppes and thickets are in evidence, the southeast, in particular, the Oaxacan coast, is marked by savanna vegetation. The seaward slopes of the Sierra Madre are covered with deciduous trees which loose their leaves in the dry season.

The landward slopes as well as the higher reaches support coniferous trees and evergreen oaks. Along some portions of the coast, lagoons and swamp vegetation can be found, and in the broader coastal zones, the commercial exploitation of the coconut is increasing.

11. The Lowland Corridor of the Isthmus of Tehuantepec

The Sierra Madre del Sur is bounded in the southeast by the lowlands of the Isthmus of Tehuantepec. The isthmus forms a low-lying, narrow corridor which crosses Mexico at its narrowest point in a north-south direction and roughly along the meridian at longitude 95 ° west. Vegetation in this area consists mainly of dense tropical forest.

For most geologists the isthmus marks the division between the North American and South American continents.

12. Southeastern Mexico

The area which lies between the Isthmus of Tehuantepec and the Guatemalan border constitutes Mexico's southeastern region and consists of the mountains of Chiapas, the plains at the foot of these mountains, and a series of low-lying zones. These zones run in a roughly east-westerly direction and are bordered by the basin of the Rio Grijalva-Rio Usumacinta in the north, and by the Isthmus of Tehuantepec in the west. In the east the low-lying zones continue with no visible break into Guatemalan territory.

Southeast Mexico covers an area of 74,000 sq. km (28,550 sq. miles), predominantly the territory of the state of Chiapas. The various geographic regions within the area have their own distinctive topographical characteristics. Moving northwards from the Pacific, these regions include the Pacific coastal plain (12a), the Sierra Madre (12b), the Chiapas Lowlands (12c), and the Chiapas Highlands (12d) – the latter slope down to the Grijalva-Usumacinta basin in the north.

The Pacific coastal plain in Chiapas, 360 km (224 miles) long and between 15 and 40 km (9 and 25 miles) wide, is an "amphibious" region of swamps, lagoons and alluvial plains (formed by small rivers which flow from the highlands). The plain is relatively sparcely populated.

The Sierra Madre of Chiapas, between 45 and 75 km (28 and 46 miles) across, runs parallel to the coastal plain. While its southern (Pacific) flank is steep, its northern flank slopes gradually to the river flats of the Upper Grijalva. The base of the Sierra Madre of Chiapas consists of crystalline rock which is in discordance with the overlying Mesozoic rock stratum. The average height of the range increases as we move from the northwest to the southeast. In the southeast there are a number of volcanoes. The highest peak is the volcano Tacana (4,060 m/13,300 ft) on the Guatemalan border.

The Chiapas lowlands, which range from 30 to 50 km (18 to 31 miles) in width, drop from an elevation of 650 m (2,130 ft) on the Guatemalan border to 450 m (1,480 ft) in northwestern Chiapas. The northern boundary is formed by the spectacular canyon, the Cañon del Sumidero. In the northeast, the lowlands are bounded by the Chiapas Highlands which are composed mainly of limestone which dates back to the Mesozoic era (there are typical karst formations in parts).

The highest peak in the Chiapas highlands is Cerro Zontehuitz (2,784 m/9,130 ft) near San Cristóbal de las Casas.

13. Baja California Peninsula
Mexico's western extremity is formed by the rocky and desert-like Baja California Peninsula which lies between the Pacific Ocean and the 100–200 km (62–124 mile) wide Gulf of California. With an area of 170,000 sq. km (65,600 sq. miles), it comprises the states of Baja California Norte and Baja California Sur.

The peninsula is 1,230 km (764 miles) long. At its widest point it measures 255 km (158 miles) across; at its narrowest point, near the free port of La Paz, 40 km (25 miles) across.

It consists of a backbone of mountains – the continuation of California's Coast Range – with elevations of around 200 m (656 ft) in the south and up to 2,000 m (6,560 ft) in the north. Its highest peak, La Encantada, reaches a height of 3,069 m (10,070 ft).

The mountains in the south are composed of "young" volcanic rock; those in the north, of granite. On both coasts, which together have a length of 3,340 km (2,075 miles), the peninsula's rugged backbone drops abruptly into the sea. Along the rugged coastline the surf has carved arches, towers and other bizarre shapes out of the rock.

For the most part, southern Baja California is covered with cacti and other succulent plants. In the north, the chaparral – vast thickets of thorny shrubs – reigns supreme. The highest reaches of the mountains support mixed forests of pine and oak.

(Schmidt)

Climate

The climate of a given region is determined by three basic factors:
1. Latitude (or distance from the equator, the imaginary line around the earth equidistant from the two poles and marking the region which receives the most direct sunlight),
2. Elevation,
3. Position with respect to the prevailing winds.

Spanning eighteen parallels (the 14th to the 32nd), the vast territory of Mexico can be divided roughly (at the 20th parallel) into two climatic zones. The **tropical rainy zone** in the south is characterized by cloudy summers with showers and thunder storms, and the **subtropical arid zone** in the north is characterized by year-round fair, dry weather and light winds.

Generally speaking, most eastern seabords (including Mexico's) do not

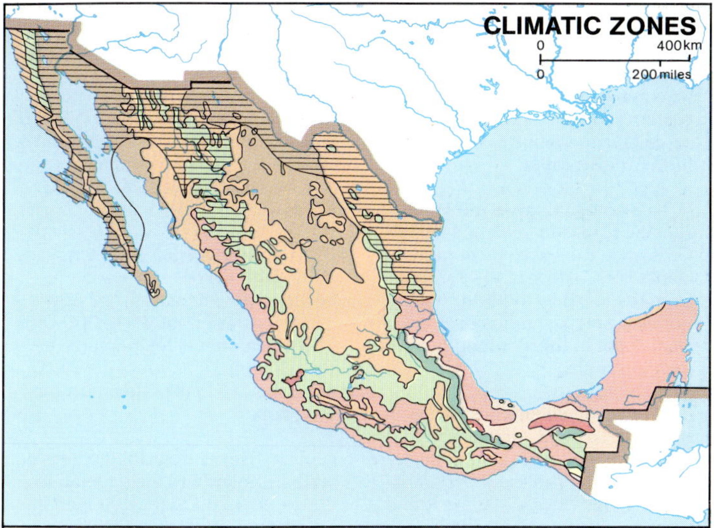

	WET ZONES			DRY ZONES: Steppe climate relatively dry			DRY ZONES: Desert climate very dry		
Main periods of precipitation	year round	summer	winter	year round	summer	winter	year round	summer	winter
Very warm	Af	Am Aw		BSx'	BSw	BSs	BWx'	BWw	BWs
Temperate	Cf Cx'	Cw	Cs						

Af Warm and humid, precipitation throughout the year
Am Warm and humid, precipitation in summer
Aw Warm, humid in parts, precipitation in summer
Cf Moderately warm and humid, precipitation throughout the year
Cw Moderately warm and humid, precipitation in summer
Cx' Temperate, humid in parts, precipitation throughout the year
Cs- Moderately warm and humid, rain in winter (Mediterranean climate)
BSw Relatively dry or steppe climate precipitation in summer
BSx' Relatively dry or steppe climate, infrequent heavy showers throughout the year
BSs Relatively dry or steppe climate, rain in winter
BWw Very dry or desert climate, precipitation in summer
BWx' Very dry or desert climate, infrequent heavy showers throughout the year
BWs Desert climate, rain in winter

experience the latter type of climate. This is due to the presence of trade winds which, especially during the summer months, bring in rain. In eastern regions, therefore, the tropical rainy zone tends to extend further northwards.

To a certain degree, a third climatic type is in evidence in Baja California: the subtropical rainy climate of California which ranges from the 32nd to the 40th north parallels and is characterized by rainfall not in the summer, but in the winter months.

In Mexico, altitude plays a greater role in determining climate than latitude does. As a result, in addition to the climatic zones mentioned above, four climatic "levels" can be found:

1. The **"tierra caliente"** (hot land), found between sea level and 700–800 m (2,500 feet), has temperatures averaging over 22 °C (72 °F). This climatic level is found primarily along the eastern and western coasts.

2. The **"tierra templada"** (temperate land) extends from 800 m to 1,700 m (2,500 to 6,000 feet) above sea level. The mean annual temperature here lies between 17 and 22 °C (63 to 72 °F).

3. The **"tierra fria"** (cold land) lies in the high valleys of Mexico between elevations of 1,700 and 4,700 metres (6,000 to 12,000 feet). The mean annual temperature here ranges from 17 °C to minus 10 °C (63 °F to 14 °F) depending on the elevation.

4. The **"tierra helada"** (frozen land) begins where the vegetation ends – at 4,700 m (12,000 feet). It encompasses the summits of the highest mountains some of which are perpetually covered with snow. Temperatures here hover around the freezing point.

(Schmidt)

Key to Climatic Table

a b	d
c	e

TT = Tierra Templada
TF = Tierra Fria
TC = Tierra Caliente

a Average monthly temperature (°C)

b Average daily variation in temperature in a particular month (°C)

c Average precipitation in a particular month (in mm)

d Mean annual temperature (°C)

e Mean annual precipitation (in mm)

Weather Station Region	Guadalajara Central Plateau (1)				Guanajuato Central Plateau (1)				Zacatecas Central Plateau (1)				Morelia Volcanic Range (3)			
	20°41′ lat. north	103°20′ long. west	Alt. 1,589 m	TT	21°1′ lat. north	101°15′ long. west	Alt. 2,037 m	TF	22°47′ lat. north	102°34′ long. west	Alt. 2,612 m	TF	19°42′ lat. north	101°7′ long. west	Alt. 1,923 m	TF
January °C	14.7	17.1		19.0	14.2	12.7		17.9	9.6	7.3		13.3	14.4	13.3		17.7
Precipitation (mm)	14.8			894.5	13.6			667.9	7.3			265.3	11.8			754.7
February °C	16.6	18.1			15.8	13.9			10.7	8.2			16.1	13.8		
Precipitation (mm)	4.3				5.1				3.1				5.4			
March °C	18.4	19.7			18.2	14.5			12.9	9.3			18.1	14.1		
Precipitation (mm)	4.0				5.1				1.8				6.6			
April °C	21.1	19.5			20.2	14.1			15.1	9.4			19.8	13.9		
Precipitation (mm)	5.2				16.3				3.6				16.7			
May °C	22.9	17.2			21.6	13.6			16.6	9.4			20.8	12.5		
Precipitation (mm)	24.0				32.7				10.8				42.5			
June °C	22.3	12.6			20.3	11.8			16.2	8.7			20.0	9.6		
Precipitation (mm)	172.2				126.8				18.4				134.5			
July °C	20.5	10.4			19.0	10.8			14.6	7.8			18.7	8.6		
Precipitation (mm)	251.4				138.1				64.1				170.1			
August °C	20.5	10.9			19.1	11.0			14.8	7.5			18.6	8.8		
Precipitation (mm)	194.3				136.0				65.6				154.0			
September °C	19.9	10.5			18.4	10.0			13.7	6.8			18.3	8.8		
Precipitation (mm)	158.1				124.0				53.8				130.7			
October °C	19.1	13.5			17.7	11.6			13.2	7.0			17.5	9.9		
Precipitation (mm)	47.8				42.6				22.9				55.6			
November °C	16.9	16.4			16.1	12.6			11.5	7.4			15.9	12.2		
Precipitation (mm)	10.1				15.3				9.8				16.3			
December °C	15.2	16.8			14.7	12.6			10.1	7.0			14.6	13.2		
Precipitation (mm)	8.3				11.3				4.1				10.5			

Weather Station Region	Monterrey Sierra Madre Orient. (4)				Salina Cruz Tehuantepec Isthmus (11)				Acapulco Southern ranges (10)				Mazatlán Pacific Coast (6)			
	25°40′ lat. north	100°18′ long. west	Alt. 534 m	TC	16°12′ lat. north	95°12′ long. west	Alt. 56 m		16°50′ lat. north	96°56′ long. west	Alt. 3 m		23°11′ lat. north	106°25′ long. west	Alt. 78 m	TC
January °C	15.4	10.9		22.3	25.6	8.3		27.4	26.7	8.7		27.7	19.8	4.8		24.2
Precipitation (mm)	18.9			633.9	4.4			1046.8	6.3			1378.7	13.1			805.4
February °C	17.0	11.5			25.9	8.2			26.5	8.5			19.8	4.8		
Precipitation (mm)	16.9				3.8				1.3				5.8			
March °C	20.3	12.6			27.0	7.9			26.7	8.6			20.5	5.0		
Precipitation (mm)	12.7				1.6				0.3				3.1			
April °C	23.4	11.8			28.4	7.8			27.5	8.2			22.1	5.1		
Precipitation (mm)	26.3				0.6				1.2				0.9			
May °C	25.9	11.1			29.5	7.7			28.5	7.4			24.6	4.7		
Precipitation (mm)	35.9				48.1				36.0				1.2			
June °C	27.8	11.2			28.3	7.5			28.6	7.1			27.1	3.8		
Precipitation (mm)	62.9				264.3				281.0				33.0			
July °C	28.1	11.5			28.4	7.7			28.7	7.6			28.0	4.3		
Precipitation (mm)	61.4				207.4				256.1				188.3			
August °C	28.0	11.2			28.5	8.1			28.8	8.0			28.1	4.3		
Precipitation (mm)	110.5				176.1				252.4				226.9			
September °C	25.6	9.6			27.6	7.6			28.1	7.5			27.9	4.6		
Precipitation (mm)	156.1				240.4				349.1				244.9			
October °C	22.5	9.8			27.4	7.7			28.1	7.5			27.2	4.7		
Precipitation (mm)	91.2				87.9				159.2				56.6			
November °C	17.9	10.1			26.7	8.0			27.7	8.2			24.3	4.9		
Precipitation (mm)	23.4				8.6				28.1				16.4			
December °C	15.6	10.8			26.0	8.2			26.7	8.4			21.5	4.8		
Precipitation (mm)	17.7				3.6				26.6				15.3			

Weather Station Region	La Paz Baja California (13)				Guaymas Pacific Coast (6)				Isla de Cozumel Yucatán Peninsula (8)				Tampico Gulf Coast Plain (7)			
	24°10′ lat. north	110°7′ long. west	Alt. 18 m	TC	27°55′ lat. north	110°53′ long. west	Alt. 4 m	TC	20°31′ lat. north	86°57′ long. west	Alt. 3 m	TC	22°12′ lat. north	97°51′ long. west	Alt. 73 m	TC
January °C	18.3	8.0		24.2	17.9	9.7		25.6	22.9	8.6		25.5	19.2	7.6		24.3
Precipitation (mm)	No figures			–	11.6			220.7	86.8			1552.8	43.0			1034.5
February °C	19.0	8.9			19.0	10.1			23.3	9.3			20.4	7.6		
Precipitation (mm)	–				7.0				63.4				15.7			
March °C	20.7	10.4			21.0	10.7			24.5	9.5			22.0	7.5		
Precipitation (mm)	–				3.4				48.2				11.7			
April °C	22.8	11.9			23.5	10.1			26.0	9.5			24.6	7.2		
Precipitation (mm)	–				1.3				53.0				22.7			
May °C	24.9	12.5			26.4	11.0			26.9	9.1			26.8	6.7		
Precipitation (mm)	–				0.0				140.8				47.1			
June °C	26.8	12.1			29.8	9.3			27.2	7.9			28.0	6.8		
Precipitation (mm)	–				2.6				200.2				121.1			
July °C	29.4	9.8			31.2	8.1			27.2	8.7			28.0	7.1		
Precipitation (mm)	–				38.8				111.5				153.3			
August °C	29.8	8.9			31.1	8.1			27.2	9.2			28.2	7.1		
Precipitation (mm)	–				60.2				152.0				134.8			
September °C	29.0	8.4			30.7	8.3			26.8	8.2			27.2	7.2		
Precipitation (mm)	–				50.7				243.4				280.6			
October °C	26.4	9.2			27.7	9.5			26.0	7.4			25.6	7.5		
Precipitation (mm)	–				21.7				234.4				132.0			
November °C	23.1	8.7			22.7	10.0			24.6	7.7			22.0	7.7		
Precipitation (mm)	–				6.7				110.8				46.3			
December °C	20.0	7.9			19.4	9.8			23.4	8.1			19.9	7.4		
Precipitation (mm)	–				16.7				108.5				26.2			

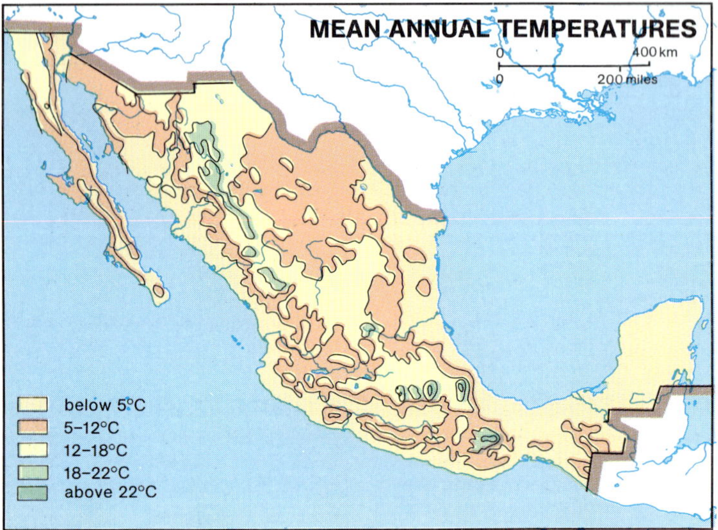
MEAN ANNUAL TEMPERATURES
0
400 km
0
200 miles
below 5°C
5–12°C
12–18°C
18–22°C
above 22°C

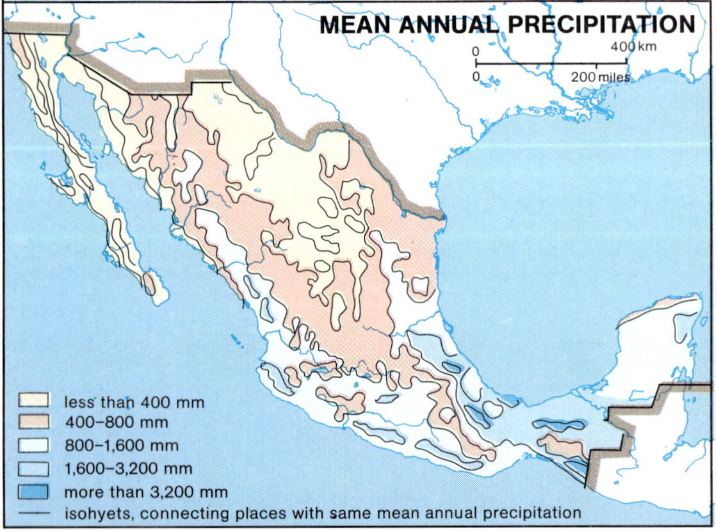
MEAN ANNUAL PRECIPITATION
0
400 km
0
200 miles
less than 400 mm
400–800 mm
800–1,600 mm
1,600–3,200 mm
more than 3,200 mm
isohyets, connecting places with same mean annual precipitation

Flora

Few of us may realize just how many of our familiar plants actually come from Mexico. Crops such as **maize** (second only to wheat in terms of acreage planted worldwide), **kidney beans** and **gourd** all originated in Mexico, as did many of our loveliest garden flowers, including the **zinnia,** the **cosmos,** the **marigold** and the many magnificent varieties of **dahlias.** Mexican plants grace our window sills and greenhouses as well: **poinsettias** (Euphorbia pulcherrima) and cacti such as **old man's head** (Cephalocereus senilis), **nipple cactus** (Mamillaria carnea) and the **spiny barrel cactus** (Echinocactus grusonii) are among our favourite house plants.

Finally, **sweet peppers** (Capsicum annum) and **avocados** (Persea americana), **cacao** (Theobroma cacao) and **vanilla** (Vanilla planifolia) – all indigenous to Mexico – add flavour and zest to our cuisine.

This list can only give an idea of the diversity of Mexican flora: in fact, the country is home to over 20,000 varieties of flowering plants alone. Due to its length (almost 4,000 km/ 2,500 miles from north to south) and the immense altitudinal differences between its deepest canyons and its loftiest mountains, the territory of Mexico encompasses a vast array of environments. These, in turn, support an extremely varied plant life. Temperature greatly affects the make-up of plant life as well, and Mexico is characterized by extraordinary temperature variances. As one travels northwards through the region surrounding the approximate dividing line between the tropics and the subtropics, a marked drop in temperature is discernible. With every increase in altitude, the temperature takes a similar plunge.

As a result, altitude rather than latitude determines Mexico's climatic zones: the "tierra caliente" (hot land) reaches up to 700/800 m (2,500 feet); the "tierra templada" (temperate land) extends between 800 and 1,700 m (2,500 and 6,000 feet); and the "tierra fria" (cold land) is found above 1,700 m (6,000 feet). In the north, of course, the transition points between zones are found at lower altitudes.

The "tierra caliente", with average yearly temperatures of over 24 °C (75 °F), embraces the Yucatán Peninsula and the lowlands of the Gulf and Pacific coasts as far north as the tropic of Cancer. Here, there is a tropical climate and heavy precipitation prevails. At one time, large portions of the states of Tabasco, Chiapas, Campeche, Quintana Roo and Veracruz were covered by tropical rainforest, but in recent years, much of it has been cleared for farming and ranching, leaving only a small concentration of forests in

Campeche, Chiapas and Quintana Roo.

With their wide variety of flora and fauna, these forests make up a complicated ecosystem, the inhabitants of which have developed interesting adaptive mechanisms in order to survive. In the case of plants, the need for sunlight has resulted in the formation of "layers" of life in the rainforests of southern Mexico. Only the tallest-growing and longest-living trees make it to the uppermost level of the forest where their crowns form a canopy at heights of between 30 and 50 m (100 and 160 feet). One such tree is the **mahogany** (Swietenia macrophylla), one of our most valuable sources of wood.

The middle level contains smaller, fast-growing trees such as the **ant tree** (Cecropia sp.); the **sapodilla** (Achras zapota) – the latex of which yields chicle, the chief ingredient in chewing gum; and **palm trees** of the genera Bactris and Chamaedora.

Because so little light filters down to the lower level, only shade-loving plants such as **ferns,** the **bastard plantain** and **dwarf palms** can be found there. Climbing plants such as the **philodendron** (Monstera deliciosa) sometimes penetrate through all of the forest's layers to eventually emerge above the canopy.

Epiphytes, which include plants of many families (orchids; bromeliads, some species of fern), are plants which live on the surface of other plants; unlike parasites, however, they derive food and moisture from the air.

Despite what its abundant growth suggests, the soil of the rainforest is extremely poor as a result of its uninterrupted growth cycle. Cleared tropical forestland is thus incapable of yielding more than a few meagre harvests. When the soil is spent, the land is abandoned and the process of deforestation continues.

Plants which grow in regions with extended dry periods (the Yucatán Peninsula, the Pacific coast and Baja California) have obviously adapted to cope with the limited water supply there. Some trees, such as the majestic **ceiba** (Ceiba pentandra), the **logwood** (Haemotoxylon campechianum) and the **calabash tree** (Crescentia cujete) protect themselves from dehydration by shedding their leaves. Succulents, such as the cactus and the agave, are structurally designed to conserve moisture. The **sisal agave** (Agave sisaliana), a native of the Yucatán Peninsula which can now be found in tropical regions all over the world, is an important source of fibre.

Savanna regions, which represent a transition zone between the "tierra caliente" and the "tierra templada", can be found not only in the tropical lowlands of the Yucatán Peninsula, but in the subtropics of the north and on central Mexico's high plateaux as well. These temperate savannas are home to many familiar species of agave. Like the **prickly**

pear (Opuntia ficus-indica), another Mexican native, the **American agave** (Agave americana) is just as common a sight along the Mediterranean as it is in its native land. Also known as the century plant or American aloe, this species flowers only once in every 10 to 30 years. Two other species of agave deserve mention here: the **maguey** (Agave atrovirens) and the **tequila** (Agave tequilana), the sources of pulque and tequila respectively. Yuccas – some of which, like the **elephant yucca** (Yucca elephantipes), can grow as tall as trees – can be found throughout the savanna.

Mexico's deserts and semideserts, the greatest of which can be found in the north (the Sonora Desert) and on Baja California, lie adjacent to the savannas. These regions boast the largest concentration of different species of cactus found anywhere in the world. Most characteristic are the giant **torch cacti** (Lemaireocereus sp.), which can reach heights of over 10 m (30 feet), and the **organ-pipe cacti** (Pachycereus sp.). The **peyote or mescal** (Lophophora williamsii), a small spinless cactus, grows in the sierra between Chihuahua, San Luis Potosí and Querétaro. Its tubercles (mescal buttons) contain mescaline, a hallucinogenic drug. The stimulating effects of mescaline have been known to Mexican Indians since ancient times – the cactus was in fact venerated as a god. The Huichol of Nayarit still hold the cactus sacred, and once a year collect mescal buttons, which are then ingested as part of a celebration.

Mexico's national tree, the **ahuehuete** (Taxodium mucronatum) thrives in the wet regions of the "tierra templada". An imposing specimen of this giant cypress (it has a girth of 42 m/140 ft and an estimated age of 2,000 years) can be seen in the churchyard in Tula near Oaxaca. Extensive stands of **ahuejote** (Salix bonplandiana) are found near Mexico City and along the canals of Xochimilco.

In the mixed forests of the north, **reticulate oak** (Quercus reticulata), **Moctezuma pine** (Pinus montezumae) and **Portuguese or Mexican cypress** (Cupressus lusitanica) can be found. These trees penetrate into the "tierra fria", which begins between 1,500 and 1,800 m (5,000 to 6,000 feet) above sea level depending on the geographic position. There they are joined by the tall Australian immigrant, the **eucalyptus.**

The 10,000 km (6,000 mile) long Mexican coast, with its many beaches and lagoons, forms a zone of vegetation all its own. Palm trees, in particular the **coconut** (Cocos nucifera), line the beaches which skirt the Yucatán Peninsula, the Gulf coast and the Pacific coast up to the city of Mazatlán.

Casuarinas (Casuarina equisetifolia), **malabar almonds** (Terminalia catappa) and **sea grapes** (Coccoloba uvifera) also grow in great numbers along the coasts. **Morning glory** (Ipomoea pes-caprae) and **Canavalia maritima**

1
2
1
3
4
5
6
7
8
9
6
10

(related to the jack bean) sometimes spread floral carpets over entire beaches.

The numerous lagoons along the Gulf coast (Laguna Terminos) and the southern Pacific coast offer an ideal environment for **mangroves.** These gain a foothold in the oxygen-poor coastal slime with their prop roots, and throw out countless aerial roots which often look like pencils sticking up out of the ooze. The red mangrove (Rhizophora mangle), the most commonly found species of this tree, forms impenetrable thickets which cover vast areas along the coast.

The best first impression of the variety and diversity of Mexican flora is provided by the ornamentals, both native and immigrant. Besides the **poinsettia,** other native flowering plants include the yellow-blossoming **golden shower** (Cassia alata); the **yellow elder** (Tecoma stans); the pink-blossoming **ipé tree** (Tabebuia pentaphylla); the **gold cup** (Solandra nitida), a climber with magnificent orange bell-shaped flowers; and the pink blossoming **Mexican creeper** (Antigonon leptopus), which is sometimes referred to as **coral vine.**

Immigrants include the **royal poinciana** (Delonix regia); the **African tulip tree** (Spathodea campanulata); the **jacaranda** (Jacaranda mimosifolia); the **hibiscus** (Hibiscus rosasinensis); the **oleander** (Nerium oleander); the **bougainvillea** (Bougainvillea spectabilis); the **frangipani** (Plumeria alba); and that tall and graceful Cuban immigrant, the **royal palm** (Roystonea regia).

No less numerous are the varieties of fruits grown in Mexico. At any market you should be able to find **avocados, cherimoyas, sour sops, guavas, papayas, maracuyas, sapodillas** and **prickly pears.** The selection of vegetables and herbs and spices is equally great. In addition to the countless varieties of **chilli peppers** – well-known as the fiery ingredient in Mexican food – you can find edible, starchy roots such as **cassavas** and **yams, plantains, courgettes** (zucchini), spiney **chayotes** and pungent-smelling **coriander.**

(Beese)

1. Saguaro cactus (Carnegiea gigantea; can grow to over 15 m/50 ft.; simple or branched trunk)
2. Barrel cactus (Echinocactus grusonii; up to 1 m/3 ft. in diameter, spines up to 8 cm/3 ins. in length
3. Notocactus leninghausii
4. Torch cactus (Cereus sp.)
5. Spurge (Euphorbia abyssinica; introduced from Africa)
6. Prickly pear (Opuntia ficus-indica; cactus with edible fruits now grown in tropical and subtropical regions all over the world)
7. Maguey (Agave atrovirens)
8. Yucca (Yucca sp.)
9. Rattail cactus (Aporocactus flagelliformis)
10. Porcupine cactus (Opuntia erinacea)

Natural World

As the map below shows, the scenery, climate and vegetation of Mexico are extremely varied, ranging from the deserts of the north to the forests of the south, from the sierras of Oaxaca and Chiapas to the plains of Veracruz, Tabasco and the Yucatán Peninsula. Due to the broken nature of the terrain, you can find in a single state both arid and humid regions; conifers alternate abruptly with tropical rainforests reminiscent of Amazonia. "Cold land" and "hot land" are often side by side, and it is not rare to find, on a single mountain, fields of potatoes and lettuces at the top and coffee plantations at the bottom.

The significance of such diversity for the visitor is that, should he find the heat or the cold unbearable, he has only to travel for a few hours in one direction or another for a complete change of air. It also makes travelling overland a pleasure.

This variety of climate is reflected in the fruit markets, where apples lie alongside coconuts, and extends to the animal world as well.

For all of these reasons, doing some travelling on foot in Mexico is certainly worthwhile. As anyone who has tried it will surely agree, there is no better way of coming into closer contact with the natural treasures of the country. *(Valerio)*

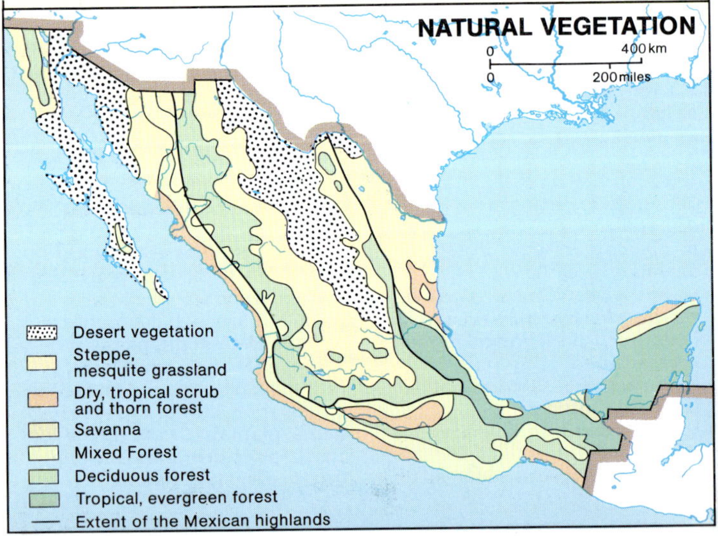

Fauna

Those hoping to find big animals in Mexico should prepare themselves for a disappointment: on the whole, the tropics and subtropics of the western hemisphere are characterized by a lack of large mammals, and the few species which do occur are rare. Furthermore, many of these are now endangered due to poaching and agricultural expansion. On the other hand, however, Mexico boasts a stunningly varied array of birds, reptiles, amphibians and invertebrates.

Mexico lies at a point where the **Nearctic** and **Neotropical** regions, the animal worlds of North and South America, overlap. These great zoogeographic regions were separated for many millions of years during the Quaternary period, during which time each developed its own unique animal life. The presence of species from both regions in Mexico today is explained by the fact that following the emergence of the land bridge between the two great continents, animals began migrating in both directions. Today, as a rough generalization, Nearctic animals are found at higher elevations, and animals which originated in Neotropical regions predominate in the lowlands. Some groups of animals – reptiles, in particular – developed in Mexico itself during the ice ages. The area of distribution of such animals – including reptiles like the rattlesnake, the sagebrush lizard (genus Sceloporus), and the mud turtle – is still centred here.

Mammals

Mexico is the northernmost range of the New World monkeys. **Geoffroy's spider monkey** (Ateles geoffroyi) occurs from southwest Jalisco to the Gulf coast and the Yucatán Peninsula. The **mantled howler monkey** (Alouatta palliata) is a rarer species whose habitat is the continually shrinking rainforest. Both of these have a long, partly naked prehensile tail which serves as a "fifth hand" when climbing.

A frequently occurring hoofed mammal is the **white-tailed or Virginia deer** (Odoceileus virginianus) which can be found throughout North America. Although it is widespread in Mexico, it is not often observable except in mountainous regions. With a little luck, however, you may be able to spot large-eared **mule deer** (Odoceileus hemionus) in the semideserts of Sonora, the northern highlands or Baja California. The **red brocket** (Mazama americana) is a small deer with unbranched antlers which you may sooner encounter on a dinner plate in southern or southeastern Mexico than face-to-face in the wild.

Two species of peccary occur in Mexico: the **collared peccary** (Tayassu tajacu), also found in the southern United States; and the somewhat larger **white-lipped peccary** (Tayassu pecari). Peccaries are fierce, omnivorous and gregarious animals which, when threatened, will attack lynxes, pumas (see Walt Disney's "The Living Desert") and even man.

Canines are represented in Mexico by various **foxes** as well as by the **coyote** (Canis latrans), which is common in the north. The **Mexican wolf** (Canis lupus ssp.), however, can be found only in small numbers in the Sierra Madre del Sur.

The familiar, North American **black bear** (Ursus americanus) is also quite rare in Mexico. Related mammals which occur more frequently include the **raccoon** (Procyron lotor) and the **coatimundi** (Nasua narica). The young of the latter, which can be quite tame but tend to be rather demanding, are sometimes kept as pets. The nocturnal, arboreal **kinkajou** (Potos flavus) inhabits only the tropical south.

An interesting variety of felines are native to Mexico. The **puma** (Felis concolor), "el leon", which once ranged throughout the entire country, is now rare and endangered. Another rare and endangered species is the **jaguar** (Panthera onca), "el tigre", which occurs primarily in the south but ranges along the Pacific seaboard as far north as southern Sonora. The smaller cats, which include the **bobcat** (Lynx rufus), the **ocelot** (Leopardus pardalis) and the **jaguarundi** (Herpailururs yagouaroundi), are more common. With a little luck, you may even spot one of these from your car on the roadside at night.

An animal you might well catch sight of during the day (its fearlessness is due to its lack of natural enemies) is the thick-skinned, ill-tempered American **badger** (Taxidea taxus). Two members of the weasel family you would do best to avoid are the striped (Mephistis mephistis) and the spotted (Spilogale putorius) **skunk.**

Mexican hares are characterized by oversized ears which serve them as thermoregulators; in other words, they keep them cool. The **antelope jackrabbit** (Lepus alleni) of the deserts and semideserts of the northwest boasts the largest ears of all – they make up one fourth of its entire body.

The **ground squirrel** is a timid, diurnal rodent which lives in colonies, particularly in arid regions. At the slightest sign of danger this creature will scamper into its burrow (actually one of a connecting system of burrows) only to poke its head above ground a short while later when curiosity gets the upper hand.

While travelling in parched, inhospitable areas at night, you may be surprised at the number of **kangaroo rats** (Dipodomys) you see along the way. Kangaroo rats are pouched rodents with short forelegs and long hindlegs which they use for leaping forward. Living as they do in areas with little moisture, they derive water from the seeds and insects they feed on.

The **coendou or prehensile-tailed porcupine** is a New World tree porcupine of southern Mexico. As its name suggests, it has a naked prehensile tail which it uses to grip tree trunks when climbing. Caution is recommended, for its bristles – which it will eject at the slightest provocation – penetrate deep into the skin and muscle tissue, leaving behind wounds which fester easily.

Mammals which can be found in Mexico's coastal waters include the

California sea lion (Zalophus californianus), which ranges primarily along central Mexico's Pacific coast, and the seal.

The **sea cow or manatee** (Trichechus manatus) is a timid mammal of tropical waters which you will only spot with a great deal of luck.

The breeding grounds of the **grey whale** (Eschrichtius robustus) are located off the coast of Baja California (see "Nursery of the Grey Whale", p. 248).

Mexico is the home of several species of tropical **bats,** a number of which (Artibeus spec. and Carollia perspicillata, for example) are fruit-eaters like the Old World flying foxes. The most famous (or rather, infamous) of the Mexican bats is the great **vampire bat** (Desmodus rotundus), a rare species native to all parts of the country. They feed on the blood of mammals (including man) by biting into the skin with their sharp teeth and licking up the blood that flows from the wound. As carriers of rabies and equine trypanosomiasis, they are dangerous both to man and domestic animals.

Armadillos, edentate (having no teeth) mammals of the American tropics and subtropics, are represented in Mexico by the **nine-banded armadillo** (Dasypus novemcinctus), which can be observed at night an in the early morning. In rural areas, armadillos also enhance the daily diet.

Another edentate mammal is the New World anteater, of which two species are found in Mexico. The 54–56 cm (almost two-foot) long **tamandua** (Tamandua tetradactyla), whose tail doubles its length, is found throughout the grasslands and savannas of Tabasco, Chiapas and Yucatán. In contrast, the silky **two-toed anteater** (Cyclopes didactylus) is a small (no larger than a squirrel), rare species which dwells in wooded areas.

Those particularly interested in the mammals, birds and reptiles of southern Mexico should visit the zoo at Tuxtla Gutiérrez in Chiapas – probably the best in Latin America.

Birds

There are at least 1,000 different species of birds in Mexico. The most notable of those occurring along the coast are the **brown sea pelican** (Pelecanus occidentalis), which nose-dives into the water to catch its prey; and the **magnificent frigate-bird** (Fregata magnificens) which can be found on both the Pacific and Gulf coasts. With their long, forked tails, their shiny black feathers and their brilliant red gular pouches (which are inflated during courtship and before mating), frigate birds are striking to look at. The so-called "man-o'-war birds" are also fascinating to watch, for rather than catching fish themselves, they often try to snatch them away from other aquatic birds by staging acrobatic attacks on them in mid-flight.

Several species of **herons** can be found not only near the water, but in fields and meadows as well. In addition, **ibises** and **spoonbills** can be found in the swamplands, and there are some **flamingos** along the Gulf coast.

The long-toed **American jacana** (Jacana spinosa), which frequents coastal marshes and ponds, is fascinating to watch as it hunts insects from atop an unsteady carpet of lily pads.

The nests you may notice hanging from the ends of the branches of trees are built by the rather plain and inconspicuous **black oriole** (family Icteridae).

Woodpeckers, some of which have bizarrely tufted crests, are easy to observe, particularly in mountainous regions. Often, you can even spot their nesting holes in tall saguaro cacti.

About 50 species of "flying jewels" – **hummingbirds** – can be found throughout Mexico. From mountainous regions to cities and villages, these seemingly delicate creatures make themselves at home anywhere they can find small insects and flowers from which to collect nectar.

Nineteen species of **parrots** live in Mexico. The **military macaw** (Ara militaris) ranges from the savannas of Sinaloa in the west and Tamaulipa in the east all the way to South America.

Of the five varieties of amazons in Mexico, those found in the south and on the Yucatán Peninsula – in particular, the **yellow-lored amazon** (A. xanthochloro) and the **white-fronted amazon** (A. albifrons) – are most common. Much more prevalent are the chiefly green parakeets of the genus Aratinga. Although these birds are readily recognizable by their shrill voices, you often have to scan the trees long and hard before spotting one climbing about.

The **turkey buzzard** (Cathartes aura), which was quite commonplace up until a few years ago, has now retreated to areas where it is not hunted. Unlike the Old World vultures, New World vultures like this one are not related to the hawks, but rather, to the storks (!). They can be seen (where else?) around animal carcasses – mostly those of pets and domestic animals which, in Mexico, wander about rather freely and often stray into the paths of moving cars. The **king vulture** (Sarcorhamphus papa) with its bright and colourful, naked head and its black and white plumage can be found only in the rainforests of southern Mexico.

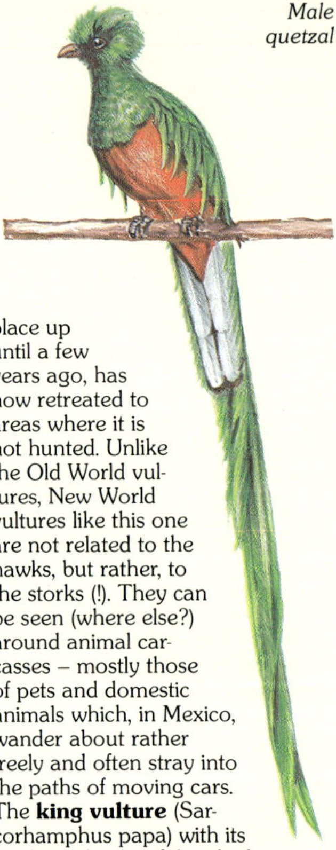

Male quetzal

The long-legged **caracara** is a true hawk, but, like the vulture, it feeds on carrion it finds on the roadsides of southern Mexico.

Toucans and **aracaris,** brilliantly feathered, fruit-eating birds with very large but light (due to air chambers) beaks, are found mainly in southern and southeastern Mexico.

The **quetzal** (Pharomachrus mocinno), the most important bird in the mythology of the Mexican Indians as well as the national bird of Guatemala, lives in the tropical mountain forests of Chiapas and southwards. This beautiful bird, a member of the trogon family, is in grave danger of extinction.

Reptiles

Mexico boasts more species of reptiles – well over 1,000 and new discoveries are made almost every day – than any other country in the world.

While freshwater or marine turtles can be found in almost every body of water, land turtles can only be found in the arid regions of northern Mexico. The most prevalent of the freshwater turtles is the **painted turtle** of the genus Chrysemys, which can often be found sunning itself on a tree trunk lying in the water. The **mud turtle** (family Kinosternidae) leads a more reclusive life and is, accordingly, inconspicuously marked. The attractive **Mexican wood turtle** (Rhinoclemmys) of the Pacific coast, on the other hand, can all too often be found stuffed and for sale at souvenir stands.

A different attitude towards turtles is displayed along the Gulf coast where even endangered species like the giant **Dermatemys mawi** (its shell can reach a length of 80 cm/ 2.5 ft) can be found tied up in bundles and offered for sale at meat and produce markets. If you find yourself in Villahermosa, visit the "mercado" and see for yourself. There you will also find **common or green iguanas** (Iguana iguana) and **black iguanas** (Ctenosaura specs.) – likewise meant to be cooked and eaten. Because of this, these large, impressive lizards, characterized by a serrated dorsal crest, have become a rare sight in Mexico. In areas where they are not hunted, however, they will even venture close to houses, where they can be "baited" with tablescraps and observed.

The wealth of smaller lizards is immeasurable: **sagebrush lizards** (Sceloporus), which can scare off rivals with a mere nod of the head, are tree, rock and ground dwellers; lizardlike **racerunners** (Cnemidophorus) can be seen shooting across streets and roads and hunting insects in refuse dumps (among other places); **anoles** dwell in trees and bushes, where they often can be seen on the very tips of the branches.

The strange, **two-handed worm lizard** (Bipes canaliculatus) is a reptile unique to Mexico and California. At first sight it resembles an earthworm, but if you look closer, you can spot its tiny eyes and its two strong forelegs with their shovel-like claws used for digging. Little is known about the biology of these animals.

The **gila monster,** of which there are two species (Heloderma suspectum, native to the American Southwest, and H. horridum, native to Mexico), is the only venomous lizard in the world. These large, impressive orange and black (warning colours!)

nocturnal reptiles hunt small animals and actually pose little threat to humans – as long as one doesn't get bitten!

Mexico also has its share of crocodiles: the **American crocodile** is found along the Gulf coast, the **Morelet crocodile** (Crocodylus moreletii) is found in Yucatán, Chiapas and Tabasco, and the small **caiman** is found throughout the lowlands of the Pacific coast region. Only with a great deal of luck will you be able to observe one of these shy creatures in the field.

Rattlesnakes, whose area of distribution is centred in Mexico, can theoretically be encountered anywhere in the country – even in the high sierra. Fortunately, the sharp rattling sound made by their tail usually gives fair warning of their presence.

The **boa constrictor** can be found along the Gulf coast, in the south, and along the Pacific coast as far north as the arid state of Sonora. A multitude of other snakes, some with colourful markings, can be found throughout the country. Most of these are difficult to observe, however, due to their reclusive habits.

Amphibians

The most conspicuous of the salientians (frogs and toads) is certainly the **giant or marine toad** (Bufo marinus) which grows to a length of over 20 cm (10 inches) and is prevalent everywhere except in the highlands. As for the other frogs, they may make a lot of noise during the rainy season, but you will rarely get a glimpse of them.

Even more reclusive are the **salamanders,** of which one very unique species lives in Mexico. The **axolotl** (Ambystoma mexicanum), whose Nahuatl name means "water doll", is a neotenous tiger salamander, that is, it does not go through metamorphosis, but lives and breeds in the larval stage.

Insects

The number and variety of **butterflies** in Mexico are enough to make the heart of a nature lover beat faster. Butterflies can be found virtually everywhere – only in areas where intensive vegetable farming is practised and crop dusting takes place (as in Culiacán) is their population scant.

Watching **parasol ants** (Atta) at work can be truly fascinating, especially when they are transporting large pieces of leaves: it looks like the leaves are moving by themselves. In their underground colonies these ants grow fungi (the spore cases of which represent their only source of food) on the chewed-up pulp of the leaf fragments. Because they sometimes cause considerable damage, these ants are considered pests.

Spiders

Bird spiders and **scorpions,** which are really not half as bad as they are made out to be, are represented by many species in Mexico. You should take care to avoid the yellow scorpions of the arid regions, however, for they are indeed highly venomous.

(Wicker)

The Mexican Indians

The figure given for the percentage of pureblood Indians in Mexico is usually somewhere between 7 and 25. This is understandable when one considers the many criteria used to determine racial identity and the varying degrees of emphasis placed on factors such as life style and cultural behaviour. Whatever the case may be, it cannot be denied that there are groups of people living in Mexico – particularly in the south – who can be defined, ethnically as well as culturally, as Indian. These include the Zapotecs of Oaxaca; the rural Mayas of Yucatán, Campeche and Quintana Roo; the highland Maya of southern Chiapas; the Lacandons; the Chamulas; and the Zinancatecs. The continued survival of these groups, particularly of the last three mentioned, is imperiled by a number of factors such as inbreeding, degenerative diseases, alcoholism, venereal disease and malnutrition, all of which are proving difficult to bring under control.

A government agency has been created to tackle these problems: the Instituto Nacional para los Indigenos (National Native Institute) administers counselling centres, health clinics and hospitals. Its primary task, however, is to instruct the Indians in modern, more rational farming methods and to introduce the cultivation of new and more profitable crops – tasks which are not as easy as they seem. Needless to say, the agency suffers from a notorious lack of funds and personnel. Furthermore, there is sometimes a lack of cooperation on the part of the traditionally-minded Indians who are diffident to change and justifiably sceptical of the white man's innovations.

The difficulties involved in surmounting these problems are more or less the same as those facing the Mexican agricultural sector in general. Following the Revolution, the large, hereditary estates were broken up: subsequent governments have encouraged a system known as "ejidismo" which was designed especially for small-scale farming. This system was based on an ideology which is still held sacred, although many critics insist that such an agricultural form is not only a failure now, but could never have functioned anyway. The ejido system can be seen as the traditional Mexican form of socialized farming, for privately-owned land was unknown in the ancient Indian civilizations.

An ejido can be described as a kind of holding: a piece of land owned by the state is transferred to a family, a village or a cooperative society for their own use. Experience shows that the difficulties begin with this simple act of granting tenure. The Indians lack experience in the employment of modern farming methods, faulty planning and organization (or even an absence of both) are often in evidence, and most of these small farms are forced to operate on a minimum of capital. The average Indian farmer does not have enough money to buy seed, animal feed and the essential pieces of equipment and machinery. Funds advanced by the government are quickly spent, the seed is quickly consumed, and the vicious cycle of debts, interest payments, minimal returns and, finally, impoverishment begins. Farmers who fall hopelessly into debt soon abandon their land to either seek work as day labourers or migrate to commercial centres in the hope of finding employment. Once they are there, however, their situation only worsens, as evidenced by the number of Indians living in slums on the peripheries of the big cities. In these dismal communities, the opportunities for advancement are virtually non-existent and there is little cause to hope for a better life for their children. Social assistance does not exist in any form, there is no possibility of acquiring a better education, and utter hopelessness prevails.

For the Mexican government, these are merely one aspect of an entire complex of problems affecting the population as a whole. Outside the cities, the INI may try to improve the situation of the Indians, but for those already in the cities there is little hope, In urban areas they merely swell the ranks of the poor, the continued growth of which poses seemingly insurmountable difficulties for the state. At present, efforts are being directed towards keeping the indigenous Mexicans in their traditional homelands and increasing opportunities for them there. Whether of not this will succeed and how the necessary contact with the technological world will affect the Indians remain to be seen. Sadly, a little scepticism is probably in order. *(Thieme)*

Contrasts in the North – Tarahumara and Mennonite

One of the greatest contrasts in this land of contrasts is that which exists between two groups of people who live in close proximity in the northern state of Chihuahua. The Tarahumara Indians of Copper Canyon and the Mennonites, their nearest neighbours, represent two cultures, two religious systems that live on here side by side, in the space of a few hundred miles. The people of both these groups are Mexicans, yet their life styles are totally different and both are far removed from, say, the Mexicans who live in the capital city.

Over millions of years, raging waters have carved deep gorges in the Sierra Madre Occidental, Mexico's western mountain range. The Barranca del Cobre, or Copper Canyon, cuts as deep as 1,700 m (5,577 ft) into this mass of land, the peaks of which rise to heights of up to 2,800 m (9,186 ft). This giant natural maze contains a complexity of topographical features which assault the eyes with the bizarre images they create. The world famous Grand Canyon of Arizona could fit four times into the labyrinth of the Copper Canyon, its walls sloping down gradually in an endless series of steep giant steps.

This awesome region is the realm of the Tarahumara, an Indian tribe which has managed to remain outside the confines of civilization up to the present day.

Who are these people? The Tarahumara, who belong to the great family of the Apaches, call themselves the Rarámuri, the running people. In a region where most of us would have difficulty walking, they run, and indeed are said to be able to run deer to exhaustion, Tarahumaras can run straight up mountains that an outsider could only surmount after tiresome zigzagging. Oblivious of sharp stones, they usually go barefooted, using their toes to grip the rocks.

They practise a "sport" (to them it is a form of entertainment) in which they run – sometimes for miles and miles without rest – while kicking a wooden ball ahead of them. The pride of a Tarahumara is to be a good runner. Families and whole communities challenge each other to races which can last up to an entire day and night (even children's races last several hours). Two teams run against each other, each with its own wooden ball. The race takes its contestants through canyons and rivers, and over fences and any other obstacles which are encountered. Wagers are placed on the teams – characteristically enough, it is the runners themselves who play for the highest stakes. To keep alert during the race contestants wear "rattle belts" made of deer hoves (to assure them the swiftness of deer) and pieces of wood. Women compete as well, but in their races a hoop replaces the wooden ball. The hoop, which is made of entwined yacci leaves, is propelled forward with a stick.

Forty thousand Tarahumaras live in the region surrounding the Barranca del Cobre and the Barranca de Urique – part of the 25,000 sq. km (9,650 sq. mile) large barranca country of northern Mexico. Each of them would have a great chance of winning Olympic gold in the marathon, but to keep up their enormous stamina, they depend largely on their environment: their mainly vegetarian diet features plants and herbs which can only be found in barranca country.

The Tarahumara move with the changing seasons. In the winter, when icy storms lash the highlands, they live at the foot of the canyons where it is warm enough for orchids to grow. In the summer, they move back up to the highlands. Some Tarahumara still live in caves, but most of them live in wooden huts built under shelves of rock which jut out from the canyon's walls. They grow maize and keep small flocks of sheep and goats, using dung to enrich the poor soil (by keeping the flocks on the move, they assure that each new maize field is properly fertilized). Their animals are the pride and joy of the Tarahumara, and they are rarely slaughtered. Maize is the source of a sweet beer called "tesquino" which is brewed for special occasions, "tesquinadas", when families from all over gather together.

The inaccessibility of their homeland has saved the Tarahumara from many of the "blessings" of civilization. Even though they have been Christianized, they continue to appeal to their traditional gods. In matters of the hereafter they pray to God, Jesus Christ and the Virgin Mary, but for their everyday problems, they turn to their own Indian gods. They believe that the spiritual world is the exact reverse of the physical world: so, while the body sleeps at night, the soul works in the spiritual fields. The other world also comes into play when a Tarahumara dies. Certain family members then wear the clothes of the opposite sex for three days, in which time the soul of the deceased reaches its final destination. When a woman dies, the observances last one day longer – women run more slowly.

The Mennonites of the region around Cuauhtémoc, the town nearest the territory of the Tarahumara, are "drop-outs" from society. At least that is what we might call them today – people who reject modern technical achievements and whose attitudes and beliefs have remained virtually unchanged for hundreds of years.

The Mennonites originated within a 16th-century Anabaptist movement (so called because of its doctrine of adult baptism) and are closely related to the Amish and the Hutterites. The Mennonites, German protestants who lived quietly and unobtrusively as "Congregations of the Cross", rallied around the Frisian reformer Menno Simons, who, in a now-famous document, refused the Pope further obedience and renounced his Holy Orders. The spirit of the Inquisition first sent the pious Mennonites in search of more hospitable lands, but wherever they went, their religious principles eventually came into conflict with the needs of the worldly authorities. In Prussia they worked to make large areas of land suitable for agriculture, but moved on to Russia when the Prussian authorities demanded they carry out military service. In Russia they lived peacefully for around a century until there too they were to be conscripted and forced to pay taxes. Finally, in the 19th century, they emigrated to Canada.

In 1874, the Mennonites, with their usual diligence and skill, began laying the foundations for their existence in the New World with the cultivation of vast tracts of land in Manitoba. But Canada, too, wanted to integrate these newcomers into their society, so many of them soon moved to Mexico. President Alvaro Obregón granted them the concessions they considered essential: the right to educate their children in their own schools and the exclusion from military service. In 1921, they received their charter and settled in the state of Chihuahua.

These hard-working pacifists may not know how to handle a sword or a rifle, but they certainly can handle a plow. The list of their agricultural achievements is long: they have turned the desert of northern Mexico into fertile farmland; they supply the entire republic with their delicious cheese; thanks to them, the state of Chihuahua is Mexico's leading oat producer; and virtually all the country's apples come from their orchards.

Some 32,000 Mennonites live scattered throughout 150 small villages and communities surrounding the town of Cuauhtémoc, where they even have their own bank. Their communities are set up according to the most basic principles of communism: goods and property are held collectively and the common good ranks above personal needs. There is no place for shirkers in their society. Mennonites marry only among themselves and raise large families. A Mennonite who marries an outlander may never hope to return to the fold again. Because of these strictures, some have felt compelled to move, this time to Central and South America – to Honduras, Bolivia and Paraguay.

Twentieth-century frivolities such as motorized vehicles for personal use, electricity for nighttime illumination, and modern appliances in the home are looked upon with disapproval: all around Cuauhtémoc, Mennonites can be seen in their horse-drawn carriages. These tall, blond, blue-eyed Mexicans do, however, employ modern technology for the benefit of production: tractors rumble over the fields and diesel generators power the cheese-making machines.

In their quaint German dialect, they greet visitors with kindness and interest. Some tour operators have even come to an arrangement with certain Mennonite families whereby tourists can visit their homes. The Mennonites use the opportunity to market their handicrafts. I've been told that they'll even take you in if you're willing to work with them. To live in the 19th century for a few months – that would certainly be appealing to someone looking for an alternative to modern civilization.

After you leave the Mennonites – the men in their blue overalls and wide-brimmed straw hats, the women in their long black skirts – you'll quickly find yourself in the desert again. The lush green of their fields will disappear, to be replaced by the harsh beauty of the Mexican countryside as it once again stretches to the horizon in shades of brown and grey. *(v. Debschitz)*

The Lacandons

Much has been written about them – more of it fiction than fact. They have been mystified and romanticized. They were once thought to be the last of the "savages" and there were some who thought they should be protected as an "endangered species". Adventure-seeking tourists, refugees from civilization, have tried to live among them – but with little success.

Who are they, the Lacandons? The answer is not easy, for linguistically they do not belong to any other Indian group in Chiapas. They are related neither to the Zoques nor to the Tzeltals, nor even to the Tzotzils, their immediate neighbours in the region around San Cristobal de las Casas. They call themselves "Masswal", which means "low class", a name which was certainly given them by the Aztecs who scorned their primitive life style.

They seem to be a people who stemmed from a variety of ethnic backgrounds and whose dissimilarities were blotted out in the course of time by the hardships of life in a menacing environment. There can also be no doubt that they are a Mayan people, although this designation is as meaningless and vague as the word "Indian". It is not even known with certainty if these people are indigenous to the area they now occupy or if they migrated there. If the latter is true, the next question is: where did they come from? Their culture gives us no clues. If they had belonged to one of the fallen civilizations of the Petén, their long journey must have signified a cultural step backwards for them.

Anthropologists have tried to answer these questions by taking anatomical measurements, particularly cranial measurements, but the results must be viewed as inconclusive because the Mayan racial type is too uniform. The results of recent linguistic research, however, are far more interesting. The phonetics and suffix endings found in the Lacandon language (and in all Mayan languages) show clearly that it originated on the Yucatán Peninsula. In fact, it has been shown that this language is an archaic dialect of Yucatán Maya. This discovery has given rise to two theories as to the origin of these people: either they were forced out of their original homeland on the Yucatán Peninsula and migrated south, or they share a common origin with the Yucatán Maya, but did not migrate to the peninsula after the collapse of their cultural centres around the year A. D. 900. Instead, they must have split from the main group of their own people and migrated to Chiapas. This second theory is supported by the little-known fact that there is a further, isolated group of Lacandons living between Palenque and Ococingo in northern Chiapas, though only those who live in the vicinity of Lacanhá Lake actually call themselves "Lacandons". This second group of Lacandons is considerably more acculturated than the jungle Lacandons of the south – only their common language betrays the connection between the two groups.

It is difficult to say just how many Lacandons there are. The Palenque Lacandons are slightly more numerous than those in the south, but altogether they number less than one thousand. Lacanhá Lake itself is home to only a 60-member clan of Lacandons and an unknown number of small, scattered groups roam the 100,000 sq. km (40,000 sq. mile) large region between the Usumacinta, Jacate and Lacantún Rivers.

An examination of the Lacandons, their life, lore and rituals need not take into account the northern group as its members no longer display the specific cultural behaviour their cousins in the south do.

The traditional dress of the Lacandons consists of a white smock which reaches to below the knees. This smock is worn by men and women alike. Women sometimes add colourfully-dyed woolen skirts to this simple dress. The hair is worn loosely over the shoulders and nothing is worn on the head. Occasionally, the men wear nose rings and the women wear necklaces made of berries or glass beads (nowadays, they can be made of plastic beads as well). Precious metals are seldom used; these people are, after all, too poor.

Hard physical labour characterizes the life of Lacandon men and women, for both sexes perform the same tasks together. Archaic methods and tools are used to work the land: digging sticks are used for seeding just as in olden days; to clear the thick underbrush, fires are set or machetes (the only iron implement they know) used. Many tasks, in particular the clearing of forestland, are ritualized: the fire, for example, may only be started by rubbing sticks together.

It would be only partly correct to characterize the Lacandons as farmers. While farming does form a part of their traditional culture, a large amount of their food is supplied through hunting and the gathering of wild fruits. While some Lacandons may keep a few chickens, domestic animals are not common among these people. Even though it could be easily done, they seldom cultivate "exotic" plants such as bananas, but instead concentrate on traditional crops: maize (which is ground into flour for tortillas), cassava (the root of which is a valuable source of food), sweet potatoes, beans and tomatoes. In addition to game such as pecaries, tapirs and birds, they eat turtles and turtle eggs and fish and crustaceans from the rivers and lakes.

Lacandon society, which clearly was at one time rather complex, is now organized along relatively simple lines. Owing to the small population, many aspects of social order once necessary for the well-being of their society have become superfluous.

Today, Lacandons live mainly in single-family units; seldom do they live in clans which together form villages. Originally they were organized in ten clans, all of which still exist today, albeit in name only, and without the social significance they once had. The breakdown of the clan system has brought about a number of problems which threaten the existence of these people. When they were still organized in clans, exogamy was the rule, but today, marrying within the family has become such common practice that it is now impossible to determine the degree to which the population is inbred. Polygamy is practised – Lacandon men take as many wives as their economic circumstances will allow. (The fact that they were only "discovered" about 100 years ago explains why these people were never Christianized.)

Lacandon houses are simple structures consisting of four posts supporting a roof which extends to the ground and is secured to the posts with lianas. Their temples, which are constructed along similar lines, in no way resemble those of their Mayan ancestors, but are merely more elaborate versions of a normal Lacandon house. In the temples, prayers are chanted and incense is burned.

The very many gods and religious concepts known to their ancestors have been reduced to a simple concept of opposing principles: a positive principle represented by the Rain God, Metsaboc, and a negative principle represented by Kisin, the God of the Underworld and bringer of earthquakes and sickness.

Unlike the ancient Maya priests, who were titled, revered and respected and enjoyed extensive social privileges, the Lacandon priest is not much more than a shaman.

It is interesting to note that in scheduling important religious observances such as holy days and days of abstinence from certain foods or from sexual relations, the priests base their calculations upon a 260-day cycle – an obvious remnant of the ancient Mexican ceremonial calendar which was based on the lunar year.

The Lacandon's view of the world is governed by his eschatological beliefs. The Lacandons believe that they live in a world which, like the previous one, is doomed to destruction. Exactly when the demise of the world will come to pass is not known. The fate which awaits each Lacandon after death is the splitting up of body and soul: the pulse, the seat of physical life, goes to Kisin in the underworld while the heart, the seat of spiritual life, goes to Metsaboc, the God of Rain, who is also seen as the God of the Heavens.

The question of whether this primitive society and ethnic identity of the Lacandon people can survive is a good one – and one which pertains not only to the Lacandons, but also to all other archaic Indian societies. As it is impossible to shield them from progress, from the encroachment of civilization, from industrialization, etc., their chances for a future do not look bright. The danger is that they will in time disappear in the southern Chiapan melting pot where they will become assimilated and cease to exist as a self-contained group. Whether they can develop a new way of life for themselves remains to be seen – but it is doubtful.

A visit to the Lacandons on Lacanhá Lake is difficult to arrange because of problems of transport and accommodation. There is a landing strip near the village, but in the interest of the villagers, it is closed to tourists.

Information on how to get there can be obtained from the travel agencies in San Cristobal de las Casas. *(Thieme)*

Black Gold

There is a good chance that the misfortunes the Mexicans once suffered on account of their gold could be brought upon them again in this century – but this time, by black gold.

It was always clear to the colonists that the country had more to offer than just gold. Mexico does indeed abound in natural resources, and it may be said without exaggeration that there is hardly another country in the world – at least not one of comparable size – that is blessed with such an abundance of minerals (see "Mining and Industry").

Of all Mexico's resources, however, **petroleum** and **natural gas** are the most important. They render the country independent of fuel imports and represent an important source of foreign exchange. In 1982, for example, Mexico was able to export more than half of its petroleum; the United States is bound by long-term agreements to purchase Mexican natural gas (this they use in order to spare their own offshore reserves).

Mexico's oil fields are not a discovery of recent date – they have been known about ever since the flourishing manufacturing industries of the Western world began to show an interest in this raw material. At the beginning of this century – in the days of Porfirio Díaz' presidency – United States oil companies were already tapping the Gulf coast reserves near the mouth of the Rio Coatzacoalcos. One of Mexico's oldest refineries is still in operation there today – at Minatitlán in the state of Tabasco (this is in fact one of the country's most important production sites).

As early as in 1921, Mexico was the second-largest oil producer in the world, but was still under the aegis of the number one producer, the United States. In 1938, President Lázaro Cárdenas nationalized the Mexican petroleum industry and compensated the U. S. oil companies involved. With this act, he became a national hero. Soon afterwards, however, and as a result of the worldwide economic depression and World War II, oil production, which had stood at 500,000 barrels per day (1 barrel = 42 U. S. gallons/35 imperial gallons), fell to one fifth of that amount. The refineries and oil-drilling rigs which had been taken over by **PEMEX (Petroleos Mexicanos),** the semi-governmental petroleum monopoly, soon became obsolete, and in the 1960's, the country was producing hardly more than was necessary to satisfy its own needs. When, in the 1970's, the population explosion occurred and Mexico's economic difficulties and foreign debt situation were deemed out of hand, oil was looked to as a cure-all.

Under President López Portillo and PEMEX Director Díaz Serrano, production was stepped up, old installations modernized, new refineries constructed, exploration carried out and the conveyance system expanded.

PEMEX owns large refineries near Ciudad Madero (on the Gulf of Mexico near Tampico) and in Minatitlán (Gulf coast), Reynosa (near the U. S. border) and Salina Cruz (on the Pacific coast of the Isthmus of Tehuantepec). By means of a network of pipelines, oil is supplied to the highland refineries outside Salamanca (between Guanajuato and Guadalajara) and outside Atzcapotzalco (a suburb of Mexico City). These refineries provide for Mexico's two largest cities, Mexico City and Guadalajara. In order to finance these installations, PEMEX has taken out high foreign loans. The company is Mexico's largest individual debtor and carries a considerable amount of the responsibility for the country's catastrophic debt situation.

In many cases, the refineries form part of extensive petrochemical plants (Salamanca, Minatitlán, Atzcapotzalco) where ammonia, used in fertilizers and processed materials, is produced. New petrochemical plants (the Pajaritos and "La Cangrejera" processing plants) are now going up along the Gulf coast.

In the 1970's, output increased to 1 million barrels per day in Tabasco alone and it is now estimated that Mexico's reserves amount to about 200 billion barrels, an unbelievable amount. Petroleum and natural gas, which have been found under Mexico's Gulf coast shelf, are now being pumped up from drilling platforms. In light of these finds, Mexico has extended its territorial waters to a distance of 200 nautical miles. Natural gas is produced mainly in the region around Reynosa, near the U. S. border. Oil production is centred around Tampico, Tuxpan and Pozo Rico and in the Coatzacoalcos/Minatitlán region. There is a small oil field near Salina Cruz (Pacific coast of the Isthmus of Tehuantepec).

As a result of increased output in the seventies, Mexico rose to the position of fourth-largest oil producer in the world. One billion dollars were invested in a pipeline to Texas and agreements over the supply of natural gas to the United States were concluded. 1978/1979 were the years of the boom, but the crash came soon afterwards. The enormous foreign debt incurred for the development of the new industry and all connected future projects had been allowed to pile up in the expectation that it could easily be paid back in oil. In 1980, the year before the crash, Mexico recorded a total output of 106 million tonnes.

After the oil crisis came the moment of truth. Rather than join OPEC, Mexico had counted on its nearness to the United States, but things were no longer working out as planned. The United States no longer wanted the natural gas, an already crowded market was glutted with oil, and prices dropped. In 1982, repayments on interest and principal to the amount of $ 20 billion fell due – a sum of money which Mexico simply did not have. The impetuous investments financed with foreign capital began to take their toll – Mexico was, for all intents and purposes, bankrupt.

Despite falling prices, however, production was stepped up by 14% in 1982, and over 50% of the total was exported. In 1983, with an output of 132.7 million tonnes of petroleum and 41.9 million cubic metres of natural gas, Mexico ranked among the largest oil producers in the world (outside of OPEC).

In 1982, PEMEX dismissed 10,000 employees, and towards the end of President Portillo's term of office, other abuses came to light which the new government is now busy exposing and rectifying. Díaz Serrano was sent to prison for embezzlement and breach of trust, and Ramón Beteta became the new president of PEMEX.

In the course of the enquiries it also became apparent that production costs in Mexico were unusually high; furthermore, it was discovered that through the underhandedness of the unions, there were six times more employees on the payrolls in Mexico than there were in the U. S. or Venezuela. A sense of imminent doom spread throughout the population. – The new government now faces the task of cleaning these "Augean stables".

Environmentalists have taken advantage of this opportunity and finally stepped in. In the previous atmosphere of euphoria, few voices were raised to call attention to the damage caused by a total lack of regard for the environment. But, in 1979, an incident occurred which did indeed bring home to all of Mexico the possible dangers involved in drilling. The platform "Ixtoc I", located in the Bahía de Campeche, sprang a leak, and nine months passed before it could be sealed. In the meantime, 500,000 tonnes of crude oil had spilled into the sea and an environmental catastrophe loomed. Providence directed wind and waves away from the coast, however, and Mexico's shores at least were saved from disaster.

The 10,000 Indian farmers armed with clubs, pitchforks and antique rifles who blocked the Cactus Refinery in Chiapas in 1981 and paralyzed production for two days to protest the contamination of their fields and of the air they breathe also wanted to avert disaster. The government promised to take steps to protect the environment after the governor of Chiapas joined ranks with the protestors.

A study compiled by the University of Mexico on the high levels of soil and water pollution in the region around Minatitlán and the Rio Coatzacoalcos was once again brought to light by the enquiry. First submitted in 1976, the study was so alarming that the decision was made to declare it classified material in order to avoid a general panic.

And so it became quite obvious that "black gold" had brought both glory and shame to Mexico – as it has to other countries as well. The government and PEMEX have started to heed the danger signs, however. In 1983, an environmental protection plan was drawn up which treats the problems thoroughly and offers solutions for the future. But all of this costs money – lots of it – and where is one going to get money in Mexico? *(Thieme)*

Mining and Industry

Important mineral resources and a well-developed industrial sector have placed Mexico among the most economically advanced nations in Latin America. The country has acquired significance as one of the world's most important suppliers of raw materials (and in particular, as a supplier of petroleum and natural gas, as dealt with in the previous chapter).

As many as 400 years ago, Mexico was already supplying a substantial portion of the world's **silver** and **gold.** Up until the end of the 19th century, precious metals formed the bulk of Mexico's exports, with other products trailing far behind. As shown by the 1983 figures (an output of 6.9 tonnes of gold and 1,900 tonnes of silver), Mexico is still an important producer of precious metals, particularly silver. Although the country was in second place behind the Soviet Union in 1980, it now hopes to regain its position as number one silver producer in the world with the opening of new mines near Guanajuato.

Other major mining products include (all figures given are in tonnes and indicate output in 1983 unless otherwise stated): **iron ore** (8,424,000 t), **zinc** (257,000 t), **copper** (208,000 t), **lead** (167,000 t) and **manganese ore** (used in steel refining; 133,000 t). Mexico is also an important producer of **antimony, cadmium** and **bismuth,** although these metals, which are also used in steel refining, make up only a small portion of its total mineral output.

Sulphur (1,602,000 t) and **phosphates** (498,000 t) are among the important nonmetals produced. With respect to sulphur, a raw material important to the chemical industry, Mexico is a leader among the world's producers. Phosphates are used primarily in the manufacture of fertilizers and detergents.

Mexico's **coal** output (5,400,000 t in 1977) may seem small in comparison with the amount of oil it produces (132.7 million t in 1983) but the coal reserves, located primarily in the northern state of Coahuila, are very important. The coal they yield is directly convertible into coke, and the latter is then used in the **smelting** of the ore deposits of the Cerro de Mercado near Durango. The oldest blast furnaces are found in the state of Coahuila; **iron and steel works** are concentrated in the state of Nuevo León around Monterrey, Mexico's second most important industrial centre.

Large steelworks are either under construction or in operation in other parts of the country as well: in southern Puebla, on the Gulf coast north of Villahermosa, and on the Pacific coast near Las Truchas, where a new steel complex and "steel city" (Ciudad Lázaro Cárdenas) have sprung up. Here, low-grade domestic iron ore and Australian coal are used in smelting.

Important copper **mines** are located near Cananea in the northern state of Sonora; copper, lead and silver mines can be found near Hidalgo del Parral and Chihuahua (both in the state of Chihuahua); iron ore is mined near La Perla in Chihuahua. Sulphur, like petroleum and natural gas, is found in the Gulf region.

Until the early 1960's, the production of raw materials (excluding petroleum and natural gas) was chiefly in the hands of foreign (and especially American) companies. As a result of national legislation, however, foreign interest in the mining sector has been greatly reduced. Nowadays, at least 51% of a company's capital must be in Mexican hands and new mining concessions are only granted to Mexican companies.

In the last 45 years, Mexico has grown into an industrialized nation, and today it produces virtually all common **utility and consumer goods** itself. The quality and, in particular, the price of these goods do not correspond with the situation on the world market, however, because high protective tariffs levied on imports essentially keep **foreign competition** out of Mexico. On the other hand, if it were not for this customs barrier, many firms in Mexico would never have been founded because they would never have been able to realize enough profit to cover the cost of setting up production.

Above all, it is the capital goods sector (machines, industrial equipment, etc.), which is underdeveloped and still largely in the hands of foreign or transnational companies. The Mexican government plays a dominant role in the industrialization of the country through its incentive schemes, customs policies and programmes for national development as well as by providing roads, ports and power plants. The investment activity of large semi-governmental companies like PEMEX is another significant factor. National policy is aimed at promoting foreign investments and, furthermore, at directing them into sectors which have so far been neglected. At the same time, however, national interests are to be placed before the capital and profit interests of foreign investors, and local investment activity is to be promoted.

State intervention is bothersome to **foreign investors,** but the Mexican government takes pains to keep up good relations. Taxation is low and, in addition, tax concessions exist in certain regions. The regulations governing the transfer of profits abroad are fair, protective tariffs guarantee a minimum of foreign competition in domestic markets, and wages are low as a result of two factors: the guaranteed minimum wage is low and the governing Partido Revolucionario Institucional (PRI) keeps a strong hold on the unions.

Industry is concentrated in the Mexico City area as well as in the areas around Monterrey in the north and Guadalajara in the west. The government has also authorized the

establishment a number of new, small, regional industrial zones.

Industrial parks have been set up in Querétaro, San Luis Potosí and Tolula, as well as in those industrial centres already mentioned in the previous chapter with regard to the petrochemical industry. Further industrial development is to take place along the coast and in areas outside the main centres of population. In this way, presently underdeveloped areas will gain jobs and economic significance.

Mexico's northern frontier constitutes another important industrial zone. In cities like Ciudad Juárez, Tijuana and Mexicali, U. S. manufacturers have, with the permission of the Mexican government, set up branches which produce solely for the **American market.** Producing such goods as electronic components for radios, televisions etc., these so-called **border industries** or "maquiladores" profit from low Mexican wages but do offer a comparatively high number of work places for Mexicans.

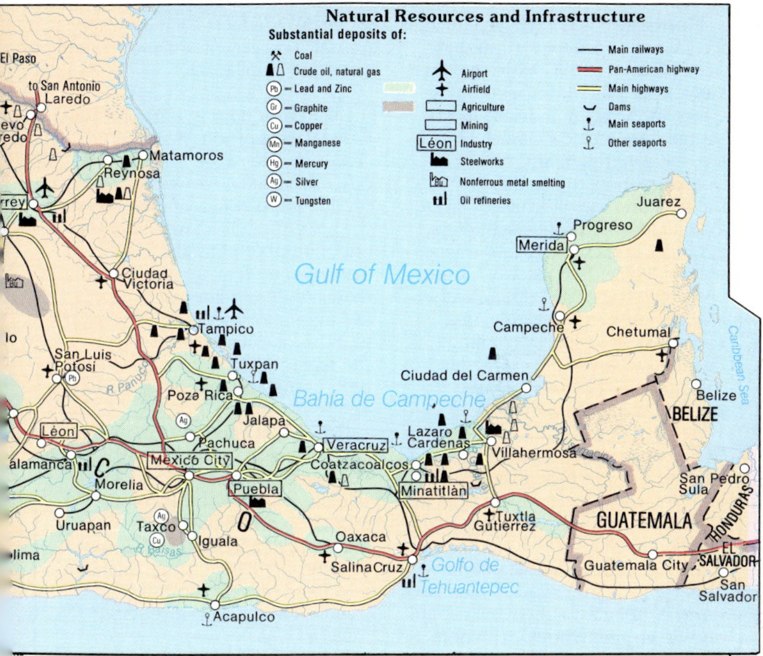

Of the industries centred around **Mexico City,** metal manufacturing and metalworking (mechanical engineering, etc.) occupy 25% of the factories; the pharmaceutical, food and drink, and textile industries together account for a further 50%. Paper, cement and tyre manufacturing, as well as the electrical engineering industry, are located on the outskirts of the city; the automobile industry has manufacturing plants which encircle the capital at a radius of around 80 km (50 miles) – some of these plants even export goods.

The mass motorization of Mexico, which had been advancing by leaps and bounds in the 1970's, suffered a setback as a result of the economic crisis which began in 1983. Since then, the production and sale of motor vehicles has decreased sharply.

The industrial centres which occupy the second and third positions in Mexico are Monterrey in the state of Nuevo León, and Guadalajara in Jalisco. Guadalajara is also an important banking centre.

Monterrey is known in particular for its iron and steelworks (Fundidora Monterrey 1903, Mexico's first large-scale blast furnace complex). Other branches of industry represented here include machine-building, metalworking, automobile manufacturing, the chemical industry, the manufacture of cellulose and paper products, of glass, ceramics and crockery and of electric appliances, the electronics and communications industries, leather and rubber manufacturing, and shoemaking. Dairying, canning and the production of mineral fodder for the agricultural sector are also important activities in this region.

Although the metal industry is not as prominent in **Guadalajara** as it is in Monterrey, the city is nevertheless a centre for iron ore smelting and for the manufacture of machinery, transport vehicles and equipment. Other important products manufactured here include chemicals, soaps and detergents, shoes, cement (near Tlaquepaque) and high-quality industrial products such as photographic equipment and electric and electronic appliances.

Lying as it does in a fruitful area, Guadalajara produces and processes a wide range of fruits and other foodstuffs. As well as the food production plants scattered about the area, there is a large brewery and a number of tequila distilleries. The town of Tequila, the heart of the tequila industry, lies just 60 km (37 miles) northwest of Guadalajara, and this popular spirit is definitely the region's best-known product both home and abroad.

Other, less important, industrial centres include: (in the north) Chihuahua/Cuauhtémoc, Hermosillo, Gomez Palacio/Torreón, Monclova and Saltillo (both near Monterrey), Durango and Tampico; (in central Mexico) Aguascalientes, León and Morelia; (in the south) Puebla, Orizaba/Córdoba and Mérida.

(Schmidt)

The Agricultural Sector and its Problems

Even though Mexico has developed in the past 45 years into one of Latin America's leading industrialized nations, the country still remains essentially an agrarian land. In 1979, 7.9 million Mexicans (40.1% of the labour force) were employed in agriculture. After petroleum and petroleum products (which accounted for 22% of all Mexican exports in 1980), agricultural products such as coffee, cocoa, cotton, tobacco, sisal, and fruits (tomatoes, strawberries) are Mexico's second most important export item. The agricultural sector also supplies most of the country's food as well as the raw materials needed for the manufacture of textiles (cotton, fibre), vegetable fats and oils.

Mexico's most important agricultural products include (figures for 1982, expressed in thousands of tonnes): **wheat** (4,468); **maize** (12,215); **sorghum,** a cereal used primarily in animal feed (4,717); **beans** (1,093); **soya beans,** used in animal feed and as a raw material in the cosmetics industry (672); **coconuts** (800); **tomatoes** (853); **cucumbers** (150); **chillis** (370); **melons** (978); **watermelons** grown primarily for domestic consumption (664); and **grapes** (598). Mexico is also a producer of wines, though these cannot be compared with wines produced in Europe and California.

Sugar cane plantations are also important to the agricultural sector: Mexico is one of the largest sugar producers in the world (34,066). Sugar is also used as a primary product in the distillation of rum and other alcoholic beverages. (Bacardi Rum has a large distillery in Tultitlán, Mexico state, which, according to their own advertising, uses only domestic raw materials in production.)

Of the many fruits grown in Mexico, the most important are **oranges** (1,995), **lemons** (819), **mangos** (701) and **bananas** (1,572). **Peaches** (189) and **strawberries** (65) are exported to the U. S., Canada and Europe in the winter months. Mexico exports 46,000 tons of natural **honey** each year, making it the world's number one exporter of that product. **Coffee beans** (313), **cocoa** (41) and **tobacco** (67) are also important products.

Despite the continued rural exodus, the number of workers in the agricultural sector rose from 5.7 million in 1970 to 7.9 million in 1979. The percentage of the population employed in this sector, however, varies greatly from state to state. States lying north of the tropic of Cancer have the smallest proportion of farm workers, while in the southern states often 80% of the labour force is in agriculture. Furthermore, two fifths of the country's agrarian population is concentrated in the small states south of Mexico City, in an area which comprises only 14% of the nation's territory. The typical farm is small (less than 5 hectares) and produces little more than what is required to sustain it. Large, modern, efficiently-run agricultural enterprises do, however, predominate in the irrigated oases in the north and along the Pacific coast. Cattle ranches are also large-scale operations covering vast areas of (non-irrigated) land.

The new **irrigated zones** which have sprung up in the deserts and semi-deserts of the northern states (thanks largely to government support) are the backbone of the Mexican agricultural sector. Such zones are located at the estuaries of the rivers Yaqui, Mayo, Fuerte and Culiacán in the west (where cotton, wheat, maize, soya beans, sorghum and rice are grown), and in the Colorado River basin, where cotton covers 65–70%, and wheat, 20–25% of the land under cultivation. Other irrigation zones can be found along the Rio Grande and in the Comarca Lagunera, an area of the northern plains located around the cotton town and industrial centre, Torreón.

The area of transition between the arid but irrigated north and the hot and humid south is formed by the **fertile valleys of the "altiplanicie central"** or central highlands (Bajio, the Valley of Mexico, the Valley of Puebla-Tlaxcala).

Crops grown here include maize, beans ("frijoles negros"), wheat, chick peas ("garbanzos"), garlic ("ajo"), onions ("cebollas") and chillis – all staple foods which appear daily, either raw or cooked, on Mexican dinner tables. Other important crops include alfalfa (basic to the diet of the dairy cattle kept on large dairy farms in the central highlands) and tomatoes and sugar cane – both of these products are exported on a large scale.

The region which was clearly at one time the centre of agricultural activity in Mexico – the southern part of the central altiplano – is now practically without importance as a supplier of food, whether it be to the country as a whole, or in particular to the urban populations, or as goods for exportation. The reason for this is overpopulation: there are just too many people trying to make a living in agriculture in this area. Furthermore, most of the farms are limited in size and resources and are only able to provide for the farm family itself – a marketable surplus is rarely produced.

In the hot and humid states of **southern Mexico,** and especially along the southern Gulf coast, plantations predominate; maize, sugar cane, coffee, citrus fruits, beans and rice are the crops grown here.

The coastal state of **Veracruz** ranks among the richest in Mexico thanks to its prospering farms – and its oil reserves. Forty percent of the maize grown here finds its way to urban markets in the country's interior. Veracruz is also an important supplier of tropical fruits to the central highlands, and an important producer of export produce such as sugar cane and coffee. In the other large state on the Gulf coast, **Tabasco,** where new oil discoveries were made in recent years, cattle raising has increased in importance despite problems posed by the hot and humid climate and the appearance of cattle pests such as "garrapata".

Conditions on the Yucatán Peninsula pose problems for agriculture there. The lack of surface drainage in this porous limestone tableland precludes the irrigation of regions with little rainfall, making the growing of crops with high water requirements virtually impossible. The cultivation of the henequen agave, a drought resistant plant which supplies fibre for ropes and sacking, provided one way out of this dilemma. Between 1880 and 1910, plantations with their own fibre mills and railways were established. These were flourishing, highly profitable operations producing an export commodity which brought a great deal of foreign exchange into Mexico – until, that is, the competition created by East African sisal and Indian jute as well as the increased significance of synthetic fibres began harming the henequen trade considerably. The Mexican state, which now supports the plantations financially, has taken over the mills and is now trying to promote the sale and use of the fibre within Mexico itself.

The above example illustrates only one of the profound problems affecting the Mexican agricultural sector today. While regional problems do not lend themselves to generalizations, it can be said that agriculture is the problem sector of the Mexican economy. A few figures may serve to illustrate this point: in 1980, 40.1% of the labour force employed in agriculture produced only about 8% of goods and services (gross national product). At the same time, it was a very small portion of the nation's farms, namely 15%, which supplied as much as 75% of the nation's food.

Several factors contribute to this permanent state of crisis in the Mexican agricultural sector. The country's population increases at an average annual rate of 3.1%, a figure which places Mexico among the countries with the highest growth rates in the world. Despite continued movement towards the cities, there are still too many people trying to make a living off the land. Productivity shows a very slow rate of increase and the availability of cultivable land is limited.

In 1970, there were 3.6 million landless campesinos (farm workers) who had to eke out a living as day or seasonal labourers. (The way in which land is distributed still puts most of Mexico's farmers at a disadvantage). Almost 52% of the farms were "minifundios" (small farms of less than 5 hectares), which due to their limited size and resources, were often not able to provide enough food to feed the farm family much less provide a surplus for the markets of the big cities. On the other hand, in 1979, there were over 5,000 farms with an area of over 5,000 hectares and a large number of medium-sized farms as well, with between 25 and 200 hectares of land.

These large and medium-sized farms in fact form the backbone of the country's market and export production. But the country could not do without its "minifundios" either: they provide work and an income for that portion of the population which as yet cannot be integrated into the more productive sectors of the Mexican economy (industry, transport, trade and services). The abandonment of the small-scale farms would deprive almost half the Mexican population of a means of livelihood.

The present state of affairs in the Mexican agricultural sector and the situation of the people who work in that sector are the products of a

Fishing

The fishing industry is often seen as the problem child of planners and nutrition experts in Mexico. The potential of the fishing industry to make a significant contribution to the feeding of the ever-growing population has been recognized but not yet exploited to the full.

Mexico did extend its territorial waters from 12 to 200 nautical miles, but to safeguard offshore oil fields and not because of fishing. It is estimated that only 14% of the possible catch has so far been realized.

The country's fishing fleet is dated and dilapidated; facilities for refrigerating and transporting this valuable commodity are inadequate. A large section of the industry is in government hands, however, and in 1980 a bank was founded, the function of which is to supply the fishing industry with capital for investment.

The main fishing areas are the coast of Yucatán near Campeche and the Gulf of California. Among the twenty or so species fished in these waters are tuna, bonito, shark, sardine, shrimp and lobster.

Ideal conditions for game fishing have resulted in numerous hotels being built and fishing fleets established along stretches of the coastline frequented by U.S. sportfishermen. This represents an important source of income for Mexico. *(Schmidt)*

continuing historical process and may not be judged merely from the point of view of economic practicality. Seventy-five years ago, impoverished and starving small farmers and day labourers sparked off the bloody Mexican Revolution with the cry "tierra y libertad" (land and freedom). In 1910, a few hundred families controlled practically all the country's arable land and the great impoverished mass of the Mexican people worked on their immense haciendas much like slaves. The Revolution and the ensuing fifteen years of civil war cost the lives of millions of Mexicans and led to the destruction of most of the haciendas.

The constitution of 1917 and the Código Agrario (Agrarian Code) provide for the expropriation and distribution to landless farmers of all privately-owned land exceeding a certain size (usually 150 hectares of cultivable land). Such redistribution has been taking place at irregular intervals for the past 50 years and has resulted in the creation of a new form of land ownership – the "ejido". Under this system, large estates are divided up and distributed to landless farmers for their sole use, but the state retains legal ownership of the land as well as the right to repossess and redistribute unused parcels. While the right to an ejido may be passed on to one's heirs, the sale, lease or mortgage of state property on the part of the "ejidatario" (the user of the land) is prohibited by law. *(Schmidt)*

Tourism

Mexico comes very close to fitting the requirements of an ideal holiday destination. It is a place where cultural and leisure activities can be enjoyed in perfect balance – culture and bikini go hand in hand, so to speak. This aspect of Mexico will definitely appeal to Europeans or anyone else facing a long flight. Most people would not choose to travel such a distance merely to enjoy sun, sea and sand, but would be happy to combine such pleasures with more serious pursuits. For tourists interested in such **combination holidays,** a two to three week stay with a few days in Mexico City followed by a week of touring (taking in the Maya sites on the Yucatán Peninsula, for example) and rounded off by a few days on the Pacific, Gulf or Caribbean coast is highly recommended. Those who do not book an "itinerario" with their flight will find that they can rely on the tour operators in Mexico to provide all the information and help in planning and booking whatever kind of vacation they want.

As is the case with every holiday spot in the world, there is indeed a **"best time" to travel** to Mexico. With respect to coastal resorts, however, month-to-month fluctuations in temperature are minimal: On the Pacific coast, for instance, (Mazatlán, Puerto Vallarta, Manzanillo, Ixtapa-Zihuatanejo, Acapulco), it gets hotter than usual from May onwards until the longed-for showers finally come – mostly at night and mostly in the form of downpours. Humidity may increase then, but the climate still remains pleasant to perfect. In the late summer, tropical storms can send strong winds and rains beating down on the Gulf and Caribbean coasts.

In the period from early summer to autumn, hotel prices in coastal resorts tend to be lower than in the high season. The period from December to Easter constitutes the high season. At this time, most **resort hotels** along the coast offer rooms only on the basis of MAP, the "Modified American Plan" (half board); some hotels only offer rooms with "American Plan" (full board). During the low season it is possible to book rooms in a hotel on the basis of the "European Plan" – meal not included. During the high season, confirmed hotel reservations are an absolute must in the resorts along the coast!

In the Mexican highlands with their **centres of cultural, historical and archaeological interest** – Mexico City, Cuernavaca, Taxco, Querétaro, San Miguel de Allende, Guanajuato, Guadalajara, Oaxaca – the same hotel prices are in effect all year round. The best time to visit this region is in the period following the rainy season, i. e. from mid-September until May.

Touristic **infrastructure** is good to excellent in the well-known centres of tourism. Outside these areas, however, it is as good as non-existent. The individual traveller should bear in mind that not every spot on the map offers suitable lodgings. Motels – where available – are, as a rule, quite comfortable. Rooms without private baths are rare in Mexico.

Due to the fact that in many areas you can travel for a hundred miles or so in any direction without finding a place to spend the night, it's definitely a good idea to plan your itinerary and to schedule your stops with care.

It should also be borne in mind that driving at night in Mexico is a sometimes hazardous enterprise and one which should be avoided if at all possible. Unlighted trucks are often recognizable as obstacles only moments before they are encountered, a bush pulled up by the roots and placed in the middle of the road just yards from the truck being the only indication of trouble ahead. Horses and cows (naturally without tail lights) pose problems for the overtired driver too. Cyclists without lamps or reflectors on the wrong side of the road, children playing in the middle of the highway, and foot-deep potholes which appear without warning are all part of the reality of motoring in Mexico.

It's best not to tempt fate, because an otherwise neighbourly and hospitable Mexican will not stop at night to help motorist in trouble. The implications of the still-valid Napoleonic Code are all too obvious to him: anyone present at the scene of an accident runs the risk of being arrested (law enforcers do not have to prove the guilt of a suspect, but rather, the suspect must furnish proof of his innocence). Furthermore, anyone who stops on the road at night runs the risk of falling victim to a violent crime. It's in your own best interest to pull off the highway at dusk and take up quarters for the night!

Mexico boasts two of the ten most beautiful hotels in the world – Las Hadas in Manzanillo and the Acapulco Princess in Acapulco – as well as a number of hotels which enjoy international renown (Mexico City's Camino Real, for example). Standards in Mexico's first-class and de luxe hotels are high – accommodation and service are excellent, prices are high! Chain hotels like Sheraton, Westin, Holiday Inn (called Posadas in Mexico), El Presidente and others offer their familiar high standards plus a charming touch of local colour.

Hotels in the medium-priced range offer comfort at reasonable prices and add a more personal touch than you find in the luxury establishments. They represent an interesting option for tourists. Hotels which offer a taste of life on a colonial hacienda (the best example is probably the Hacienda Cocoyoc, 60 miles or so south of Mexico City between Cuautla and Cuernavaca) are worth looking into as well.

Those who are more interested in mingling with the "people" than in bathing in luxury at an exclusive hotel should seek out smaller hotels in the medium-priced range at the resorts as well. These charming hotels have literally sprung up in the shadow of the giant resort complexes with their eccentric architecture and sumptuous gardens and parks. Unfortunately, however, it is virtually impossible to book a room at these smaller hotels from abroad – telex costs are too high and mail service is slow and unreliable.

Visitors to Mexico who are between the ages of 12 and 35 and on a tight budget may like to take advantage of the economical package tours offered by the CREA. The **national youth club** organizes tours of the most interesting parts of Mexico for tourists in this age group (tours last from one to three weeks). Transportation is provided in de luxe buses; lodgings are provided in dormitory rooms in hostels or economy hotels.

For more information on these tours (which are open to all young people regardless of nationality) contact the Agencia Nacional de Turismo Juvenil, Glorieta Metro Insurgentes, Local CC-11, 06600 México, D. F.

Although **camping** is not as popular in Mexico as it is in the U. S. and in Europe, there are a number of well-equipped camp and trailer sites in the country. Those who plan on travelling to Mexico with a tent or a motor caravan might like to join the Club Monarca de Acampadores (named after the monarch butterfly which migrates yearly from Canada to Mexico).

The club offers a series of organized trips which start at different points in the country. Membership can be taken out for the duration of one trip or for an entire year. The trips are scheduled to correspond with the Mexican fiesta calendar. For example, trips are organized to the "Fiestas Patrias" in the state of Guanajuato (the birthplace of Father Miguel Hidalgo, the father of Mexican independence) on or around September 16th, Independence Day. Another example is the 11-day trip to Oaxaca in July to see the famous Guelaguetza Dances.

For more information write to the Club Monarca de Acampadores, Aptdo. Postal (P. O. Box) 31-750, 45050 Guadalajara, Jalisco.

The Mexican Ministry of Tourism, the Secretaría de Turismo (SECTUR), is one of the country's most important government departments for the simple reason that tourism is an important source of foreign exchange. The tourist industry is now once again challenging oil for the distinction of being the country's number 1 foreign exchange earner, the position it held until 1979 when PEMEX (Petróleos Mexicanos) took over. The importance of foreign exchange is clear in a land which finds itself heavily in debt.

Today, Mexico attracts as many tourists as Hawaii – roughly 4.7 million annually. 83% of these visitors come from north of the border. Foreign tourists pump over one billion U. S. dollars into the Mexican economy every year – in 1984, the exact figure was $ 1.7 billion. Of that, a good $ 1.1 billion remains in the country – Mexican tourists, for their part, spend between 500 and 600 million dollars abroad annually.

The important role played by border tourism in Mexico's balance of payments should never be underestimated. It's clear, however, that the 170 million border crossings which take place every year – either into or out of Mexico – cannot but leave their mark along the Mexican-U. S. frontier. This is especially true of the Mexican side. The tourist should bear in mind that these border towns, some of which are even "twinned" with towns north of the border, are not typical of the rest of Mexico. The crass display of commercialism evident in these towns and the reputation they "enjoy" are a direct result of both the interests of the tourists who frequent them and the desire on the part of the towns themselves to satisfy these interests.

Despite the treasures that Mexico has in store, its portion of the world tourism market (1.5% in 1979) is still quite small. Tourism specialists maintain, however, that "only the surface has been scratched" in terms of Mexico's touristic potential. For this reason, the Mexican government, through an organization set up to finance tourism projects, FONATUR (Fondo Nacional de Fomento al Turismo), is developing more and more coastal areas into tourist centres.

The number of suitable sites, especially along the Pacific and Caribbean coasts, is enormous. The training of a sufficient number of suitable hotel and service personnel could pose problems, however.

It's all too easy to forget that Mexico's "hospitality industry" does not have the thousand-year-old tradition of Europe, for example. The waiter who serves you a coco-loco at a beach restaurant or bar may, just a few years ago, have been employed as a harvester of the coconuts in which the drink is served.

(v. Debschitz)

Resorts from Acapulco to Cancun

As the plane approaches Acapulco, the mood of its passengers seems to change. During the half-hour Aeromexico or Mexicana shuttle – which flies from Mexico City to Acapulco with the frequency of a commuter train – the trials and tribulations of the big city are forgotten. Neckties, which in Acapulco are worn only at funerals, have been left behind.

No sooner has the plane completed its climb than it begins making its landing approach. The barren, craggy peaks of the Sierra Madre can be seen below. After a little turbulence – a sure sign that the Pacific is near – the plane flies in a wide arc over the coastline, giving its passengers their first breathtaking glimpse of the bay which Alexander von Humboldt called "one of the most beautiful in the world".

Stepping off the airplane, the passengers are hit by a wave of humid, tropical air. The difference between the dry, mild climate of the capital city and the sun-drenched coastal climate of Acapulco is breathtaking in the true sense of the word! The airport is modern and efficient; some sections are even air-conditioned. Luxurious indolence overcomes the travellers waiting for their luggage. Outside, palm trees sway in the breeze.

As soon as the airport taxi turns onto the broad motorway which heads toward the Bay of Acapulco, the magic begins. Long lagoons surrounded by tens of thousands of palms flank the road to the right: the water is as warm as bathwater. After a few miles, one of the largest and most beautiful hotel complexes in the world appears on the left: the Acapulco Princess and its sister hotel, the Pierre Marqués. The "Princess", as everyone here calls the queen of Revolcadero Beach, lies directly on the white, sandy beachfront, separated from the ocean by 50 metres (165 feet) of beautiful pools and tropical gardens.

The hotel complex comprises three buildings, one of which (the middle one) is shaped like a pyramid. Insiders joke that the Princess is the hotel with the most pious guests: there is hardly a "gringo" who doesn't say "oh my God!" when he walks into the hotel's atrium lobby for the first time and gazes upwards past cascades of flowers to the glassy firmament above the hotel's 20-plus floors. Later, when guests approach the check-out desk after a few sun-drenched days of rest and recreation and are presented with the bill, a muffled "Jesus" can often be heard. Naturally, a hotel of this type is not exactly inexpensive!

The Acapulco Princess boasts 1,000 rooms, two 18-hole golf courses, more than a dozen tennis courts (including two air-conditioned indoor courts) and four – or is it already six? – swimming pools. Imagine a day in the tropical garden: behind you, the imposing backdrop of the hotel pyramid and before you, the entrance to the mile-long beach; at your side, a grotto bar under a waterfall and around you, "beautiful people" from the four corners of the globe – that is certainly something special!

As your taxi continues towards Acapulco, you will next catch an enchanting glimpse of the small Bay of Puerto Marqués and its sandy beach skirted by restaurant huts. Here, squealing pigs run about freely – a tropical paradise without jet-set pretensions. The bay is ideal for sailing and water skiing.

The highway continues climbing until it reaches its highest point – 100 metres (330 feet) above the sea – the site of the Las Brisas Hotel. You'll only be able to see the arch which spans the road. But here, gentle traveller, lies the luxury upon which Acapulco's reputation as a playground for the jet set is based.

Steep roads lead up to the 250 bungalow-like hotel rooms (almost every one equipped with its own swimming pool and a red-and-white striped jeep) and the homes of the rich and super-rich, concealed from the eyes of the curious by hedges of bougainvillea. Fitted out with every imaginable luxury, some of these villas can be rented – personnel and all – for prices of around $ 2,000 a night. High above all this are a chapel and a giant cross, erected by a wealthy Mexican in memory of his son who died when his plane crashed into the bay. Today, the cross stands as a landmark over Acapulco.

After the road passes over a hill, you get your first glimpse of the sight that makes the heart beat faster: the Bay of Acapulco, looking like a giant soup tureen below you. The level bayshore is lined with landscaped parks interspersed with boldly designed high-rise hotels. Just beyond, the landscape becomes very hilly; some hotels and apartment complexes are situated high above the bay. Further beyond lie the mountains of the Sierra Madre.

Yes, of course, there is some truth to all the negative things said about Acapulco. As far as old Acapulco worshippers are concerned, the beachfront has been marred by too much construction (but the volume of guests gives the contractors justification). Of course, the water in the bay is not as clean as it could be (but there are a lot worse examples of water pollution in the world). Naturally, Acapulco is loud, often overrun, overpopulated (it does, after all, have a good quarter of a million inhabitants) – but it offers more than the other comparable beach resorts in the world. Insiders say that in Acapulco, there is nothing which cannot be had.

In Acapulco, there are some 200 tiny, small and medium-sized hotels, some of which offer a surprising degree of comfort for prices which, when subjected to international comparison, can certainly be called reasonable. Then there are the dozen luxury hotels which offer everything a holidaymaker could possibly wish for. No other resort in Mexico provides its guests with such a wide range of hotels. The same holds true for restaurants: from hamburger joints to luxurious gourmet restaurants with menus of sterling silver, there is something here for every palate and purse.

If you like thinks cozy and familiar, however, you will need to come here equipped with a strong sense of well-being and contentment, for you will be confronted with an amazing amount of glitter and wealth. Those who come here on a tight budget but with the intention of rubbing shoulders with the "beautiful people" will soon find themselves relegated to the stands from where they may only participate as spectators. Life at this resort is clearly dominated by cash-heavy "gringos" who hope to spend as much as possible in the short time they plan to stay. Travellers and holidaymakers with less available cash who stay in medium-priced hotels, walk to the beach and feed for the most part on tacos because their holiday funds have to last several weeks can easily feel disadvantaged.

My advice: stay away from Acapulco if your resources are low – or plan only a short visit, but one with all the trimmings. Otherwise you'll find yourself feeling like a poor "country cousin" (like I did the first time I came here – it's not fun to have to listen to other people telling you about all the interesting and "in" things you've missed because you're staying in the wrong hotel or you eat in the wrong restaurants or got to the wrong discos).

Lets take a look at the swimming pools of Acapulco. Avenida Costera Miguel Alemán, which was named after the former Mexican president who did much to further the industrialization of the country and tourism (until his death in 1983 he was president of the Mexican Tourist Board), runs parallel to the beach along the entire length of the bay. Up and down this avenue are hotels with swimming pools that are anything but rectangular. There are pools which form rings around islands-cum-dance floors or restaurants; pools with waterfalls; pools with real ships on the sand; pools with canals which run through landscaped parks... No one pool is identical to another; each one seems to possess something extra which makes it just a little more interesting than the one next door.

It was in Acapulco, by the way, that the famous pool-bar was invented. If you're thirsty, just swim up to the bar, take a seat on one of the underwater bar stools and enjoy a coco-loco (coconut blended with rum and other kinds of liquor). Payment is always by signature (at the hotel where you are staying, of course!).

Restless souls usually spend their day roaming up and down the beach (which is accessible to everyone – private beaches are forbidden in Mexico) and wandering in and out of the various hotel gardens. This is the best way, of course, to discover where the prettiest bikinis are – or where your own bikini causes the greatest stir.

Acapulco has a trifling total of 23 beaches. Insiders say that the most interesting beaches for pre-noon sunning and swimming are Playa Caletilla and Playa Caleta (opposite Isla la Roqueta and Isla Yerbabuena with its underwater statue of the Virgin of Guadalupe). After lunch, it's Playa Hornos and Playa Hornitos; in the late afternoon, Playa Condesa is the place to be. In the evening, people in the know drive – or have themselves driven – to Pie de la Cuesta outside Acapulco. Those who have been there won't easily forget the combination of sunset and roaring surf. But swimmers should beware – if you suddenly find yourself cast up on the beach with your mouth full of sand and no swim trunks, count yourself lucky – these waves have been known to break swimmers' backs.

In the evening, Acapulco really starts to stir. As soon as night begins to fall, the queues start forming outside the trendy restaurants. Go ahead and inch your way inside as well – it could be worth your while! Acapulco is still a prime celebrity draw. Check the table next to yours – there's a good chance you are dining next to a star. Three hundred and sixty days a year of sun and caressing breezes have a way of attracting ex-Beatles, ex-secretaries of state, ex-prime ministers and first ladies and show-business people from all over the world. The selection of "in" restaurants is utterly inexhaustible. Especially charming are the rustic fish and steak houses found along the Costera overlooking the beach.

The evening is also the time to enjoy the thrill of watching the death-defying Quebrada divers – best seen from the restaurant of the El Mirador Plaza with a drink in your hand. The young men dive (not without first having called upon the Virgin Mary and a battery of saints!) 40 metres (130 feet) down into a small cove between the cliffs which fills with water as the tide comes in. One miscalculated dive and...

Midnight is the time for a visit to one of Acapulco's discos – famous not only on account of the slender beauties who frequent them. The latest thing is the laser disco, an ingenious combination of noise and light. A disco which has managed to remain an "in place" for a number of years is one which is called simply "UBQ" (Ultimate in Beauty and Quality). If you come alone, don't be surprised if you are refused entry – here, equality of the sexes is striven for. Often, a reasonable tip (in addition to the fee at the door) will help you gain entry into paradise. Here, a long-standing rule is, never wear the same outfit twice. Ladies, keep an eye on your men.

Those looking for another, particular form of distraction need not look far: Acapulco is, after all, a port town. Its "zona roja" or red-light district is located in the city centre. If you just can't seem to get into one of the chic discos, go to La Huerta instead. There the ladies always leave a small donation at the shrine of Our Lady for every new customer. When it starts getting light, go down to the docks for fresh oysters right off the truck.

Cancun

Another fashionable beach resort is Cancun, the small peninsula which extends into the Caribbean from the tip of the Yucatán Peninsula. This L-shaped piece of land was chosen a little over ten years ago by computers in Mexico City to be the site of a new resort. Climatic conditions as favourable as those in Acapulco (actually not so, as hurricanes often influence the weather in the Caribbean in the late summer), its nearness ot the U. S. east coast, the quality of its beaches and the archaeological attractions in the vicinity all made Cancun seem like the ideal spot to build a resort. Today, this former island (now connected to the mainland by a bridge) "possesses" an array of luxury hotels, a conference centre and even a town. Still, Cancun, the pet project of former president Echeverría, has little cosmopolitan flair. The selection of restaurants outside the – pardon – sinfully expensive hotels is limited. The hotels are, it must be added, at a par with their international counterparts – architecturally as well as in terms of service and facilities. Cancun also has an interesting history: 15 years ago, it was inhabited by a few coconut gatherers; 1,500 years ago, by the Maya. Small temple pyramids still overgrown with vegetation can be found at the southern end of the island.

Cancun is a surf and snorkel paradise. For those who go out more for daytime than night-time sports, Cancun, with its beaches of powdery coral sand, is the place to be. The brackish lagoon enclosed by the "L" of the island is ideal for sailing and waterskiing. Deep-sea fishing and diving are fantastic in the open sea, which stretches out in shades of light-green to turquoise from the shoreline to the violet-blue horizon.

The exceptional opportunities for diving offered by the coral reefs off the island of **Cozumel** – Mexico's largest – located off the Yucatán coast south of Cancun are described in the next chapter.

Ixtapa-Zihuatanejo

The secret "getaway" for capital city dwellers who wanted peace and quiet for a few days was, for many years, the fishing village of Zihuatanejo, 200 km (124 miles) northeast of Acapulco. Here, there were two hotels, no air conditioning, good fish – it was paradise. Now, however, civilization has taken over. But romantics need not despair: the new town of Ixtapa, where all the modern hotels have been built, is located about 8 km (5 miles) away from the tiny port of Zihuatanejo, whose name, by the way, comes from the Nahuatl word "Cihuatlán", which means "land of women". Zihuatanejo, as the Spaniards later called it, was for centuries an important port for the shipment of timber. Papayas, bananas and mangos are grown in this region of the Pacific coast. And now there's tourism.

Zihuatanejo has four beaches, one of which has a rather interesting history: Las Gatas was designed as a swimming hole for a Tarascan princess by her father, King Calzonzin, who had stones placed at the entrance to the bay to hold back the tide.

The islands off the coast – the largest of which is called Ixtapa – comprise a wildlife sanctuary. Parrots, pelicans, seagulls, iguanas and raccoons can be ovserved here in the wild. Naturally, the new resort town of Ixtapa provides facilities for every type of sport which can be enjoyed in the water: scuba diving, snorkeling, surfing, sailing, waterskiing and para-sailing (practised with a parachute, a boat and a long rope). The people of Ixtapa are especially proud of their 18-hole golf course designed by Robert Trent Jones.

Puerto Vallarta

The world first became aware of this small fishing port on the Pacific thanks to an especially volatile Hollywood couple. Elizabeth Taylor and Richard Burton, who came here to film "The Night of the Iguana", found this place so romantic that they built a house here and stayed on. Rumour has it that the whisky flowed freely for years on end.

The tourism experts were the next to discover the romance of the place. This little town with cobblestone streets lies on the Bay of Banderas against a backdrop of tropically-forested mountains. Tourists can experience jungles and mangrove swamps by taking the tour boat out to the small bay of Yelapa or by going up the Ameca River in a dug-out canoe.

The town of Puerto Vallarta is tranquil and pretty. A broad beach promenade stretches between the bay and the town's old colonial centre; on either side, new hotels are spreading out further and further, some of which are architectural jewels. Entertainment is well provided for in the form of restaurants, discos, etc.

Naturally, in Puerto Vallarta, every imaginable type of aquatic sport can be enjoyed. The deep-sea fishing here is excellent.

Mazatlán

Mexico's northernmost Pacific resort – now we are doing an injustice to developing resorts such as Playa Blanca – is an important port town with a population of about 200,000. (See town plan on page 256.) It boasts the second-tallest lighthouse in the world (after Gibraltar), a large market, and a transport rarity: three-wheeled vehicles called "pneumonias" which serve as taxis. El Malecon, the beachfront boulevard with its restaurants and hotels (some of which are exquisite – the El Cid, for example, is completely surrounded by a swimming pool), extends for miles beyond the nucleus of the city. Mazatlán is proud of having the largest shrimp fishing fleet in Mexico – some say in the world. Needless to say, Mazatlán's speciality is seafood and Mazatlán's seafood is excellent.

Every conceivable form of aquatic sport, up to and including para-sailing and deep-sea fishing, as well as golf on either the 18- or 9-hole course belong to the favourite pastimes of holidaymakers here. Mazatlán – Nahuatl for "place of deer" – is also the starting point for hunters who want to try their skill in the highland jungles of the nearby mountains.

Manzanillo

Manzanillo first made headlines when Bolivian tin king and billionaire Antenor Patiño made his dream of a hotel come true: Las Hadas ("the enchanted dream") is a 200-room resort centre built in a style reminiscent of Disneyland and Saudi Arabia. This white "hotel city" on a small bay ranks among the ten most beautiful hotel complexes in the world. All the beautiful, the rich and the famous of this world have basked in the sun by its swimming pool and have let themselves be nipped by the impudent parrot on the hanging bridge. Las Hadas offers restless souls an advantage: this is where it's happening. Unlike in

Acapulco, where the restless search for the next sensation can go on without end, all the action here is concentrated in one place – on the small sandy beach in front of the gleaming white backdrop of Las Hadas.

This unassuming port town now houses a number of other hotel complexes, but none of them is quite as exclusive as Las Hadas. So if you can afford it, why not make this "enchanted dream" come true for you? *(v. Debschitz)*

Underwater World

Ten thousand kilometres (6,000 miles) of coastline on three bodies of warm water – the Pacific Ocean, the Gulf of Mexico and the Caribbean Sea – make Mexico a favourite holiday destination for diving fans. It is impossible to list here each of the hundreds of excellent diving sites along the Mexican coast; instead, the country's foremost divers' paradise, the island of **Cozumel** on the Caribbean side of the Yucatán Peninsula, will be described in detail.

Mexico's largest island (measuring 53 by 14 km/33 by 9 miles) was called Cuzamil, "land of the swallows", by the Mayas, whose temple ruins can still be seen in the island's interior. Wherever you go, you will meet descendants of these people, many of whom still speak the melodious, sing-song language of their forebears. First-time divers will find them to be friendly, patient, and persistent helpers in times of need.

The second largest coral reef in the world, the **Palancar Reef,** is located about 200 metres (650 ft) off the southern coast of the island. It was here that Jacques Cousteau discovered vast beds of the valuable and rare black coral while exploring the area in 1960. Palancar, which has attracted some 100,000 divers from all over the world since that time, is only one of a total of 20 reefs located between Cozumel and the Yucatán coast some 18 km (11 miles) away. A deep trench in the ocean floor provides for a constant supply of crystal-clear ocean water which nourishes the wealth of marine life found here in a variety of forms. The coral colonies off the coast of Cozumel are among the most intact in the world.

Some 30 hotels are found along the 15 km (9 mile) stretch of beachfront which faces the mainland. San Miguel, with a population of 30,000 is Cozumel's main city. Scattered throughout the town, and in the hotels, are a total of over 15 diving schools with just as many modernly equipped boats, some of which can hold up to 24 divers. Each school has its own diving sites and many also offer tours for non-divers. Especially "fashionable" is the trimaran which belongs to the island's newest luxury hotel, the Sol Caribe – it's fitted out with underwater photography equipment and floodlights for nighttime dives.

Cozumel is not only a scuba divers' paradise, but a snorklers' one as well. Some coral gardens are located just a few metres beneath the water's surface, and a downward visibility of 50 metres (160 ft) is no rarity. Those interested in the undersea world which begins just beyond the hotel beaches, may first like to visit the sea aquarium in San Miguel to get a preview of what's in store for them.

Scuba divers will find an underwater aquarium off La Ceiba Beach, set up by the energetic owner of the La Ceiba Hotel. Water-resistant signs pointing out the various types of corals, sponges and other forms of marine life guide you along a 120 m (400 ft) long "educational tour" through the coral reef.

The 30 km (18.5 mile) long belt of coral reefs off Cozumel Island was designated a marine park a few years ago. The use of harpoons as well as the collecting of corals and other "souvenirs" is strictly prohibited. Many divers come here not only to enjoy one the most intact coral reefs in the world, but also to see the sunken airplane it harbours. The underwater wreck of the 40-seater Convair even served as a backdrop for the Mexican disaster film "Survival II".

Excellent diving grounds can be found off **Cancún Island,** the fashionable new seaside resort 70 km (43 miles) north of Cozumel; as well as off **Isla Mujeres** ("island of women" – so called because of the many Mayan clay figures of women found here), which is likewise to the north of Cozumel and a few miles from the mainland port of Puerto Juárez. Island hopping by plane is possible, and diving gear can be rented all over.

Near Isla Mujeres, a sensational discovery was made a few years ago: at a depth of about 20 m (66 ft), divers found a cave containing "sleeping" sharks. Brave souls can swim down to these otherwise so dangerous creatures, touch them, try to lift them up and even look them in the eyes, which stay open while these up to 6 m (20 ft) long sharks recline here in a state of temporary lethargy.

Marine biologists are still puzzled. This obviously dispels the myth that sharks must "swim or die" – that only through the continuous movement of their powerful fins can enough water pass through their gills to furnish their massive organism with the oxygen it needs – but they still do not know why they need rest. One theory is that the sharks which seek out the cave off Isla Mujeres are pregnant females.

Another paradise for divers is **Akumal,** a holiday village on the Yucatán Peninsula about 100 km (60 miles) south of Puerto Juárez. Up until a few years ago, Akumal was a private club. Now it is a hotel with one of the best – some say "the" best – diving shops in Mexico. Some 50 coral reefs lie within a half hour's boat trip of the coast. For a grimly romantic adventure, you can dive down to the frigate "Matanzeros", sunk in a sea battle in 1742. Interesting pieces from the wreck and unusual Mayan sculptures are on view in Akumal's small museum.

From here, it's only 10 km (6 miles) to the **Xel-há Lagoon** – actually four interconnecting lagoons which together form a giant pool for saltwater fish. Through an underground stream, they have access to the open sea and its crystal-clear water. Divers can admire a Mayan shrine which lies just a few yards beneath the surface.

(v. Debschitz)

Deep-Sea Fishing

The much-used term "paradise" still carries meaning when used by experienced deep-sea fishermen to describe the waters off the Mexican coast. After all, Mexico does have an incredible 10,000 km (6,000 miles) of coastline. Four different bodies of water come into consideration: the Pacific Ocean; the "Sea of Cortés" (Golfo de California) between the 1,700 km (1,000 mile) long peninsula of Baja California and the mainland; the Gulf of Mexico, with Florida on the other side; and the Mexican Caribbean.

All the well-known resorts in Mexico can provide sportfishermen with the best of equipment: the boats, as a rule, are between 7 and 10 metres (22 and 30 feet) long, fully equipped with fishing tackle, "combat" seats, and powerful engines. A hire fee of about $ 150 (for one person) to $ 250 (for two persons) is charged for an 8-hour excursion including crew and equipment. The prices vary from region to region and according to the season.

Perhaps the largest population of fishes in the world – including some of the most spectacular fighting fishes – can be found along Baja California in the "Sea of Cortés" and near **Cabo San Lucas** off the peninsula's southern tip. In Cabo, however, you'll have to pay dearly for the hire of a yacht. In **La Paz, Loreto** and **Mulege,** the oasis by the sea, the rates are far more reasonable. The season for marlin and sailfish is from September to November and again in June and July; roosterfish and other fighters can be pursued all year round. Mulege is famous for black snook which can weigh up to 30 kg (65 pounds) and grow to a length of 1,80 metres (6 feet). La Paz, the capital of "Baja" is the centre for marlin (from mid-March to November); sailfish (late May to November); billfish (in the summer months); as well as bonito, yellowtail, roosterfish and tuna all year round. The Presidente Hotel south of the city is recommended for sportfishermen as it can take up to three hours to travel through the bay and out into the open sea.

Mazatlán, Guaymas and other mainland resorts on the opposite side of the Gulf of California are also popular hunting grounds for fighting fish. From Mazatlán, the striped marlin is pursued from January to May; the black marlin from May to November; and the sailfish, the yellowfin tuna, the bonito, the dorado, the black and the white sea perch, the sierra and the roosterfish, all year round. An international sportfishing tournament is held each July at Guaymas; and in September, regular tournaments are held in nearby San Carlos Bay. The waters here are ideal for marlin, sailfish and dolphin from June to October: yellowtail can be fished during the winter months.

Topolobampo, the port of **Los Mochis,** located about half-way between Mazatlán and Guaymas, is the place to be in August and September for marlin and sailfish; from November to April for pompano; and from August to October for dolphin. Roosterfish and yellowtail are prevalent all year round.

In the Pacific resort of **Puerto Vallarta,** the sailfish-season, which runs from November to May, is ushered in with a deep-sea fishing contest. Summer is the time for marlin; the autumn months for wahoo. Dolphin, roosterfish, bonito, tuna and red snapper can be caught off the coast near Puerto Vallarta all year round.

In **Manzanillo** and further south in **Ixtapa** and **Zihuatanejo,** the ideal time to hunt sailfish is from mid-November to March. Marlin, dolphin, roosterfish, sea perch, madregal and many others can be caught here as well.

The International Sailfish Rodeos take place in Acapulco each April and November. Here, off the coast of this world famous resort, you can catch marlin, tuna, barracuda, bonito, red snapper and sailfish all year round. The fishing in the freshwater lagoons near Acapulco is also interesting.

The resorts of **Cancun, Cozumel** and **Akumal** offer the best opportunities for deep-sea fishing in the Mexican Caribbean. Cancun even offers the double fun of fishing either in the saltwater lagoon that separates the peninsula from the mainland or in the open sea, where blue and white marlin can be caught in April and May; sailfish and dolphin from March through July; bluefin tuna in May; and wahoo and kingfish from May through September. Bonefish, tarpon and barracuda can be fished in the lagoon. The waters surrounding the island of Cozumel provide equally varied opportunities for sportfishermen: sailfish, bonito and dolphin are prevalent from March to July; and kingfish and wahoo from May to September.

Fishing permits may be obtained by tourists for the duration of one day, one week, one month or one year. Visitors who come with their own boat must pay a small fee for its registration. The Oficina de Hacienda and the Secretaría de Pesca (Department of Fisheries) are responsible for issuing import licences. For more information on sportfishing, competitions, etc., contact:
SECTUR (Secretaría de Turismo),
Sub-Direccion de Aquaficion,
Presidente Masaryk 172,
11550 México, D.F.

(v. Debschitz)

Mexican Fiesta Calendar

January 1: National holiday. New Year's Eve is traditionally celebrated within the family. In smaller towns, New Year's Eve festivities take place in the main square, and on New Year's Day, there are local fiestas complete with fairs, music and folk dancing, horse racing and cock fighting.

January 6: All over Mexico. Epiphany or Three Kings' Day is a second Christmas for the children – they place their shoes before the door in the hope that they will be filled with gifts and sweets. In those Mexican villages which recognize the Three Kings as their patrons, the day is celebrated with fireworks, dancing and a fair.

January 8–14: Ahila in the state of Puebla. At the fair which takes place during this week, the incomparable "voladores" (fliers), dressed in feathered costumes dating from pre-Columbian times, perform thrilling acrobatics from a 13-metre (43-foot) tall mast.

January 18: Taxco in the state of Guerrero. The feast of Santa Prisca, the patron saint of Taxco, is celebrated with religious processions, a carnival and folk dancing performed by groups from surrounding villages.

February 2: All over Mexico. "Candelaria" (Candlemas) is the day for blessing the farm animals and the seeds preliminary to planting. The observances are particularly colourful in Cholula, San Juán de los Lagos, Talpa, Taxco and in Cuajimalpa near Mexico City.

February 5: National holiday. Constitution Day in commemoration of the promulgation of the Constitution of 1917, the event which officially ended the Mexican Revolution. Modern Mexico was founded upon the principles of this constitution.

February 27: Ocoyoacac in the state of Mexico. A festival of Indian dances including Indian versions of Roman gladiatorial fights and charming dances performed by children in old costumes. Following the performances, there is a banquet featuring regional specialities.

Late February/early March: All over Mexico. Carnival season, the time of merrymaking and abandon before Ash Wednesday. The Mardi Gras festivities in Veracruz and Mazatlán are especially exuberant.

March 4: Taxco in the state of Guerrero. Religious dance festival with performances of medieval dances and children's dances.

March 21: National holiday in honour of Benito Juárez' birthday.

Late March/early April: Easter Week (some shops close the entire week; others, only on Holy Thursday, Good Friday and Easter Sunday).

April 15th to 17th: Fortín de las Flores in the state of Veracruz. The annual flower show is as famous in Mexico as the flowers which are grown in this pretty town.

April 25: The feast of Saint Mark is celebrated in all towns and villages where this saint is venerated. The grandest celebrations are those held in Aguascalientes, where the carnival lasts from ten to twelve days. The best mariachis, guitarists, charros (rodeo riders) and toreros gather here to test their ability. Hotel reservations – three months in advance if possible – are a must.

May 1: National holiday. Labour Day is observed with much colour and activity in the squares of the small towns of Mexico.

May 3: All over Mexico. The Feast of the Holy Cross. On this day, every building contractor throws a party for his workers complete with beer, "barbacoa" and fireworks. A flower-adorned cross is placed atop each unfinished building. The festivities in Milpa Alta (near Mexico City), Santa Cruz Acalpizcan (near Xochimilco), Tonalá (near Guadalajara), Tehuantepec and in Ozumba in the state of Mexico are especially interesting.

May 1st to 6th: Jalapa in the state of Veracruz. Regional fair with celebrations, bull fights and dancing. This fiesta dates from 1720, when it took place in celebration of the arrival of the Spanish fleet which brought wine and other luxury goods from Europe.

May 5: National holiday in commemoration of the Battle of Puebla where the Mexican army defeated the French. Special celebrations take place in Acapulco and Puebla.

May 31: Tehuantepec on the Isthmus of Tehuantepec. May 31st marks the beginning of a fiesta that lasts an entire month and climaxes on June 21st, 24th and 29th. The festivities include processions, riding competitions, dances and a big fair. The famous handicrafts produced in this region are exhibited during the festival.

June 24: All over Mexico. The Feast of Saint John the Baptist. The observances begin on the evening of the 23rd with serenades and songs, student parades, pilgrimages and picnics. It is customary to go for a swim or take a bath at twilight on the 24th.

July 3: Oaxaca. A fair with dancing, cock fighting, racing, fireworks and pilgrimages in honour of Saint Marcial.

July 16th to 28th: Oaxaca. The Cerro del Fortín, a mountain near Oaxaca, is the site of an Indian festival which dates from pre-Columbian times. Dances are performed in splendid costumes.

August 13: Mexico City. Day-long dance performances at the foot of the Monument to Cuauhtémoc at the intersection of Reforma and Insurgentes in honour of the last Aztec prince. The performances are repeated one week later.

August 15: Assumption Day is observed with celebrations in most parts of Mexico. The greatest festivities take place in Aguascalientes, in Amozoc and Cholula in the state of Pueble; in Milpa Alta in the Federal District; and in Izamal in the state of Yucatán.

September 1: National holiday. President's report on the state of the nation.

September 8: Taxco in the state of Guerrero. Performance of a dance which dramatizes the battle between the lord of Tepotzlán and the neighbouring chieftains. Dances are performed atop a tall mast and rites are held at the monument to the god of Tepotzlán. From this monument, which is located at the summit of the mountain, one has a magnificent view of the city.

September 16: National holiday. Independence Day. At 11 pm on the night of the 15th, Father Hidalgo's cry of "Viva México" ("El grito de Dolores", which signalled the start of the Mexican revolt against Spanish colonial rule in 1810) is traditionally repeated. In some areas, the 15th is observed as a holiday as well.

September 29: Feast of Saint Michael. Wherever cattle are raised, the patron saint of horsemen is revered. In villages named San Miguel, this day is observed with fiestas, rodeos and banquets.

September 30: National holiday in honour of the birthday of one of the heros of the Mexican struggle for independence, José Morelos. Big celebrations take place in Morelia and in Cuautla in the state of Morelos.

October 4: In honour of the Order of the Franciscans and their great contribution to the development of colonial Mexico, the Feast of Saint Francis of Assisi is observed in most parts of Mexico. Fiestas with music, dance and fireworks take place in Pachuca in the state of Hidalgo; Salina Cruz in the state of Oaxaca; Tala in the state of Jalisco; Uruapan in the state of Michoacán; Zopopan near Guadalajara; and Valle de Bravo in the state of México.

October 12: Columbus Day or "The Day of the Race" is celebrated throughout the country in a variety of different ways. In Tlaquepaque on the outskirts of Guadalajara there is a fair featuring performances of Indian dances.

November 1st and 2nd: All over Mexico. On All Saint's and All Soul's Days, villagers carry food and drink to the graves of their loved ones as a token of their respect. (See "Night of the Dead", page 72).

November 20: National holiday in commemoration of the Revolution of 1910.

November 22: Feast of Saint Cecilia. As she is the patroness of musicians, this is an especially popular holiday in Mexico. The celebrations in Zapotitlán in the state of Jalisco, the home of the mariachis, are especially lively.

November 30: Tequila in the state of Jalisco. This day marks the start of a long and lively series of celebrations in honour of Our Lady of Guadalupe in the birthplace of the famous Mexican drink, tequila. The "big day", December 12, is celebrated with bull fights, rodeos. mariachi music and dancing in the streets.

December 12: The Feast of Our Lady of Guadalupe is observed all over the country, but the biggest celebrations take place in and about the Basilica of Guadalupe outside Mexico City.

December 16–24: This is the time of the "posadas", an observance which symbolizes Mary and Joseph's search for a room at an inn ("posada") in Betlehem. Special celebrations take place in Oaxaca, Querétaro and San Miguel de Allende.

December 25: Christmas Day

December 28: The Day of the Innocents. Like April Fool's Day, this is a day "set aside" for the playing of practical jokes.

(v. Debschitz)

Food and Drink

The image of the tourist who starts spitting fire after his first Mexican meal is terribly exaggerated. Naturally, an important ingredient in Mexican dishes is the chilli pepper, of which there are countless varieties (an old Indian cook spoke of at least 200). Chillies range from the tiny, red, infernally hot ones to pungent black ones and mild ones the size of sweet peppers. They can be had fresh, dried or in jars. Depending on the strength of its aroma, a chilli pepper can round out the flavour of a dish – or determine it. A tip for those who bite too heartily on one: a pinch of salt on the tongue takes away some of the fire.

In Mexico, you can eat like a king in a variety of ways. Go ahead and send your taste buds on a voyage of discovery – it will be worth your while! Mexico boasts 4,000 (!) different dishes. Each province, each region, each city and town has its own specialities. Insiders will tell you that that "cocina mexicana" comes close to being as varied as the cooking of China.

Like pasta in Italy and rice in Asia, **tortillas** form an intrinsic part of every Mexican meal – starting with breakfast. Tortillas are made of meal ground from maize, Mexico's main crop. The thin round cakes are rolled up, sprinkled with a little salt and eaten warm in place of bread. If you are not already familiar with it, the flavour of cornmeal takes some getting used to. Its aroma envelopes

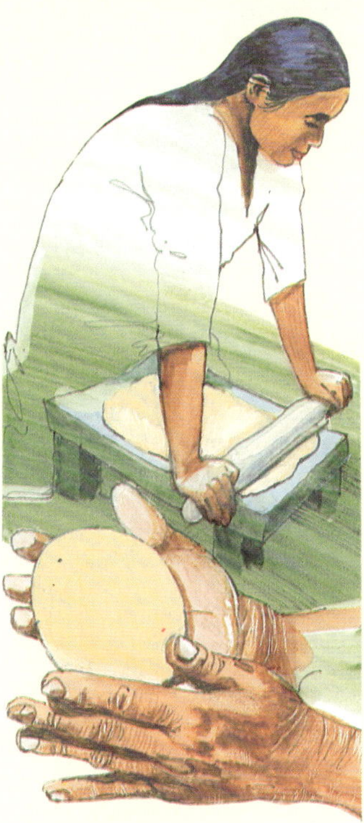

you at every corner, for tortillas are baked on the move, so to speak – on tortilla griddles heated over small ovens in the street.

Tortillas can be eaten in dozens of ways. Here, a few of the best-known specialities: **tacos** consist of diced pork, beef or chicken, cheese, eggs or vegetables wrapped in a tortilla; **enchiladas suizas** (Swiss enchiladas) are chicken-filled tortillas in a hot tomato sauce sprinkled with cheese and baked; **enchiladas verdes** (green enchiladas) are pork-filled tortillas in a hot sauce made from ripe green tomatoes, chillies and garlic; **quesadillas** contain a filling of melted cheese and are served sprinkled with grated cheese; **chilaquiles** are tortilla "sandwiches" made of deep-fried tortillas and layers of cheese and chillies or onions.

At breakfast time, tortillas are served in the form of **huevos rancheros,** a fried egg atop a fried tortilla served with salsa roja, tomato sauce with lots of chilli and onions. **Huevos mexicanos,** eggs scrambled with diced tomatoes, chillies and garlic, are equally popular. Fruit is an important part of a Mexican breakfast: **mangos, papayas, honeydew** and **watermelons, piñas** (pineapples) and **plátanos** (bananas) are favourite breakfast fruits.

Mexican soups include **sopa de tortilla** with fried tortillas cut into strips; **caldo tlalpeño,** a broth with chicken, avocados, chilli, onions and rice; **sopa de aguacate,** cream of avocado soup; and **sopa de elote,** cream of maize. **Calco de carne** is just the thing for queazy stomachs after a long night – beefstock heavily spiced with chilli and reduced to a bouillon. Another popular pick-me-up is the **coctel de ceviche,** marinated raw fish served well-chilled with onions, chillies and tomatoes.

In addition to the above-mentioned "platos mexicanos" whose basic ingredient is the tortilla, **tamales,** made from dough consisting of cornmeal and water to which hydrated lime has been added, are

Margaritas

1 lime wedge	Coarse salt
2 cups (500 ml) tequila	2½ cups (600 ml) grapefruit juice
1½ cups (400 ml) orange-flavoured liqueur	½ cup (120 ml) fresh lime juice

Rub the rims of 16 stemmed glasses with the lime wedge. Dip into a plate of coarse salt; set aside for up to 6–8 hours.

In a large pitcher (or in the blender) combine tequila, grapefruit juice, orange-flavoured liqueur (Cointreau, Triple Sec, etc.) and lime juice. Add ice and blend, or stir and pour into salt-rimmed glasses over crushed ice.

Makes about 16 margaritas. Salud!

also extremely popular throughout the Republic. The dough (called "masa") is usually covered with a filling of chicken, wrapped in maize husks, steamed, and then eaten with **atole,** a sweet maize gruel. Like tacos, tamales are sold all over from small street stalls.

Dishes enjoyed by Mexicans on special occasions (and ones which you will also encounter on the menus of the better restaurants) include: **guajolote con mole poblano,** turkey with a spicy black sauce made by cooking together chocolate and several varieties of hot peppers; **carne asada,** thinly-sliced, grilled meat with chillies and vegetables; **frijoles refritos** or refried kidney beans, a staple of the Mexican diet; and **guacamole,** avocado sauce with onions and tomatoes which is scooped up with baked tortilla chips. Other favourites include **cabrito** (grilled kid); **chiles rellenos** (stuffed peppers); and, of course, **filete** (fillets of beef from cattle which graze on the open plains of Sonora). Another speciality, **filete a la mostaza,** is served with a delicate mustard sauce flavoured with spices and spirits.

Grilled offal, such as **riñones de carnero** (sheep kidneys), is also very popular. If you are honoured with an invitation to a "barbacoa", don't pass it up. At these Mexican barbecues, mutton is cooked in a pit lined and topped with agave leaves upon which a fire is built.

Favourite fish dishes include **huachinango,** red snapper from the Gulf of Mexico, which is filleted and fried or grilled whole; and **pescado blanco,** a tasty, white-meat, freshwater fish. **Ostiones** (oysters), **camarones** (shrimps) and other seafood can be had in abundance in Mexico's larger cities and, of course, along the coast.

The list of popular main dishes could go on and on. Before we come to the **postres,** desserts, just a word about the Mexican speciality known as **chicharrones.** These crisp, fried pork skins sprinkled with the juice of small, green, highly aromatic limones (limes) make a delicious snack before, after and between meals.

Favourite postres include **flan de queso** (cheese custard with caramel sauce); **chongos** (a coagulated milk dessert much like junket); and **arroz con leche** (rice pudding with cinnamon).

A glass of delicious Mexican beer, **cerveza,** accompanies most main meals. The Mexican brewing tradition originated with German brewmasters who came to the country many years ago. There are many popular brands; most are served in bottles, but some are available on tap. Mexicans often sprinkle a little lime juice into their beer, thus giving it an interesting flavour. "Tecate" beer is drunk from the can – after the edge has been sprinkled with salt and lime juice. **Mexican wines,** which are produced in Baja California and in the region around Aguascalientes, are also popular. Their quality, especially that of the red wines, corresponds to that of a better-quality table wine. Before meals, Mexicans will drink a **tequila** or a **margarita** (a tequila cocktail); vodka and tonic and white rum and cola ("cuba") are also popular. After-dinner favourites include brandy and the coffee-and-cacao liqueur **Kahlua.**

You will do your Mexican hosts a great favour by passing up imported alcoholic beverages like German wines or French cognac when dining out together. Because of the prohibitive import duties on foreign spirits, a round of cognac in a better restaurant could cost as much as the entire menu.

Mexicans love to eat out – restaurants and cantinas are like second homes to them. Business lunches – in Mexico, business is conducted primarily over meals – can last for hours and often end up in an evening of drunken revellry. Today, however, "la crisis", the present period of belt-tightening, is forcing many Mexicans to give up such dearly-held habits. The business lunch is increasingly being replaced by the "working breakfast" – it's faster and cheaper.

(v. Debschitz)

Pulque, Tequila, Mescal

From deep inside the heart of the Agave tequilana comes the fiery Mexican distillate known as tequila. This clear to amber-coloured liquid – depending on its quality – takes its name from a town located 60 km (37 miles) outside Guadalajara in the state of Jalisco, where millions of spiny-leaved **maguey plants** blanket the highlands.

Of the over 400 species of agave indigenous to Mexico and neighbouring countries, only the blue agave may be used in the making of tequila. Mexican law limits its cultivation to an area comprising the state of Jalisco along with a few adjoining areas in the states of Michoacán and Nayarit.

The massive agave – not a cactus but a member of the amaryllis family – is a very slow-growing plant. Some species take up to 24 years to mature: the flower stalk emerges from the plant's "heart" (the base from which the spiny, sword-like leaves radiate) and the plant dies. The first white settlers in the American Southwest called this particular agave the century plant. Spanish ships brought the agave to southern Europe where it encountered a hot and arid climate similar to that of the Mexican highlands, but only in its homeland can it be found in such great numbers and in so many varieties.

According to Indian legend, the maguey plant first sprouted from the bones of the goddess Mayahuel, who was stolen from the sky by the plumed serpent Quetzalcoátl. Long before the conquest, the Indians discovered the secret of making **pulque** from the juice extracted from this plant... and the aromatic beverage has been enjoyed ever since!

Sweet maguey juice (called "aguamiel" or honey water) flows from the plant's heart, which is cut open by skilled "tlachiqueros" just before the time comes for the flower stalk to emerge from the leaf cluster. With a curved knife, they cut a hollow in the upper part of the plant's spiny base. Mornings and evenings, the "honey water" that collects inside is sucked out into a gourd. After fermenting slowly for three days, the pulque is ready.

This milky, frothy beverage may smell and taste a bit sour, but it is very refreshing and only moderately alcoholic. Pulque is the preferred drink of the Indians: on Saturdays they tend to patronize "pulcherías" – cantinas serving only pulque – rather than bars serving beer. And – a triumph for modern technology! – pulque is also available in cans. While this is nothing for purists, it doesn't taste as bad as one might expect and it provides the tourist with a convenient way of enjoying the Indians' "nectar of the gods".

For the making of **tequila,** the entire centre section (or "piña") of the maguey is cut out. Robbed of its heart, the plant folds its leaves as though in resignation, and dies. The "piña" (pineapple), which looks like a large turnip and can weigh up to 70 kg (154 pounds), is cooked, minced and crushed. The resulting mash is pumped into fermenting barrels to which yeast is added. The fermented mash is then distilled twice.

Colourless "tequila blanca" or "de plata" is diluted with distilled water to a potable proof and bottled direct from the barrel. Older tequila has a golden colour from having been aged in oaken vats which earlier contained brandy, bourbon or wine. After 6 months of ageing it is called "de oro", after 1 year, "añejo". After 7 years, tequila becomes as costly as V. S. O. P. cognac. The Sauza distillery calls its premium distillate "Conmemorativo".

Of the some 60 distilleries located in and around the town of Tequila, the best known are Sauza, Cuervo, Virreyes, Orendain, San Matías and Herradura. In 1980, 26 million litres of tequila were sold in the United States alone, and the drink is fast gaining popularity in other countries as well.

There is a ritual involved in the drinking of tequila: a Mexican first sprinkles salt on the back of his hand, then he bites into a slice of lime and, with the juice still in his mouth, licks up the salt. Finally, he washes everything down with a shot of tequila. In the mouth, the three ingredients blend together to create an incomparable symphony of flavours. It is said that a shot glass of "sangrita" (a spicy hot mixture of fruit and chillis) between each shot of tequila will ward off drunkeness – but this is just a myth.

The "gusano de maguey", a worm whose habitat is the maguey plant, is often added to special casks of tequila. It can be found either floating big and fat and dead in the bottle or in powdered form, mixed with salt, in a small sack wrapped around the bottle's neck.

More frequently, however, this worm can be found in **mescal,** a maguey liquor which is the special pride of the Oaxaca region where it is sold in attractive black pottery jugs. Distilled from a narrow-leaved species of maguey, it is more potent than tequila. The short leaf base is cooked in a pit (similar to a "barbacoa" or barbecue pit), then fermented and distilled. With mescal, you can unwittingly spoil a happy gathering: it contains traces of mescaline, a substance which affects the mood and can cause one to become aggressive at a moment's notice – especially if large amounts of alcohol have already been consumed. So, even though it may taste good, please be cautious when dealing with mescal! *(v. Debschitz)*

Gastronomy

Dining out is an important aspect of the Mexican way of life. The social behaviour of the Mexican is responsible for the fact that restaurants, cantinas and bars are central points of communication in Mexican communities. This puts the tourist at an advantage: because a neighbourhood's social life doesn't take place exclusively within the four walls of private homes, the tourist often finds himself a part of it and can, with a little luck, meet the nicest people at the very next table. There is an endless variety of places to eat in Mexico, and for the tourist who seeks to discover the essence of the Mexican lifestyle, these can be highly interesting. Some of the "gastronomic forms" which have developed are worth taking a closer look at.

Let's begin with the description of a career in gastronomy which began out of sheer frustration: Carlos Anderson, the pampered son of wealthy parents, fell into evil ways and got involved with drugs out of boredom with his life of indulgence. In order, on the one hand, to maintain his large circle of friends, and, on the other, to do something useful, Carlos, along with a number of his "amigos", came up with the idea of opening a restaurant. The concept – first put to the test in Mazatlán – was simple. The restaurant's guests – young people from good families – should be served not by menial personnel, but by their peers – more young people from good families. This put the guests and the waiters on an equal and friendly footing, so to speak. Everyone who was part of the operation shared in its profits and its losses. The concept was an instant success. The flagship of the operation, which now includes a dozen restaurants and bars all over Mexico and even in Los Angeles, is **Anderson** on the Reforma in Mexico City. Rich and influential Mexicans hold stock in the small company – and make up its clientele. It's worth patronizing one of the restaurants just to see the old photos depicting life in Mexico at the time of the Revolution and the curious antiques which serve as its decor. It takes a good half hour to get through the queue and to a table at **Carlos & Charlie's** in Acapulco.

A gastronomic experience of another kind can be had at one of the two **Los Comerciales** restaurants in Mexico City. There, the guest is not only treated irreverently, as a buddy and friend, but he will also find himself spectator and sometimes target of the circus antics of the waiters. Almost as an added attraction, he can also order something to eat – and what he is served will be of superb quality. These restaurants are decorated entirely with advertising posters, which hang from the ceiling and cover every inch of wall space. The menu is presented in the form of a funny newspaper.

Mexico City, and in particular the Zona Rosa, has an array of high-class restaurants which can satisfy the demands of even the most pampered of guests. Within the "golden rhombus" – between Reforma, Insurgentes, Av. Chapultepec and Sevilla – there are a dozen or so restaurants whose cuisine meets the highest international standard. At **Delmónico's, Focolare, La Calesa de Londres, Estoril, Normandie, Piccadilly Pub, Rivoli** and **Chalet Suiza,** Mexican elements are deliciously incorporated into French or international cuisines. Here, Mexican notables from the worlds of business and politics dine side by side with the international crowd.

A class apart from the already large selection of fine restaurants are two haciendas in Mexico City: the **San Angel Inn** in southern Mexico City and the **Hacienda de los Morales.** With their high ceilings, high-backed chairs, high prices and culinary achievements of the highest order, both have the aura of the glory of colonial times about them. Another of Mexico City's exceptional restaurants is the **Del Lago** which is situated on an artificial lake in Chapultepec Park, and features French cuisine with a Mexican touch.

An important meeting place for young people and an important part of urban life in Mexico are the chain restaurants **Vips, Denny's** and **Sanborns'** (actually a drugstore chain, but well-known for its restaurants). Here, good food is served fast, without fuss and, in most cases, round the clock. The "platillos mexicanos" (Mexican specialities) are especially good. These restaurants are also popular for breakfast which, in Mexico, has the dimensions of a full meal.

Regional restaurants can be found everywhere in the country. If you happen to be in Mexico City but have a craving for a touch of Veracruz, go to the highly popular **Fonda del Recuerdo,** which is decorated with the typical cut-out streamers of the Gulf coast. To the sound of jarocha music, specialities like toritos, vuelve a la vida (a fish platter) and jaiba rellena (stuffed crabs) are served. Other "fondas" (typical Mexican restaurants) offering delicious local fare include: the **Fonda del Refugio,** which features mole de gallina (chicken mole); the **Fonda las Delicias,** which features sopa de tortilla with Oaxaca cheese; and the old **Fonda Santa Anita,** which is said to have been one of the city's first three eating places. In Mexico City alone, there are at least fifty more restaurants which specialize in regional cooking.

Mexico's hotel restaurants are of a quality which is not to be underestimated. Whether in Cancun or Acapulco, in Puerto Vallarta or the capital city, the places to go for exciting shows accompanied by excellent meals are always the large hotels. Those in the know will tell you that the restaurant in the Hotel Presidente Chapultepec called **Maxim's** definitely lives up to its name – the chef de cuisine from Paris sees to that!

There is a restaurant (in a tiny hotel) in Cuernavaca near Mexico City which enjoys a special reputation among friends of fine dining. Not that its cuisine is of a quality that would draw gourmet critics from all over the world – that would add only little to the attraction of **Las Mañanitas.** It is the ambience of this restaurant that makes it so unique. Behind a row of colonial housefronts, a vast, subtropical garden, with ponds around which peacocks strut, lies hidden. Before the guest is led to a table in the patio restaurant, he waits in the L-shaped lounge. The lounge rooms are decorated with valuable paintings, authentic colonial furniture, and a functioning fireplace: as if that weren't enough, they have an unobstructed view of the illuminated garden (the rooms are missing one wall). When the waiter holds a candle up to the blackboard where the specialities of the day are written down in chalk, and you make your selection with a margarita (a tequila cocktail) in your hand, you'll almost feel like you're in heaven!

After having burned your tongue on high-proof alcohol and then on hot Mexican food, you can burn it again in one of Mexico's **cantinas.** Although these officially opened their doors to women a few years ago, the smart ones still stay away. Cantinas are the domain of machos who come here to drink, roll dice, tell jokes and feel as though they were on top of it all. Tourists (of the male sex) who can speak at least a few words of Spanish might like to visit the **Mirador** near Chapultepec Park in Mexico City – it can get quite interesting on Fridays from the early afternoon onwards. Here, even distinguished economic leaders spit on the floor, down "copas" one after the other and come near to losing their shirts in a game of dominos or dice. This revelry is accompanied by language which would make a lady blush. Presumably, that is why they remain outside or go to the restaurant next door, where they wait, as they have been doing for centuries, until it's time to drive the "borracho" home. Ah, Mexico!

(v. Debschitz)

Arts and Crafts

According to statistics, 2 million Mexicans earn their living by producing handicrafts or **artesanía,** as it is called in Mexico. Their employers are, so to speak, the tourists who buy souvenirs at markets, from street vendors, and in souvenir and arts-and-crafts shops. The economic situation of these small artists and craftsmen is often dismal: as they are only the first link in the usual marketing chain, they earn very little. Many tourists look for cheap souvenirs, so prices must be kept low. In addition, the middlemen and the retailers are interested in making their profits. …

The manufacture of handicrafts in Mexico is primarily a cottage industry. It is usual for family members to work together at home or in small workshops. Many of these predominantly Indian families produce handicrafts as an extra source of income in addition to, say, being employed in agriculture; others work exclusively as artisans. Some people find only occasional employment as homeworkers, and still others work year round under factory-like conditions, for instance in the production of ceramics, one of the most important and diverse branches of the Mexican handicrafts industry.

In most of these small operations, only one material is utilized. It is not at all uncommon for whole villages or even regions to specialize in the manufacture of one particular product. As a result, the tourist can find a "typical" souvenir at almost every stop on his Mexican tour.

Some of these things can be quite heavy… and heavy on the purse as well. **Onyx** (a crystalline quartz with a fine ribbon structure) and **obsidian** (a natural glass formed by the rapid cooling of molten rock), two smooth materials which are fashioned into necklaces, figurines modelled after pre-Columbian originals, or lovely chess pieces, are not only heavy, but they make some of the most expensive souvenirs that can be had in Mexico.

Lighter (and more reasonable in price) are the inventive **straw items** from Tzintzuntzan, a small village near Pátzcuaro in Michoacán. The state of Michoacán, one of central Mexico's most scenically beautiful, is the centre of the production of artesanía – and with good reason. In the 16th century, Bishop Don Vasco de Quiroga made an appeal to the consciences of the Spanish landowners ("encomenderos") and succeeded in freeing the Tarascan Indians of the region around Pátzcuaro from the "encomienda" system of forced labour. In order to provide the Indians with an income which would save them from falling back into dependence (in the form of bondage to pay off debts, for instance), the bishop decreed that in each village, a different trade should be pursued. Furthermore, the villages should trade their products amongst each other, thus supplying each other's necessities and even achieving a modest level of prosperity. When the standard of living of the people of this region today is compared to that of the people in Mexico's other predominantly Indian regions, it can be said that this programme was at least in part successful. In any case, "Tata Vasco" (Daddy Vasco), as the bishop is affectionately called by the descendents of the Tarascans, has not been forgotten: a monument stands in his memory in Pátzcuaro's zócalo.

Pátzcuaro boasts a small but beautiful "museo de artes populares" which exhibits the many forms of folk art that are sold in village markets and shops. Folk art from all over Michoacán can be admired at the regional museum in the state capital of Morelia: fine **lacquerwork** that compares favourably with that of East Asia, as well as artistically carved and painted **masks** come from Uruapan; lacquered trays and bowls ("jicaras") and **wooden boxes** come from Quiroga; imaginative **copper miniatures** and durable objects for household use (such as kettles) come from the copper town of Santa Clara del Cobre; **guitars and mandolins,** from the simplest of instruments to those suitable for concert use, come from Paracho. A large percentage of the population of La Piedad de Cavadas are occupied in the weaving of **rebozos,** the traditional shoulder wraps worn by women. Rebozos can serve as a scarf or as a wrap to take away the morning and evening chill of the highlands. They are used to carry babies and other loads such as groceries; furthermore, they seem to be absolutely necessary for church visits.

A green glaze is applied to the surface of the **pottery** of Michoacán, produced primarily in Patamban. As this glaze probably contains lead, these wares should be used for decorative purposes only. Black ceramic is the trademark of the pottery of the state of Oaxaca. The workshops in the village of San Bartolo Coyotepec not far from the city of Oaxaca are open to visitors. The craftsmen of the village of Atzompa specialize in the making of animal figurines.

As in Michoacán, crafts production in the state of Oaxaca is divided among the different villages. **"Sarapes",** woolen blankets decorated with animal designs and an ornamental border, are woven in Teotitlán del Valle. In Santo Tomás Jalietza, women use an age-old technique – a belt loom with one end tied around the waist and the other tied to a tree or a post – to weave colourfully-patterned **belts, shawls, bags** and small **wall hangings.** The **skirts, blouses, ponchos** and other articles of clothing offered at the markets of Oaxaca are mostly hand-woven, often richly embroidered and sometimes dyed with expensive, natural dyes. But because cheap, industrially-produced goods are also prevalent, it's a good idea to check the quality carefully.

This applies in particular to "specially priced" articles offered by street vendors in places frequented by tourists. Often, the very same article can be had for much less in the shop around the corner. You can get an idea of the going prices for individual articles by visiting one of the government-sponsored fixed-price shops such as Fonart or the "casas de artesanía". Equipped with this information and some skill in bargaining, you can save money at the markets – you'll only have yourself to blame if you pay more! At the same time, however, you should keep in mind that for you, the tourist, a few hundred pesos may be nothing, but they could buy a small meal for a hungry artisan or vendor.

Mexican handicrafts are also appreciated by the Mexicans themselves: middle- and upper-class Mexicans enjoy them as decorative objects. For people of the lower classes, who with much creativity and skill fashion an array of useful items from simple materials such as agave or palm fibre, straw, cane, wood, paper and shells, they serve as articles of daily use. Ornamentation is usually patterned after traditional motifs – flowers and animals appear most frequently. Many hand-crafted items also have religious significance. The best known example of these is the "árbol de vida" or **tree of life** made in Metepec in Puebla state: an allegorical tree fashioned of clay and decorated with polychrome ceramic figures.

In addition to traditional handicrafts, there are new forms which have developed only recently. An example of this is **bark-paper painting,** which originated in Hidalgo – a state with a pottery-painting tradition – only 25 years ago. The dark, course-fibred "papel amate", which is obtained from the wild fig or "amatl" tree, was originally used for magical purposes. An inventive mind came up with the idea of combining the two crafts, painting and paper making, and the art of bark-paper painting was born. At first, the bark paper was painted with the same animal and flower designs found on pottery; now, genre scenes of village life predominate.

The list of flourishing Mexican crafts could go on and on. The industry is not without its problems, however. For example, as a result of the success of bark-paper painting the amatl tree has almost become extinct in the state of Hidalgo.

With its abundance of workshops, the former mining town of Taxco, once famed for its deposits of copper and silver, is still the **silver-working** capital of Mexico. For the past ten years, though, this once-flourishing craft has been plagued by difficulties. The increased world-price of sterling silver (925 parts pure silver) makes it impossible to pay the silversmiths fairly for their high-quality workmanship. Only a small number of the prospective customers who enter the workshops to learn about the art of silverworking and to admire the "articulos de plateria", from fingerrings to flatware, are prepared to pay the prices asked.

Those who travel to Taxco in the hope of picking up silver at bargain prices will be sorely disappointed. Nevertheless, a visit to this charming colonial town is worth the trouble: the countryside is impressive and the town's position on the slope of a mountain is unique.

Mexico's **leather** craftsmen are being confronted by the same problems with which the country's silversmiths have to contend. Quality hides must be imported, with the result that briefcases, suitcases and small leather articles from León in the state of Guanajuato are expensive. Just as everywhere else, good quality has its price in Mexico, too.

(Schmidt/Egelkraut)

Art in Mexico

The art of New Spain and of independent Mexico has a history which spans about 450 years; in contrast to that, the art of Mesoamerica has been in existence now for over three thousand years.

The 16th century – the age of **destruction and reconstruction** – was not only the century of the conquistadores and the missionaries, but also that of architects, stonemasons and stuccoworkers. Hundreds of fortresses, monasteries, churches, chapels, palaces, aqueducts, fountains and bridges – all inspired by Spanish models – were built. Entire cities were constructed, in some cases upon the ruins of Indian cities.

Mexican art began as a transplanted art but soon acquired its own characteristics. **European styles of art and architecture** prevalent at a particular time (Mudéjar, Gothic, Plateresque, Baroque) were adopted, modified, combined – albeit at a later date and with a certain lack of respect for the originals. This modification and combination of styles is typical of all of Hispanic America; in Mexico, however, architecture took on special forms.

The battlemented walls of Mexican monasteries made it possible to integrate the central forecourt, the "atrio", into the area consecrated for the purpose of celebrating Mass. (Their aim being the conversion of the Indian population, the monks endeavoured to offer them something equal in immensity to the pyramids to which they had been accustomed.) During processions, consecrated Hosts were deposited in chapels, "capillas posas", in the four corners of the forecourt.

Monastery portals were often designed in the form of an "open chapel" (the so-called "capilla abierta"). These portals opened out like shells and meant that religious ceremonies could take place in the forecourt and even those standing outside the monastery walls could participate. The largest of these open chapels is located in Cuernavaca.

In the 17th century, baroque was adopted and given a whole new look. **Churrigueresque,** a style of Spanish baroque architecture of the late 17th and early 18th centuries always associated with rich **ornamentation,** became even more ornate in Mexico. Churrigueresque survived well into the 18th century and left Mexico with some very remarkable pieces of architecture.

During this period, **figurative representation** was an important part of church architecture, and, together with other decorative elements, created a unified whole. For this reason, baroque sculptures and oil paintings should never be viewed close up, but always from a distance. In this way, the ornamentation can clearly be seen as an intrinsic part of the entire artistic concept.

On church façades, churrigueresque decorations project from plain walls of ground volcanic rock ("tezontle"). The interiors of these churches are characterized by profuse ornamentation and the generous use of gilding.

The Indians and mestizos who had the task of decorating these interiors were granted far more liberties than were the architects who had designed the buildings themselves. In the latters' case, there were European models with which they were obliged to conform. This freedom in decoration is reflected not so much in the incorporation of Indian motifs (as is the case in Peru) as in the material used for the rich stuccowork. A mixture of reeds and clay called "quincha" was used – this could be worked easily into the desired forms. Examples of this decorative style can be found in the churches of La Soledad and Santo Domingo in Oaxaca, the monastery church in Tepozotlán, the Chapel of the Rosary in Puebla and the church of Santa Maria in Tonanzintla (a "peoples'" version of the Chapel of the Rosary, it looks like a man-made grotto overgrown with vegetation). In all of these churches, the decoration has the tendency to dazzle and overwhelm the viewer. "The delight in the style breaks with the norm by emphasizing the line and complicating the design. The art of New Spain betrays the desire to go beyond the model." (Octavio Paz)

The young Mexican republic was marked by French-inspired neoclassicism, a style which corresponded neither to the condition of the country nor to the character of its people.

It was not until the middle of the **20th century,** after "the discovery of Mexico by the Mexicans", as the Revolution has also been called, that Mexican architecture regained international acclaim. Once again, fresco painting and sculpture (and the technique of mosaic) played an important role.

Fine examples of Mexican architecture of the 1960's include: Ciudad Universitaria, the campus of the National University of Mexico (sadly, the original concept behind the campus is no longer apparent, subsequent annexes having inevitably altered the planned layout; certain buildings remain outstanding, however – Juan O'Gorman's library is probably the best example); the Museo Anahuacalli, a building which Diego Rivero presented to the Republic of Mexico along with his collection of pre-Hispanic art; Unidad Independencia, the exemplary housing estate in southern Mexico City.

The Museo de Antropología, one of the most important examples of museum architecture in the world, stands as a tribute to monumental architecture and to Aztec centralism. Architecture as the manifestation in stone of invisible powers – it is in the light of this Mesoamerican tradition that one should also view the gigantic dimensions of the Museo Tamayo, the Colegio de México and the Escuela Militar. The new cultural centre of the National University in Pedregal (once a bleak, volcanic area) belongs in this list as well. With their "Espacio Escultórico" (Sculptured Space or Space as Sculpture), Helen Escobedo, Mathias Goeritz, Manuel Felguérez and others have created a valid synthesis of volcanic landscape and marshalling reason, of pyramid and circle, three-dimensional and four-dimensional space, and open and closed form.

In contrast to architecture and sculpture, **painting broke away from its European models only very slowly.** From the 16th century on, there have been frescos (in monasteries) and panels (on view today in the Pinacoteca Virreinal). After the printing press was introduced, woodcuttings became very popular, too. An entire room at the Museo del Arte Moderno is dedicated to the important 19th-century artist, **José Maria Velasco** (1840–1912), who created watercolours of the central Mexican countryside in the style of the German Romantics.

Unmistakeably Mexican, on the other hand, was his contemporary, **José Guadalupe Posada** (1851–1913), whom André Breton saw as perhaps the first master of pure, robust humour in art. In addition to his famous "calaveras" (skeletons in comical poses), he created posters for theatre pieces and illustrated lives of the saints and "corridos", rhyming ballads sung on the street narrating current events and tales of horror. In 44 years, Posada produced about 20,000 prints in all.

The work of Posada also ushered in the age of modern Mexican painting. The latter is synonymous with names like **Diego Rivera, David Alfaro Siqueiros** and **José Clemente Orozco** and with "muralismo" (the painting of politically-inspired murals in and on public buildings).

The **muralist movement** can be seen as having risen out of the encounter between the Mexican social revolution and the revolution in the world of art in Europe in the 20th century. Rivera subscribed to Cubism, Siqueiros was interested in Futurism and Orozco had much in common with the Expressionists. The majority of the work of these three painters represents an artistic commentary on Mexican history and on the revolution in particular. In spite of all their differences, the work of all three displays artistic power and a multiplicity of artistic forms.

Muralism can be seen as the art of a young, nationalistic nation. The revolution rediscovered traditional Mexico, and artists were summoned to participate in this new beginning of Mexico's history.

The minister of education at that time, José Vasconcelos, believed in the responsibility of art towards society, but he also believed in freedom of artistic expression and thus never forced aesthetic or ideological dogma upon the artists. His successors did not share his ideas, but they did recognize the **political value of "muralismo":** a government that had never been Marxist and had ceased being revolutionary donned the guise of populistic and progressive nationalism by commissioning, promoting and financing works of art which portrayed Mexican history in a pseudo-Marxist, simplified light.

Rivera and Siqueiros were adherents of a party with aesthetic and political programmes; Orozco, an anarchist and conservative in one, was the true rebel.

Between 1920 and 1940, Mexican art combined two ostensibly incompatible elements: an international aesthetic vocabulary and inspiration based upon native tradition. Towards the end of this period, muralism degenerated into ideology, and a new generation of artists came to the fore. The most important of these was **Rufino Tamayo,** now the "grand old man" of the Mexican art scene. In what has become a tradition in the 20th century, he presented the Republic of Mexico with his collection of pre-Columbian art, now on exhibition in the innovative Tamayo Museum in Oaxaca.

The Museum of Modern Art (Museo del Arte Moderno) in Mexico City contains a permanent exhibition of contemporary art (Arte Contemporáneo de México) in which photography is also included. In addition, those interested in the current Mexican art scene can learn more by visiting galleries, particularly those in the Zona Rosa, in Polanco, in San Angel and now in Coyoacán as well.

(Siefer)

Mexican Music

"... and evenings on the Plaza Garibaldi..."

This is one item which never fails to find its way onto tourist itineraries. For it is here, on this square in the centre of Mexico City, that the **mariachis** gather every evening to entertain passers-by and café clientele. Dressed in traditional black suits with silver buttons, and wearing wide sombreros, these musicians have become a symbol of Mexican music. Definitely a "must" for anyone visiting Mexico. It should be borne in mind, however, that these ensembles, which seem to engage in a contest of voices and blaring trumpets to the accompaniment of violins and guitars, represent only a small part of Mexico's musical palette.

Music is an integral part of everyday life in Mexico, and can be enjoyed by the traveller in every corner of this enormous land. Many concerts are performed out of doors – in streets and squares, in shady parks and romantic courtyards – and are free of charge. The zócalo, the main square in Mexican cities and towns, usually contains a "kiosco", a wooden or wrought-iron pavilion where bands play full blast on some evenings – and almost always on Sundays – for the entertainment of the passers-by.

The type of music performed at these concerts depends on the region. Mariachi music, whose home is in the state of Jalisco, is popular throughout the country. The origin of the name has never been fully explained, but many sources trace the word "mariachi" to the French word "mariage". When the French were masters of the haciendas, it was customary to have musicians play at weddings ("mariages") and other festive family gatherings – hence, the connection.

Marimba music is at home in the southern states of Chiapas and Tabasco as well as in and about the city of Veracruz on the Gulf of Mexico. With almost breathtaking virtuosity, the musicians beat a wooden xylophone, a **marimba.** This instrument is thought to have been brought over by slaves from Africa, but it also displays similarities to the pre-Columbian "teponaztli", a notched drum made from a hollow tree trunk.

On the Gulf of Tehuantepec near the city of Oaxaca, **"bandas"** can be heard: bands made up of brass and percussion instruments which are said to have been modelled after American military bands. The enthusiasm of the musicians is always apparent and a few wrong notes here and there never seem to bother anyone.

In addition to traditional tunes, the programmes of the open-air concerts also include waltzes, polkas and marches, musical forms which were introduced by Europeans and modified by the Mexicans to suit their own tastes. One of the most popular waltzes in Mexico is "Sobre las Olas" by Juventino Rosas (1868–1894). The name of this composer may hardly be known outside his country, but when waltzes are played in other parts of the world, "Over the Waves" can often be heard together with the best of Vienna.

Mariachi, marimba and banda music, waltzes, polkas and marches have been played in Mexico since about the middle of the 19th century. The country's musical tradition, however, goes back much further.

Long before the arrival of the Spaniards, **the Aztecs, the Mayas, the Coras, the Zapotecs and the Mixtecs,** to name only a few Indian groups, **had had a highly developed musical culture.** That of the Aztecs has been most thoroughly studied and will be featured here as representative of the achievements of all the other pre-Columbian civilizations.

Music was connected with religious ceremonies, which were often accompanied by choral music and stylized dancing. Strict rules were laid down for the temple rituals:

according to contemporary sources, anyone who broke these rules risked punishment by death.

At the same time, exceptional musicians enjoyed a high degree of recognition in the Aztec state, where gods such as Macuilxochitl, the god of playing, and Xochipilli, the god of flowers, love, poetry and song, were also venerated as gods of music.

Depictions in painting and sculpture of musicians with instruments and dancers in characteristic poses bear witness to this recognition (many of these can be seen in the Tamayo Museum in Oaxaca; in the Anthropological Museum of the University of Jalapa; and in the difficult to reach but extremely worthwhile Diego Rivera Museum on the outskirts of Mexico City).

The Aztec melodies of yore can be reconstructed today only with the greatest of difficulty: the native Mexicans did not have a system for writing down music. The best source we have are the writings of the Franciscan monk Bernardino de Sahagun who gathered and recorded information on Aztec life, customs and religion in the 16th century. He was the first person to attempt to put Indian melodies on paper.

The instruments used by the Aztecs throw some light upon the **music of pre-Columbian times. Flutes** and **whistles** capable of producing many different tones were fashioned out of cane, bones, metal and jadeite. **Trumpets** were made out of shells or clay. Drums such as the previously mentioned **"teponatzli"** and the three-legged **"huehuetl",** which was made from the wood of the ahuehuete tree (a kind of cypress) and had a head of skin, were important percussion instruments. Stringed instruments, without which Mexican music today would be unthinkable, were obviously unknown: as far as we can tell, the Indian languages did not even have words for such instruments.

The musical abilities of the Aztecs even impressed the bellicose Spaniards when they were first exposed to them. Later, the colonizers made use of the Indians' love of music in their missionary work: the success was greatest where music was used to convey the message of Christianity.

The **conservatories of music** which were **set up by churches** throughout the country were much frequented by the Indian population. Archives show that in the 16th century, Indians were already composing sacred music. Just what was accomplished within the walls of Mexico's cathedrals at that time is still (and in some cases, finally) being divulged today. The most successful conservatories seem to have been those attached to the cathedrals of Mexico City, Puebla, Oaxaca and Morelia.

Secular music was also influenced by far-away Europe. At first it was Spanish forms like the **"villancico"** – a folk song which developed via the cantata into a kind of Christmas carol – which set the tone. **"Sainete"** and **"tonadillas escénicas",** musical interludes with a satiric character, were also popular.

Following independence in 1821, **Italian opera** caught on; and towards the end of the 19th century, at the time of the dictatorship of Porfirio Díaz, it was **French music** which set the example for Mexican compositions. Salon music – composed by Gustavo Campa, Melessio Morales, Ricardo Castro and others – was very popular then and is still a favourite at open-air concerts today.

Sadly, other 19th century compositions have been forgotten. Luis Baca (1826–1855), for example, is known to have written seventeen operas, one of which is said to have premiered at the Scala in Milan. The scores of all these works, however, have been lost.

Some **traditional pre-Columbian dances** have, fortunately, been preserved, and they still play an important role on festive occasions in Mexico such as "Semana Santa" (Holy Week). Examples of these are the **"Danza del Venado"** or Dance of the Stag of the Yaqui Indians of northwest Mexico; and the **"Danza del Tigre"** or Dance of the Jaguar of southern Chiapas.

The "dance of those who fly" originally had a ceremonial function. Now, the **"voladores"**, descendents of the Totonacs of the tropical Gulf coast region, regularly demonstrate their daring aerial acrobatics as a tourist attraction in Acapulco and other resorts.

Authentic, colourful dances can be seen at many local fiestas, and artistic adaptations of traditional pieces are staged twice a week at the Palacio de Bellas Artes (Palace of Fine Arts) in Mexico City. The exciting performances of the Ballet Folklórico also include "newer" folk dances from all parts of the country which have been markedly influenced by European (but also by South American and African) forms.

Spanish fandangos, jarabes, zapateos and seguidillas are recognizable in many Mexican **folk dances,** for which the rhythmic basis is the "son" – a syncopated rhythm in triple time with six beats to the measure which combines Spanish and Indian elements. Various regions have developed their own form of the "son": the jarabe tapatio in Jalisco; the huapango, the son huasteco, the bamba and the malaguẽa or son jarocho along the east coast from Tamaulipas to Veracruz. The dances and songs of the states of Michoacán and Guerrero are designated "sones de tierra caliente".

The make-up of the "son conjuntos" also varies from region to region, but guitars and rhythm instruments are always part of the ensemble and the Indian harp or "carpa" appears frequently.

The **"sones"** consist of short songs with four-line verses which deal with love and beautiful women or describe the beauty of a city or region. They can also be improvised to suit a special occasion.

North Mexico is the home of **"musica norteña",** cheerful dance music, the most popular form of which is the polka. In the northern states of Chihuahua and Sonora, the **"corrido",** a street ballad and form of news broadcast which experienced its heyday during the revolutionary years from 1910 to 1928, achieved great popularity. In those days, not surprisingly, narratives extolling the deeds of the heros of the Revolution like Pancho Villa or Emiliano Zapata replaced the usual love stories and tales of bandits and federales.

"Musica ranchera", whose lyrics, like those of American country music, deal mostly with lost love and loneliness, is considered to be the extension of the old corridos. This is the form of popular music, by the way, which, when measured in terms of recordings produced, is best-loved by the Mexicans.

In the 20th century, Mexico's composers of "serious" music went back to the musical heritage of the Indians and to newer folkloric traditions for their inspiration. Like Mexico's muralists, the composers of the "national epoch" (between 1928 and 1950) reflected upon their own heritage. Their music can be seen in part as a protest against the overwhelming influence of European forms, which, however, are still recognizable in the work of **Manuel M. Ponce** (1882–1948). Ponce is generally considered to be the "father of Mexican music".

Carlos Chávez (1889–1978) treated Indian themes in his "Sinfonia India". "La Noche de los Mayas" (The Night of the Mayas), originally written by **Silvestre Revueltas** (1889–1940) as a film score, is considered to be a musical masterpiece. In his 4th Symphony, **Candelario Huizar** (1883–1970) captured the atmosphere of Cora Indian ceremonies.

Contemporary composers like **Manuel Enriquez, Hector Quintanar, Mario Lavista** and **Federico Ibarra** combine Indian rhythms and modes with avant-garde forms.

Examples of symphonic works based upon folkloric themes are **Pablo Moncayo's** "Huapango" (1941) and a work by **Blas Galindo** that takes us back to the mariachis: his "Sones de Mariachi" (1940) for full orchestra is based upon what is probably the most famous of all mariachi songs – "La Negra".

(Egelkraut)

Literature

For many a visitor to Mexico, a sightseeing trip in the capital city may lead to a unique encounter with her literature – provided that the Ciudad Universitaria (University City) is part of the itinerary. There, just outside the city proper, stands the ten-storey-high, windowless building that houses the central library – an oversized stack of approximately two million volumes. This imposing structure, which could be described as the "key" to Mexican literature, seems at the same time to be a symbol of the barriers which hinder our understanding of it. For, despite the many fine translations available, language is still a considerable barrier. The recent prominence of Latin American writers has not yet led to a significant increase in their readership. For many, the first literary encounter with Mexico still occurs through the works of foreign writers. D. H. Lawrence, B. Traven, Malcolm Lowry, Graham Greene –

all have enriched world literature with their impressions of this Latin American country. The works of Oscar Lewis, which rank among the classics of non-fiction, provide us with fascinating sociological portraits of its people.

But Mexico's own writers are still waiting to be discovered by a wider public. It is probably safe to say that more tourists are familiar with the University Library's façade (designed by Juan O'Gorman) than with any volume contained within. Language and cultural differences are not the only factors restricting the accessibility of Mexican literature, however. In his tribute to **Octavio Paz,** the 1984 winner of the German Booksellers Association's annual peace prize, the president of the Federal Republic of Germany, Richard von Weizsacker addressed the problem of attitude: "As far as knowledge of Latin America goes, we are among the underdeveloped nations of this world. This can only be to our disadvantage. The feeling of political and intellectual superiority prevalent in the Old World has changed into a belief that we lead the world in terms of economic and technical advances. Octavio Paz opens the door to a better understanding of his continent when he says, 'Latin America is a culture.'"

Indeed, no one has pondered Latin America's – and particularly Mexico's – social, economic, political and cultural problems as deeply as Octavio Paz. This prolific writer and statesman, who was born in Mexico City in 1914, has published a wide variety of works, from poetry to articles and essays.

Paz' writings, as well as his own biography, are symptomatic of 20th-century Mexico: all important is the search for identity – the sense of being Mexican – and the search for intellectual roots. From 1519 onwards, the Conquest systematically destroyed intact cultures, attempting to replace them with an imported culture which never quite took root. Hernán Cortés' fateful words, "Acabar con el alma del Indio!" (wipe out the very soul, i. e. erase from existence, the Indian) had, and still have, the effect of a curse. The princely and priestly classes, and with them the upholders of the ancient civilizations, were eliminated; the temples were razed; the sacred images destroyed; and the codices burned (of the Maya codices, for example, there are only three extant specimens, and these can be found in, of all places, Dresden, Paris and Madrid). The auto-da-fé of Maní, staged by Bishop Diego de Landa of Yucatán in 1562, attained tragic notoriety.

Two centuries later, **"Chilam Balam",** the books of the Jaguar priests of the Maya, eventually appeared in a Latin transcription. "Records of the debacle" – according to W. Cordan.

"The story", writes Carlos Fuentes in his novel, "Terra Nostra", a brilliantly constructed panorama of Mexican history and culture covering over 1,200 pages, "was the same: tragedy then and farce today, farce then and tragedy afterward, everything was a lie; the same crimes were repeated, the same mistakes, the same foolishness, the same omissions as on each of these authentic dates in this linear, relentless, exhausting chronology: 1492, 1521, 1598 ...".

Mexico's literature has never been one which professes to have all the answers: it is, rather, one which probes. It does not show the way, but is searching for ways (Paz). This motif – whether expressed in symbols, signs, metaphors and allusions or addressed in actual interviews, discussions, articles, essays or, above all, in films – pervades Mexican art. Mexico's literature offers no cure-alls: it does, however, reveal the realities of life in Mexico – whether in the country's maize fields or its urban centres – in poetry and prose. Mexico's literature functions as a seismograph in a country which, while presently being spared great upheavals, is resting on a shaky foundation of unsolved problems. The poet **Alejandro Aura,** born in Mexico City in 1944: "Let's be on our way .../ For here nothing happens,/ Time is official."

A chronological account of Mexican literary history offers very little to go by, for it was not until the second half of this century that Mexico's writers began assessing their country's development since the Conquest – never losing sight, of course, of the glories of their native ancestors.

In "Quetzalcoátl in Myth, Archaeology and Art", the former Mexican president **José López Portillo y Pacheco,** one in a long line of Latin American politicians and diplomats who have also been productive writers, tells the story of the Aztec creator of man and the winds, a story which symbolizes the rise and fall of a great but ill-fated empire.

A different treatment of the classic, mythological motif is found in the absorbing short story "Chac Mool" by **Carlos Fuentes.** In this surrealistic tale of a Mexican golem, an initially harmless, soulless creature comes alive. As a monster, it discovers its destructive power and drives a desperate man to his death. "Monsters have simply come into fashion", writes Fuentes.

Death, by the way, is a recurring theme in countless Mexican narratives. Death, and returning.

In the works of many Mexican authors, an involvement with native roots is apparent: to a certain extent, however, these same authors also focus on the problems faced by the "indigenas" in Mexico today.

The socialist **Elena Poniatowska,** born into the old French-Polish aristocracy in Paris in 1933, recounts in her "testimonial novel", "In Face of Everything", the story of Jesusa Palancares, a woman as old as this century. "Jesusa walks" – like countless others in her country – "with shoulders bent, she keeps close to the walls, huddled up inside herself. Jesusa belongs to the millions of men and women who do not live, but rather, survive." Elena

Poniatowska, a highly respected critic in Mexico: "Jesusa represents the people who have gotten nothing from the country – a country that doesn't even notice them, that is pushing them more and more off to the side."

In his novel based on the film "The Golden Cock" ("El gallo de oro"), Juan Rulfo (born in Sayula, Jalisco in 1918) provides us with a penetrating study of social dependence. After the death of his mother, Dionisio Pinzón, a poor, unfortunate town crier, leaves his dilapidated hut on the edge of the village. By chance, he becomes the owner of a wounded fighting cock which he nurses back to health and which eventually brings him happiness and prosperity. What might correspond to a successful career in another society, is here, on the edge of the Third World (to which Mexico may or may not belong, depending on one's set of criteria), a never-ending test of power and worth – even in times of prosperity. The fight up the ladder is always a fight for survival. Wealth inhibits the ignorant, the weak, the disadvantaged, those who cannot find a place on the social pyramid. Dionisio, who wanders from fairground to fairground with the singer Bernarda "Caponera" Cutiño, dividing his time between cockfights and the roulette table, between the card table and the bar, discovers, when he tries to storm the barricades of birth and background, that there are limits to what he can achieve. He is lonely to the very day of his death – and beyond. The supposed freedom, the footloose life of a vagabond is also what his daughter subscribes to: "There she – Bernarda – stood and sang, as her mother had once started to sing, and with her songs, she cried out her loneliness into the world".

The history of Mexican literature is also a history of solitude, a topic which intrigues many authors – like Octavio Paz, who offers some excellent analyses of the phenomenon in his volume of essays, "The Labyrinth of Solitude", first published in the early 1950's.

The mask is an important symbol in Mexican literature: behind a mask, a Mexican can give up his identity and take on another. **Xavier Villaurrutia** (1903–1950) in his poem "Poetry": "... and you leave me by myself,/ without pulse, without voice,/ without face,/ without mask, a naked man/ on a street full of gazes." Carlos Fuentes writes of a costume ball to which the guests are invited to come dressed as "Mexican murals". Decadence? More – in a society which vacillated for centuries between the clergy and the Reform, it is almost an ideology. "Señor Juárez made libraries out of the churches, and the best proof we have that our poor country is going to the dogs is that the books have now been carried away and the holy water fonts re-installed." So laments one of Fuentes' protagonists.

The Mexican tradition of the masquerade can be traced back at least to the 17th century and one **Juana Inés de la Cruz** (1651–1695), a nun and woman of broad learning who embodied – according to Chávez –

"the Middle Ages, the Renaissance, the Baroque period and modern times in one person." Juana Inés de la Cruz, with all her complexes and repressions (she was a lesbian), her sexual neuroses and her almost pathological thirst for knowledge, was a much sought-after figure in educated circles in late 17th-century Mexico City. She could only allude to the condition of her soul: "While divine grace lifts me up to the heights of sanctity, the weight of my mental afflictions drags me down to the depths". The legendary Juana, who was also known as the "Musa Mexicana" or "Mexico's tenth muse", wrote poetry and mystery plays, theological treatises and comedies. She masked her psychoses in a cycle of 973 verses entitled "El Primero Sueño" (The First Dream) in which nocturnal dream images are embedded in poetic reveries.

Two hundred and fifty years later, **Gabriel Zaid** (born in Monterrey in 1934) contemplates sarcastically in "Archimedes' Proof": "Where is the soul?, the surgeons ask". Likewise **Carlos Pellicer** (1899–1977) who, along with **José Gorostiza** (1901–1973) and Xavier Villaurrutia, was one of the eminent figures behind the literary journal "Los Contemporáneos", which was launched in the late 1920's: "... let us create our own image of what the soul is ...".

The life of the poet **Rosario Castellanos** (1925–1974) reflects the difficulties encountered by a woman of literary inclination in the land of "machismo". The daughter of a landed proprietor of Indian extraction, Rosario Castellanos began the study of philosophy at the early age of 16 and went on to become a lecturer at several universities in Mexico and the United States. In addition to poetry, she also wrote essays and short stories and, like so many of her literary colleagues, she was in diplomatic service. Octavio Paz:

> In saying what the names
> say, which we say,
> they say time: ourselves.
> We are names of time.

This century alone has seen at least half a dozen literary movements, each one grouped about certain writers or literary journals. Through the years, literary trends have come and gone, but their ideological battles are still being carried on today with an unbelievable degree of intensity, severity, and – unfortunately – intolerance. While the post-modernists have defended and are defending their position to the point of declaring it a dogma, the literary clubs and secret political societies of the 19th century proclaimed to the educated classes the ideals of the French revolution. The Literary and Social Club of Querétaro, for example, counted among its membership the commander of the local militia, Captain Ignacio Allende, who went on to become one of the foremost military leaders of the independence movement. A quarter of a century earlier, Father Miguel Hidalgo y Costilla had been a member of the same club.

Thanks to this liberal and tolerant spirit, Mexico was later to become a haven for political emigrés from many parts of the world. Many writers who fled Nazi Germany in the 1930's and '40's found asylum in Mexico. Later, the country became a home for exiled Spanish writers, and today it receives exiles from South American dictatorships.

A turning point for Mexico – and for Mexican literature – was the Revolution of 1910, which, despite all of its horrors, is still glorified today. It was – after the long years of dictatorship under Porfirio Díaz – a time of chaos, of lawlessness, of brutality. In "Pedro Páramo" and "The Burning Plain", two works which have had a lasting effect on the literature of Latin America, Juan Rulfo portrays that period in Mexico's history when it was possible to "buy salvation with money" and to "wipe one's backside with court records". On the haciendas, intrigue and revenge reigned supreme: "From now on, we make the laws ourselves. You got a strong hand among your men at Medialuna?" Killings and assassinations were an everyday occurrence: "I'm just a shepherd. Killing murderers – it's fun. It must be a wonderful feeling to be able to help the Lord get rid of this Satan's brood."

In his novel, "The Heredias", Carlos Fuentes (born in Mexico City in 1928), Mexico's foremost novelist, lets Mexican history pass in review as he recounts the story of a Mexican family. "Mexico is", one of his protagonists says, "a land of upheavals: they are almost always violent, and then of a certain epic proportion; but more lasting and cruel and insidious, I assure you, when they are peaceful disturbances like those of the last sixty years." Elsewhere he writes, "Our wounds never heal."

(Skupy)

Mexican Architecture

Under this heading fall three clearly defined architectural styles, each of which was wholly independent of the others. The **monumental architecture of the native Mexicans,** as exemplified by their magnificent temples and palaces and their splendid cities, was destroyed by the conquering Spaniards; it had no effect on the architecture of the following epochs. It was replaced by the **architecture of the Conquistadores,** which was imported from Spain and naturalized in Mexico. **Modern architecture** is also an import, but once it took root in Mexican soil, it developed a quality all its own which has given it a special position in the world of architecture.

Clearly, these three categories pertain only to Mexico's monumental and representational architecture. What is said in each case does not apply to the rural architecture of the Indian peasants. This dates from ancient times, survived the Conquest and its aftermath, and has lasted up to the present day. Only now, with the increased acculturation of the remaining Indian peoples, is it going through a process of change.

As evidenced by the codices containing depictions of the so-called Chichimec huts and, especially, by the reliefs found in the Quadrangle of the Nuns at Uxmal, the Indian dwellings of today are built along the same lines as those of their forebears – dwellings which were products of the environment and of the way of life of their occupants. The materials used (wood, natural fibres, loam) were, and still are, easily obtainable. Now, as before, the walls are made of the trunks of young trees; the gaps are filled in with rope made of sisal and brushwood. The outer walls are plastered with a smooth layer of mud which is then painted. The floor is also made of mud. The walls, which are barely taller than a man, are topped by a mostly oversized, carefully built hip roof. The roofs consist of a sturdy lattice covered with maize, palm or agave straw; they often have a smoke outlet, but in most cases, the cooking is done outside. These roofs are remarkably solid and durable – they can last a good seven to eight years, even in areas with high rainfall. The sturdiness of construction and the materials used often vary according to climate and vegetation.

The Ethnographic Section of Mexico City's Museum of Anthropology provides a comprehensive survey of rural Mexican architecture.

From top to bottom:
Round Huaxtec hut in Veracruz;
Zapotecan hut in Oaxaca;
"bahareque" or "embarro" from the region of Chiapas.

The **ancient Mexican monumental architecture** originated with the Maya in the jungles of the Petén region of Guatemala during the first century B. C. The oldest structures discovered thus far – they date from around the year B. C. 400 – are temple platforms located in Uaxactún (Building E VII sub) and under the north acropolis of Tikal. E VII sub, a temple platform with stairs on all four sides, already displays the characteristics which were later to typify temple architecture in all of Mexico. At the same time, the Pre-Classic cultures of the central Mexican highlands developed a temple platform at Cuicuilco which was identical in concept but somewhat more primitive in its execution. While the Mayas built a "perfect" structure of closely and decoratively set stones, the early temples of the central plateau were crude, circular structures consisting of a mound of earth covered with volcanic rubble. The sacred objects placed upon these platforms must have been, at this early stage, of non-durable materials, as no traces of them have ever been found.

The Early Classic phase was a period of parallel development in the architecture of both the Maya and the peoples of the central plateau. Substantial advances began in both cases at the turn of the era; the Early Classic phase was characterized by the exchange of concepts and styles between the two regions and by a high degree of mutual influence. During this phase, a whole series of new achitectural forms were developed – forms which are now as typically and unmistakably "ancient Mexican" as are the famous temple pyramids. These "new" structures included the ball court, shaped like two T's end to end, and the extensive palace or residence, often accessible by only one entrance or stairway. What is remarkable about these palaces is the marked emphasis which was placed on the façades. In addition, the sunken courtyard was developed in Teotihuacán; this would later be adopted by both the Zapotecs and the Mayas.

In most cases, the monumental architecture of the early Mexicans served a religious or ceremonial purpose; none of the ancient civilizations developed a secular architecture of any great significance.

It's interesting to note that a remarkable similarity exists between the layout of these palaces and that of the "patio houses" introduced to Mexico centuries later by the Spaniards: the rooms, which together formed a labyrinthine compound enclosed by a wall, were grouped around one or more courtyards or patios.

Throughout the long history of ancient Mexico, existing temple pyramids were never destroyed to make way for new ones; rather, they were enlarged or used as a base for a new structure. Examinations of structural ruins also indicate that the ancient Mesoamerican architects possessed very little knowledge of statics – a remarkable fact when we consider that these civilizations acquired a level of mathematical knowledge hardly matched in the Old World. The lack of "practical" knowledge in these matters is documented by the instances of unbelievably thick, crudely-laid stonewalls, which do, however, serve their purpose in supporting the heavy roofs.

It almost seems at times that the sole purpose of this architecture, and of Classic Mayan architecture in particular, is to serve as a foundation for ornamentation – the yield in terms of interior space often appears insignificant in relation to the expense in terms of construction.

The Spaniards who arrived in the early 16th century encountered only the civilizations of the Aztecs and the Mixtecs, two peoples who had produced significant feats of architecture, but whose cultures can only be described as inferior followers of those which had preceeded them – that is to say, they had borrowed much but had developed little themselves.

The Spaniards, after destroying what they found, systematically replaced it with their imported **Spanish architecture.** Churches were built in the baroque style of the motherland, but incorporated a few colonial variations – changes in style and construction which were necessitated by the new location. Because of the frequent earthquakes which always damaged, if not destroyed, such structures, the walls were made thicker, the cupola placed lower and the steeples shortened.

The architectural model for private homes was the patio house, a concept which, as mentioned above, was already known in Mexico. Obviously, however, colonial Mexican homes were not patterned after Indian models, but were copies of Spanish homes which, in turn, had long before been copied from the shady architectural forms the Romans had devised for their sunny Mediterranean empire.

Only a few of the Mexican cities and ceremonial centres destroyed by the Spaniards were later repopulated (this was the case with the capital city). Most of the Spanish cities were new settlements, each built according to a definite plan set down by the "Reglamientos de las Indias", an administrative order issued by the Spanish king. The Reglamientos left nothing to chance. The city plan was based on that of ancient Roman cities and incorporated the principles of engineering which had been laid down by Vetruvius and others. Like that of an army camp, the layout was totally logical and practical: the city was square-shaped and surrounded by a wall, the streets constructed at right angles to each other to allow for the optimal use of all available space.

At the centre of the city complex stood the most important buildings. In a Roman settlement these would have been the residence of the general in command, the curia and the temple of Jupiter. In the Mexican city we find the cathedral, the governor's palace and the Ayuntamiento, the seat of administration. These buildings were grouped around a large square (which might be either rectangular or quadrangular in shape) called the "Plaza de Armas".

Even today, this is the picture most Mexican cities present to their visitors. It is important to point out that this architectural concept based on logic and geared to practicality is a typically European phenomenon which stands in marked contrast to the architecture of ancient Mexico.

Following the colonial period, Mexico remained for quite some time under the influence of European and, in the 20th century, American architecture, all the while keeping up with every new trend which came along.

A change came about after the Revolution when Mexico, while continuing to pick up all kinds of ideas eagerly, began executing these new ideas in often unusual and surprising ways. All over Mexico, but particularly in the capital city, buildings began going up which sent out their own signals abroad – buildings which are the subject of architectural studies today.

In the late 1920's, during the period of consolidation towards the end of the Revolution, the first apartment houses in the style of the Bauhaus, and, in particular, in the style of Le Corbusier, were erected in San Angel. An important architect who began working at this time was **Juan O'Gorman.** The son of Irish immigrants, O'Gorman advocated on the one hand the principles of functionalism, but was, on the other hand, also affected by the then burgeoning sense of Mexican-Indian identity and purpose. His best-known work is, without doubt, the University Library in Mexico City, in which he combined functionalism (the structure itself) and the ideals of Mexican patriotism (as symbolized in its mosaic façade). This was in 1952. His earlier works show him as an attentive pupil of Bauhaus.

The most important figure in Mexican art and architecture during this period was certainly **Diego Rivera.** Rivera is best known for his murals portraying the Indians and their Spanish oppressors in a style which may be identified as a Mexican variation of socialist realism. As an architect, he tried to put into practice the concept of "look to the past" – a bold venture which was often plagued by failure.

A good example of this is the old archaeological museum of Mexico City. Built between 1950 and 1960, the museum was abandoned soon after its completion. Diego Rivera had designed it in the style of an Aztec stronghold – solid and massive and with only tiny windows. It was Juan O'Gorman's task to translate this design into a functional piece of architecture – an undertaking which was doomed to failure from the start because a museum needs light. What resulted was a structure which stands as a monument to a politically motivated style, but which serves no useful purpose.

O'Gorman and Rivera, **Juan Legorreta, Yanez** and **del Moral** were the leading figures in the field of architecture in the years prior to World War II. All were students of Dr. Villagrán Garcia, whose name is known only in architectural circles today. It was he who put forward the theory of "contemporary Mexican architecture as the result of the historical development of our art in search of a doctrinary, theoretical orientation and of a form of expression suited to our culture."

This old guard of ideologists eventually found itself opposed by a new generation of architects. The Bauhaus architects **Walter Gropius** and **Mies van der Rohe,** who had established themselves in the U. S. after fleeing Nazi Germany, came to wield much influence over Mexico's architects. For, while Louis Henry Sullivan's Chicago School had had little impact on Mexican architecture, Bauhaus in Chicago did. The purism and scholastic logic of van der Rohe found both ardent adherents and decided opponents in Mexico.

Contemporary Mexican architecture seeks to unite both forms: uncluttered functionalism according to the concepts of **Adolf Loos** who postulated "lack of ornamentation as a sign of spiritual strength and maturity", and a dynamic, brightly decorated architecture as exemplified by the university, the Olympic stadium and the Teatro Insurgentes.

The best and certainly most recognizable example of this blending of styles is the new **Museum of Anthropology** in Chapultepec Park. Its architect, **Pedro Ramirez Vazquez,** has succeeded in creating a building which is functional as well as decorative. It is a low building (only two storeys) situated around a spacious patio; its large picture windows allow for ample light in the rooms. Vazquez was not interested in re-creating the splendour of Aztec architecture; instead, with the use of new methods and materials, he created an exemplary work of contemporary Mexican architecture, doing justice to both the principles of the Bauhaus and the pride and purpose of 20th-century Mexico.

New methods and materials play an important role in the solution of a specifically Mexican problem in the field of high-rise construction: earthquakes and the soft clay and sand of the old lake bed upon which Mexico City rests. Tall structures such as the Torre Latinoamericano, the multistorey buildings along the Reforma and Matias Goeritz' enormous concrete towers at the entrance to the "satellite city", Ciudad Satélite had to be earthquake-proofed. This is done in Mexico in one of two ways: either the building is erected upon concrete posts and steel girders which are driven deep into the ground – like Max Cetto did in the 1950's –, or it is erected in a heavy concrete trough which "floats" on the underlying ooze. The building's structural steelwork gives it the necessary elasticity to vibrate in an earthquake at certain set frequencies. Only through the selection of light-weight materials and the careful calculations carried out by Leonardo Zeevaert for the design of the foundation was Mexico able to allow itself the construction of a building like the 182 m (600 ft) high **Torre Latinoamericano** which has withstood every earthquake it has experienced – from the great earthquake of 1957 to the most recent one on September 19, 1985.

(Thieme)

Regional Section

There are no clearly-defined regions in Mexico. It is not possible to use uniform landscape, a shared economic structure, or even cultural background in order to set regional borders. Should Chiapas be included in the section on the south or in that on the southwest? Should Zacatecas be considered to lie in the north? Different criteria are used to settle such questions in almost every book on Mexico one reads.

The following regional division of Mexico aims at simplifying coverage of this extensive land. It, as any other, can never be anything but arbitrary.

Regions, Towns, Cities **Page**

Mexico City
The Splendour of America's Oldest Capital

The Conquistadores were dazzled by its beauty – México-Tenochtitlán, the capital of the Aztec empire, its immense temple complexes rising out of a white sea of houses in the middle of Lake Texcoco's azure waters, was bigger and more magnificent than any city in Europe. The Spaniards called it the "Venice of America" because of the canals which connected its various quarters. Four broad causeways spanned the lake, connecting the island capital with settlements on the lake's banks. Huge wicker baskets filled with soil and pumice and planted with trees, flowers and maize (a forerunner of today's hydroponics!) floated on the water like flowery islands. Grouped together, these artificial islands, their roots gradually settling into the soft lake bed, formed the foundation of new city quarters. In this way, the territory of the natural island grew larger and larger.

The great city of México-Tenochtitlán, which housed over 200,000 people within its walls, was already over 200 years old when a handful of Spaniards, aided by trickery and by firearms which spread fear and terror throughout the population, successfully completed its conquest on August 13, 1521. Hernán Cortés, who defeated the last Aztec ruler, Cuauhtémoc, ordered that the city, and particularly its religious centres, be razed to the ground. Then, from the rubble of courtyards and temples, pyramids and palaces, he built the capital of New Spain. The enormous wealth of the new domain was reflected in the magnificence of the city's colonial buildings, which soon earned it the name "the city of palaces". This city built by the Conquistadores forms the nucleus of today's Mexico City – known to the Mexicans themselves as "La Capital", or quite simply as "La Ciudad", the city.

There is a good chance that this city, once the largest in the New World, is now the largest in the entire world. Having long since spread beyond the actual territory of the "Distrito Federal" (abbreviated to "D. F."), Mexico City together with its satellites towns now covers an area of 1,500 sq. km (580 sq. miles).

Millions of people live in the state of Mexico (which surrounds the Federal District like a horseshoe) and in the state of Morelos to the south. Population figures can only be guessed at: the Federal District is thought to have a population of over 13 million; the figure for the entire Valley of Mexico is nearly 18 million. Mexico City has, in the language of the demographers, a net daily growth rate of 1,000 inhabitants: number of births plus number of new arrivals minus the number of deaths. For the traveller, however, this amazing growth rate remains abstract. The area which Mexico City encompasses is so vast that it is impossible for one to form a mental image of the city as a whole. Only from the sky at night – from an aeroplane making its descent – can one get an idea of its vastness as it sparkles like a galaxy as far as the eye can see. The slum quarters are far removed in every sense from the affluence of the Zona Rosa.

While the headaches of the city fathers, who have to provide the largest conglomeration of people in the world with the necessary infrastructure – water and sewerage, electricity and roads – do not affect the tourist, the city's air probably will. On some days, Mexico City's smog, which is said to contain three times as many pollutants as the smog in Los Angeles, can be truly unpleasant (although Los Angeles' smog is considerably more irritating to the eyes and nasal passages). "Breathtaking" is the right word to describe an inner city intersection at rush hour.

Only seldom do the winds manage to sweep the 2,300 m (7,500 ft) high Valley of Mexico clean, allowing its inhabitants a view of the two snow-covered mountains in the west (Popocatépetl and Ixtacíhuatl are both volcanoes of over 16,000 ft). The sight of these two mountains rising up in the distance, however, has the effect of a revelation – one beholds the majesty of the vast landscape formed by the city and its surroundings.

(v. Debschitz)

A Tour of the Capital City

The pulsating rhythm of this city caught between the ancient and the ultramodern has an excitement all of its own. No visitor ever lasts very long in his hotel room – everyone itches to get out and be taken along by the magic of this giant metropolis. Mexico City is full of attractions and to get the most out of them, you will have to plan your time well that's to say, efficiently but not too rigidly.

The magnetic effect of the sidewalk cafés in the Zona Rosa, the tranquillity of the colonial streets in the southern suburb of San Angel, the bustling activity of a market – all belong to the experience that is Mexico City.

Take your time. Don't try to "do" Mexico City in three days – it would almost be a waste of the airfare. The treasures of this city cannot be taken in at an emotional distance like pieces exhibited at an open-air museum. Keep your ears tuned to the special rhythm of this city and let yourself by swept away by its Latin

Getting Around in the Capital City

Mexico City has an excellent public transportation system which can be recommended highly to each and every one of its visitors. The city's modern **underground system** now covers a distance of over 100 km (62 miles). Line 3, for instance, which spans the entire city from north to south over a distance of 22 km (13 ½ miles), is one of the longest underground lines in the world. The modern trains, which were supplied by the French, run on rubber wheels – the current of air created by the approaching train can be felt long before the train itself can be heard.

When the metro was built, prior to the 1968 Summer Olympics, many of the Aztec relics found during construction were incorporated into its design. Tracks were even laid through an Aztec temple which now forms part of the underground terminal near the Zócalo.

The cost of a ticket on the underground is minimal. Foreign visitors will also appreciate the system of symbols the city fathers thought up to make underground travel easier. Each station (many of whose names are difficult to pronounce and remember) is symbolized by an easy-to-recognize pictogram. This system was not devised solely with tourists in mind, however, but rather out of consideration for the many inhabitants of the city who cannot read.

The stations are clean, smoking is prohibited, classical music fills the air. Women appreciate the metro cars reserved for their use only – especially during the 8 am and 6 pm rush hours when it's everyone for him (or her) self. Mexico City's metro carries more than 4 million passengers daily.

Those who would like to see the city above ground (and choose to do so via public transportation) will find a **bus** stop at almost every street corner. Many buses, however, are not in the best of repair, and furthermore, they are mostly overcrowded. The modern "dolphin" buses, on the other hand, will only take on as many passengers as there are seats available (a ticket for this bus costs a little more than normal bus fare). After you have become familiar with the bus lines and their routes, you are sure to find bus travel a quick and inexpensive way to get around.

The city's main thoroughfares (the Reforma, for example) are served by "peseros", **taxis** which pick up and drop off passengers (up to six at a time) anywhere along a fixed route. The drivers of these taxis, mostly vintage American models, hold a finger up in the air to signal that there is space available. The peseros cost only about a third of a regular taxi fare (also in fact quite low in Mexico). *(v. Debschitz)*

American flair – you're bound to lose your heart!

The four most attractive sections of the city are centred around Chapultepec Park, Alameda Park, the Zócalo and the Zona Rosa.

Chapultepec Park

Our tour of the city begins on the Hill of the Grasshopper, in Nahuatl "Chapultepec" – the place where Aztec princes once hunted deer. With an area of 10 sq. km (almost 4 sq. miles), the **Bosque de Chapultepec,** which contains woods and meadows, a zoo and botanical gardens, playgrounds. lakes for rowing, and museums, is one of the largest city parks in the world. **"Los Piños"** (The Pines), the official residence of the Mexican president, stands here as well.

A 61 m (200 ft) high hill dominates the park. In 1783 the Spanish Viceroy Gálvez decided to build a castle on this hill where Aztec rulers had once resided. Construction of the castle was never completed, however. After Mexico had shaken off the yoke of Spanish rule and had become a republic, the building was turned over to the National Military Academy. In 1847, in the decisive battle of the Mexican-American War, American troops stormed the fort. Six teenage cadets fought bravely and died – today they are Mexican heroes.

In 1866, the Hapsburg emperor Maximilian and his young wife Charlotte moved into the castle and, during the three short years of their reign, transformed it into a magnificent residence. Charlotte even designed portions of the park's gardens herself. Today, Chapultepec Castle, one of the few legacies left by Maximilian, houses the National Museum of History, **Museo Nacional de Historia** (closed Tuesdays).

On your way up to the castle, take a look at the **Gallery of Mexican History,** officially known as "La Lucha del Pueblo Mexicano por su

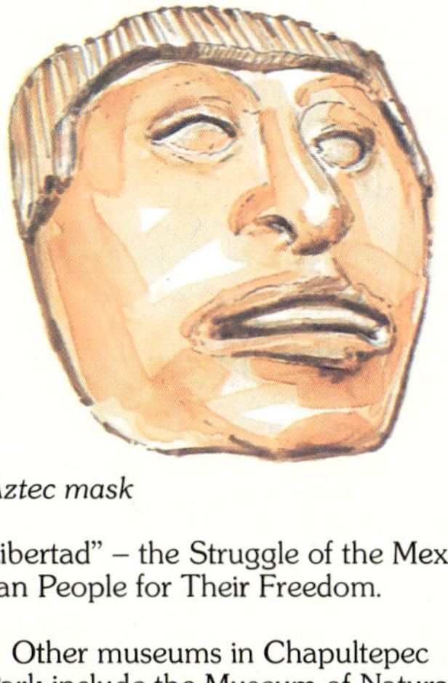

Aztec mask

Libertad" – the Struggle of the Mexican People for Their Freedom.

Other museums in Chapultepec Park include the Museum of Natural History **(Museo de Historia Natural)** and the Museum of Modern Art **(Museo de Arte Moderno).**

Certainly the most important museum in the park – and in all of Mexico, for that matter – is the National Museum of Anthropology **(Museo Nacional de Antropologia e Historia),** in which the important relics of Indian cultures from all over Mexico have been brought together. Those interested in ancient Mexican history will want to devote an entire day to this museum (see separate chapter).

At the Young Heroes Monument **(Monumento a los Niños Heroes)** – dedicated to the courageous cadets who lost their lives in Chapultepec – a pedestrian bridge takes you out of the park and over the traffic of the **Paseo de la Reforma,** which extends for its entire length before your eyes. This broad avenue, another of the few legacies of Emperor Maximilian's short reign (1864–67), was modelled after the Champs Elysées. Ironically, however, it was eventually named after the reform championed by his political vanquisher, Benito Juárez.

Take a stroll down this beautiful boulevard. For the first mile or so – as far as the intersection with the Insurgentes, Mexico's longest city street – it is flanked by modern high-rise buildings, small colonial villas, hotels, restaurants and cinemas. Further along, the buildings increase in size: it is here that airlines and banks have their offices. Here too, shops alternate with sidewalk cafés.

"Glorietas" are what the Mexicans call the city's many traffic circles, at the centre of which stand famous monuments. As you leave Chapultepec Park behind you, you will see to the left of the Reforma the statue of **Diana Cazadora** – this figure of the naked huntress caused quite a furore in the straitlaced days when she first graced this spot. As you walk up the Reforma, the first statue you will encounter will be that of the **Angel de la Independencia.** To the Mexicans, this golden angel atop its high pillar is known simply as "El Angel" – or jokingly as "the fallen angel", for it actually did fall from its pedestal during an earthquake more than 20 years ago.

At the centre of the bustling intersection of Mexico City's two main thoroughfares, the Reforma and the Insurgentes, stands the **Monumento a Cuauhtémoc,** a monument to the courageous last ruler of the Aztecs. The Reforma's next monument is dedicated to Christopher Columbus **(Monumento a Cristobal Colón).** To the left of the next intersection you can see the imposing **Monumento a la Revolución.** Originally built to serve as Mexico's capitol, it was turned into a pantheon after the Revolution and now holds the remains of revolutionary heroes. To the right is the Avenida Juárez which leads to the heart of the city.

Alameda Park

For a good part of its length, the Av. Juárez is flanked by Alameda Park. Dating from 1592, the park once served a grim function: during the Inquisition, heretics were burned here at the stake. Today, beautiful statues (brought back from Italy by President Porfirio Díaz) and the marble semicircular monument to

Juárez (Hemiciclo a Juárez) stand here amidst the park's ancient trees.

The Palace of Fine Arts **(El Palacio de las Bellas Artes),** which houses the National Opera, the National Theatre, the Ballet Folklórico de México, as well as various art exhibitions, is located directly opposite the park. Completed in 1934, this white marble building was constructed in a style which incorporates elements of Maya, Mixtec and Classic architecture. The famous **Ballet Folklórico de México** (Mexican Folkloric Ballet) can be seen here on Wednesdays and Sundays in several performances. Tickets should definitely be booked in advance (your hotel concierge or a travel agent will be able to arrange this).

The stage curtain created by Tiffany out of coloured glass and depicting the two volcanoes Popocatépetl and Ixtacíhuatl provides the backdrop for an impressive show of lights between ballet performances.

Since its completion, the Bellas Artes has sunk some 5 m (16 ft) into the soft subsoil of the Mexican capital.

Opposite the Palacio stands the 44-storey Latin-American Tower, **Torre Latinoamericana** – stable and earthquake-proof thanks to a special floating foundation. The view from its tower at 180 m (almost 600 ft) up is extensive and very impressive, but still does not truly convey the dimensions of this monstrously large city.

A mural by **Diego Rivera** in the Hotel del Prado opposite the park is the focus of a 37-minute long sound-and-light show.

Walk up and down the Avenida Lazaro Cárdenas and you will find yourself amidst a confusion of shops and stands, pawnshops and restaurants. Tourists are hardly to be found here – but the effervescence of Mexican life is!

If you continue up the Av. Juárez straight onto the Av. Francisco I. Madero, you will pass two magnificent examples of colonial architecture. The Casa de los Condes del Valle de Orizaba, called the House of Tiles **(Casa de los Azulejos),** was built in 1596 and now houses a Sanborn's department store and its well-known restaurant. The Palacio de los Marqueses de San Mateo de Valparaiso, also called Iturbide's Palace **(Palacio de Iturbide),** is an example of Mexican baroque with Italian influence

Many of the small intersecting streets you pass on your way to the Zócalo are traffic-free zones with cobblestones and colonial streetlamps. Quite a number of jewelry shops can be found here.

Zócalo

The **Plaza de la Constitución,** better known as the Zócalo, is the second-largest city square in the world (only the Red Square in Moscow is larger). The site of the square was once the heart of the Aztec empire, the centre of México-Tenochtitlán. The Cathedral

Plaza Garibaldi

Would you like to give yourself or a friend a gift of music? No, don't buy a record – hire a mariachi band to play a few romantic tunes, or to play the whole night through! To do so, head for the Plaza Garibaldi, the musical heart of the city located off the Central Lazaro Cárdenas in old Mexico City, six blocks north of Alameda Park.

You'll know when you're close by because of the unmistakeable confusion of sounds and melodies spreading from the square in all directions, In a single evening, up to 70 different bands can be seen and heard, all offering their services for a price, but offering samples of their musical ability free of charge – for their own pleasure as well as that of their audience! With their members all dressed in identical black costumes – silver-studded, narrow trousers, short jackets, embroidered, wide-brimmed sombreros – the bands can hardly be told apart, but the connoisseur can hear in a matter of minutes which Mariachis are good and which are more amateurish.

The word "mariachi" is said to derive from a play on words and from a Mexicanization of the French word "marriage". During the short period when the Hapsburg emperor Maximilian and his wife Charlotte ruled the country at the behest of Napoleon III, it was customary to have four musicians in "charro" uniforms play at festive weddings. It was at this time that the typical mariachi sound – created by a harp, a guitar and a violin – developed. Trumpets were added later, and today, a mariachi band would be unthinkable without them.

Love and pain always go hand-in-hand in Mexican songs. In Garibaldi Square, you can abandon yourself to the strains of songs which can be melodious and sweet, rousing, romantic, or defiant. Mariachi music turns the hearts of its listeners inside out. In Mexico, everyone can sing, and many possess a repertoire that can last an entire night. Young men croon sweet songs into the ears of their sweethearts, accompanied by a mariachi band.

In the cantinas surrounding Garibaldi Square, the Mexican soul bares itself as never before. The most famous of these, the "Tenampa" and the "Plaza St. Cecilia", are true bastions of mariachi culture – anyone who wants to do field studies will find that these offer the best opportunities! "A song, Señor?" Every few minutes there's another mariachi at your table. The price (one song costs about as much as a record album) and the formation of the band are quickly agreed upon. These negotiations are usually carried out by the "first violinist" who also sings the solo parts. The mariachi band takes its position in a half-circle around the table and starts up. It is customary to invite the "host" to sing the solo voice.

"Con dinero, o sin dinero, hago siempre lo que quiero, y mi palabra es la ley" is sung with great feeling to the accompaniment of the mariachi choir. It's one of the most popular songs in Mexico and is "muy macho", very masculine. "With or without money, I always do what I want, and my word is law – I'm still the king", goes the refrain. These are the defiant words of a man who realizes that his beloved doesn't want him anymore. "But when I die, I know you'll cry" – "llorar y llorar", cries the choir. That's how they are, these Mexican men. There is a feeling of brotherhood in the air and the tequila flows freely.

Cars continually pull up alongside the square, especially at the weekend, and the mariachis pounce upon their prospective customers. One or two demo songs and a whole band disappears into a car (the bass guitar usually ends up on the roof). An hour later, the band spills out of a taxi and back onto the square. Some well-to-do Mexican had hired them to do a late-night rendition of "Las Mañanitas", the Mexican's birthday song, whose cheerful melody, when interpreted by a mariachi band, makes a fitting accompaniment to the beginning of a new year of life.

(v. Debschitz)

Metropolitana, the largest church in Latin America, stands on the north side of the Zócalo. The first church that went up on this spot (shortly after the Conquest) was torn down to make way for the cathedral. The latter was planned in 1567, started in 1573 and finally completed in 1813. Its style incorporates Doric, Ionic and Corinthian elements.

In a small square in front of the cathedral, itinerant workmen wait for customers. Each has a sign announcing his own particular craft mounted in front of his tool box. And each is ready to jump up at a moment's notice to leave with a prospective employer.

El **Sagrario,** the sanctuary, adjacent to the cathedral, was built in 1750 in Spanish baroque style.

The National Palace **(Palacio Nacional),** once known as the "New Houses of Moctezuma", is the seat of the Mexican government. The building, which encloses 15 courtyards, was a gift of the Spanish King Philip to Hernán Cortés in 1529. The original structure, however, was almost completely destroyed by rioting mobs in 1692. The giant murals in the National Palace, painted by Diego Rivera, are important examples of Mexican "muralismo".

Over the main portal hangs the bell which Father Miguel Hidalgo y

Costilla rang on the night of September 15, 1810 to call the people to arms.

Every year, on the anniversary of this date, the Mexican president stands before a crowd of thousands gathered on the Zócalo and rings this bell to commemorate the "grito de Dolores" which sparked the Mexican War of Independence against Spain.

Opposite the National Palace stand the National Pawnshop **(Monte de Piedad),** formerly the palace of the Aztec ruler, Axacayatl.

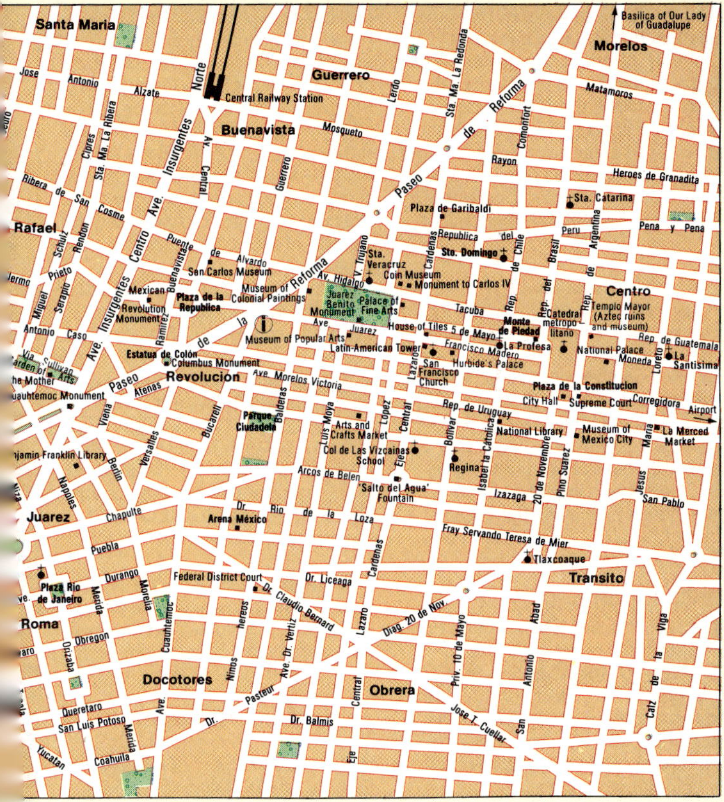

and the Merchants' Arcade **(Portal de Mercaderes).**

On the south side of the Zócalo stand the two city hall buildings of the Departamento del Distrito Federal. One of these was built in 1532 and, in its long life, has functioned as a grain exchange, a city jail and a mint office.

Just one block north of the Zócalo lies the most important pre-Columbian excavation site of the past 20 years. Here, in 1978, a massive stone disk depicting the moon goddess Coyolxauhqui in relief was discovered solely by chance just 2 m (6 ½ ft) under the ground. This discovery led archaeologists to the Temple Mayor, the most important temple pyramid in the entire Aztec empire (see separate chapter). When in Mexico City, don't miss the opportunity to see the fabled heart of the once greatest city in the world.

Zona Rosa

To see and be seen.... In Mexico City there's a whole district set aside for such activities – the Zona Rosa, or Pink Zone. Previously an affluent residential district, the rather unusual name is said to have originated in the local custom of painting the small colonial houses pink. Today the Zona Rosa houses most of the city's hotels as well as the greatest concentration of restaurants, cafés, nightclubs and discotheques.

The Zona Rosa is located – when approached from Chapultepec Park – to the right of the Reforma between "El Angel" and Avenida Insurgentes Sur. Many of the little side streets in the vicinity of Calle Niza and Calle Hamburgo are paved with cobblestones and illuminated by colonial streetlamps.

Here, where the restaurants and cafés stand side by side and their outdoor tables fill up entire streets (on the Calle Copenhague, for example), Mexico City is particularly chic. Here, the local jeunesse dorée, prominent figures in business and politics, and tourists from all over the world come together to form one big happy family. The Zona Rosa is the place where "one" meets one's business associates for dinner at an expensive restaurant, one's friends at a sidewalk café or disco, or other tourists for a stroll and a little sightseeing. The Zona Rosa never sleeps – when the last disco guests start heading for home or for their hotels, early-rising businessmen are already ordering breakfast.

As far as **shopping** goes, expensive but mostly quality antiques, exquisite examples of Mexican crafts ("artesanía") and exclusive silver and leather goods can be found at a myriad of boutiques and shops in the Zona Rosa. Here too, the Alta Moda of Milan can be found side-by-side with Burberry's and Rolex. For many travellers in the know, shopping in the Zona Rosa belongs to the musts of a trip to Mexico City.

But Mexico City also has a great deal to offer once we move away from the Zona Rosa, the Zócalo, and the capital's two best-known parks.

South Mexico City

The Avenida Insurgentes Sur leads to the southern part of the city and then on to the University. About 5 km (3 miles) south of the intersection with the Paseo de la Reforma stands Mexico's tallest building, the 51-storey **Hotel de México.** Although its revolving restaurant is in operation, this 1,340-room hotel has still not been completed. Up until now, the project has been thwarted by the gigantic costs involved – costs which even strain the financial power of its owner, the multi-industrialist Manuel Suarez. The hotel's two ballrooms can hold up to 14,000 people.

At the foot of this giant (which has been part of Mexico City's skyline for more than ten years now) stands the **Polyforum Cultural Siqueiros** – a rather unusual monument to an artist. The 4-storey, 12-ribbed circular structure contains the world's largest three-dimensional, semi-sculptured mural, a work by the celebrated artist David Alfaro Siqueiros. Called "The March of Humanity", it depicts the progress of mankind through history. By means of a revolving auditorium, the 2,700 sq. metres (29,000 sq. ft) of the mural are brought closer to those viewing it.

Continue along the Insurgentes Sur and you will come to the district of **San Angel,** a sleepy little town graced by elegant homes in the middle of the big city. The Saturday Bazaar **(Bazaar Sábado)** in San Angel's Plaza San Jacinto is always an interesting experience. Here you can find some of the most unusual examples of Mexican craftsmanship (in most cases, artistic adaptations of Indian originals). Many of the artists who display their work here are North Americans or Europeans who come to Mexico to gather inspiration from the artistic legacy of the ancient civilizations. San Angel boasts one of Mexico City's most exclusive restaurants, the San Angel Inn, a former hacienda.

A few miles further south lies the residential district of **Pedregal,** built upon black volcanic rock. Here, the imaginativeness of modern Mexican architects has created a fashionable residential district which can stand comparison with any other millionaires' quarter in the world.

It was here in the south of the city, in the district of Tlalpan, that the oldest known structure in the Americas, the circular Cuicuilco Pyramid, was uncovered just a few years ago. Its origin is obscure, but it is estimated to be 2,500 years old.

The pyramid (height 18 m/almost 60 ft), diameter 118 m/almost 390 ft) had been buried under lava since an eruption of nearby Mt. Ajusco.

South of Mexico City lies the **Universidad Nacional Autónoma de México.** As its name implies, the campus (which occupies an area of some 4 sq. km/1 ½ sq. miles) forms an autonomous city. The University, whose student body numbers 260,000, claims the distinction of being the oldest in the New World (it was founded in 1553). The celebrated **façade of the University Library** was designed by the artist and architect Juan O'Gorman. Stone mosaics (glass was used only for the colour blue) covering all four walls depict Mexico's main cultural epochs.

Nearby the University is the **Olympic Stadium.** Built in the form of a crater of a volcano and adorned with a bas-relief by the muralist Diego Rivera, it can hold up to 100,000 spectators.

A short distance south of the Olympic Stadium lies another stadium of enormous proportions, the **Estadio Azteca,** which can hold up to 105,000 spectators. Eight thousand private boxes, some equipped with air conditioning, bar, etc., have been leased to moneyed football fans for a period of 99 years. This is where the opening ceremonies and the final of the first World Cup Football Championship held in Mexico (1970) took place – and this is where they will take place again in 1986.

A cultural attraction of another kind can be found here in the south as well. The **Sala Nezahualcoyotl** is North America's first circular concert hall and one of the largest concert halls in the world. An audience of up to 2,500 can enjoy optimal sound quality made possible by specially developed acrylic "clouds" positioned over the central stage.

Continue south through Tlalplan and you will come to the famous **Floating Gardens of Xochimilco.** The gardens may not float anymore, but the vegetation in this confusion of canals is indeed abundant and well worth seeing. The name "Xochimilco" originated in Aztec times when artificial islands – large wicker baskets filled with soil and pumice – were used for the cultivation of maize and other grains.

A trip through the canals on one of the flower-adorned gondolas can be quite a romantic experience. "Floating" Mariachi Bands pull up alongside the excursionists' boats to offer their services, taco pedlars row up and down the canals, and even sarapes are bought and sold from boat to boat. Xochimilco is especially lively on Sundays when its boats are filled with Mexican families on outings.

West Mexico City

Those who enjoy sightseeing in lovely residential areas should not miss **Las Lomas,** the Hills, the neighbourhood of villas and residences to the west of Chapultepec Park. Well-to-do Mexicans, diplomats and the heads of foreign companies all reside here – as befits their station.

Las Lomas is really quite aptly named – its streets wander uphill and down, through barrancas (gorges) and over hilltops. Here, even the Paseo de la Reforma changes its appearance – from a bustling thoroughfare to an elegant avenue lined with palm trees.

Those who want to see more of elegant Mexico are directed to the **Polanco** district north of Chapultepec Park, a neighbourhood characterized by stately villas, smart department stores, posh shopping malls, and lovely parks.

North Mexico City

Mexico City's northern reaches also offer a number of attractions. Avenida Insurgentes Norte leads northward to **La Villa,** the heart of Catholic Mexico and site of the **Basilica de Nuestra Señora de Guadalupe,** the Basilica of Our Lady of Guadalupe, the dark-skinned Madonna who is revered as a symbol of racial unification.

According to the legend, on December 12, 1531 (not long after the conquest), the Virgin Mary appeared on **Tepeyak Hill** to a poor Indian farmer named Juan Diego and bade him to have a church built in her honour on that spot. Juan Diego told not only his parish priest of the vision, but the bishop as well, who ordered him to produce proof of the Virgin's request. When Diego returned to Tepeyak Hill, the Virgin appeared to him again and instructed him to gather up the roses which appeared suddenly from between the rocks, and carry them in his cloak to the bishop. He did as he was told, but when he opened up his cloak, the bishop beheld an image of the Virgin – her face as dark as an Indian's – imprinted on the cloth.

Juan Diego's cloak with the image of the Virgin is kept in a sanctuary in the new basilica. The old cathedral, which had become too small to accommodate the masses of the faithful, now serves as a museum.

The new basilica's circus tent construction means that it can hold up to 10,000 persons. When its 70 doors are opened, however, 25,000 more people can take part in the mass from the square outside.

If you are planning a trip to the Pyramids at Teotihuacàn, two side-trips – one to La Villa and the other to the **Plaza of the Three Cultures** in **Nonoalco-Tlatelolco** – should be part of your itinerary.

Next to the remains of an Aztec pyramid (the traces of a city founded in 1337 by renegade Mexicas) stands the colonial church of Santiago de Tlatelolco, formerly part of the Colegio de la Santa Cruz, a school for wellborn Indians who had managed to excape persecution after the Conquest. The third culture is that of today's Mexico: modern office buildings form the backdrop for Aztec pyramid and colonial church.

Tlatelolco, once the most famous market in the Aztec empire, and unrivalled in Europe for its orderliness and fair prices, was the site of the last battle between the Aztecs and the Spaniards. Under the leadership of the youthful prince Cuauhtémoc, the Aztecs fought bravely against Cortés and his Indian allies. They suffered a crushing defeat, however, and Cuauhtémoc was taken prisoner and later hanged.

On a marble slab in front of the church, the following words can be read: "On August 13, 1521, Tlatelolco, heroically defended by Cuauhtémoc, fell under Cortés' assault. It was neither a triumph nor a defeat, but rather, the painful birth of a new race which embodies Mexico today."

(v. Debschitz)

Museo de Antropología

Even those who have honed their ability to understand historical causes and effects through the study of Tacitus' "Historia" will find Mexican history a bit confusing at first. Difficulties arise at the very outset, when it comes to learning the names of Indian peoples and civilizations and of the exotic-sounding places which they inhabited. These words seem alien to our ears because they've been – thank heavens! – handed down to us in their original form. Although they were, of course, transcribed using Spanish orthography, they were not Westernized to make their pronunciation easier or their meaning clearer. In Mexico, you will have to deal with these indigenous names, for Mexican history will pursue you wherever you go. Just let yourself be carried away by their novel melody, and do the best you can with their wealth of consonants. You might find it easier after a shot of tequila!

Those who would like to probe the sources of Mexico's deep-seated pride and exuberant vitality must first acquaint themselves with at least a little pre-Columbian history. The best way to get an overall, concise picture of pre-Conquest Mexico is by spending several hours in the National Museum of Anthropology in Chapultepec Park. Inaugurated in 1964, the museum was first constructed in wood as an experiment to see if it would harmonize with the park scenery. The moment of truth did not arrive, however, until this unique architectural concept had finally been realized in seven different kinds of marble and stone and the 4,000 exhibition pieces had been placed throughout its many rooms. The museum's creators had chosen the 7 metre (23 foot) high, 150-tonne stone figure of the rain god Tláloc, the largest pre-Columbian monolith in the Western Hemisphere, to stand as a landmark in front of the building. This statue was transported from its place of discovery, a river bed in the Valley of Mexico, to the capital city with great technical difficulty. The Mexicans recount that on the day the god was erected on the museum grounds, dark clouds covered the sun and a three-day tropical storm unleashed its fury over the high plateau – in the middle of the dry season! Since then, they say, the weather in the capital city has never been the same. Earlier, it was possible to plan one's day around the rainy season's downpours which always started at 1:30 in the afternoon and ended at 4:00 pm. Now, however, the rains no longer come and go according to schedule.

Water whirls down the ornamented pillar which supports the giant parasol covering the patio around which the museum is centred. This lovely entrance sets the stage for your excursion through the museum's twelve rooms – rooms which will demand your undivided attention.

The Introductory Hall to Anthropology provides a survey of pre-Columbian and modern Mexican anthropology (this encompasses physical anthropology, archaeology, linguistics and ethnology). Following that, the Mesoamerica Room gives an overall view of the native cultures throughout the entire region. Then it's back to the beginnings: you will learn that the first migrations to the American continent took place approximately 40,000 years ago and that man first set foot upon Mexican soil around 12,000 years before the birth of Christ.

The pre-classic (dating back to the year 2000 B. C.) cultures of the central highlands already had notable funeral customs, village communities and ceremonial centres. Evidence of the last is the circular pyramid of Cuicuilco, located in the suburb of Pedregal, one half hour by car from the museum.

An entire room is dedicated to the culture of a people whose name we do not know and to their "city of the gods", Teotihuacán, 20 km (12 ½ miles) northeast of the capital's city limits. The influence of the then greatest political and religious centre in Mesoamerica lasted a millenium, but virtually nothing is known about the people who built this famed city. A life-sized replica of the Temple of Quetzalcoátl is on display here. The original, with its massive platform, is considered to be the most beautiful temple in all of Mexico and Central America.

In the next room, Mexican history begins to take on a more tangible shape. This room is dedicated to the Toltecs, whose empire sprang from the fading civilization of Teotihuacán. On display here are the art of Xochicalco, a cultural centre influenced by Teotihuacán and the Mayas (600 to 900 A. D.); and the art of Tula, which was founded by nomadic tribes from northern Mexico. The museum also houses

Model reconstruction of Tenochtitlán

one of the famous atlantes of Tula, four of which once supported the (completely unpronounceable!) Temple of Tlahuizcalpantecutli. A replica can now be seen alongside the three authentic colossal (4.6 m/ 15 ft) statues of warriors in feathered dress still in Tula. Incidentally, this site is just one and a half hours drive from Mexico City and makes an interesting destination for a half-day outing.

Hall 7, dedicated to the civilization of the Aztecs, is the largest and most important in the museum. The Mexica, as this nomadic tribe was actually called (the name Aztec was given them by their less-than-cordial neighbours), migrated from the north to the Valley of Mexico. There they settled, merely tolerated by their disdainful neighbours, and eked out an existence that was anything but glorious. According to legend, they were instructed by their god (careful, it's another tongue twister) Huitzilopochtli to look for a sign that would lead them to their new homeland: an eagle perched on a nopal cactus, devouring a snake. This symbol now appears on the seal of the Republic of Mexico and can be seen, among other places, on the back of every coin. The history-making event finally occurred in the year 1325: the cactus, the eagle and the snake were spotted on an island in the middle of Lake Texcoco. Humbly, the Mexica asked permission of the people who dominated the area to settle on that isolated piece of land. Approval was given and in due course the magnificent city of Tenochtitlán was built.

The Aztec-Mexica soon developed into a dominant military force, surpassing all other nations in wealth and influence. The Aztec empire reached the height of its expansion in the second half of the 15th century. The exhibits in the Aztec Room clearly show the unusually pronounced religiousness of these people. This religiousness was the impetus behind their advanced culture – a culture which reached its zenith a few decades before the arrival of Cortés.

Among the most interesting objects exhibited here are the Sun Stone or Aztec Calendar (see the following article), which is 3.6 metres (12 feet) in diameter and weighs 24 tonnes; and a model representing the temple district of Tenochtitlán during the golden age of Aztec culture.

The next room is devoted to the civilizations which blossomed around present-day Oaxaca: the Zapotecs of the central valley and the Mixtecs of the surrounding mountains. Known as excellent architects, the Zapotecs built the city of Monte Albán atop a mountain (which they levelled themselves) near the provincial capital of Oaxaca (on hour by plane from Mexico City). The Mixtecs, known for their goldwork and their picture writing, gradually conquered the area during the waning years of Zapotec civilization (between 800 and 1200 A. D.).

Mexico's oldest known culture – also known as the mother culture of Mesoamerica – is that of the Olmecs. The giant stone heads displaying Negroid features which can be found in La Venta Park near

Villahermosa (two hours by plane from Mexico City) are eloquent witnesses to their advanced cultural development. Other Gulf coast cultures include the Totonacs and the Huaxtecs north of Veracruz.

The civilization of the Mayas, described in detail in the next room, flourished for 700 years (from 200 to 900 A. D.). Their territory extended from the Yucatán Peninsula to Honduras, but the most interesting relics of this advanced culture can be found in Mexico. The museum focuses on their art and architecture (there is a model of the world-famous, richly frescoed Temple of Bonampak in the museum garden), as well as on their cult of the dead (a stairway leads down from the room to the Vault of the Dead). Two further halls of the museum are devoted to Northern and Western Mexico.

I strongly recommend comfortable shoes for a visit to this museum: the feet suffer from standing in one place supporting a tilted body while you stare upward at some massive statue. Not to mention the wear and tear they undergo in the course of walking and stopping and trying to take in the host of fascinating details throughout the museum! Because the captions and explanations of the pieces on exhibit are in Spanish only, it may be a good idea to purchase a museum guidebook or, better still, to take an escorted tour through the museum.

Those who still have some strength left after visiting the rooms on the ground floor should go upstairs to see the interesting dioramas depicting scenes from the daily life of Indian peoples in Mexico today. Films illustrating the development of the Mesoamerican cultures up to the conquest are shown in the museum's lower level.

The Museum of Anthropology is open daily except Mondays. It's best to stay away on weekends when multitudes of young Mexicans flock to the exhibits, attracted by reduced admission prices.

(v. Debschitz)

The Aztec Calendar

The Sun Stone or Aztec Calendar is cherished by Mexicans today as their second national treasure – after the Mexican flag. This massive carving – a basalt disk 3.6 metres (12 feet) in diameter and weighing 24 tonnes – was discovered in the layers of rock under the Plaza Major on December 17th 1790. Initially embedded in the base of the western tower of the cathedral, it was brought to the former anthropological museum in Moneda Street in 1885. Finally, in 1964 when the National Museum of Anthropology opened, the Sun Stone was given its rightful place in the Mexica Room – the largest and most important in the museum – where it forms the centrepiece of a dazzling exhibit.

When I asked a Mexican friend of mine what he could tell me about the Aztec Calendar that wasn't in the guidebooks, he gave me a terse reply: in the first place, it is not a calendar, and in the second place, the name of the people whose universe it represents is Mexica (also spelled Mejica) and not Aztec. That name was given them by the peoples of Lake Texcoco after the place from whence they had come: Aztlan, which means "Place of the Herons" in Nahuatl. For the sake of simplicity, we'll continue to call this giant stone relic of an ancient culture by the name by which it is widely known – the Aztec Calendar – even though we now know better!

The "calendar", dedicated to the sun as the central deity, actually depicts the Aztecs' concept of the creation of the world. This was based upon their "century", which lasted 52 years. At the end of every 52 years, the gods were expected to make their will known as to the future of the world. On the last night of each of these eras, the priests studied the heavens and the heavenly bodies to discover if mankind would be granted a future of another 52 years. If their divinations proved positive, the Aztecs would then commence to show their gratitude for divine favour through the ceremony of the New Fire – a ritual in which the New Sun was fed with human hearts and human blood. These were thus bad times for the prospective sacrifices – most of them prisoners of war.

This knowledge is the basis for the scientific theory that the Aztec Calendar was actually a giant sacrificial altar used in the veneration of the lord of all celestial bodies, the sun.

The following is a short lesson in Aztec mythology. If you pay close attention, you'll also learn a few words of Nahuatl, which is still spoken by the majority of the six million Indians in Mexico today.

The Sun Stone's central figure is that of the sun god, Tonatiuh, the lord of the universe. Depicted with fair hair and an obsidian tongue, his head is flanked on either side (east and west) by claws grasping human hearts: these illustrate the necessity of making human sacrifices to him. Tonatiuh is surrounded by symbols of the four "creations" of the world previous to the one during which the Sun Stone was carved. Above his head is a ray of sunlight, and below it, a sacrificial thorn. Together, this entire central relief symbolizes the Movement Sun or Ollin Tonatiuh, the fifth and last creation of the world.

The animal which represented the sun god was the eagle. The eastern or morning sun was called Cuauhtehuatl, "the soaring eagle"; the afternoon to evening sun was called Cuauhtemoc, "the falling eagle".

The symbols of the four previous epochs are contained in four square panels surrounding the head of the god. To the upper right is the first, Ocelotonatiuh (ocelot is one of many Nahuatl words which have found their way into the English – and other – languages) or "jaguar sun". The race of giants which populated the earth at this time was devoured by jaguars at the epoch's end. The next one, represented to the lower right, was Ehecatonatiuh or "wind sun". A hurricane destroyed the world at the end of this epoch and the survivors were transformed into monkeys. The god of this epoch was Quetzalcoátl, who appears more than once in Mexican history. The third epoch (depicted to the lower left) was Quiauhtonatiuh or "rain sun", and its god was Tláloc, the god of rain. At the end of this epoch, humankind was destroyed by fiery rain and the survivors transformed into birds. The fourth epoch was called "water sun": this time, a great deluge swept over the earth and its survivors were transformed into fish. Chalchiuhtlicue was the goddess of this epoch.

The Mexica year consisted of 18 months of 20 days each, plus 5 extra days (known as the "nemontemi") at the end of the year. On the Sun Stone, the symbols of the 20 days form a ring around the central relief. Starting to the upper left of centre with the symbol of the first day, Cipatli (crocodile); it continues on to the eleventh day, Ozomatli (monkey) directly opposite; and ends with the symbol of the twentieth day, Xochitl (flower). Visitors to the capital city will encounter this word when they go to see the flower-bedecked boats of Xochimilco in the southern part of the city – a popular destination for a Sunday outing.

Two fire serpents (Xiuhcóatl), their bodies dotted with tongues of fire, encircle the stone. Their tails meet at the top. At the bottom of the stone, Xiuhtecutli, the ruler of the night, and Tonatiuh, the sun, stare at each other with mouths agape.

With this knowledge, you will now be able to understand and explain the significance of the symbols on your Mexican souvenir – for which traveller to Mexico does not come home with an Aztec Calendar in the form of a silver pendant, an ashtray or a model cast in plaster suitable for hanging on the living room wall?

(v. Debschitz)

El Templo Mayor

For nearly two centuries, the Aztecs dominated Central Mexico and carried out campaigns of conquest with the discipline and precision of the Roman legions. Their feathered array, which gave them the appearance of the feared "Plumed Serpent", sent terror into the hearts of their neighbours.

The tribute that the subjugated peoples had to pay was high: in addition to foodstuffs, precious metals, blankets and cocoa beans (which were used as money), the Aztecs were especially interested in warriors taken in battle. They were designated as sacrifices for the appeasement and pleasure of the Aztecs central deity, Huitzilopochtli, the God of War. If a campaign did not produce enough prisoners, slaves were bought to increase their ranks. In effect, Aztec traders procured human sacrifices on the free market.

Accounts of excessive blood sacrifices have been handed down to us by the Aztecs themselves. On one occasion during the reign of Moctezuma II, 20,000 victims perished under the stone knives of the priests. The Aztecs were convinced that, without such sacrifices, the world would end. Ironically, this religious custom ended up playing a role in the demise of their world. Despite the greed of the Spaniards, they seemed more tolerable to the subjugated peoples of central Mexico than the blood-thirsty inhabitants of the island-city in Lake Texcoco, México-Tenochtitlán.

When Hernán Cortés and his 500 men stood before the gates of this city, they could hardly believe their eyes. More than 200,000 people lived here – more than in any city of the Old World. Tenochtitlán was divided into four parts, each one symbolizing a corner of the world. In the middle of this "cosmos" stood a temple complex which represented the centre of the spiritual and religious life of the Aztec people. The highest temple – as high as a 15-storeyed building and thus higher than most of Europe's cathedrals – was a step pyramid with two altars on its upper platform, one dedicated to the Rain God, Tláloc, and the other, to the God of War, Huitzilopochtli. This temple, called **El**

Two worlds collide

Templo Mayor by the Spaniards, was the place where the bloody human sacrifices took place.

Like cattle, the victims were driven up the pyramid to priests waiting at the top who then cut out their hearts and shoved the mutilated bodies back down the steps. The flesh of some victims was eaten as part of the ritual.

On August 13, 1521, the fate of the Aztec capital was decided at the battle at Tlatelolco (now the Plaza of the Three Cultures). The Aztecs were utterly defeated by the combined forces of the Spaniards and the Indians who fought with them under Cortés, and the religious centres of Tenochtitlán were destroyed.

The Spaniards built a new city upon the rubble of the old, and the Templo Mayor sunk into oblivion. It was not until 1790, 269 years to the day after the Aztec capitulation, that the first remnant of the past was found – the **Coatlicue monolith.** In the same year, the 24-tonne sun stone or **Aztec calendar** was found during the course of further excavations in the middle of the **Zócalo,** the capital city's main square.

For almost 200 years, scholars argued amongst themselves about the exact location and size of the Templo Mayor; they surmised that the foundations of the temple lay under the cathedral on the main square. In 1900, and later, in 1913/14, further pieces of Aztec constructions were found all around the Zócalo; a small museum was even set up to display these finds. The door to the Aztec past was not opened completely, however, until February 1978, when workmen from the city power company, working just 2 m (6 ½ ft) under ground, uncovered the great stone disk (3 m/10 ft across, 30 cm/12 inches thick, and weighing 8 tonnes) of the **Moon Goddess, Coyolxauhqui.** It lay intact under a layer of plaster.

Coyolxauhqui or "the one with the bells on her face" is an important figure in Aztec mythology. According to legend, she conspired with her many brothers to kill their mother before she could give birth to the god Huitzilopochtli. The god, however, sprang fully grown and armed from his mother's womb, cut off his evil sister's head, cut up her body, and chased off his brothers. Anthropologists see the story as a cosmic drama symbolizing the struggle the sun (represented by Huitzilopochtli) must win every day against his sister, the moon, and his brothers, the stars (whom he scatters into the four winds), in order to protect his mother – the earth.

With this discovery, it became clear that the site of the central temple complex had been found. After 4 ½ years of careful excavation work under the direction of Mexico's chief archaeologist, Eduardo Matos, all four sides of the Templo Mayor were exposed.

The entire structure is far more complex than anyone had ever suspected. A total of eleven different structures have been uncovered and identified; each one is superimposed over the previous one like icing on a cake. From the year 1325 onward, each Aztec ruler had "his" temple built over the one of his predecessor. The best preserved is the second one which was completed in 1390 – even the bases of the altars of Huitzilopochtli and Tláloc are intact.

A total of 6,770 different cult objects were found. These include life-sized stone figures known as "standard bearers", giant stone serpent heads, obsidian knives and sacrifical altars.

An especially interesting discovery was that of a figure of the **goddess Mayahuel** carved out of serpentine, a rock resembling jade. The statue is 1.32 m (just over 4 ft) high and weighs 285 kg (628 lbs.). The "green goddess", whose body is completely covered with symbols and hieroglyphics etched into the jadestone, was found right next to the Moon Goddess Coyolxauhqui.

The Moon Goddess, Coyolxauhqui, "the one with the bells on her face."

Many of these up to 600-year-old pieces (the "green goddess" included) had to be given on-the-spot first aid to prevent them from crumbling upon contact with the air. The Aztecs had concealed them in specially made niches in the pyramid walls. Now they are on exhibit in their own museum in Tacuba Street.

At the site of the Templo Mayor there is an interesting representation of the temple complex of Tenochtitlán in the form of a fountain. The scale model of the ceremonial centre (as seen by archaeologists in the light of the new findings) covers an area of several square yards and is clearly visible under a thin film of running water.

(v. Debschitz)

Spectator Sports

In addition to the "charreadas", Mexican rodeos (see "Charros" in the Impressions section), Mexico City offers a number of spectator sports which are well worth looking into.

Corrida de toros

The Mexican's Spanish heritage is quite apparent in their enthusiasm for the bullfight, and Mexico City offers the best in the republic! The city also boasts the largest bullfighting arena in the world: the Plaza Monumental, better known as the Plaza México. Located one block off Avenida Insurgentes Sur about 5 ½ km (3 ½ miles) south of the intersection of Reforma and Insurgentes, the bullring can seat up to 50,000 aficionados. The city's other arena, El Toreo, is located north of the Hipódromo de las Américas (4 km/2 ½ miles northeast of Chapultepec Park).

The main bullfighting season (when all the world's great toreros and matadors are to be seen in Mexico) lies between the months of November and March. But the "corrida" can be interesting at other times of the year as well. "Novilladas" is the name given to the bullfights of the young toreros who are still building up their reputation.

The bullfight is one of the few events in Mexico which begins on time: Sunday afternoons at 4 o'clock sharp. (Only when there is a game in the neighbouring football stadium is the start postponed until 4:30 – in the interest of traffic!) It's best to arrive at least a half hour early. This spectacle of human courage and brute strength is best experienced from the "barrera", which encompasses the first seven rows; the "primer tendido", the following nine rows, can also be recommended.

Even though it costs more, a seat on the "sombra" (shady) side of the arena is your best bet, as it can get quite uncomfortable in the hot sun!

Frontón

A popular sport to bet on in Mexico is frontón or **jai alai,** a Basque court game which is reputed to be the fastest game in the world. Played by professionals on a court 61 m (200 ft) long, the game consists of a player hurling a hard ball (about the size of a tennis ball) against a wall to his opponent, who catches it with the help of a "cesta", a special glove in the form of a wicker basket. During the game, the ball can fly at speeds of up to 100 mph. Jai alai is also played by specialists with the bare hand.

This high-powered and dangerous game can be seen at Frontón México, located near the Plaza de la Republica (and the Mexican Revolution Monument) daily except Mondays and Fridays from 7:30 pm.

Frontón tennis or frontenis, played on a three-walled court with rackets instead of "cestas", is played by women at Frontón Metropolitano from 4:00 pm.

Horseracing

The great attachment the Mexican has to the horse shows up clearly at the horse races. It's always racing season at the Hipódromo de las Américas in west Mexico City. From October 12 until the end of September, races and serious betting take place here four times a week. Tourists who present a tourist card can get in on reduced admission.

Other spectator sports which are well worth seeing include bicycle racing, auto racing (on the 3-mile course of the Autodromo de México) and, of course, football in the Estadio Azteca in the south of the city.

(v. Debschitz)

"Land's End" – Baja California

This quirk of nature, known as the Peninsula of Baja California, stretches out into the Pacific Ocean like an appendage of the state of California. Longer than the Italian peninsula (there are over a thousand miles of road between Tijuana and Cabo San Lucas) but only half as wide, this poor and hostile region is Mexico's wildest and most desolate.

The peninsula's interior is characterized by a forbidding mountain range known as the Sierra San Pedro Mártir in the north and the Sierra de la Giganta in the south. The mountains form part of the Coast Range which extends along the entire western coast of North America. The Sierra San Pedro Mártir contains the highest peaks: the Cerro de la Encantada (3,069 m/10,070 ft), Baja California's highest mountain, is located inland from San Felipe (on the eastern coast of the peninsula).

Canyons and gorges dotted with saguaros and organ pipe cacti, and populated by rattlesnakes, tarantulas and scorpions make for very dangerous territory, negotiable only on the back of a mule. The temperature can easily reach 50 °C (over 120 °F) at midday and you'll find that you'll be in constant need of water to keep your body temperature at a comfortable level. In the valleys, you'll find some ramshackle farms or "ranchos", dogs, a few goats.

This phenomenon of heat and isolation can be approached in either of two ways. The first possibility is to sail down the Pacific coast and back up through the Gulf of California with stops along the way in sheltered coves or on sandy beaches – and perhaps to include a few trips into the interior. Or, in order to experience this forbidding but majestic land to the full, you could drive along the 10-year old state highway, Mx 1. The highway begins at Tijuana on the U. S. border, crosses the narrow peninsula twice from east to west as it runs southwards, and ends at "land's end", Cabo San Lucas.

If you choose to go by road, do be careful, and avoid travelling after dark. The shoulder of the highway is dotted with "vados", drainage ditches which seem to be popular with cud-chewing cows at night. Car wrecks, some as old as the highway itself, stand as witnesses to the serious accidents which often occur. Grotesque crosses made of exhaust pipes, trim mouldings, brake pipes – anything long enough to be bent into shape – can often be found next to the wrecks. Old tyres function as wreaths. The road is dangerous during the day, as well: heat causes fatigue, and lack of traffic and monotony of landscape lead to boredom at the wheel.

There are some beautiful stretches of road, however. In the north, the highway hugs the Pacific coast for some 300 km (almost 200 miles), and in the south, the Gulf coast for about 200 km (120 miles). Other stretches of road pass through majestic deserts like the Desierto Vizcaíno.

Here, near the town of Guerrero Negro (which means black warrior), stands the largest saltworks in the world. The works centres around a hot laguna which, due to a high rate of evaporation, is very rich in salt deposits. Giant tractors carry the salt to the loading port of Guerrero Negro. This operation is run by a Japanese conglomerate; the biggest customer for the salt is the Japanese chemical industry.

San Ignacio

South of the desert, in the Sierra San Francisco, lies San Ignacio. No more than a hole in the wall, San Ignacio is, nevertheless, a centre for the "rancheros", the mountain farmers who live in the vicinity. "Vicinity" is a rather flexible term – some of them have to ride for two days before arriving here to pick up provisions. The shops and stands in San Ignacio carry only the barest necessities. The little money the rancheros make from the sale of goat cheese or perhaps from an ox is just enough to cover the purchase of essential items such as clothing, spare parts for machinery, and batteries.

Geographically, this region forms the centre of Baja California; civilization is close by. Seventy-three kilometres (forty-five miles) from here, the Mx 1 turns toward the Gulf coast and the port of Santa Rosalia, where there is a small air field serving local traffic, and a ferry to the mainland – to Guaymas, Sonora.

While in San Ignacio, those who are in good health and have strong nerves may like to consider visiting the **Cueva Pintada** (Painted Cave). The road to the village of San Francisco may be negotiated by car, but you should reckon with a bumpy ride. Although it consists merely of a few adobe-brick huts with palm-leaf roofs, the village does offer accommodation (of the humblest sort), food and the mules necessary for continuing on to the cave. Depending on the adroitness of mule and rider, the trip can take from a little less to a little more than a day. The unspoilt landscape more than makes up for the discomforts of the journey and the inevitable rear-end soreness. And besides, your destination is the most beautiful of the approximately forty painted caves in Baja California.

The paintings, executed by Paleo-Indian hunters, possibly to gain the favour of gods and conjure up the animals they wished to kill, are truly impressive. Scenes of an obviously succesful hunt show hunters standing with their game: horned animals

Nursery of the Grey Whale

They travel for two to three months before arriving in their thousands in the warm waters off the Peninsula of Baja California. Grey whales (Eschrichtius glaucus), among the largest mammals in the world, return each year to their breeding grounds in the bays and lagoons along the peninsula's rugged coastline. Here, their young are born and reared under the protection of their mothers.

In October, when icy winds start blowing over the Bering Strait, between fifteen and twenty thousand grey whales start on their 5,000-mile journey from Alaska to Mexico. These rare giants, some over 18 m (60 ft) in length and weighing 100 tonnes, travel along the coasts of British Columbia, Washington state, Oregon and California. In December, the first arrive at their destination, the warmer waters of the western coast of Baja California.

In 1960, the Mexican government made an important contribution toward the preservation of the grey whale by declaring the Laguna Ojo de Liebre (Eye of the Rabbit) a grey whale sanctuary. In 1979, the Laguna San Ignacio, 200 km (124 miles) south of the Ojo de Liebre, was granted the same status. From a guard station on the island of Guadalupe, it is seen to that, in accordance with an order enacted in 1920 under President Alvaro Obregón, grey whales are left undisturbed in Mexican waters.

(possibly deers or goats) are pierced with arrows. The paintings' brick-red colours are still in good condition.

Santa Rosalia

Santa Rosalia is a small port town – nothing special, but nevertheless, the "big city" for the rest of central Baja California. A few small tourist hotels have gone up along the beaches nearby and amazing tales are being told of hotel corporations which want to invest in the area's development. The people are giving in to dreams of big money – or at least hoping for tourists, jobs, and a little prosperity.

Santa Rosalia, which was founded by a French mining company, today contains two monuments to its Gallic past. The town boasts the best bakeries (supposedly) in all of Mexico, and the country's most unusual church stands here. The structure's prefabricated iron parts were sent here from half way around the world in Europe. The engineer who designed it also designed a famous monument which stands in Paris. His name was Gustave Eiffel.

In the shallow, warm bays of Baja California, these peaceful giants, who enjoy being petted and scratched, have acquired a rather mean reputation. In the nineteenth century, a whaler from San Francisco, Captain Melvin Scammon by name (the Laguna Ojo de Liebre is also known as Scammon's lagoon), noticed large numbers of grey whales off the coast of Baja California. He cast anchor before one of the bays and sent boatloads of whalers into the shallow waters. Confused by the hulls of these boats, some of the calves became disoriented and lost sight of their mothers. The mothers, in desperate search of their young, dove under the boats and hurled them up into the air, causing them to break apart. Terrified to death by these "belligerent fish", the unsuccessful whalers escaped back to their ship. Since then, the grey whale has had the reputation of attacking and destroying boats. Moby Dick, are you out there?

Not because of their supposed ferocity, but more because of their friendliness, it has been made illegal to observe the whales from boats anchored off the coast. For years, genuine whale sightseeing jaunts were organized from San Francisco, but because the tame young whales often swam right up to the ships and motor yachts and injured themselves on their propellers, these are now banned by the Mexican government. It is, however, possible to observe these "nurseries for whales" from land: in Baja California Sur, the San Carlos turn-off from state highway Mx 1 leads directly to the coastal region of the Bahía Magdalena where, between the months of December and March (and with a little bit of luck), you may catch a glimpse of this spectacle of nature.

(v. Debschitz)

From Santa Rosalia, the highway continues along the coast of the Gulf of California for about 200 km (just over 120 miles). A few American yachts may be seen bobbing up and down in the waters of the beautiful and isolated Bahía Concepción, but there is no infrastructure to speak of here, although you may hear talk of big plans.

For the sake of the Gulf coast's still-intact environment, however, one can only hope that care is taken in implementing any such plans. When the hoped-for masses of people appear, a unique and irreplaceable biotope could be destroyed – and the waters of Baja California may well play out their role as breeding ground for whales.

Villa Insurgentes

After following the east coast as far as Ligui, the Mx 1 crosses the Sierra de la Giganta and continues on to Villa Insurgentes on the peninsula's western side. Here you should pick up supplies of food and petrol as this will be your very last chance between here and La Paz – 210 km (130 miles) away. There's a golden rule in Mexico: you should always start looking for the next petrol station when your tank is half empty. That way, you won't find yourself pulling up to a pump on your last drop only to hear the words, "no tenemos gasolina" – "we don't have any" – and the next filling station is miles away!

La Paz

You'll know you're approaching La Paz, the capital of South Baja California, first by the increase in the number of auto wrecks left and right of the highway, and then by the first houses, or rather, shacks, which appear. These form part of the town's outlying slums, evidence of the rural exodus which affects even this part of the country.

With its checkerboard layout, this town of 130,000 (or more) inhabitants appears to be fresh off the drawing board. Actually, however, it is the oldest city in the region. The first Spaniards arrived here in 1534 – only to be killed by the Indians.

Up until about 1915, La Paz had been famous for its pearls, but the oyster beds in the Bahía de la Paz are now long gone. In Mexico, it is whispered that the Japanese, with whom La Paz used to compete on the pearl market, had a hand in the demise of the beds....

Today, La Paz is a free port which thrives on tourism from the mainland. If you plan to travel by car from the U. S. to La Paz and then cross over to Topolobampo/Los Mochis or Mazatlán by ferry, you must have a temporary import permit for your car (obtainable along with your tourist card) and you must get it stamped shortly after Ensenada – otherwise, you won't be allowed on the ferry.

Signs of a burgeoning infrastructure can be found all along the Bahía de la Paz, a resort which has been exceptionally well-favoured by nature. More or less attractive examples of hotel architecture now dot the coastline and the number of hotels is steadily increasing – evidence that this formerly isolated region of Mexico is gaining in popularity.

The traffic routes between La Paz and the mainland have been considerably expanded: there are several flights daily to Mexico City and two ferry connections between La Paz and Mazatlàn and Los Mochis. It is obvious that a new coastal resort is in the making here.

(Thieme, v. Debschitz)

San José del Cabo

The flight in Aeroméxico's 40-seater turboprop from La Paz to San José del Cabo is a spectacular (if turbulent!) experience. The air beneath the wings is unbelievably clear – you can look straight down upon a lunar landscape or see the waters of the Sea of Cortés (another name for the Gulf of California) shimmering on the horizon.

The airport at San José del Cabo, which serves flights from Mexico City as well as from several U. S. cities, is designed to accommodate small jets. At the airport, you'll notice that most of the luggage handed out consists of bulky fishing equipment – an early sign that you've landed in a fishermen's paradise. From the airport, it's around 15 km (9 miles) through sandy terrain to the little town of San José del Cabo and its few modern hotels scattered along the beach.

Here, at the tip of the Baja California peninsula, the desert mountains drop directly into the sea. Their sharp contours stand out against the horizon in a somewhat paler blue than the inky sea from which they are separated by a yellow ribbon of fine sandy beach. Not a trace of humidity in the air – the dryness of this spectacular lunar landscape seems to absorb all the moisture from the sea. Behind you, you have cacti and other spiny plants, in front of you is a body of water which literally teems with fish – a total of 857 different species of fish have been counted here.

The road from San José del Cabo winds its way southwestwards for 30 km (18½ miles) to Cabo San Lucas. At the halfway point stands a hotel complex which has become a Mecca for sportfishermen from all over the world – the Hotel Cabo San Lucas. Here, almost every inch of wall space is covered with trophies from the sea (the hotel organizes celebrated deep-sea fishing contests). Yachts bob in the water along the pier in front of the hotel; the latter's restaurant terrace enjoys a picturesque location upon the cliffs. Here, only the best will do – money seems to be no object. Those who try to pay with pesos, however, will be given a withering look, for the dollar is king – as it was in the days when a room could be booked only through a U. S. representative, and the hotel could only be reached by private jet or yacht.

Cabo San Lucas

The town of Cabo San Lucas offers a number of new, very attractive hotels, a large port with a ferry service to Puerto Vallarta as well as special mooring facilities for sportfishing boats, and a few shops and restaurants. – But the greatest attraction here, on the southern tip of Baja California, is, without doubt, that offered by nature. The warm waters of the Gulf of California meet the cooler waters of the Pacific Ocean, creating a spectacular show of colours. (It is worth coming this far to see this alone.) If you wade through the water along the approximately 100-metre-wide beach, you will notice gentle fluctuations in temperature: the currents from the Gulf are lukewarm while those from the Pacific are quite cool. Practised divers can observe another natural phenomenon underwater: a "sandfall", created when the current drags fine sand (tons of it per second) over an undersea crag and into the deep.

The landmark of Cabo San Lucas is the natural arch which has been formed in the rocks along the coast by the erosive action of the sea over millions of years. As part of a sightseeing boat trip you can circle around this bizarre rock formation and see sea lions basking in the sun.

(v. Debschitz)

The North

North Mexico contains the country's largest states, but has the country's lowest population density. The states which constitute North Mexico (and, in brackets, their capitals) are: Baja California Norte (Mexicali), Baja California Sur (La Paz), Sonora (Hermosillo), Chihuahua (Chihuahua), Coahuila (Saltillo), Nuevo León (Monterrey), Tamaulipas (Ciudad Victoria), Sinaloa (Culiacán), Durango (Durango), Zacatecas (Zacatecas), San Luis Potosí (San Luis Potosí) and Aguascalientes (Aguascalientes).

The Peninsula of Baja California is a special case both geographically and culturally – due to its isolated position, its development differed from that of the rest of the country – even from that of the rest of the north. It has therefore been dealt with as a separate region.

Up to a little over one hundred years ago, the U. S. states of California, Arizona, New Mexico and Texas were also part of northern Mexico. Although the Rio Grande (or Río Bravo, as the Mexicans call it) now forms the border between the U. S. A. and Mexico, the states of the American southwest share a long history and a wealth of traditions with those of the Mexican north.

The mainland states of Sonora and Sinaloa on the west coast are characterized by the wild mountainous scenery of the Sierra Madre del Norte and a relatively narrow coastal strip. With a population density of just 8 inhabitants per square kilometre, Sonora is one of the most sparcely populated Mexican states; Sinaloa, with a population of 32 per square kilometre, is in the bottom third of the Mexican scale.

In the northwest, the border Mexico shares with the United States could well be described as a badly-healed wound. The frontier separating Baja California and Sonora in the south from California and Arizona in the north can hardly be controlled and, in the interest of good Mexican-American relations, may not be sealed off. This area has thus become a playground for smugglers, who do a booming business in industrial goods to Mexico and in illegal workers and narcotics (a recently developed but fast-growing field) to the U. S. The illegal cultivation of marijuana and poppies, and the production of drugs from these plants, have become genuine growth industries in Sonora, Sinaloa and western Chihuahua, and no one has any idea how they can be quashed. The police are always making attempts – spectacular as well as half-hearted – to take action against the farmers and the dealers, but to no avail. It is even whispered that certain sections of the police actually co-operate with the drug mafia, that they look the other way – and make a profit.

Tourism in this immense region is primarily border tourism. Americans who live along the 3,200 km (almost 2,000 miles) of the Mexican frontier visit border towns like Tijuana, Mexicali, Nogales, Ciudad Juárez, Nuevo Laredo, Reynosa and Matamoros to pick up leathergoods and spirits at low prices, to go to the jai alai matches or to the dog races, or maybe to indulge in a little betting or whatever.

The resorts along the west coast facing the Gulf of California have merely local significance. The beaches, which are relatively clean and pleasant, are frequented by people from towns like Hermosillo, Ciudad Obregón and Los Mochis, but they offer no touristic infrastructure whatsoever.

The main gateway to Mexico for travellers coming overland from the United States is the **border crossing** over the Rio Grande at **Laredo, Texas/Nuevo Laredo, Nuevo León.** From there, the Pan-American Highway takes you the 150 km (93 miles) to **Monterrey,** capital of Nuevo León and Mexico's second-largest industrial centre after Mexico City. (There is another important border crossing northwest of Laredo/Nuevo Laredo. At the point where the Rio Grande leaves the Mexican border and heads northwards stand **El Paso/Ciudad Juárez.** It is here that the Christopher Columbus Highway begins – it can take you the 1,830 km (1,140 miles) to Mexico City.)

Monterrey

Founded in 1579, Monterrey has been growing at a breathtaking pace since the end of the 19th century and now has over 2 million inhabitants, making it **Mexico's third-largest city.** To an extent found nowhere else in the country, business and industry here are organized along U. S. lines. The city also boasts the country's most prestigious institute of higher education in the field of science and technology, the Monterrey Institute of Technology, abbreviated M. I. T. like its great American counterpart, the Massachusetts Institute of Technology.

Monterrey's centre consists of its main square, the **Plaza Zaragoza,** and the adjacent cathedral. Its most attractive specimen of colonial architecture is the Bishop's Palace **(El Obispado),** located on a hill, the Cerro del Obispado, in the southwestern part of the city. Built at the end of the 18th century, it now houses a museum. From the palace, you can enjoy a fine view of the city and its landmark, the **Cerro de la Silla** (Saddle Hill).

Nuevo Casas Grandes

From the border at Ciudad Juárez, it's around 375 km (230 miles) to Chihuahua, capital of the state of the same name. Those interested in Pre-Columbian sites might like to make a detour, however: turn west onto state highway 2 after Juárez, and then at Janos south onto highway 10; this road will then take you to Nuevo Casas Grandes. Outside this rural town lie **Casas Grandes,** the most important ruins in northern Mexico. The Indian name, Paquime, means the same thing: "big houses".

The site lies in an arid plain on the eastern slopes of the Sierra Madre. Its excavation in the years 1958–1961 under the sponsorship of the Amerind Foundation brought theretofore unknown but very significant data to light.

The architecture is typical for the region in which it originated – the excavators call it Gran Chichimeca, the territory of the Chichimecs (the "barbarians" of the north). Here, two architectural elements come together. Domestic dwellings, the so-called pueblos, are similar to those of the American southwest, while the sacred architecture resembles that of the Toltecs. Round ritual dance platforms are modelled after those of the Central Plateau; a cross-shaped platform has been so built that its four points are exactly aligned with the four compass directions, suggesting that it may have served as an observatory.

Several ball courts in the usual double-T form represent another southern import: the ball game and the ball court were developed in the Maya region and brought to the Central Plateau by the Toltecs, for whom they assumed a central role in ritual life.

The dwellings, on the other hand, stand clearly under northern influence. Multi-storeyed adobe structures grouped about a communal patio, and containing rooms with sleeping niches and rooms where household activities took place, resemble the "apartment houses" of the Hohokam and Anazazi cultures. With only one entrance, which could be sealed off in case of danger, the dwellings were closed to intruders like a fortress. The occupants moved from floor to floor by means of a series of ladders which could be pulled in in the event of an attack.

The archaeological zone of Casas Grandes is easily accessible: a paved road leads to the parking lot and the site itself can be negotiated on foot without any problems. Those who would like to consult a qualified source for more information on the site should contact Señor Piñon, owner of the motel of the same name in Nuevo Casas Grandes. Señor Piñon is very familiar with the local archaeology and even keeps a museum in his motel with objects from the surrounding area.

From here, it's about 350 km (217 miles) on good, even roads to Chihuahua. To get there, continue on highway 10 through Buenaventura and on to El Sueco, where you can pick up the Christopher Columbus Highway.

If time allows you could, however, turn southwest at Buenaventura and drive towards Cuauhtémoc. Shortly before arriving in the town you will arrive at the Mennonite settlements described in the chapter, "Contrasts in the North – Tarahumara and Mennonite".

Las Varas

The road from Buenaventura to Cuauhtémoc offers another possible excursion, this time to the ruins of the Cuarenta Casas (forty houses). Roughly 100 km (60 miles) south of Buenaventura, at Gomes Farías, leave the main road and head west until you reach Las Varas. The ruins are located 8 km (5 miles) outside the village.

The site is easy to reach and may be visited without a guide. The main point of interest here is a large cliff dwelling similar to the ones in Mesa Verde, Colorado. The "cave of the windows" is a cliff dwelling of some 30 m (almost 100 ft) in length, incorporated into a natural cave. Dendochronological dating shows that it must have been inhabited between the 11th and the early 13th centuries. The population of the village is estimated to have been around thirty. The living and working quarters are still distinguishable today, and rooms designated for the storage of food are recognizable as well. Burials were found toward the back of the cave.

The descent into the cave is a little difficult, but well worth the effort. As suitable accommodation is lacking in this region, you may have to consider spending the night in Cuauhtémoc – so plan to visit this site early in the day to give yourself enough time to get there.

Chihuahua

Chihuahua, population 500,000, capital of the largest of the Mexican states, is the busy commercial centre of a large hinterland. Founded in 1709, the city has an attractive **colonial centre** featuring a late-baroque cathedral (situated on the Plaza de Armas) that was financed (not exactly voluntarily) by the employees of the silver mines in the vicinity.

Chihuahua figured significantly in the Revolution of 1910 – it was the seat of government and headquarters of **Francisco "Pancho" Villa,** to whom a small museum is now dedicated. Run by one of his widows until her death in 1981, it is now in the hands of the city. A further museum of local historical interest is located on a former estate, the Quinta Gameros. The Quinta Carolina, located outside the city, will give you an idea of the opulence of a late 18th century Mexican country estate. (Chihuahua is a possible starting point for a trip on the scenic Chihuahua-Pacifico railway. See page 263.)

Hidalgo del Parral

There are several ways to get from Chihuahua to Mexico City. The fastest (though least interesting) is via Highway 49 through Torreon, Fresnillo, Zacatecas, San Luis Potosí and Querétaro. A slight diversion is highly recommendable, however.

If you turn west at Jiménez, approximately 220 km (136 miles) south of Chihuahua, you can visit the pretty rural town of Hidalgo del Parral with its well-preserved **colonial architecture.** The church of Our Lady of Fatima is built entirely of micaceous rock and is well worth seeing.

From here, Highway 45 heads south for 410 km (255 miles) to Durango. This road goes on and on for miles through steppes inhabited solely by an occasional herd of cattle. The endlessness of the wide open spaces the Mexicans call "El Norte" becomes apparent, and one understands why the Mexican cowboy no longer tends his herd from the saddle, but instead, from the helicopter.

When driving on roads like this one – and the following applies to the entire northern region – one should always keep an eye on the level of petrol in the tank and fill up at every opportunity. Petrol stations are few and far between and many are "fresh out" when you get there. The words "no tenemos gasolina" can easily conjure up nightmares.

Durango

Durango (like Chihuahua, capital of a state of the same name) is a typical sleepy, dusty northern town. Its colonial past is represented by a cathedral and by a monastery that has been converted into a hotel.

From Durango, you can take one of the few roads which runs west to the coast – Highway 40 which winds its way up to the Los Mimbres Pass (2,500 m/8,200 ft) and through the rugged mountain world of the Sierra Madre Occidental to **Mazatlán.** This stretch of highway is particularly scenic but demands strong nerves from the driver who uses it – often you'll encounter timber transporters on the road, and the asphalt is badly worn in parts.

Mazatlán

A fishing port on a peninsula which juts out into the Pacific Ocean, Mazatlán has now developed into a holiday resort with excellent facilities for fishing. The town also has fine beaches and an extensive promenade, the "Malecon". It's quite an experience to stand at the rock "El Mirador" and watch while young locals dive into the sea far below, timing the flow of the tide exactly. A ferry sails from Mazatlán to La Paz, Baja California. (Mazatlán is also featured in the chapter "Coastal Resorts" and in the section "Chihuahua-Pacifico".)

Along Highway 45 as it continues south from Durango are two important archaeological sites, **Chalchihuites and La Quemada.** These have been the object of considerable research in recent years. They are seen as only the tip of the iceberg, however, as remains of ancient cultures are continually being unearthed in this trackless and impassable territory. While the study of the northern Mexican cultures has only just begun, these finds have already dispelled the myth that ancient Indian cultures were found only in the south.

Chalchihuites

At Sombrerete (service station here!) about 120 km (75 miles) south of Durango, a small, unpaved but passable (in dry weather) road leads west to the village of Chalchihuites. Six kilometres (approx. 4 miles) outside the village, on open farmland belonging to a hacienda, lie the remains of a fortified city. On the basis of the ceramics and remnants of paintings found in the lower sections of the still intact walls, it can be said that this complex dates from the heyday of the **Teotihuacán civilization** of the Central Plateau – perhaps it was a commercial centre and fortified post on the northern frontier of their territory. (For La Quemada, see p. 265.)

(Thieme)

Zacatecas

After another 165 km (102 miles) on Highway 45, you'll come to Zacatecas, capital of the state of the same name. The city lies at an elevation of approximately 2,600 m (8,500 ft), in a wide depression at the foot of three hills – the Cerro La Bufa, Cerro de la Mala Noche and Cerro del Padre – which are all part of the so-called Sierra de Zacatecas.

Zacatecas, best known for its **silver mines,** is a **picturesque, historic town** with many impressive buildings as well as a fair number of hotels and restaurants – yet relatively few tourists.

A town of approximately 61,000 inhabitants (1975), it serves as an important way station and "middleman" between, on the one hand, central Mexico (including the industrial centres of Mexico City, Puebla/Orizaba and Guadalajara) and, on the other, the few centres of population along the northern Mexican "frontier". Zacatecas boasts two universities, the Universidad Autónoma de Zacatecas and the Instituto de las Ciencias (Institute of Sciences). The mines in the vicinity yield silver, gold, lead, zinc, copper and mercury ores. These mines, as well as of course the town's attractive historic centre, its architecture and art treasures, mean that both Zacatecas and its environs have much to offer the tourist.

In recent years, efforts have been made to make this region even more attractive to tourists: there is now a cable railway to the Cerro de la Bufa, and the mine "El Eden" has been opened to visitors.

The city's shade arcades and its cathedral are among the most beautiful examples of **colonial architecture** Mexico has to offer. The city is

Tlahuizcalpantecutli – The Pleasure of Disorientation

Much has been written about the pre-Hispanic ruins of Mexico: the pyramids and temples of Teotihuacán, Monte Albán, Palenque, Chichén Itzá and Uxmál are a "must" for any visitor. These sites are not only valuable records of the various Indian cultures that built them, of the Mayas, Mixtecs, Zapotecs, etc., but also landmarks in world history. As the Sphinx belongs not only to Egypt, they belong not only to Mexico, but to Man. Along with the Inca ruins of Peru they could be called the Wonders of the New World.

Comparisons have often been made between the Mayas and the Greeks, and archaeologists, in dividing up the different Indian cultures into phases, use labels like "preclassical, classical, postclassical" which encourage Old-World analogies. This parallelism, however, is deceptive: in some respects the ruins of Mexico are very different from those of Rome and Greece. Most importantly, their discovery and exploration is far more recent, dating only from the early years of this century. Consequently, far less is known about them. The visitor to Knossos experiences the pleasure of recognition: "Ah! here is that labyrinth the legend speaks of". What thrills us at all the Hellenic sites is to meet, face to face so to speak, the gods and heroes that have indelibly marked our culture, that we were told about in school, that have influenced centuries of literature and art that is familiar to us. The visitor to Teotihuacán, Uxmál or Palenque experiences a different pleasure – the pleasure of disorientation. Instead of familiar Apollo, Bacchus or Dionysus, he is confronted with strange, barbaric gods whose names he cannot even pronounce: Coatlicue, Tláloc, Tlahuizcalpantecutli! And the mythology, the cosmology, the concepts behind those names are no less strange.

taking remarkable pains to preserve the unique character of its historic nucleus which, aside from necessary modernizations, has undergone no great changes over the years, thanks to the fact that Zacatecas has never been a centre of migration (its industrial development was never significant enough).

The city of Zacatecas ("The Place Where the Zacate Plant Grows in Abundance") is said to have been founded in 1546 on the occasion of a military campaign in the Zacatecas region undertaken by the conquistadores Juan de Tolosa, Cristobál de Oñate, Diego de Ibarra and Balthasar Término de Bañuelos. During and after the campaign, large deposits of precious and base metals were found in the area. The Spaniards, however, were interested pri-

Moreover, while what is known about these cultures is certainly fascinating, what is not known is in some ways more attractive.

The mysteriousness of these relatively recently unearthed cultures is enhanced by the mysteriousness of the locations – arid plains, mountain tops, jungles – and the way their architects seemed to deliberately harmonise their works with nature as they found it. The slope of the Pyramid of the Sun in Teotihuacán echoes the shape of the surrounding mountains; the lushly carved stone of Palenque echoes the lushness of the forest out of which it only half emerges.

And then – another difference with the Old World – in Mexico there are so many ruins that have not yet been unearthed, that are tacitly known about but not officially discovered. Most visitors will be amazed to see, in the middle of an otherwise flat valley, small geometrical "hills" which are obviously small pyramids that no one has bothered – or dared – to unearth. Or in the Sierra, a precipitous road will take them past a high mountain, entirely covered with grass and bushes but with a top so neatly and geometrically layered and terraced that it cannot possibly be natural.

Often the attitude of the local people to these concealed constructions is reserve, jealousy and suspicion. American archaeologists have been known to disappear in such places and, though the causes were almost certainly natural, investigations were not always made.

This strange reserve of the Mexicans (well, not so strange if one remembers how many treasures have been stolen from them by foreign dealers) is part of the reason their ruins have not been subjected to the cool, systematic exploration and analysis that has brought the treasures of the Old World into the daylight. The treasures of Mexico, centuries after the conquest, are still half-submerged in shadow.

(Valerio)

marily in the gold and silver mines – these had been in operation since pre-Spanish times.

The ore mines attracted countless colonists to the settlement, and in 1588 King Philipp II granted it its city charter. A number of religious orders also established monasteries here (the Franciscans in 1616, for example) and undertook the Christianization of the north.

Zacatecas reached its height in the 18th century. Even though considerable amounts of the ore mined were shipped to the motherland to fill the crown's coffers, enough wealth remained in the city to allow the leading families and the monastic orders to build to their heart's content.

From 1810 to 1905, coins, primarily silver ones, were struck in the city's own mint. Official records show that silver to the value of 350 million silver pesos, an unimaginable sum in terms of today's money, passed through the mint in those years.

During this century and up until about 1970, the city experienced a period of stagnation (especially noticeable in the field of construction) accompanied by a return to its traditional functions as a seat of administration, a centre for the surrounding mining industry, an educational centre, a garrison town, a stop along the route from El Paso to Mexico City, and the centre of a small tourist industry.

One of the greatest attractions Zacatecas has to offer is its cityscape and its **unique location,** the beauty of which can be best appreciated when viewed from the Cerro de la Bufa. This hill, along with the other two which encircle Zacatecas, is illuminated at night, creating a picturesque backdrop for the dark silhouette of the city.

Due to its position in the hills, Zacatecas has an irregular street plan (the so-called "plato roto plan"). While it shares this feature with other mining towns such as Taxco and Guanajuato, the city must seem quite confusing to Mexicans from other areas who are used to the checkerboard layout of most of their cities. Furthermore, Zacatecas does not have a main square or "Zócalo" as most Mexican cities do. Instead, its nucleus, which contains a high concentration of mostly one-storey or two-storey buildings with thick walls that shield from the heat and the cold, has a roughly triangular shape formed by Benito Juàrez Street in the south, by Zamora, Aldama, Tacuba and Hidalgo Streets in the east and by Galeana Street in the west. Benito Juàrez, which runs in a roughly east-westerly direction, contains the city's covered market, the telephone and telegraph office, a number of banks, and several hotels and restaurants.

The city's points of interest can be found primarily in the vicinity of Hidalgo and Genardo Codina – Miguel Azuza Streets.

Calle Galeana and Calle Hidalgo with their majestic buildings in reddish "cantera" are just two of the many lovely, picturesque streets in Zacatecas.

The city's most impressive structure is certainly the **cathedral.** The richly sculpted façade is probably the most striking example in Mexico of what is called churrigueresque style – even the upper storeys of its two towers are richly ornamented. This imposing church located on Hidalgo Square was built between 1730 and 1760 – its almost overly opulent facade is evidence of the **wealth and artistic sense** of the city (Zacatecas' silver mines were among the viceroy's most productive). The cathedral's cupola was remodelled in 1836 after the one in the church of Maria de Loreto in Mexico City.

It may be hard to believe, but the ornamental masonry on the cathedral's imposing facade has never been finished. According to the story, the artisan responsible was condemned to death for a crime he had indeed committed, but was given a suspended sentence until he could finish the work....

Facing the cathedral is the **Palacio del Gobierno** (the state government building) which dates from the 18th century. Calle Veyna begins here and leads uphill to the church of **Santo Domingo.** Built between 1746 and 1759 by the Jesuits, the church has a decorative baroque façade. In front of it stands a fountain surrounded by a wide, horseshoe-shaped double staircase which leads to the entrance. The church is shaped like a Latin cross with a nave and two aisles and a cupola over the altar. The altars decorated with gold leaf in churrigueresque style are not its only art treasures: the sacristy contains paintings depicting the passion of Christ by the 18th-century painter Francisco Antonio Vallejo.

Next to the church on the small **Plaza de Santo Domingo** stands the former Jesuit college to which the church originally belonged. Through a portal you can enter the beautiful cloister of the college.

Other points of interest in Zacatecas include the **Plaza Miguel Auza** with its palatial buildings with wrought-iron embellishments, the little **Jardin Juárez** and its surrounding buildings, the **Portal de las Rosales** in Calle Allende, a long shopping gallery, and **Calle Tacuba** with its pretty colonial houses.

Another of the city's impressive structures is the **Aqueducto del Cubo.** Built in the late 18th/early 19th centuries, the aqueduct is almost 2 km (over a mile) long and spans the southern arterial road of the city, the Calzada Gonzales, in a series of arches.

Just before the aqueduct, near a small park on the right-hand side of Calzada Gonzales as you head out of town, you'll find the tourist office of the state of Zacatecas. From the park, a footpath leads the few hundred yards to the **abandoned mine "El Eden"** which is now open to the public.

The Convent of Our Lady of Guadalupe in the village of Guadalupe, about 7 km (4 miles) east of Zacatecas, is not only an architectural attraction in itself but also contains a remarkable collection of paintings mainly from the 17th and 18th centuries.

From August 27 to 31, an **annual festival** takes place at Cerro de la Bufa. On this occasion, the "Morisma", a theatrical dance based on the "legendary battle fought by Charlemagne and the twelve princes of France against the Saracens under their leader Mohammed" is performed. A symbolic battle of Christians against Moors – one based on legend and not on fact.

Religious celebrations take place primarily at the end of the year (December 31).

Typical **Zacatecan dances** include the "barreteros", the "diablo verde" (green devil) and the dance of the "gorgoros" which is accompanied by rhythmic foot stamping ("zapateado"). *(Schmidt)*

La Quemada/Chicomoztoc

From Zacatecas, it is "only" 610 km (340 miles) to Mexico City by the most direct route, but the 320 km (200-mile) scenic detour to Guadalajara shouldn't be missed. Fifty kilometres (30 miles) south of Zacatecas along the route to Guadalajara lie the ruins of the fortified city of La Quemada, built in terraces on a ridge. A paved road leads up to a parking lot and a guard house which also contains a small museum. The site's Indian name, Chicomoztoc, means "seven caves" and alludes to the legendary home of the Mexica in Aztec mythology. This allusion is unfounded, however, as the names were given to the site at a later time. Its original name is, as is so often the case, unknown.

The site was known to the Spaniards as early as in the 16th century; they mentioned it in a set of directions to the silver mines at Zacatecas. Its architecture and the ceramics found indicate that it is older than the site at Chalchihuites. Founded during the height of Classic Teotihuacán about the middle of the 1st century A. D., it was still inhabited at the time of Toltec domination of the central highlands (until about A. D. 1200). Elements such as sunken colonnaded courtyards are borrowings from Teotihuacán, while the temple platforms were obviously Toltec.

From the parking lot, you must proceed uphill on foot. A "palace" constructed of rough-hewn stone without the use of mortar, and surrounded by a wall, rises up from the first terrace. Courtyards and thick pillar stumps indicate that this functioned as a refuge for the people of the area. An avenue leads west from the foot of the fortress to a steep and pointed pyramid. At its summit, there is a platform which contained an altar of some sort of which only traces remain. South of the pyramid, moving uphill, we find great retaining walls which must have offered the people protection and defence against enemy attacks. Here, there are also ruins of dwellings and pyramids.

Due to the heat and the difficult terrain, the climb up to this site should only be undertaken after careful consideration.

From here, Highway 54 continues on to Mexico's second-largest city, Guadalajara. Towards the end of this 270 km (167-mile) stretch, the highway winds its way downhill and into the plain where the city – considered to be the loveliest of Mexico's big cities – is located.

(Thieme)

Chihuahua-Pacifico

The railway line which runs through the wild mountains of the Sierra Madre and along the majestic Copper Canyon is not only one of the most exciting and scenic railways in the world, but also represents a technical achievement of the first order.

The construction of the 653 km (405 mile) long track began in 1898. By 1912, only the mountain pass at Creel (elevation 2,500 m/8,200 ft) had been reached. During the confusion of the revolutionary years. construction was halted and the work dragged on for decades. The most difficult stretch was begun in 1952, and it took nine years to complete those last 100 miles. The engineers had to struggle here with 86 tunnels and 39 bridges through the mountainous terrain before reaching the Pacific coast at Topolobampo/Los Mochis, the end of the line.

The trip today takes about 13 hours; the trains run in both directions on a single-track line. While there are daily departures, it is best to take the "Vista", a train with comfortable Pullman cars, a dining car and sight-seeing car. It leaves Chihuahua on Mondays, Tuesdays, Thursdays and Saturdays at 8.00 am and Los Mochis on Tuesdays, Wednesdays, Fridays, Saturdays and Sundays at 9.00 am.

From **Chihuahua,** the train runs along flat terrain until it gets to **Cuauhtémoc,** where it begins winding its way up the sierra (some ascents are so steep that the train has to back up first to manage them). In the late afternoon, the train reaches **Creel,** a small town, but nevertheless the most important in the region. At the next station, **La Divisadero,** the train makes a 20-minute stop to give the passengers a chance to take in the beautiful panoramic view of the Copper Canyon – as spectacular a sight as the Grand Canyon in Arizona. From here, the train continues along a scenic but hair-raising route down to the Pacific coast. The drop in altitude is accompanied by a marked rise in temperature and humidity. At around 7.00 pm, the train reaches **Los Mochis.**

It is probably best, however, not to try to cover the entire distance in one day, but instead, to do it in four day's time. A two-day stop-over in Creel serves to intensify the experience of the countryside, and gives you the opportunity to get to know the area well. In Creel, there are a number of hotels which cater to foreign tourists, but the nicest place to stay is definitely the Copper Canyon Lodge, a log cabin inn with comfortable rooms (but no electricity – in keeping with its solitary, tranquil setting) located about 40 minutes from Creel near the entrance to the canyon.

Hotels in and around Creel itself offer organized tours into the surrounding countryside. A day-long excursion can be made through the majestic, unspoilt Sierra Madre, and into the famous **Copper Canyon** – a treat for those interested in geology. A trip to **La Bufa,** site of an old silver mine (prospecting still goes on here), is also to be recommended. You can see die-hards panning for gold in a stream – reputedly with little success. The trip to the waterfalls of **Basaseáchic** is also lovely.

The town of Creel and the vicinity are inhabited by large numbers of Tarahumara Indians, the native people of this region. The Tarahumara are easily recognizable, whether dressed in their traditional long, white cotton shirts and bright red headbands, or in blue jeans, as is often the case nowadays. Up until recently, this was a cave-dwelling people – true descendants of the ancient cliff dwellers. Today, there are still a few families in out-of-the-way places living in large, comfortable cave dwellings, but those who live near town gave up their caves for houses or huts long ago. Not far from Creel, there is an "inhabited" cave which is open to the public. The occupants, however, are only there as tourist attractions; they sell arts and crafts and handmade violins, a speciality of the Tarahumaras, and they collect tips from photographers. Although it resembles a museum in many ways, the cave is still well worth visiting.

At noontime on the second day you can continue on to the Pacific coast – or head back towards Chihuahua.

If you chose to do the former, once at the coast, Los Mochis could be your point of departure for a trip south via Culiacán to the seaside resort of Mazatlán, and from there either north to Durango or southwards via Tepic to Guadalajara. From Topolobampo, you could head for Baja California via the ferry to La Paz.

Highway 15 along the Pacific coast is a gateway to Mexico for Americans coming either from California (via Tijuana or Mexicali) or from Arizona (via Nogales). For the most part, the highway runs along the coast through rather rough terrain. The foothills of the Sierra Madre often extend right down to th coast and the strip of land between the mountains and the often marshy littoral zone is narrow. Bays, lagoons, peninsulas and islands characterize this stretch of coastline. Attractive beaches and touristic infrastructure are rare.

This obviously does not apply to the resort of **Mazatlán,** which can be reached in an easy day's drive from Los Mochis. The resort consists of a small fishing town with a ferry port and a collection of hotels and restaurants along an 8 km (5 mile) long "costera" or coastal road. The beach is clean and pleasant; the water clear and calm – there is no surf and only in a few areas are there high waves. The water is shallow – you can wade out a good distance before losing ground under your feet. Mazatlán is a quiet resort which can be recommended wholeheartedly to families with small children. Those who want nightlife after a day at the beach are better off in Acapulco!

Culiacán, the capital of the state of Sinaloa, hasn't a great deal to offer the visitor and, as the distance between Los Mochos and Mazatlán can easily be covered in a day, will hardly come into question as a stopover point.

From the town of **Tepic,** located on the road from Mazatlán to Guadalajara, day trips can be made by sportsplane into the nearby territory of the Huichol, an Indian people who live in tribes in the wild terrain surrounding the border between the states of Nayarit and Jalisco. The main Indian communities all have landing strips, but not all of these are accessible to tourists at all times of the year. Especially during periods of local celebrations, the Huichol do not welcome outside visitors. The organizers of the charter flights in Tepic are familiar with Huichol customs, however, and only fly tourists to communities which may currently be visited. Pilots may be contracted through the hotels and travel agents in Tepic.

The Huichol are obviously the heirs of an ancient cultural tradition, but the question is, which one? According to what is currently known about them, it can be said that they come from the same cultural background as the Chalchihuites civilization, but that they separated from that group and migrated to the lowlands of the western Sierra de Nayarit. Their ethnography and customs have been the object of study since the beginning of this century.

Although these people live in villages, they can almost be described as nomads due to an important cultural and religious tradition which is still practised today: the wanderings or "pilgrimages" which the Huichol undertake on foot over distances of anything between 200 and 400 km (125–250 miles). Alone or in small groups, they visit holy places – mountain caves, lakes or streams which have a magical function – bearing offerings to be placed before them. Of course, these wanderings have a long tradition, but the Huichol are not prepared to divulge any information about it.

Many of these wanderings are undertaken in order to collect peyote (or mescal) buttons from the cactus Lophophora williamsii. The button-like tubercles of this rare cactus, difficult to find because of its perfect adjustment to the environment, contain mescaline which, as a hallucinogen, figures importantly in Huichol rituals. Under the influence of the drug, the Indians perform rites the meaning of which is known only to themselves. And they create artwork which has found acclaim on the art market and now fetches high prices. It is obvious that while performing these rites, the people do not welcome outside observers.

However, the fact that they have virtually no source of cash income forces them to put aside their xenophobia at least occasionally and invite tourists into their villages in the hope that they will buy their paintings, their weavings and their ceramics. These villages, most of which can be reached by plane, are located near Acaponeta, Sta. Caterina and Sta. Teresa. From Tepic, State Highway ("carretera") 15 takes you to Guadalajara, 230 km (143 miles) away. From there, you could also fly into Huichol territory, but the flight route is longer and, therefore, more expensive. *(Thieme)*

The West

At a distance of 40 km (25 miles) from Guadalajara, Highway 54 crosses the state line between Zacatecas and Jalisco, and, with that, the imaginary line between north and west Mexico. The other western states (and their capitals) are: Nayarit (Tepic) and Colima (Colima) which border on the coast, and Michoacán (Morelia) and Guanajuato (Guanajuato) which border on the central highlands.

Guadalajara

Guadalajara is the capital of Jalisco and Mexico's second most important commercial and political centre. In terms of industry, it ranks third behind Monterrey.

The city has a rich cultural tradition, numerous places of historical interest and institutions of higher education (such as the University of Jalisco). The lovely **colonial city,** its cultural attractions and the touristic attractions in the vicinity (Tonalá, Tlaquepaque, Lago de Chapala) draw visitors from Mexico as well as from abroad. All visitors will find a wide range of good to first-class hotels and restaurants.

Guadalajara lies at an altitude of 1,500 m (5,000 ft) in the wide, flat basin of the Valle de Atemjac. The history of the founding of this city is rather eventful. First, the name Nuño Beltrán de Guzmán comes up. He was the Spanish conquistador who set out to conquer the northwest on his own, and who went down in history as one of the most ruthless and cruel of the conquistadores. It was Guzmán who founded the original settlement. This was moved twice to protect it from Indian attack – first, to Tonalá, and finally to its present location.

The actual founder of Guadalajara, however, was Cristóbal de Oñate. He had the city built in 1542. The Spanish crown had already granted it its city charter and coat of arms in 1539, and in 1560, it became the capital of Nueva Galicia. The city continued to grow and eventually became the seat of an "audiencia", directly responsible to the Spanish crown.

In 1810, Guadalajara joined the Mexican **independence movement** led by the parish priests Hidalgo and Morelos. Following the defeat at Aculco, Hidalgo retreated to Guadalajara and organized a government opposed to the Conservatives and Royalists who supported Spain, but the Royalists soon captured the city.

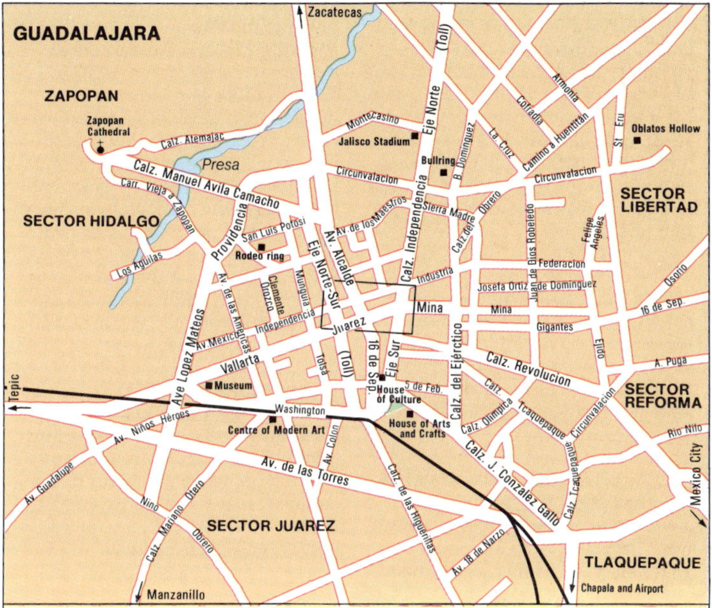
GUADALAJARA
ZAPOPAN
Zapopan Cathedral
Calz. Atemajac
Presa
Calz. Manuel Avila Camacho
Carr. Vieja a Zapopan
SECTOR HIDALGO
Los Aguilas
Providencia
San Luis Potosi
Rodeo ring
Zacatecas
Montecasino
Jalisco Stadium
Eje Norte
(Toll)
Bullring
Circunvalacion
Av. de los Maestros
Sierra Madre
Calz. Independencia
B. Dominguez
La Cruz
Cofradia
Armonia
Camino a Huentitán
St. Eru
Oblatos Hollow
SECTOR LIBERTAD
Obrero
Calz. del Obrero
Juan de Dios Robeledo
Felipe Angeles
Federacion
Josefa Ortiz de Dominguez
Industria
Mina
Gigantes
16 de Sep.
Osorio
Av. Alcalde
Eje Norte-Sur
Munguia
Clemente Orozco
Av. de las Americas
Independencia
Juarez
Av. Mexico
Ave Lopez Mateos
Vallarta
Tolsá
16 de Sep.
Eje Sur
Calz. del Ejercito
Ejido
Calz. Revolucion
A. Puga
SECTOR REFORMA
Tepic
Museum
House of Culture
5 de Feb.
Washington
House of Arts and Crafts
Calz. Olimpica
Tlaquepaque
Circunvalacion
Rio Nilo
Av. Niños Héroes
Centre of Modern Art
Av. Colon
Calz. J. Gonzalez Gallo
Calz. Tlaquepaque
Mexico City
Av. Guadalupe
Av. de las Torres
Calz. de las Higuerillas
Nino Obrero
Calz. Mariano Otero
SECTOR JUAREZ
Av. 18 de Marzo
TLAQUEPAQUE
Manzanillo
Chapala and Airport

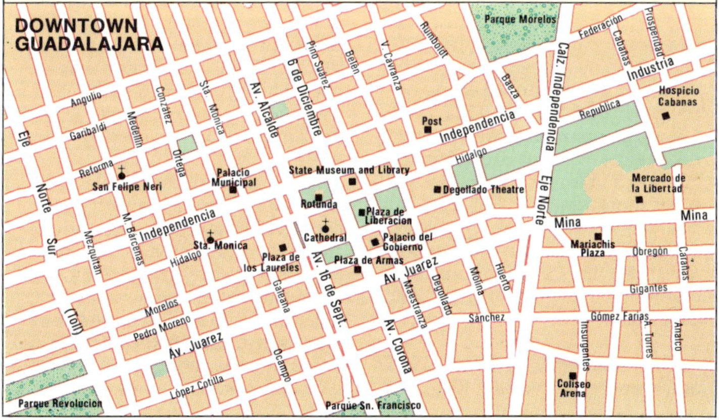
DOWNTOWN GUADALAJARA
Parque Morelos
Rumboldt
Federación
Cabañas
Prosperidad
Industria
Calz. Independencia
Pino Suárez
Belén
V. Carranza
Baeza
Hospicio Cabanas
Angulio
Conzález
Sta. Mónica
Av. Alcalde
6 de Diciembre
Republica
Garibaldi
Medellín
Post
Independencia
Eje Norte
Reforma
Ortega
Hidalgo
San Felipe Neri
Palacio Municipal
State Museum and Library
Degollado Theatre
Mercado de la Libertad
Rotunda
Plaza de Liberación
Mina
Norte
Independencia
Cathedral
Palacio del Gobierno
Mariachis Plaza
Obregón
Cañas
Sur
Mezquitán
M. Bárcenas
Sta. Monica
Hidalgo
Plaza de los Laureles
Av. 16 de Sept.
Plaza de Armas
Av. Juarez
Degollado
Molina
Huerto
Gigantes
Galeana
Maestranza
Sánchez
Gómez Farias
A. Torres
Analco
(Toll)
Morelos
Pedro Moreno
Av. Juarez
Av. Corona
Insurgentes
Ocampo
López Cotilla
Coliseo Arena
Parque Revolucion
Parque Sn. Francisco

Following the declaration of Mexican independence (in 1821), Guadalajara became the capital of the state of Jalisco (1823). The city was again the site of combat between the years 1856 and 1858. From 1863 to 1866, it housed a garrison of French occupational troops sent by Napoleon III to support the monarchy set up by him.

The city's main points of interest are centred about the main square, the **Plaza de Armas,** which is surrounded by the cathedral and sagrario, the Palacio del Gobierno del Estado de Jalisco (the seat of the state government) and two lovely shopping arcades.

Completed in 1774, the **Palacio del Gobierno** still serves as the state capitol (during a short interim from February 14 to March 19, 1858, it served as the seat of the federal government under Benito Juárez). The building, whose architecture unites classic and churrigueresque elements, possesses a beautiful two-storey patio whose levels are connected by a grand staircase. The Palacio contains three **murals** by the celebrated Mexican artist **José Clemente Orozco.** One of them depicts the figure of Padre Miguel Hidalgo in glorified dimensions; another mural, entitled "Political Circus", depicts the people's eternal struggle for freedom. The mural in the Hall of the Legislature depicts celebrated figures in Mexican political history.

The **cathedral,** begun in 1558 and consecrated in 1616, is located north of the Plaza de Armas. The structure represents a text-book example of ecclecticism: besides Gothic arches and baroque ornamentation, it also displays features of classic architecture and of a style known as "Mudejar". Of the many paintings inside (most of which can be found in the cathedral's auxiliary chapels), two deserve special mention: the painting entitled "La Purisima", located over the entrance to the sacristy, is attributed to Murillo; in the sacristy itself is an oil painting by Cristóbal de Villapando.

West of the cathedral lies the **Plaza de los Laureles,** a small, almost quadratic square graced with a fountain and laurel trees, from which it got its name. North of the square stands the Municipal Palace **(Palacio Municipal),** a relatively new colonial-style building.

In the centre of the Plaza de la Rotunda east of the Municipal Palace stands the **Rotunda de los Hombres Illustres,** a temple-like monument to Mexicans from the worlds of politics, culture and science who have earned themselves a place among the "illustrious". There are statues of certain leading figures.

A beautiful building with a two-level patio dating from the 17th century stands on the other side of the Plaza de la Rotunda from the Municipal Palace. This is the former Seminario de San José, which now houses the State Museum **(Museo del Estado de Jalisco).** One of its attractive, tree-filled gardens contains statues, pieces salvaged from demolished buildings of architectural importance, and a number of cannons. The museum's ground floor contains a collection of paintings by leading Mexican artists of the last four centuries. Works by members of the famous artist families of Echave and Juárez, by Juan Correa, Cristóbal de Villapando, José de Ibarra, Miguel Cabrera and a recent mural by José Guadalupe Zuno can be admired here.

Between Morelos and Hidalgo Streets, opposite the Plaza de la Liberación, stands the Degollado Theatre **(Teatro Degollado),** built in 1865 during the reign of the Habsburg Emperor Maximilian. The cupola of this impressive neo-classic structure is decorated with a fresco by Gerardo Suarez depicting themes from the 4th canto of Dante's "Divine Comedy". Two former monastery churches are located near the theatre: **San Agustin** with its baroque façade and **Santa Maria de Gracia,** the sacristy of which is worth visiting. The Palace of Justice **(Palacio de Justicia)** with its plateresque ornamentation is also nearby.

The church of San Francisco and the Plaza San Francisco lie south of this central zone, at the intersection of Priscilliano Sanchez and Avenida 16 de Septiembre near **Parque San Francisco** with its laurel trees and cast-iron benches. San Francisco, likewise a former monastery church, was built in baroque style in 1684 upon the foundation of an even older church.

Other places of interest can be found in the southern and eastern parts of the city. Take Av. Morelos past the Calzada Independencia and continue about 150 yards on Calle D. Rodriguez to the **Mercado de la Libertad.** This two-storeyed covered market offers the usual market wares and probably the largest selection of **handicrafts** to be found in Mexico. Basketry, ceramics from the outlying villages of Tlaquepaque and Tonalá, and a wealth of leather goods are offered for sale. Leather working is a traditional craft in this region – Guadalajara is one of the centres of the Mexican shoe industry.

From the market, take Cabañas Street to the Cabañas Orphanage **(Hospicio Cabañas),** a massive neo-classic structure built after 1801. Commissioned by Archbishop Ruíz de Cabañas, and planned and executed under the supervision of Manuel Tolsa, the leading architect of the time, it contains no less than 23 courtyards. Facing the main courtyard, there is a chapel (no longer used as such) the walls of which are covered with murals painted by José Clemente Orozco in 1939. Considered to be his masterpiece, this work features a mingling of Christian, antique and Indian religious elements and the use of a sometimes mystic visual imagery.

The **Plaza de los Mariachis,** actually a little street lined with arcades and cafés where one can sit and listen to the mariachi bands, lies directly south of the Mercado de la

Libertad. The musicians wear the typical costumes embellished with embroidery and studs (which, according to tradition, must be of pure silver).

If you proceed southwards along the Calzada Independencia, you will soon come to the enormous park and exhibition grounds known as the **Parque Agua Azul,** where local arts and crafts fairs and exhibitions of industrial products manufactured in the state of Jalisco are held at various times of the year.

The park, occupying land which used to be a railway yard, also contains an experimental theatre and the **Casa de Artesanías del Estado de Jalisco** – a permanent exhibition of Jaliscan handicrafts. If you are interested in the genuine and the unique, you should come here to buy.

Sales exhibitions featuring ceramics and other handicrafts are also held in **Tlaquepaque,** 6 km (less than 4 miles) to the south. Pottery and papier-mâché workshops and exhibitions can be visited in Tonalá, located about 14.5 km (9 miles) west of Guadalajara centre (connections by bus from Tlaquepaque).

The canyon of the **Rio Grande de Santiago** – more than 3,000 ft across and over 1,000 ft deep – is located 16 km (10 miles) to the north of the centre of Guadalajara.

Buses leave regularly from the "Central Camionera" in Guadalajara heading for the **Lago de Chapala** 51 km (32 miles) south of the city. Here you can spend a leisurely afternoon boating on the lake or relaxing on the shore.

After Mexico City, Guadalajara has the best system of traffic communications in all of Mexico. As a main junction for traffic between north and central Mexico, it is a stop on most bus routes. Its train station is the most important along the Mexico City-Mexicali-Tijuana-U. S. A. route and also serves rail traffic along the Mexico City–Ciudad Juárez route. *(Schmidt)*

Those who are in a hurry to get from Guadalajara to the capital can take State Highway 90/110 to Irapuato and from there, the motorway which leads via Celaya and Querétaro to Mexico City. The 356 km (220 mile) stretch can easily be accomplished in half a day.

Those who aren't in such a hurry, however, may like to consider making the trip in three days with one overnight stop on Lake Pátzcuaro and then two nights in Guanajuato.

The scenic route from Guadalajara to Lake Pátzcuaro takes you first to Lake Chapala (arriving there at Chapala itself), along the lake's eastern bank to Ocotlán (where there is a 16th century cloister) and then onto Zamora (in Michoacán state).

Lake Pátzcuaro

From Zamora, 119 km (74 miles) along good roads will bring you to Lake Pátzcuaro, considered by many to be Mexico's most beautiful lake. The Indian fishermen who fish its waters with "butterfly nets" from strange-looking boats are well-known in Mexico. They live in tiny villages around the lake which, because of its inaccessibility, has managed to remain largely unspoiled. Even the main village of Pátzcuaro, which can accommodate visitors, has managed to maintain its rural-colonial atmosphere despite the presence of hotels, restaurants and arts-and-crafts shops. Those who stay the night here should arrange through the hotel to take a boat trip on the lake the next morning.

From the lake it's well worthwhile making an excursion to Tzintzuntzan, the "Place of the Hummingbirds", one of the few archaeological sites with monumental architecture in this region. A magnificent view of the lake can be enjoyed from Cerro Yahuarato, which rises up over the village of Tzintzuntzan. A giant raised platform which once supported the temples of the former ceremonial centre can be found on the slope of the hill. Twelve such "yacatas" – a rectangular platform connected with a round platform and formerly surmounted by a temple – have been reconstructed so far.

From what is known about the religion of the Purepechas (or Tarascan Indians), it can be assumed that the cult of the elements and natural phenomena (the sun, moon, water and wind) existed here. Near one of the yacatas, graves containing objects made of precious metals

have been found, suggesting that the followers of this cult were buried here.

Ihuatzio, the "Place of the Coyote" lies 14 km (8.5 miles) to the east. This site has not been fully unearthed yet but an avenue and two temple platforms can be clearly made out.

Morelia

From Lake Pátzcuaro, it's another 60 km (37 miles) to Morelia, the capital of the state of Michoacán. This well-preserved colonial town, whose nucleus about the Plaza de Armas has been declared a national monument (as have the old centres of Taxco and other towns), is an ideal place to spend an extra night for travellers who are in no hurry. The cathedral and the former seat of the Spanish government are excellent examples of the 17th-century churrigueresque baroque style.

One of the country's most scenic but at the same time most difficult roads, the Ruta de Mil Cumbres, "road of a thousand hills", leads from here through the rising foothills of the Sierra Madre Occidental and into the central Mexican plateau. The state highway passes through Tuxpan (mineral springs) and Toluca before reaching Mexico City, 310 km (192 miles) away.

Another road leads northeast from Guadalajara to Guanajuato, capital of the state of the same name. In Irapuato, turn north on State Highway 45 to Aguascalientes. To the west lies the Cubilete (dice cup), a ridge which marks the centre of Mexico – on its summit stands a huge statue of Christ with arms outstretched in a sign of blessing the land. From here, it is 70 km (43 miles) to Guanajuato.

(Thieme)

Guanajuato

Guanajuato is the capital and centre of administration of the state of the same name (abbreviated Gto.). During colonial times, it was a centre of silver mining; today, it is still a centre for the mining of ores containing important metals such as silver and zinc.

With its unique position (at the bottom of a narrow canyon), its attractive cityscape and its internationally known cultural events ("Entremeses Cervantinos", a drama festival), Guanajuato is also a centre of tourism in Mexico.

The town lies in the narrow Cañada del Marfil or Marble Canyon within the Cordillera de Guanajuato, a small chain of mountains ranging in height from 2,500 m (8,200 ft) in the west to 2,900 m (9,500 ft) in the north. The craggy, treeless peaks of the Cordillera form an imposing backdrop to the town.

The Marble Canyon is a narrow, winding, dried-out river bed which extends over a length of approximately 8 km (5 miles) and is between 500 m and 800 m wide (between 1,640 ft and 2,625 ft). Its steep walls are between 120 m and 140 m in height (between 394 ft and 460 ft) and cut deep into a sparsely-vegetated, high plateau which is, in turn, surmounted by the craggy peaks of the Cordillera de Guanajuato.

Due to the peculiarities of the topography, Guanajuato has an irregular layout which stands in sharp contrast to the checkerboard design of most of Mexico's larger towns and cities. The so-called "plato roto plan" or "broken plate plan" is characterized by winding streets and alleys and a large number of cul-de-sacs and small squares.

The upper boundary of the town is formed by the **Ruta Escenica,** the "scenic road". This affords a good view of the city and the plateau. It can be reached via two steep access roads at the western and eastern extremities of Guanajuato – the exit to the east lies near the Presa de la Olla, a reservoir.

From up above, you can enjoy an excellent view of the town with its narrow, winding streets and its colonial buildings, many of which have lovely old patios. The best panoramic view can be had from the **Monumento a Pipila** located on the "ruta escenica". The monument – a giant, gold-plated figure of a man hurling a torch – stands in memory of Juan José de los Reyes Amaro, a martyr of the Mexican war of independence (1810–1821). Known as "Pipila", it was Amaro who blasted open the heavy gates of the Alhóndiga de Granaditas, thus making possible its capture by the "insurgentes".

The name Guanajuato is derived from "Cuanaxhuata" which means "Hill of the Frogs". This was the name the Purepecha (also called Tarascans) gave to a small Otomí settlement which came under their domination. The name was later corrupted to Quanachuato and then became Guanajuato.

The valley was conquered in 1529 by the conquistador Nuño Beltram de Guzmán. The small valley settlement, originally no more than a village, quickly grew in size and importance after Juan de Rayas and other miners discovered silver in the Cordillera de Guanajuato in 1548. "Veta Madre", one of the richest silver ore mines in the world, furnished silver to the value of some 280 million pesos. The mines' high productivity encouraged the rapid growth of the town originally known as Santa Fe de Guanajuato. The population of this mining and administrative centre (it was the seat of one of the twelve intendancies set up by the Spanish government in colonial Mexico) in fact reached 80,000 (today it stands at 36,000). The wealth of the mine owners and the prosperity of the middle class is reflected in the buildings which were constructed at the time and in the works of art with which they are embellished.

At the beginning of the 19th century, Guanajuato played an important role in Mexico's war of independence. With the help of the miner Juan José de los Reyes Amaro ("Pipila"), the Insurgents were able to drive the Conservatives from their main stronghold, the Alhóndiga de Granaditas, a massive grain storehouse turned into a fortress and prison in Guanajuato's old quarter.

Their victory was short-lived, however, for the Royalists under General Calleja soon advanced upon the city. After the initial defeat of the "insurgentes" at the hands of the Spanish troops, the heads of their executed leaders (men such as Padre Miguel Hidalgo, Allende, Jiménez and Aldama) were sent to Guanajuato and displayed on the wall of the Alhóndiga. There they remained until 1821 when independence was finally achieved. Today the Alhóndiga is a national monument and museum.

In 1858, Guanajuato was made the seat of the Mexican federal government for one month when President Benito Juárez sought refuge there, thus foiling the attempt on the part of General Comonfort to overthrow the government. Today, the town has little national significance save as a centre for the mining of copper, lead, mercury and cobalt and as a tourist attraction.

Guanajuato's main points of interest include its attractive location, its lovely streets and squares and its wealth of beautiful buildings and the valuable works of art contained inside.

Of its streets, the **Calle Subterranea,** or "underground street", deserves special mention. It winds its way in an east-westerly direction following the course of the river which once flowed through the Cañada de Marfil. The waters of this river (which was drained to allow for the construction of the road) now collect in the Presa de la Olla ("cooking pot reservoir") and are fed into the town through an underground canal.

One of Guanajuato's focal points is its Zócalo, the **Plaza de la Unión.** This is a park shaped like a lancehead and surrounded by imposing old hotels with attractive façades. Some of the town's best restaurants and cafés can be found around the park as well. At its centre is a "kiosquito", a small concert pavillion.

The park is dominated by the **Teatro Juárez,** a neo-classic structure begun in 1873 and completed in 1903 featuring high columns, roof sculptures and lovely cast-iron lanterns at its entrance.

Next to the theatre is the church of **San Diego,** which was reconstructed after 1780. Its façade is in plateresque style, a Spanish ornamental style which combines Moorish, late Gothic and early Renaissance elements. ("Plateresco" literally means in the manner of a silversmith.)

If you proceed northwards on Avenida Juárez, you will soon arrive at the Arches **(Los Arcos),** a shopping mall, and at **Plaza de la Paz,** a small square surrounded by a number of imposing buildings.

The most important of these is the **Basilica de Nuestra Señora de Guanajuato** (Our Lady of Guanajuato). This late 18th-century baroque church is on a terrace with a stone balustrade and has a rather remarkable appearance. Facing the square is a façade with two steeples of dissimilar form. The one on the right is massive, square-shaped and has a platform on top, one corner of which is surmounted by a pointed bell tower. The left steeple rises up in three levels to the top, each of these levels embellished with arches.

Two tall, ornamented portals face the square. The church appears expansive due to the chapels on either side. Above the altar is a large dome with a louvre. The interior of the church houses a number of important works of art: the sacristy contains a painting of the Last Supper by Vallejo (1777), and in one of the small chapels there is a wooden statue of Our Lady of Guadalupe which was given to the city in 1557 by King Philip II as a token of his favour. The statue stands on a pedestal made of solid silver.

The Plaza de la Paz also boasts three 18th-century patrician villas: one of these, the **Casa Rul y Valenciana,** was built at the end of the 18th century by the architect Eduardo Tresquerras for the Count of Rul and Valenciana, the owner of the Valenciana silvermine. The German naturalist Alexander von Humboldt stayed here in 1803 during his expeditionary travels in Mexico.

Other buildings on the square include the 18th-century **House of the Count of Pérez Gálvez** and a state government building whose façade was reconstructed in neoclassic style in the 19th century.

Guanajuato's **university,** which despite its age (only 30 years) fits in well with the city's older buildings, can be reached via Alfredo Duques or Ponciano Aguilar Streets.

To the west of the university stands the church known as the **Templo de los Hospitales,** which can be reached via a steep stairway. To the east stands the **La Compañía** church which was built by the Jesuits between 1747 and 1765. This structure has an imposing façade decorated in churrigueresque style. The eastern portal of the church also bears sculptured embellishments. Its most impressive feature, however, is its many-storeyed steeple surmounted by a dome with towering louvre. The steeple has large windows which allow a great deal of light inside.

The birthplace of the Mexican artist **Diego Rivera** is located on Calle Pocitos south of the university.

Also located here is the **House of the Marquesas of San Juan de Rayas.** Built in 1696, it features a large patio and a chapel, the portal of which is decorated in baroque style.

If you continue west, you will arrive at the **Alhóndiga de Granaditas,** the unadorned building with massive walls and few windows which has served many purposes over the years. Built between 1798 and 1803, it originally served as a grain storehouse; later in its history it functioned as a fortress and a prison; now it is a national monument and museum. Two **paintings by Chavez Morado** hang inside. The first of these glorifies the Mexican struggle for independence; the second, painted in 1966, illustrates various elements of the culture of Guanajuato state.

Near the Alhóndiga you will find the picturesque **Plaza San Roque** and the baroque church of the same name. The square contains an open-air stage where performances are held during the Entremeses Cervantinos, Guanajuato's international drama festival. Here as well, you will find the lovely **Jardin Morelos,** a landscaped square which resembles an Andalusian garden.

From the Jardin Morelos, take the Avenida Juárez to the **Mercado Hidalgo,** a fruit and vegetable market. This cantilever steel construction with a vaulted roof and a small clock tower was built towards the end of the 19th century. A "distant cousin" of the famous Parisian market, Les Halles (no longer standing), of the Eiffel Tower and of the Museo del Chopo in Mexico City, the Mercado Hidalgo is one of the few remaining examples of late 19th century industrial architecture in Mexico. In addition to fruits and vegetables, local handicrafts are sold at the market.

One of the interesting attractions found outside the city limits of Guanajuato is the church of **La Valenciana,** recently renovated at great expense. Located about 4 km (2½ miles) north of Guanajuato on the road to Dolores Hidalgo, this structure built of light red "cantera" is a gem of churrigueresque style: it boasts a richly sculpted façade and two tall, slim steeples. Its interior is elaborately decorated as well; especially impressive is the main altar which is embellished in gold leaf.

From the terrace you can enjoy a marvellous view of Guanajuato and the surrounding mountains.

Nearby is the **Valenciana Mine,** a massive, fortress-like structure with high walls. This silver mine had been abandoned for some time but is now once again in operation – it is hoped that new, profitable ore deposits will be found.

Tourists interested in the bizarre might like to visit the "momias" (mummies) at the cemetery in west Guanajuato. To get there, just look for the city bus with the destination "Momias" written across the front – it must be the only one in the world with a destination like that!

In addition to the Entremeses Cervantinos, Guanajuato's annual festival of drama and dance, there are a number of other important local festivals which take place here. The Fiesta de la Presa de la Olla (Festival of the Olla Reservoir) takes place between the 16th and the 24th of June; the Fiesta de la Bufa takes place on July 31st; as in other parts of the country, there are "posadas", festivities and candlelight processions at Christmastide, and colourful parades and celebrations during Holy Week ("Semana Santa").

(Schmidt)

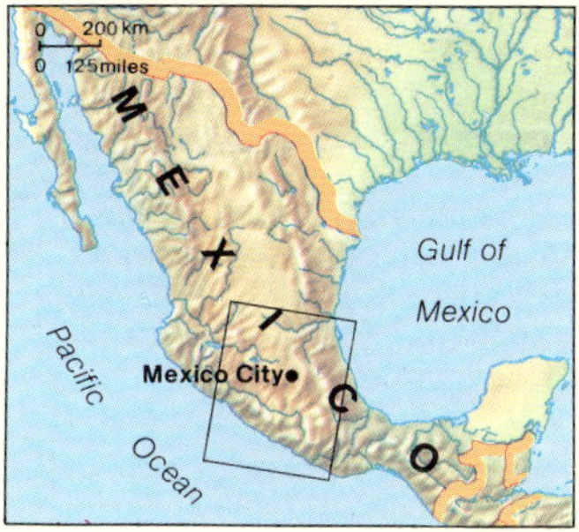

The Central Highlands

The central highlands comprise the vast region which encircles Mexico City. They reach elevations of between 1,300 m and 2,000 m (4,265 ft and 6,560 ft). The states (in brackets their capitals) which make up this region are: Hidalgo (Pachuca) and Querétaro (Querétaro) in the north, the state of México (Toluca) in the west, Morelos (Cuernavaca), Guerrero (Chilpancingo) and Puebla (Puebla) in the south, and Tlaxcala (Tlaxcala), Mexico's smallest state, in the east.

As is the case with Mexico's other regions, the central highlands cannot be defined in terms of a uniform culture or a uniform economic structure or a uniform topography. There is a certain uniformity of climate, however. Conditions here are mild and pleasant to an extent found nowhere else in the country. The towns of Cuautla, Ixtapan de la Sal, Puebla and Cuernavaca are famous for their "eternal springtime".

Tula (Tollan)

This important archaeological site lies a good 100 km (62 miles) north of the capital city in a region known as the "mesa central" in the state of Hidalgo.

The visitor will note immediately that this region has a charm all of its own: its barren, treeless landscape is positively awash with shades of grey (in recent years, these have been enhanced by the dust emitted from the two largest cement factories in the country, the Tolteca and the Cruz Azul plants!).

Tula, the capital of the Toltecs, a people who arrived here in the 10th century, has not yet been fully excavated. Its focal point is the ceremonial square which surrounds the main temple platform dedicated to the God of the Morning Star, Tlahuitzcalpantecutli ("Lord in the House of Dawn").

The excavation site can be entered via the newly-erected museum. The most interesting piece is the chacmool figure which originally stood in the palace next to the Pyramid of the Morning Star.

In front of the ceremonial square is a large ball court carefully laidout in the usual double-T form. On the back of the temple platform is the Snake Wall with its relief images of snake heads facing east and west and clutching human heads between their jaws – a highly symbolic depiction of the planet Venus, the Morning Star. The decorations on the body of the pyramid are also intact: eagles and jaguars, the animals representing the Toltec warrior castes.

Head of one of the atlantes, Pyramid of the Morning Star, Tula

Atop the temple platform stand Tula's best-known works of art: the **atlantes.** These 4.5 m (15 ft) high figures represent eagle warriors and once supported the temple roof.

Teotihuacán

A visit to Mexico City is not complete without a visit to the archaeological site of Teotihuacán, popularly known as **"The Pyramids"** because of its two most conspicuous structures. The site's tongue-twisting name is a Nahuatl (Aztec) word meaning "The Place Where Men Become Gods". Teotihuacán lies only 40 km (25 miles) from the Mexico City limits and is easy to reach from there – the hard part is getting from your downtown hotel to the outskirts of town!

The road leads via La Villa and the shrine of Our Lady of Guadalupe to the motorway heading towards Pachuca/Texpan. With a little luck, you can reach Teotihuacán in just under an hour.

The visitor can enter the archaeological site by any one of three ways: by the main entrance near the Ciudadela, by the entrance near the Pyramid of the Sun or by the entrance near the House of the Quetzalmariposa. The last one is best if you are pressed for time or have little desire to do much walking. For the best and most comprehensive look at the site as a whole, use the entrance near the Ciudadela and walk from there to the House of the Quetzalmariposa.

Teotihuacán was the main centre of the first Classic highland civilization – the civilization which also bears its name. The significance this great intellectual and religious centre had for the development of ancient Mexican cultures cannot be overemphasized – its influence carried as far north as Zacatecas and as far south as the Maya region of the Petén in Guatemala.

Atlantes and Messengers of the Gods

While Toltec culture is generally considered to have been an epigone, an imitator of its predecessors (it adopted architectural forms and other aspects of civilization from previously existing cultures in the Central Highlands), the Toltecs did show considerable individuality in the sphere of architectural sculpture.

We know that for their cult of the God of the Morning Star, whom the Toltecs named "Lord in the House of Dawn", the Toltecs favoured temples in the form of spacious, open halls. This meant that the temple walls were no longer sufficient on their own to support the expansive temple roofs, and that pillars had to be integrated into the buildings. This led to the development of a special kind of architectural sculpture. The famous Tula atlantes (See photos 32+33), colossal pillars in the form of Toltec eagle warriors, supported the temple roof just as the warrior caste of Toltec society supported the state itself. Similar figures were also used by the Toltecs as supports for altar tables (in the Temple of the Warriors at Chichén Itza, for example).

Another fascinating element of architectural sculpture which, with the arrival of the Toltecs, became an integral part of Central Highland culture was the figure of the chacmool. The name comes from modern Maya and basically means "messenger of the gods". The ancient name of this figure has not survived and so we do not know if it actually had the function implied by the modern name. The chacmool represents a warrior-priest reclining with knees bent and arms drawn towards his body, holding a small vessel above his stomach (See photo 25 for an example). He looks towards the sky, as if wishing to carry the sacrificial gifts of mankind to the gods. We can reasonably assume that the chacmool is another manifestation of the Toltec warrior-priest caste as mediator between man and the gods, a caste representing the "pillars" of the state and the world. *(Thieme)*

Unfortunately, however, our knowledge of this culture will always remain limited – just as we will never know Teotihuacán's real name but will have to be content with the name the Aztecs gave to the site. Names like that of the "Ciudadela" (Citadel), the "Pyramid of the Sun" and the "Pyramid of the Moon" are also incorrect but are, at the same time, familiar and convenient and therefore remain.

When you enter the site via the Ciudadela, the entire length of the complex stretches out before you. The so-called **Calle de los Muertos** (Street of the Dead) begins here and extends for a little over one mile past palace compounds, atrium houses and temple platforms to the Pyramid of the Sun and then on to the Pyramid of the Moon at the opposite end.

The **Ciudadela** is certainly one of the most interesting complexes in Teotihuacán. It can be entered via a broad staircase which leads inside into a sunken patio, typical of the architecture of this area and this period. In the middle of the patio is a platform which may have been used for ceremonial dances. At the opposite end of the patio is a flat, squat temple platform with a staircase leading to the top; its façade was painted in fresco, traces of which can still be seen.

If you walk around this façade, you will come to the most important monument found at this site – the façade of another, older pyramid hidden under this first one. Why this masterpiece of the Classic period was later covered over and replaced with an inferior work is unfathomable. The older façade (which can be viewed from a sidewalk surrounding it) is covered with alternating images of the Rain God (called Tláloc by the Aztecs) and the Plumed Serpent, a dragonlike being which, for the Toltecs and Aztecs, symbolized the god Quetzalcoátl. On the basis of this mural, we are now sure of the connection between this pyramid and the God of Water and Rain.

Although the Street of the Dead **(Calle de los muertos)** will probably always be known by that name, recent excavations have shown that it is not a street at all, but a series of sunken courtyards, one right next to the other, leading in a straight line to the Pyramid of the Moon. The purpose and significance of these courtyards is something we can only guess at – no sure knowledge exists.

From the Ciudadela, proceed up the Street of the Dead to the **Pyramid of the Sun.** This is not only one of the most massive structures to have been built in ancient Mexico, but also one of the mightiest to have been built in the ancient world altogether. Its base measures 220 x 225 m (720 x 738 ft), the pyramid towers up some 63 m (206 ft) and has a volume of almost 1 million cubic metres (over 35 million cubic feet).

A double staircase leading to the top of the platform, where a shrine once stood, unites to form a single staircase two-thirds of the way up. Of the shrine, no traces remain, and we have no idea as to which deity this temple was dedicated. The same holds true for the Pyramid of the Moon. It is certain, however, that it was not dedicated to an astral deity, but rather, to the deity of one of the elements. It's a strenuous climb up the stairs, but the view from the summit of the pyramid is worth the effort – especially if you have a camera.

From here, go back to the Street of the Dead and continue towards the Pyramid of the Moon. After about 30 metres, you will notice to your right a colourful fresco, well-preserved thanks to the fact that this too was covered over by a later structure. A jaguar is depicted in brilliant yellow and red; rain and clouds flow from its body – another symbol of the God of Rain. This important element seems to have stood at the centre of the religious concepts of this culture – as the murals on the next building, the House of the Quetzalmariposa, also illustrate.

Located to the left of the Street of the Dead, the **House of the Quetzalmariposa** has two levels. The upper level can be reached via a wide, open stairway leading from the "street". An open courtyard leads to a series of rooms on all four sides of the house, which may have been living quarters for the temple custodians, or storage rooms – obviously, nothing was ever found inside. The pillars in the courtyard are decorated with the motif which gave the building its name: a butterfly-like bird with the long tail feathers of the quetzal. The eyes of the animal were represented by pieces of obsidian.

This motif can be found again in the building's lower level, but this time in well-preserved fresco paintings. The entrance to this level – actually an older structure upon which the upper level was later built – is located at the back of the building. It leads through a labyrinth of patios and chambers.

As was customary in all Mesoamerican cultures, existing structures were not demolished, but rather, covered over. Thanks to this practice, large portions of these older structures have been preserved and archaeologists today are able to unearth traces of two (or more) cultural periods at the same time.

Here below, you can see the original pyramid with the famous frescos on its base: the quetzal bird in green, black, yellow and red with rain flowing from its body – once again, a symbol of the God of Rain.

At the House of the Quetzalmariposa, the Street of the Dead opens up into a wide plaza surrounded by temple platforms, the most imposing of which is the **Pyramid of the Moon.** Measuring some 44 m (144 feet) in height, this is the second-largest structure on the site. It is situated in direct alignment with the Street of the Dead. Only the temple's filler is intact, but archaeologists have managed to reconstruct the façade and the massive staircase, thus offering the visitor an impression of the temple's former splendour.

A visit to this enormous archaeological site should definitely include **Tepantitla** (just beyond the Pyramid of the Sun). Here you can marvel at the most extensive mural created during the Teotihuacán period. The mural, "Tlalocan" represents the paradise of Tláloc, the Rain God, and is painted on the walls of an atrium house. This image of paradise as a "land of plenty", a concept which, as we now know, ori-

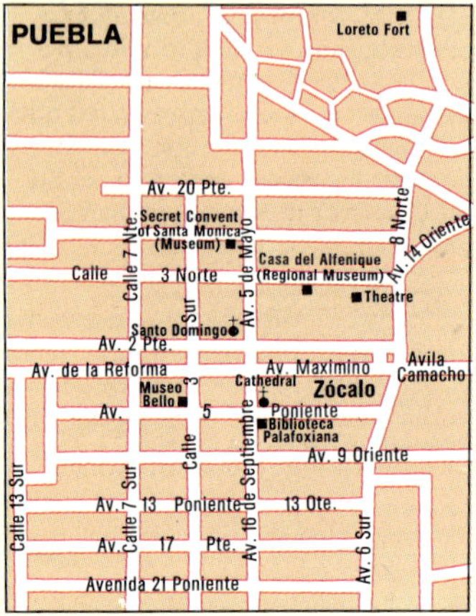

ginated in Teotihuacán, carried through all the way into the Aztec period.

Teotihuacán is well-equipped to cater for the needs of hungry tourists. "Teocalli" is not a house of god as its name might suggest (in Nahuatl, "teotl" means god and "calli" means house) but a place where you can enjoy a good hot buffet lunch. For those who prefer a more romantic setting, there's the "Gruta", a restaurant built in a huge natural cave.

Acolman

On the way back to Mexico City, you can visit Acolman, a restored 16th-century Augustinian monastery which was, at one time, an important centre for the Christianization of the region, and now serves as a museum.

The church is relatively plain, but the double courtyards, the communal rooms and the monks' cells are definitely worth seeing. There is even a bathtub here – the height of luxury!

For the trip back to Mexico City, you'll need to arm yourself with a great deal of patience, for you will inevitably end up in rush hour traffic – a situation which could prove to be quite fascinating, however.

At the beginning of the motorway which heads north to Pachuca, and right next to the cathedral of Our Lady of Guadalupe, there is an arts and crafts centre called Indio Verde where you can find quality handicrafts at reasonable prices.

The motorway which runs southeast from Mexico City to **Puebla,** 136 km (84.5 miles) away, is one of the country's most scenic. From the central plateau, it leads through mountain forests and up to the Rio Frio Pass (3,100 m/over 10,000 ft above sea level), and from there slowly winds its way down to the Valley of Puebla, situated at an elevation of approximately 1,600 m (5,250 ft).

This last stretch of road is the most interesting because it affords you an unforgettable glimpse of **Mexico's highest mountains** – atmospheric conditions permitting, of course.

To the west of the motorway, near San Martin Texmelucan, you can spot Mexico's two most famous volcanos, the Ixtacíhuatl and the Popocatépetl. As you continue towards Puebla, La Malinche comes into view in the east, and with luck, you may even spot Mexico's highest mountain, the Pico de Orizaba (5,700 m/18,700 ft) further off in the distance.

Puebla

Puebla, which has a population which is soon to reach the million mark, is Mexico's fourth-largest city. Like Guanajuato, Morelia and Guadalajara, it is considered to be one of the jewels of colonial Mexico and is high on the list of the "favourite cities" of the Mexican people.

The city was founded in 1531, obviously as a Christian counterpart to the "heathen" city of Cholula, the largest Indian settlement in the area. As a stopover between Veracruz and the capital, Puebla quickly grew in wealth and importance. In particular during the second half of the 17th century, the city blossomed thanks to the activities of the energetic Archbishop Juan de Palafox y Mendoza.

Puebla figures importantly in Mexico's more recent history as well. In 1846, during the Mexican-American War, it was the site of a battle between the Mexican army and American troops under General Scott. And on May 5, 1862, the Mexicans under General Zaragoza defeated the French here and drove them back to Orizaba. In commemoration of this victory, May 5 is observed as a national holiday.

Like most cities founded by the Spanish, Puebla is laid out like a Roman settlement. It is quadratic in form and its streets intersect at right angles. Its centre is formed by the Zócalo, the **Plaza de la Constitución,** a vast, tree-filled square with sidewalks, benches and fountains.

The **cathedral,** the second-largest in the country, stands on this square. Its thick walls and low cupola are concessions to the demands of geography – Puebla lies in a seismic zone. Although the interior is decorated in baroque style, the church is the best example of Renaissance architecture in Mexico. Like the cathedral in Mexico City, it was built over the course of many years – from 1588 to 1649.

On the main shopping street, 5 de Mayo (a pedestrian zone), a few hundred yards from the Zócalo, stands one of Mexico's most famous buildings: the **Dominican church of Santo Domingo.** Built in 1611, it is – like most Dominican churches – extravagantly decorated and richly gilded. Its lateral walls are covered part way up with lovely old tiles. "Azulejos", once a speciality of Puebla and a reason for its fame, were first manufactured here in the 16th century. The altar, made of wood and stucco and covered with a thick layer of gold leaf, contains deep niches in which holy statues have been placed.

Santo Domingo's most spectacular feature, however, is the cruciform **"Rosario"** or Chapel of the Rosary, built in 1690. The ornateness of the

Spanish baroque ornamentation on the walls and the cupola is probably unmatched in the world. In the middle of the cupola, every inch of which is decorated, God the Father can be seen surrounded by heavenly musicians and choirs of angels. A few years ago, the chapel was extensively renovated and freshly gilded so that it now radiates in its former magnificence. Above the altar, the Madonna of the Rosary can be seen in her luxurious robes.

Continue 50 yards up the 5 de Mayo and you'll reach the entrance to the **Puebla market.** A stroll through will give you an idea of the typical consumer goods and food items used in Mexican households. This is a peoples' market – no concessions have been made to the sensibilities of the genteel tourist, so be prepared to hold your breath if you must, and do watch out for pick-pockets.

Walk a short distance along 4 Oriente Street and you will come upon another of Puebla's attractions – the **Parrian, an arts and crafts market** built in the 17th century for this purpose and now restored. Here you can buy woodcarvings, items made of onyx, and Pueblan glazed tiles, all at reasonable prices.

Opposite the other end of the market stands the **Casa del Alfenique,** a magnificent late-18th-century patrician house with a richly decorated and tiled façade. The house serves today as a **regional museum** documenting patrician life in late-colonial Puebla. Furniture, household objects and clothing are on display. Of particular interest is the famous "china poblana", the costume worn by the ladies of this period. It comes in a few variations, each one just as stunning and expensive as the next. Silk and a definite East Asian flavour are unmistakable features of this style of dress.

Further attractions include La Compañía, the Jesuit church near the Palacio Municipal, and the convents of Santa Monica and Santa Catalina. A lovely panoramic view of the city can be enjoyed from Fort Loreto, situated on a hill, the slopes of which are graced with the homes of Puebla's prominent citizenry.

Cholula, which lies about 20 km (12 miles) to the west of Puebla (in the general direction of Oaxaca), can be reached in no time via the "Ruta del Quetzalcoátl", a four-lane motorway built during the administration of President Lopez Portillo. If instead, you take highway 190 in the direction of Atlixco and Oaxaca, you can stop at Acatepec.

Acatepec

Located right on the main road, the small church of Acatepec is a gem of the style known as "Indian baroque". After the fashion of the Rosario of the church of Santo Domingo in Puebla, this late-baroque church is also replete with ornate decorations. Here, however, "educated" artists were not at work, but rather, Indian artisans who knew very little about the rules of perspective and proportion.

Cholula

From Acatepec, a small road takes you northward via Tonantzintla to Cholula. (The church of San Tomás de Tonantzintla features the same ornamentation as that of Acatepec.)

7 km (4 miles) beyond Tonantzintla you'll arrive at Cholula, once a powerful Nahua city and now a small town of approximately 15,000 inhabitants. What immediately strikes the visitor is the mass of churches and chapels in Cholula and vicinity – and there is said to be a temple platform under each one!

In a letter, Cortés informed the Spanish king, Carlos V, that there were "more than 400 temples" here. Now, the people of this area say that there is a church for every day of the year. Whether or not this is true, it does serve as an indication of the former importance of this ancient Mexican ceremonial centre.

The town is dominated by a hill surmounted by a church – the church of Santa Maria de los Remedios. The "hill", however, is actually what remains of a temple pyramid which is not only the largest in Mexico, but, in terms of volume, is the **largest structure built by human hands** in the entire world.

Upon a base which measures 485 x 485 metres (1,591 x 1,591 feet), the "hill" rises up 61 metres (200 feet). In recent years, the pyramid has been the object of extensive study, but the work of excavation is proving to be extremely difficult. Since care must be taken not to damage the church in any way, only the face of the pyramid and the grounds in front of it have been excavated and reconstructed. Much has been learned about the temple's age and the history of its construction by means of tunnels dug from all directions through the body of the structure. At its very centre, a

Clay idol, Highlands' Classic Phase

temple has been found which dates from Classic Teotihuacán. This temple served as the framework upon which other temples were successively built. The final temple dates from the age of the Mexíca.

A portion of this tunnel system is open to the public. It can be entered from the rear of the pyramid and exited towards the front. This journey into the past is an experience not to be missed.

Equally interesting are the grounds in front of the temple where a large number of structures dating from the various phases of ancient Mexican history have been unearthed. Traces of an Olmec-influenced level (older than Teotihuacán) have even been identified.

Cacaxtla

On your way to Puebla or on your way back to Mexico City, you might like to make a side trip to Cacaxtla to see the beautiful murals there. Plan to arrive in the morning, however, because at noon they are draped over to protect them from direct sunlight. To get there, turn off the motorway at **San Martin Texmelucan** and head towards Tlaxcala; after about 25 km (15 miles), you will reach Cacaxtla, situated in the mountains east of Cerro Xochitecatl.

This place, the circumstances under which it was found, and the sensational discoveries made here are all rather characteristic of the situation surrounding archaeological research and excavation work in Mexico today. Although Cacaxtla's existence had been known about for a long time (it is mentioned in the "Historia de Tlaxcala"), it nevertheless remained neglected. Cacaxtla shared this fate with a few dozen other sites in this region – due to the vast number of sites yet to be excavated and the limited amount of money available for archaeological research, the INAH has no idea where to begin – until a graverobber (as is so often the case) brought to light what Cacaxtla had in store. He uncovered a small piece of the fresco which is now celebrated as the sensation of Mexican archaeology.

Cacaxtla's architecture does not date from one single period, but is rather the result of a long history. The oldest sections date from the second half of the 1st century A. D. Defensive structures and retaining walls show that, in the 10th century, the population had to defend itself against the advancing Toltecs.

The focal point of Cacaxtla, though, is the building which contains the **mural paintings.** After a 10-minute walk from the parking lot, you enter the site at its lowest point and ascend a modern wooden stairway to the raised North Plaza. There, the ceremonial centre and the chambers of the high priest were located. The North Plaza consists of a large, open, paved courtyard with a raised "palace" on its eastern side. The palace's lower level consists of a long hall of pillars whose back wall is covered with colourful murals clearly depicting a grim battle scene. The victors and the vanquished can easily be distinguished: the latter have darker skin and wear eagle headdresses. The chieftain stands out in his magnificent attire, his legs bedecked with armadillo skins. Because the lighter-complexioned victors are dressed in jaguar skins, this scene is said to depict a battle between eagle and jaguar knights.

This terminology is misleading, however, for members of these two Toltec warrior castes could not have fought in a battle at Cacaxtla. The similarity in style between this painting and paintings found in the Maya region (particularly at Bonampak) leads experts to believe that this scene was executed in the 8th century A. D. The battle depicted must have had historic significance for the people of Cacaxtla – but today, we can only guess at what this was. Perhaps it dates from the time of their conquest and settlement of this region, or perhaps it was a battle fought later against invaders. The prominent location of the painting shows the importance these people placed upon the event it depicts.

Next to this "Hall of Victory" and a few yards higher up stands another building decorated with frescos. The layout of the interior suggests that it was most likely used either for religious ceremonies or for audiences held by the temple priest. Only the large-format murals in the front section of the building complex are intact, but traces of paintings on other walls indicate that, at one time, murals must have decorated the entire complex.

The most beautiful murals here are probably those which cover the walls to either side of the entrance: slightly larger-than-life figures representing high priests in magnificent array are depicted here. A "jaguar man" and an "eagle man" can be seen standing opposite one another; in their arms they both hold a bundle of arrows, the symbolic significance of which is unknown. The jaguar man stands upon a jaguar serpent while the eagle man stands upon a feathered serpent. Behind him, the quetzal hummingbird hovers over a date glyph; the glyph behind the jaguar man denotes a place and a number. There is, once again, no recognizable connection between these two animal symbols and their use by the Toltecs; the Maya influence is, however, quite obvious.

Just as in the mural in the "Hall of Victory", the eagle man here is darker in complexion than the jaguar man, but whether or not the two murals are related is a matter of conjecture. Perhaps this mural represents a mythic transfiguration of the battle scene. Both figures are surrounded by plants and water symbols – an obvious reference to elemental concepts of fertility. It's a matter of personal taste if you want to connect these two figures with Tláloc and Quetzalcoátl.

In the hall leading into the inner room are two further figures whose clothing and attributes link them to the figures in the front of the building. Their array is less elaborate, however, suggesting that these must be temple attendants.

Scholars may find it difficult to date and interpret the murals of Cacaxtla, but they are certain of one thing – that these are the **best-preserved examples of ancient mural painting in all of Mesoamerica.**

Toluca

Toluca, the capital of the state of Mexico, can be reached by motorway from Mexico City via Chapultepec in about an hour's time. The town lies in a broad, fertile valley at an elevation of 2,670 m (8,761 ft). Famous for its mild climate, Toluca is a favourite retreat for city dwellers who come here to enjoy the town's tranquil, rural atmosphere in their holiday or weekend houses.

Toluca's "zócalo", and the capitol and church which flank it, all date from the 19th century – very little colonial architecture remains. Its most prominent avenue is the Constitución with its "portales", shopping arcades which extend along its entire length.

The town's greatest attraction, however, is its **market,** located near the baroque cloister of El Carmen. This market, one of the largest and most fascinating in all of Mexico, has a strong Indian flavour due to the many Otomí and Matlantzinca people who come here from their villages in the vicinity, all wearing their own local costumes and all bearing their own local specialities: basketry from Lerma and Santa Ana, ceramics and leathergoods from Tenanzingo and the famous woollen blankets (sarapes) from Santiago Tianguistengo. The market is held every day, but on Fridays it is at its busiest and liveliest.

Calixtlahuaca

Calixtlahuaca, an important archaeological site, lies just under 11 km (7 miles) from Toluca on Highway 15. After you pass the village, turn left at the river of the same name. The complex is situated on terraces on a hill and is clearly divided into two districts. It probably existed in pre-Classic times and it displays evidence of the influence of Teotihuacán (which was found all over the central plateau) in all its phases. Later, the Valley of Toluca fell under the sway of the Toltecs.

In ancient times, the region was populated by the Matlantzinca, an Otomí people who were conquered by the Aztecs at the beginning of the 16th century. Relations between the Atzecs and Matlantzinca remained tense thereafter. Because the latter were forced to provide Tenochtitlán with human sacrifices, they often rebelled against their Aztec conquerors – the last time was in 1519.

The circular **temple dedicated to Ehecatl,** Calixtlahuaca's best-preserved structure, dates from this later period (its core, however, dates from the Teotihuacán phase). A palace-like complex of rooms, courtyards and altars dating from Aztec times is also intact. Archaeologists refer to this as a **"calmecac",** a sort of academy for the training of priests and knights. While this is possible, there is no definite evidence to support this theory.

The most interesting structure in the older section of this complex (called **Tecaxic)** is the **Temple of Tláloc,** a pyramid-shaped platform built of black and red volcanic rock ("tezontle") whose outermost layer dates likewise from Aztec times. Nearby lies the cross-shaped **Altar of Skulls,** whose low wall is decorated with 469 stone skulls. Ashes were found inside, showing that this had been a place of sacrifice. The skull rack was probably a sort of "tzompantli", a memorial to the people whose lives were sacrificed during Aztec times.

Teotenango

In ancient times this place was known as Tenanco Tepopollan, and today it is also called **Tenango de Arista.** Located about 30 km (18 miles) south of Toluca on Highway 55 (100 km/62 miles from Mexico City), it is the **largest and oldest archaeological site in the Valley of Toluca.** Its position 200 m (650 feet) above the level of the valley gives it a commanding view of the entire region – and served as a defence against intruders in ancient times. The aspect of defence, however, did not play a role at the time the complex was built by the Teotenanca, a people who lived and worked in the valley. Initially it was meant to serve as a religious and administrative centre and residence for the elite class of priests and artisans. Traces of all the typical structures have been found: temples and palaces flanking immense ceremonial squares, secular buildings and market places.

It is clear that by the year A. D. 1200, this centre had been taken over by the Matlantzinca, who themselves had already been "Toltequized". They rebuilt the entire complex and added ball courts, and they ruled with cruelty and force – as evidenced by the mass graves containing mutilated and decapitated skeletons found here. It was also the Matlantzinca who turned Teotenango into a fortress. They surrounded the entire complex with a wall which, as the extensive ruins show, was up to 2 metres (6.5 feet) thick in parts and up to 6 metres (20 feet) high.

As soon as you enter this site (from the parking lot on its southeastern side) you will see to your right its largest temple pyramid rising up over the edge of the plateau. The site itself is situated to the west of the entrance on terraces which can be ascended via stairways and by crossing from courtyard to courtyard. Above the ballcourt, at its highest point, you can enjoy a magnificent panoramic view of the entire valley including the over 4,400 metre (14,400 feet) high **Nevado de Toluca,** the highest mountain in the region.

Unfortunately, Teotenango has been rather carelessly reconstructed in parts (too much concrete was used to make it weather and earthquake proof); nevertheless, a visit to this site and its scenic surroundings is highly recommended.

Malinalco

After travelling south on Highway 55 for another 30 km (18.5 miles), turn east at **Tenancingo** and head towards **Chalma.** Here, in a romantic valley, lies the little town of Malinalco against a backdrop of towering cliffs. Houses built of unhewn volcanic rock and gardens in full bloom conjure up images of a rural town in colonial times. The town's main attraction is the Augustinian monastery which dates from the year 1540 and still dominates the Plaza de Armas today. To reach Malinalco's archaeological site, head a short distance from the centre of town in the direction of the steep walls of the **Cerro de los Idolos.** Then, after you pass by the church of Santa Monica, you can begin the ascent to the monuments, about 230 metres (750 feet) above the valley.

Once a very strenuous undertaking, the ascent can now be made via a concrete stairway which winds its way up to the platform of Malinalco. It takes about 20 minutes, and, depending on the season and the time of day, could mean the loss of a lot of perspiration. Fortunately, there are benches along the way to accommodate those who want to take a rest. While this site cannot be called "spectacular", it is unique and well worth a visit.

The sources have much to tell us about the history of its construction: Malinalco was part of the territory of the Matlantzinca until the end of the 15th century when it was conquered by the Aztec ruler Axayacatl. Soon afterward, the Aztecs began building here – in the year "9 Calli" (9 House) to be exact. That was 1501, during the reign of Ahuitzotl. He and his successor, Moctezuma II, renewed the building contract year after year until the year "10 Reed", 1515. Why the work was halted at that time is not known. When the Spaniards arrived in 1521, the temple was not yet completed – at least according to an account by Andres de Tapia. At any rate, this temple, the most important building in the complex, does show unmistakable signs of wear, proving that it must have been "in use".

The meandering stairway leads up onto a gallery on the side of the mountain which extends around the "nose" of the precipice. Facing the Valley of Malinco is a building which consists of an open hall preceded by a hall of columns. Whether or not this was a temple dedicated to the sun is really of no matter; we do know with certainty that it was a religious structure of some sort, because there are no secular buildings here at all. The other four structures on the gallery are clearly temple platforms – their altars were circular in shape, just like the small "altar" on the edge of the precipice.

From here, a steep stairway leads up to Malinalco's most important structure and greatest visitor's attraction – a **temple carved out of the rock.** A jaguar sculpture and a stone drum stand before the entrance to the temple and a standard-bearer stands to either side. The temple's façade is made up of the sheer rock face; the enormous relief at its centre represents the face of a dragon whose open mouth forms the entrance to the temple. To walk inside, you must step over the dragon's forked tongue. Without a doubt, this was meant to suggest an entrance into the centre of the earth.

The interior of the temple represents **a unique achievement on the part of the architects of Tenochtitlán:** it is a circular room with a diamater of not quite 6 metres (20 feet) carved entirely out of the rock. A jaguar skin with the head propped up and facing the entrance is draped over the middle of a bench situated towards the back of the room. An eagle skin adorns both ends of this same bench. Another eagle skin, its head turned towards the door, stands in the middle of the room next to an opening in the floor. This could have been a "cuauhxicalli" or "eagle vessel", which was meant to receive the blood and the hearts of sacrificial victims.

There can be no doubt that Malinalco – and especially the temple hewn out of the rock – was a cult centre for members of the two Aztec warrior castes, the eagle and the jaguar knights. The question as to the exact purpose of this site remains unanswered, however. Perhaps it was a centre of meditation for members of these castes, or it may have been a place of initiation where "cadets" were received into the order. To which god the temple was dedicated is also unknown: it may have been the Aztec god of the earth, Tepeyollotli, who himself had sprung from Tezcatlipocas, the god of war. In Aztec codices, the entrances to caves and other openings in the earth were likewise depicted as a dragon's mouth.

Ixtapan

From Malinalco you can continue your journey along a number of interesting routes without having to return to Toluca.

One possibility is to travel south via **Ixtapan de la Sal** to Taxco/ Morelos. Ixtapan is a well-known health spa and holiday resort in Mexico featuring salt and sulfur springs and rather expensive hotels. The town lies at an elevation of ca. 1,600 metres (5,300 feet) and enjoys a mild, subtropical climate all year round. Its atmosphere is peaceful and unhurried; gardens full of palm trees, bougainvillea and jacarandas add splashes of colour to the lovely townscape.

Chalma

To get back to Mexico City from here, first travel eastward and then northward on the Toluca motorway to **La Marquesa.** On the way, you will encounter one of Mexico's most interesting and characteristic towns: Chalma, a place of pilgrimage famous in Mexico for its high rate of "therapeutic" success, especially with regard to mental disorders. While pilgrims are drawn here all year round, the great pilgrimages take place during the first week in January when thousands arrive on foot or by bus. Unlike most shrines in Mexico, Chalma is not dedicated to the Blessed Virgin, but to Jesus Christ and the miracle-working crucifix over the main altar in the cathedral.

The cathedral and the monastery were founded by Augustinian friars who introduced the Indians to the worship of Jesus Christ to replace their cult of Otzocteotl, whose image was worshipped in a cave. Today, when you look into the faces of the simple peasants who come to worship here (and in many other places in Mexico), the question comes to mind, "To whom are they really praying?" Perhaps Jesus Christ and the old god Otzocteotl are one and the same?

The cathedral's cupola, which dates from 1683, has recently acquired a fresh coat of gold plating.

The town of Chalma lies in a deep canyon near a torrential river. The road leading down here takes you past a market where pottery, pastries and sweets are sold. In addition, a selection of souvenirs and devotional articles which are probably unsurpassed in the world in terms of "kitschiness" are on offer.

Another route from Malinalco leads via Xochicalco to Cuernavaca, but the road is bad and in wet weather could prove treacherous in parts. While it is negotiable in dry weather, it could nevertheless put a great strain on the vehicle and the driver.

Xochicalco

Xochicalco, Aztec for "the place of the house of flowers", lies about 12 km (7 miles) south of Cuernavaca on the old road to Taxco. It is a mystery how this site got such a name, for it was already in ruins when the Aztecs dominated the central plateau. The name seems to have been given in reminder of a time when a god of vegetation was venerated

Xipe Totec, god of vegetation and the spring

here – something which was as typical for Teotihuacán as it was atypical for the celestially-fixated Aztecs.

Xochicalco lies in a mountain saddle 500 metres (1,600 feet) above the valley in the midst of a magnificent landscape marked by the foothills of the Sierra Madre.

From this vantage point, you can see the **Lake of Tequesquitengo** and enjoy a distant view in the direction of Cuernavaca.

From the parking lot, a stairway leads up to the first terrace. From here, you can either stay on the right and visit the lower part of the complex first, or you can turn to the left and proceed upwards to the main terrace.

It is recommended that you first visit the upper section of the complex where its most important monument is located: a low platform with a profile typical of the architecture of Teotihuacán. This flat pyramid is surmounted by the ruins of a temple, a rather large structure with a patio surrounded by several rooms. Especially interesting are the reliefs which decorate the platform. Carved out of dark grey andesite, they depict the Plumed Serpent, the symbol of the God of Rain and Water of the Teotihuacán era. In the niches formed by the winding body of the serpent there are figures sitting cross-legged – their facial features (especially the profile of the nose) and their garb and headdress clearly identify them as Maya priests or kaziks.

This scene bears a strong resemblance to the so-called "Astronomers' Conference", a stela located in Copan, Honduras which dates from the 6th century A. D.

The figures of the sitting kaziks alternate with date glyphs and the number nine, which had a special significance for the traditional (but inaccurate) lunar calendar. These calendric allusions continue on the front side of the platform: warriors with bundles of spears, a priest with a date glyph and three day symbols entwined in human arms can be seen here.

These reliefs are more than just mere illustrations – they tell a story, the content of which is unfortunately unknown. It may be assumed that they were created to celebrate a calendric reform – perhaps the introduction to the central highlands of the astronomic and mathematical system devised by Maya scholars. If this is true, it would mean that the reliefs of Xochicalco were a historic document of singular importance.

From this platform, the highest in Xochicalco, you can enjoy a view of the entire valley below and see **Mt. Ajusco** as well, the volcano which dominates the Valley of Cuernavaca. With an elevation of over 3,800 metres (12,500 feet), it is the highest in the region.

On the southern end of the same platform stands another pyramid – one which displays similar characteristics to the aforementioned one. Next to this, a portal leads down a steep slope to the next lower terrace. Here, two temple platforms face each other, each flanked by a rectangular "spectator stand". Between these two buildings is an altar-like structure with a stela whose carvings are, unfortunately, no longer visible.

The third group of monuments – obviously secular buildings – lies on the slope and at the foot of the mountain saddle. A long "avenue" leads west to a platform flanked by two characteristic structures: a ball-court in the well-known double-T form – clearly a Mayan import, as such courts were unknown in Teotihuacán; and a palace – clearly a residential palace, as shown by the layout of its rooms and the presence of drains and a kitchen. The remains of a "temazcal", a sweat room, also support the theory that this palace was used for secular rather than religious purposes.

Much more excavation work has to be done in and around Xochicalco before we can learn exactly how large and how old this site really is.

Cacahuamilpa

From here, you can return to the motorway and continue southwest to Taxco or Acapulco – or, if you're not in a hurry, you could stay on the old road and visit a further attraction located south of Xochicalco: the **caverns of Cacahuamilpa.** After about 40 km (25 miles) on a winding road, you will come out of a curve and see a deep canyon to your left. There is no way you could miss the site – a house stands near the entrance and there is a large parking lot nearby. These "grutas" comprise the most extensive system of stalactite caverns that has been found in Mexico so far. While it is possible (and perfectly safe) to visit the caverns on your own, it is best to take advantage of the services of one of the qualified geologist-guides.

Taxco

From the caverns of Cacahuamilpa, it's another 25 km (15 miles) to Taxco, a town of approximately 30,000 (1970) inhabitants and a popular destination for excursionists from Mexico City and Cuernavaca.

Deposits of silver, gold, lead, mercury and zinc which are still being mined (or are being mined once again) can be found in the Sierra de Taxco and elsewhere in the vicinity. The town's economy, however, is based primarily on tourism. It possesses a number of smaller, older hotels and inns as well as a few newly-erected, modern hotels.

The town of Taxco is spread over several hills situated on the steep slopes of Cerro Atachi, a foothill of Cerro de Bermeja and part of the mountainous countryside of the Sierra de Taxco. Like other mining towns, it does not have a planned layout – the various sections of town are connected to one another by stairways.

In addition to its lovely panorama and its fascinating layout, Taxco's architecture represents another of its attractions. Although there are sections of town which date only from the late 1950's, these do not necessarily stand in crass contrast to the old parts of town. Taxco's building code is far more stringent than that of other Mexican towns: it even includes exact instructions as to the architectural style of a building to be erected. For instance, the use of rounded arches on doors and windows is a requirement.

Taxco, whose name is derived from "tlaxco", ballcourt, was the centre of the Tlahuica population in pre-colonial times. Their original settlement, now known as Taxco el Viejo (Old Taxco), can be found near a number of tin and silver mines about 12 km (7.5 miles) from the town's present location.

During the reign of Itzcoatl (1428–1440), the fourth Aztec king, the Aztecs conquered this region. Thereafter, the Tlahuicas were forced to pay tribute. In 1522, the Spanish conquistadores besieged and conquered the settlement. Prospectors sent out by Cortés to search for tin found small deposits of silver on Cerro de Bermeja. Near the mines which were dug soon afterward, a settlement sprang up which was referred to as "El Real de Tetelcingo" in a document dating from 1529. This first settlement now forms the nucleus of Taxco's old town.

Other mining settlements went up nearby: Tlaxcotecapan, which is now the San Miguel quarter of Taxco; and Acayutla, located on the slopes above the old town near the church of Our Lady of Guadalupe.

All of these settlements were gradually absorbed by the growing town of Taxco, whose name was first mentioned in 1581 in a text by Pedro de Ledesma.

In the 18th century, the San Ignacio Mine yielded so much profit that its owner, the (presumably) French-born aristocrat José de la Borda, was able to build himself a palatial residence in the centre of Taxco (Palacio Borda). José de la Borda was also the benefactor of the church of Santa Prisca.

Following the drop in mine production which set in during the late 1930's, silverworking, a traditional craft which was revitalized through the initiative of Canadian-born William Spratling, increased in importance. In Taxco, silver of a high level of purity (sterling) is generally used. Silver articles are marked with the number "950" or with the stamp of an eagle, the two official hallmarks used to attest to their purity. Because silverware and silver jewellery are not cheaper in Taxco than they are in Mexico City, a visit here for that reason alone is not worth the trouble.

Most of Taxco's points of interest can be found around the Zócalo, an attraction in itself with its wrought-iron benches, shade trees and historic buildings. The Zócalo, or Plaza de Borda, is also Taxco's commercial centre: here you can find "platerías" (silver shops) as well as hotels and restaurants.

The most important building in this area is the **church of Santa**

Prisca, constructed between 1748 and 1758 in baroque style and incorporating some of the decorative elements of the late-baroque Churriguera style (which corresponds approximately to the European roccoco style in terms of characteristics and the period in which it flourished). The church has two tall, slim towers decorated in part with sculptures in the Churriguera style. Its façade, already impressive due to its perfected design and the combination of the various supporting and nonsupporting elements, is also ornately decorated with sculptures of plants, fruits and animals. The glazed tiles ("azulejos") which cover the large dome of the church can be seen from afar shining brightly in the sunlight.

Of special interest in the church's interior are the altars decorated in gold leaf and the oil painting by Miguel Cabrera (1696–1768) in the tympanum above the entrance to the Capilla (chapel) del Padre Jesús. This painting depicts the martyrdom of Santa Prisca who was decapitated in A. D. 268 in the Colosseum in Rome.

Above the Zócalo stands the palatial **Casa Borda,** the former residence of the Borda family. Behind the house is Calle Juan Ruíz de Alarcón, which is lined with lovely historic homes: to the right is the back of the Casa Borda, to the left, the richly sculpted façade of the **Casa de Villanueva,** also called the Casa Humboldt (the German naturalist was a guest here in April 1803). This house with its Mudéjar-style embellishments was built in the 18th century by Juan de Villanueva.

On the corner of Calle Ruíz de Alarcón and Calle Ex-Convento stands the **Palacio Municipal** (town hall), a beautiful building with a high tower. If you continue down Calle Ex-Convento, you will come to the former Convent of San Bernardino, which was founded in the late 16th century by the Franciscan order. It was destroyed in a fire in 1805 and rebuilt in 1823 in neo-Classic style.

If you ascend Calle del Arco from the Zócalo you will arrive at Plaza del Toril, a small marketplace which is especially lively on Saturdays and Sundays. From here, Calle Real de San Nicolás leads up to Jardin Guerrero, a small park, and the La Santisima church.

Calle Real de San Nicolás can also take you west to Plaza de San Juan, flanked to the right by the massive façade of the **Casa Grande** or Casa Real. Built in the 18th century, this building served as the seat of the mine administration under the Spanish crown. The Mexican freedom fighter and general José Maria Morelos y Pavón stayed here in 1811.

If you make the somewhat strenuous ascent up Calle Progresso or Calle de Ojeda you will be rewarded by some beautiful views of Taxco's old town. A walk up to the church of **Santa Maria de Guadalupe,** located in the northern part of the old town (make sure you've got sturdy and comfortable shoes on your feet), is worthwhile not only for the view from the top, but also for the "beyond-the-Baedeker" insights it offers into Mexican life.

If you choose to return to Mexico City from here, you cannot help but pass through Cuernavaca.

(Schmidt)

Cuernavaca

The capital of the state of Morelos lies only 75 km (46 miles) south of Mexico City on the road to the Pacific coast. Once an insider's tip for city dwellers discouraged with urban life, Cuernavaca is now, for all intents and purposes, a suburb of the capital city. The Valley of Mexico is connected to Cuernavaca by motorway: with luck and little traffic, the drive can be made in just under an hour.

Many affluent Mexicans have moved their residences to Cuernavaca while keeping their businesses in Mexico City. In light of this trend and the otherwise high number of unregistered new residents, it makes little sense to give population figures for Cuernavaca. The actual number of inhabitants certainly exceeds the official figure of 180,000. Cuernavaca is also known for its high number of foreign residents (although no official figures exist). As a result of the large number of retired Americans who have settled in Cuernavaca, the town's cost-of-living is the highest in all of Mexico.

Cuernavaca is situated, for the most part, at an elevation of about 1,500 m (5,000 feet): its climate is typified by low relative humidity and year-round springtime temperatures. Although the town was once known for its clean air, this now holds true only to a certain degree, for traffic and the presence of industries in the peripheral zones have taken their toll on the environment. Cuernavaca is a pretty, friendly town. Around the small Zócalo which marks its centre there are elegant cafés and restaurants. Here, too, stands the **Palacio Cortés,** built in 1531 by the great conquistador for his second wife, the Marquesa del Valle (de Oaxaca). In later years, it served as a town hall and now serves as a museum. While the outer walls and the first-floor veranda have held up well, the interior has undergone renovation. The frescos by Diego Rivera portraying the conquest of Mexico and the life of the Indians date from the same period as those painted on the walls of the National Palace in Mexico City.

The hills surrounding the small centre of Cuernavaca are dotted with the villas of the town's moneyed citizens. You won't be able to see much more than their lavish gardens, however, for these villas are all surrounded by high walls. The residences of the politicians even stand under 24-hour guard.

Another of Cuernavaca's attractions can also be found near the Zócalo: the **cathedral and adjacent monastery.** Under an arcade in the churchyard stands an altar where outdoor masses were once celebrated. The church's interior, which was at one time completely destroyed, has now been renovated and modernized. In the course of the renovations, remains of 17th-century frescos came to light which have proven to be of considerable historic value. They illustrate the journey of Felipe de Jesús and his followers to Japan where they hoped to spread the Christian faith. Instead, they suffered martyrdom and were nailed to crosses in mockery of the crucifixion of Christ. It is interesting and amusing to see how the fresco painter envisioned the landscape, the people, the costumes and the mechanical implements of medieval Japan. He also tried to portray the creatures of the sea, but created instead monsters which defy taxanomic classification.

Several theories exist as to the origin of the town's name. According to one, Cuernavaca, "cow horn", was a nickname coined by the Spaniards because of the shape of the valley in which the town lies. According to another, the name – as is so often the case – is a corruption of the town's Aztec name, Cuauhuahuac.

Excavation work carried out in the immediate vicinity of the Cortés Palace has brought to light the remains of Aztec structures which, unfortunately, lie for the most part underneath the palace and therefore cannot be positively identified. In the northwestern outskirts of Cuernavaca, barely 500 metres (550 yards) from the train station, lie the ruins of what was probably the main temple of this Aztec centre: the **Temple of Teopanzolco,** built by the Aztec ruler Acamapichtli following the conquest of the region. Archaeologists have identified two phases of construction. Modelled after the Templo Mayor in Mexico City, this structure is a double pyramid with temples dedicated to the gods Huitzilolpochtli and Tláloc on the upper terraces.

Now carefully reconstructed, this stunning pyramid nevertheless receives only few visitors. Most of the tourists who pass through this area are in too much of a hurry to get to Taxco or Acapulco. The summit of the pyramid offers a beautiful view of Cuernavaca and the valley and, in clear weather, one of the best vantage points from which to photograph **Mt. Ajusco.**

Tepotztlán

From here, you can drive the 100 km/60 miles back to the capital (its city limits, that is!) in about 50 minutes. But those who have some time on their hands might like to schedule an overnight stop in order to get in another day of sightseeing.

From Cuernavaca, there is a road which takes you the 48 km (30 miles) via Tejalpa to Cuautla. It is recommended, however, that you take the motorway to Mexico City instead and turn off after 15 km (9 miles) onto the new highway which leads via Tepotzlán to Cuautla.

Tepotztlán is a pretty, quiet rural town frequented on the weekends by escapees from the capital city. Surrounded by beautiful countryside at an altitude of 1,500 metres (5,000 feet), it enjoys an exceptional climate.

The Valley of Tepotzlán, in which it is located, is closed in on three sides by high, steep volcanic walls. As the centre of the cult of one of the four gods of intoxication (whose veneration involved the taking of drugs), Tepotzlán was an important place of pilgrimage during Aztec times.

The ruins of the pyramid dedicated to the God of Pulque can be found on the slopes above the town. The ascent, which takes approximately one hour, is very strenuous, but you will be rewarded at the top by a singular view of Tepotzlán and its **monastery.**

Following the Spanish conquest, in the second half of the 16th century, the Dominicans built a monastic complex here which became the most important centre for the Christianization of the Indians in the southern central plateau. The relatively well-preserved monastery, decorated in the platesque style, is now the town's main attraction.

Tepotztlán has an interesting market (especially on the weekends) which offers "artesanía" articles (arts and crafts) for sale.

Cuautla

The road from Tepotztlán to Cuautla takes you through the canyons and mountains of one of Mexico's most beautiful sierran landscapes. In the vicinity of Cuautla there are a number of partly excavated and poorly investigated ruins of Tlahuica sites, such as Yauhtepec and the temple at the summit of Cerro de Tepozteco.

The town of Cuautla, with its 80,000 inhabitants, serves not only as a regional centre but also as a fashionable, urbanite's retreat. The mild climate and subtropical vegetation for which the town is known actually characterize this entire region of the state of Morelos.

For an overnight stay, the Hacienda Cocoyoc, which was converted into a stunning hotel a few years ago, is highly recommended. Having been skilfully incorporated into the hotel's garden and swimming pool, the ruins of the old hacienda impart upon the entire complex a touch of elegance and romance which should be enjoyed at leisure. Unfortunately, the necessary peace and tranquility is often difficult to find on the weekend when visitors descend upon the hotel in hordes, thus raising the round-the-clock noise level considerably.

From here, the drive back to Mexico City can be made in one and a half to two hours, depending on the traffic.

(Thieme)

The Gulf Coast and the Southeast

"Tampico" is a popular song which sings the praises of a port city on Mexico's Gulf coast – a good point of departure for a trip along the coast to southern Mexico. Those coming from the north on the Panamerican Highway should continue south on the motorway at Monterrey and then take Highways 85 and 80 to the coast. The roads are good and the 575 km (356 miles) can be travelled in one day. The highway runs via Ciudad Victoria along the eastern slopes of the Sierra Madre Oriental and southward through the varied landscape of the state of Tamaulipas.

Tampico

The town of Tampico on the mouth of the Rio Pánuco has about half a million inhabitants. Mexico's largest fishing fleet is stationed here, and it is the country's largest (or second-largest after Veracruz – the figures vary) port. Tampico is also the site of a modern oil refinery: from here, a pipeline leads into the country's interior.

The history of Tampico and its satellite town of Ciudad Madero is closely tied to that of **Pánuco,** a small town 20 km (12 miles) to the southwest on the river of the same name. Pánuco was founded by Hernán Cortés in 1521 in the course of a military expedition against the Huaxtecs. By 1530, however, the town had begun to lose importance and it was soon overshadowed by Tampico, the port city.

Like every port city in the world, Tampico bustles with activity. As far as special attractions go, though, it has only the **Museo de la Huasteca** to offer. Housed in a wing of the Instituto Tecnologico, the museum presents a vivid and comprehensive look at the civilization of the Huaxtec-Totonacs, particularly in its early phases.

Climatically, the coastal region belongs to the tropics, meaning that it experiences continuous heat and humidity. Whenever Highway 180, which leads south from Tampico via Tuxpan and Poza Rica to Veracruz, veers away from the coast and heads toward the interior, you find yourself in the midst of some of Mexico's most lavish vegetation. Citrus fruits of all kinds, bananas, coffee beans and cacao are cultivated here on cleared land where they flourish with virtually no help at all thanks to this favourable climate.

El Tajin

The highway between Tampico and Veracruz extends over 500 km (310 miles). It would be a shame to drive the entire distance in one day, though, because of the many attractions (including inviting sandy beaches) along the way. While there are no real resorts along this stretch of coastline, a beachfront hotel complex like the newly-renovated Balneario in **Tecolutla** might tempt you to make a stop. This is also an ideal starting point for a visit to El Tajin, 50 km (31 miles) away. The ancient cult centre of the Totonacs and largest archaeological site in the region can be reached from Tecolutla via Gutiérrez Zamora and Papantla on Highway 125.

In the midst of the tropical vegetation of the gentle foothills of the Sierra Madre lie the ruins of an ancient city whose monumental architecture ranks among Mexico's

most important. So far, an area of approximately 60 hectares has been cleared of vegetation and studied, but beyond this central zone, there are still some 1,000 hectares of ruins waiting to be excavated. Hundreds of structures have been located here, but their identification is still pending.

From the parking lot/picnic grounds, it is only a short walk to the main ceremonial square and the excavated temples surrounding it.

This site had been long abandoned and forgotten by the time the Spaniards arrived – there is no mention of it in any document of the period. It was first rediscovered at the end of the 18th century: Alexander von Humboldt visited it in 1811, but its excavation did not begin until the 1930's, at which time its significance finally became clear. Clearly, it had been the centre of Totonac culture in the Classic period, long before these people moved to Misantla and Cempoala, the centres which existed at the time of the Spanish conquest.

In the 7th and 8th centuries A. D., El Tajin was **one of three great cult centres in Mesoamerica** (the other two were Teotihuacán in the central plateau and Monte Albán in the southwest). Because of the countless signs of Maya influence (ball courts, for instance) as well as the signs of Toltec sacrificial practices found here, El Tajin can be seen as something of a link between the Classic period and the period of the Nahua conquests.

On your way to the main ceremonial square, you will first pass by a number of unreconstructed ruins of platforms and galleries. Then, on your left, you will see one of the most interesting **ball courts** to be found at this site. The well-preserved reliefs on the wall of the court show that the game was part of a cult of sacrifice (in particular, one of human sacrifice) as it had been in Toltec times. It is interesting to note that the sacrifice performed here was a "toxcatl" (heart sacrifice), while the famous scene at the ball court of Chichén Itzá depicts sacrifice by decapitation.

Next you will arrive at a square and see before you "Monument V", a **temple platform** which stands atop an immense pedestal. A well-preserved stela in the form of a "palma" with a carving of a seated, bent figure (a ball player?) stands before the stairs which lead up to the temple. These stone sculptures shaped like a ship's prow are characteristic of Huaxtec art and are presumed to be connected with the ball game. Beyond this monument lies the **principal court,** the heart of El Tajin, where the main pyramids are located: steep platforms with staircases leading to sanctuaries at the top.

The most important of these monuments is the **Pyramid of the Niches,** a pyramid which resembles all others in form, but is unique on account of its decoration. The body of the pyramid is covered in sedimentary rock which was originally hidden behind a thick layer of plaster. The stairs of the platform are dotted with small niches which were earlier thought to have contained statues: it has since been proven that these niches, of which there are 364, were purely decorative. When the sanctuary atop the platform is considered as well, the niches number 365, an obvious allusion to the solar year.

From the Pyramid of the Niches a road leads northward up a gentle slope to a second complex of buildings known as **El Tajin Chico** (Little El Tajin). The most important monuments here are "Building A" and the "colonnaded building", approximately 5-metre (16-foot)-high platforms supporting temples so immense that they seem to be palaces. These temples had self-supporting, vaulted roofs, a special feature of ancient Mexican architecture. The decorations on the outside walls and on the columns and pillars are markedly different from those on the buildings surrounding the main ceremonial square. Narrow, shallow niches alternate with trapezoids and meanders; the columns in the "colonnaded building" bear Toltec-type figures of warriors.

Little El Tajin is considerably younger than the Pyramid of the Niches and Monument V, but the reliefs on the wall of the ball court mentioned previously also date from a later period. It is clear that the oldest buildings here date from the age of Classic Teotihuacán, while the more recent ones date from the 12th century, the era of Toltec predominance in the central highlands.

If you want to return from here to the capital city, drive first from Papantla to **Poza Rica,** a town dominated by a giant oil refinery and the grimy clouds of soot it emits – no wonder it is reputed to be the ugliest town in Mexico! The refinery, the country's oldest, was nationalized in 1938 by then President Lázaro Cárdenas. From here, highly scenic Highway 130 takes you along a winding route over the Sierra Madre Oriental and through Huauchinango and Tulancingo before reaching the central Mexican plateau and Mexico City, 250 km (155 miles) away. The highlight of the trip is the drive from Gilberto Camacho via Xicotepec de Juárez and the Nexaca reservoir to Huauchinango.

Misantla

If you choose to continue along the Gulf to Veracruz 215 km (133 miles) away, drive from Papantla back to Gutiérrez Zamora and turn south on the coastal road which, in parts, has been expanded into a four-lane highway. The scenery along the way is lovely but a bit monotonous: to the left (east) are beaches, stands of palm trees and the sea; to the right (west) is the silhouette of the Sierra Madre. Those interested can make a detour to visit the archaeological site at Misantla: after 110 km (68 miles), turn west at Vega de Alatorre in the direction of Jalapa and continue for 30 km (19 miles) until you get to Yecuatla. At Yecuatla, turn north (right) and continue for another 15 km (9 miles) until you reach Misantla, a small rural town which contains the partly excavated and restored ruins of a **Toltec ceremonial centre.**

The temple platforms are decorated with basalt sculptures of turtles, shells, cat-like creatures and warriors which obviously date from Nahua times, while the complex itself is Totonac. The smaller sites in the vicinity – Los Idolos, La Lima, Tapapulum – are difficult to reach and worth the effort only if you have a special interest in ancient Mexican ruins.

From Misantla, return to the coast road and continue on to Veracruz.

Cempoala

Before completing the drive to Veracruz, you might like to visit the old Totonac city of Cempoala which lies 2 km (just over a mile) to the west of the coast road. It was with the inhabitants of this city that the Spaniards had their first contact with the people of ancient Mexico. The details of this encounter are known to us not only from the Spanish side, but from Indian sources as well.

Today, this ancient city – now an archaeological park with a small museum – lies on the edge of the village of the same name. The entire ancient site covers an area of 20 hectares. Many buildings, including temples, are scattered about the village and in nearby fields, but the park comprises solely the city's ceremonial centre. In a way, the impression the site makes in modern times seems very similar to the impression it made upon the conquistador who wrote in 1519, "The whole thing was like one single pleasure garden with trees so big and tall that one could hardly see the houses".

The architecture of the three temple complexes on the ceremonial square features balustrades along the steps and corresponds to the Chichimec-Aztec style. To the east (to the right of the entrance) stands the **Temple of the Fireplaces** upon a broad platform with galleries. The name comes from the subdivisions of the upper temple which, in their ruined state, look like fireplaces.

The other two temples (they lie to the north and to the west of the square) are **step pyramids.** The larger of the two lies to the west but its staircases, with a broad balustrade, turns towards the east. The 11-metre (36-foot)-high platform was once surmounted by a temple which, according to Spanish accounts, had a straw roof. We may assume that this held true for the other temples as well.

The small **circular temple** here (which has a twin elsewhere at this site) is rather interesting. Scattered about the entire plaza are circular sacrificial altars which are familiar to us through Aztec codices (illustrated manuscripts).

In the sugar cane fields to the east of the walled-in plaza another interesting temple platform is found: the **Temple of the Little Faces,** so called because of the small, clay skulls which once decorated its outer wall. Inside the temple, whose walls are still intact, traces of colourful paintings can be seen.

In order to visit Cempoala's second circular temple, exit the plaza and cross the main road. From there, another road will take you through the village and to this well-preserved temple, the form of which, while being typical of the Gulf coast, was adopted by Aztec architects as well. It was probably devised for the cult of the wind god Ehecatl, whose functions were taken over by Quetzalcoátl in Aztec times. With the spread of this cult, this temple form spread as well – to Tenochtitlán and as far northwest as Michoacán.

The circular temple of Cempoala is of a rather unique construction: it actually consists of two loosely connected structures – a rectangular front section which contains the staircase, and behind it, the structure which supported the temple. On the grounds in front of this complex are sacrificial altars and platforms which were used by secondary cults.

La Antigua

Return to the coast road and head towards Veracruz and you will soon come upon La Antigua, also known as "Veracruz Viejo" (Old Veracruz).

The site of **the first Spanish settlement on Mexican soil,** Villa Rica de la Vera Cruz was established here by Cortés after he landed at this spot in 1519, but it was not until after 1525 that the town was actually built. La Antigua's Plaza de Armas is flanked by a renovated church and the ruins of the Ajuntamiento, the seat of colonial administration. Parts of the aqueduct which brought in water from the mountains are also intact.

Today, La Antigua is a pretty, neat village of approximately 100 souls. In addition to the Indian fishermen and farmers who have always lived here, there are now a modest number of artists and drop-outs who appreciate the village's beauty and tranquility. La Antigua lies under a high, shady canopy of trees; its houses are almost concealed by the hibiscus, bougainvillea and other subtropical plants that grow here in profusion.

Veracruz

From La Antigua, Highway 180, now a full-fledged motorway, takes you the remaining 20 km (12 miles) to Veracruz. Before reaching the city, you pass through its industrial suburbs where a refinery and a loading port are being constructed and an oil pipeline leading to the sea is to be laid. After passing the warehouses and wharves of the freeport of Veracruz, you will soon find yourself in the city centre.

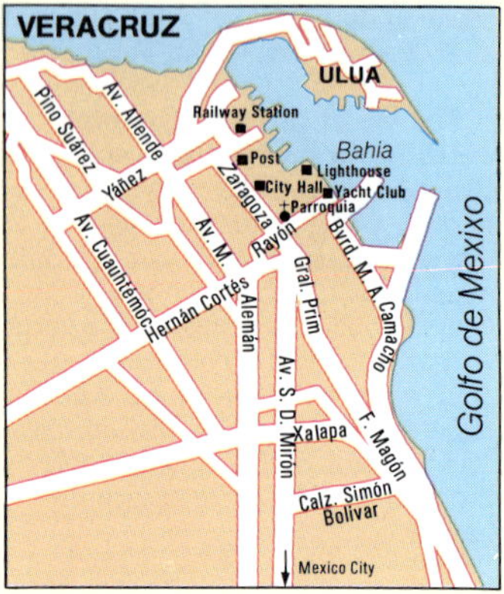

Veracruz may be the most important city in the state of Veracruz, but it is not the state capital (Jalapa is). Despite the fact that it is Mexico's most important port, next to Tampico, and despite its considerable population (in 1980, there were 340,000 people; by now, this figure could easily have risen to 400,000), Veracruz is a peaceful and attractive city – and well worth seeing.

Veracruz is the most **important centre for the transfer of goods** on the way to the capital city. In terms of passenger traffic, however, the port is no longer as significant as it originally was.

The city is situated along a shallow coast, a location which is hardly conducive to the establishment of a major port. In fact, due to its shallow shipway, Veracruz was originally only a roadstead (where lightened ships may ride at anchor), but through the construction of large jetties and the inclusion of the island of San Juán Ulua in the port complex, the city was able to improve its facilities.

Although the region in which Veracruz lies is characterized by small, low (no higher than 50 metres/160 feet) hills, the terrain nevertheless allowed for the construction of a city with a checkerboard design. The **city centre is located close by the port.**

Veracruz is a charming city with a well-kept appearance, but not much of the old town has survived and there are relatively few historic attractions.

Veracruz was founded on April 27, 1519 by Hernán Cortés. Originally called Villa Rica de la Vera Cruz (Rich Town of the True Cross), the settlement was moved twice. It was not until the year 1600 that the present city of Veracruz was built.

In its early years, Veracruz was hardly more than a place to drop anchor. Even in 1625, the town was still no more than a collection of wooden huts. Development was slow and progress was often interrupted: several devastating yellow fever epidemics took their toll on the population and the town suffered as well from pirate attacks – in particular in 1653 and 1712.

Veracruz acquired the monopoly over the exchange of goods

between the colony and the motherland. Mexico's main exports were precious metals (in particular, silver coins), dyestuffs such as cochineal and indigo, and cane sugar. In exchange, Spain furnished products which were not allowed to be produced in the colony.

The city later became **a gateway for invasionary forces** and a base for incursions into the central highlands, the most notable of which were the French landings in 1838 and 1861 and the American landings in 1847 (during the Mexican-American War) and in 1914 (during the Mexican Revolution).

This naturally impeded urban development and also explains the lack of historic buildings. With the exception of parts of the fort of San Juán Ulua, Veracruz' oldest stone structures date from the 18th century.

Of special interest to the tourist is that part of town bordered to the northeast by the coast; to the south by M. Doblado Street up to Plaza Zamora; to the west by Av. Madero; and to the north by J. Montesino Street. Most of the city's hotels are located on Av. Manuel Avila Camacho to the south of the old town.

Veracruz is clearly centred about its **Zócalo or Plaza de Armas** – the place to be, especially in the evening. Here, under the arcades, you can find a wide selection of restaurants and cafés – something for every budget – as well as one of the city's finest hotels, the Diligencias.

In addition to its lovely galleries and colonnades, the Zócalo is also notable as the site of the **Palacio Municipal** and the **cathedral of Nuestra Señora de la Asunción,** built in 1734 in the colonial baroque style.

Veracruz is famous throughout Mexico for its Mardi Gras. Not surprisingly, the centre of carnival festivities there is the Zócalo, where parades take place, marimba bands play and lots of dancing and drinking goes on on the days before Ash Wednesday. If you want to join in the fun, you'll have to plan ahead as you will be competing for hotel rooms with countless other merrymakers from Mexico and abroad.

From the Zócalo, walk down Av. Independencia, Veracruz' busiest commercial thoroughfare, to Plaza Gutiérrez Zamora where you will find the only building here which dates from the 16th century: the **church of Santo Cristo de Buen Viaje.**

In the **Baluarte Santiago,** a fortification dating from the mid-18th century, there is a small regional museum containing pre-Columbian artefacts and exhibits documenting the history of the city. Near the customs house, the Aduana Maritima, not far from here, there is a market which specializes in Mexican handicrafts (Mercado de Curiosidades).

The **Biblioteca Juárez** is housed in the bell tower of a former church located directly on the harbour: nearby is a hotel which is comprised in part of buildings which once formed part of a monastery. Harbour tours originate every half hour from the quay opposite the Emporio Hotel.

Ships for the fortified island of San Juán Ulua depart from the main wharf. **San Juán Ulua** was originally (1528) no more than a guard station and lighthouse on a small island at the entrance to the harbour. In the years from 1746 to 1771, however, it was converted into a veritable fortress for the increased protection of the city. In the 19th century, this Mexican "Chateau d'If" was a notorious prison.

Another recommended boat trip is the one which takes you to the **Isla de Sacrificios** (Island of Sacrifices) further off the coast. In precolonial times, this small island with a lighthouse was sacred to the Indian inhabitants. Here, they are said to have performed human sacrifices, the traces of which were discovered by the shocked Spaniards. The objects found here are on exhibit in the museums of Mexico City.

Because of the dangerous currents, this trip can normally be made only in the morning – and sometimes not at all. While the island is highly recommended for bathing, these same currents make its waters suitable for only expert swimmers.

The beaches near Veracruz are more on the unattractive side – you'll have to head south to find nice ones. The increased exploitation of oil deposits in the region has clearly impaired the area's suitability as a resort.

Jalapa

The road from Veracruz to Mexico City is one of the most scenic in the country: head back along Highway 180 for about 25 km (15 miles) until you get to Cardel and then turn west on Highway 40 towards Jalapa/Puebla. The drive from Veracruz to Jalapa, which covers a distance of 120 km (74 miles), can be made in two hours. The road, however, is much-used, as it is the most important traffic lane connecting Mexico City and the industrial region around Puebla with the port of Veracruz. You'll notice that this road is frequented by huge commercial trucks.

Highway 140 winds its way, first gently, then steeply, upwards through subtropical vegetation to an elevation of 1,400 metres (4,600 feet) where the pretty capital of the state of Veracruz is situated. As you approach the flat Valley of Jalapa, you can already see beyond the craggy slopes of the **Cerro del Perote** which you will later pass as you continue on towards Puebla – a strenuous drive through magnificent countryside!

The city has just over 300,000 inhabitants and very little industry.

What is especially noticeable is that it is not an oil-producing centre, but rather **a city of flowers and spacious gardens** which ranks among the most beautiful in Mexico (and among the best loved by "retirees" from Mexico City and the U. S.). In addition to its lovely cityscape, Jalapa boasts an important museum, the **Veracruz State Museum of Archaeology** – the country's no. 2 museum after Mexico City's Museum of Anthropology and a must for anyone interested in anthropological studies.

Olmec "cabeza", a colossal stone head from Villahermosa

In recent years, the museum has undergone large-scale expansion and improvement as part of a government move to "regionalize" ancient treasures. Originally, this was basically an open-air museum, but now two large circular pavillions have been built to hold the most important sculptures as well as ceramics, jewellery and grave finds.

The main emphasis of the museum is on its exhibits of artefacts found in the state of Veracruz. These exhibits make this museum **one of the most important institutions for the study of Olmec, Huaxtec and Totonac culture.** Some of the best examples of "cabezas", oversized stone heads, are housed here. These heads, to which a body never belonged, are characteristic of Olmec culture. They were found in "sacred groves" – those exhibited here come from San Lorenzo Tenochtitlán. Other highlights of the museum include "The Prince", from Cruz del Milagro; and the "Señor de las Limas", a seated male figure with a child in its lap. The faces of both figures – but especially of the child – display the jaguar features typical of Olmec art.

A special room has been set aside to hold a set of newly-excavated, clay, female figures, some of which are almost life-sized. These figures, referred to as "cihuateteo" or "cihuacóatl" are Huaxtec and were found near Veracruz.

The road which runs from here towards Puebla leads upwards out of the Valley of Jalapa and through the lava fields of the **Perote,** which can be seen to the south. While this volcano is still active, it has not erupted since 1957. From Jalapa it is just under 200 km (125 miles) to

Puebla, the last 50 (30) of which are spanned by a motorway.

From Veracruz, Highway 180 continues south along the Gulf coast for 490 km (304 miles) to Villahermosa, the capital of the state of Tabasco. After about 140 km (87 miles), you will reach the region of **Santiago Tuxtla,** where several important Olmec sites are located. The most important of these are Cerro de las Mesas and Tres Zapotes, where one of the most stunning "cabezas" (heads) was found. Low mounds which mark the spots where temples once stood can still be seen. As the Olmecs did not build out of stone or any other durable material, these sites have very little to offer the visitor. Furthermore, they are difficult to reach, boggy and are serviced only by unpaved roads.

Via **San Andes Tuxtla** and **Matacapan,** where a number of platforms and graves from the Teotihuacán era are located, the road continues on to Minatitlán, 290 km (180 miles) south of Veracruz. The climate here is hot and humid; the vegetation, tropical. On both sides of the highway lie lagoons and swamps which represent some of Mexico's most valuable biotopes. Here, rare, tropical grasses grow and snakes and alligators have found a place of refuge. Unfortunately, this refuge is being increasingly threatened by the petroleum industry. Chemical waste, which in Mexico is often not handled with the proper care, endangers the country's flora and fauna. Lately, environmental protectionists have been drawing attention to this problem and the government has promised to take preventative measures.

Coatzacoalcos and Minatitlán

The port of Coatzacoalcos and the town of Minatitlán, which lies 20 km (12 miles) inland, are synonymous with petroleum in Mexico. The refinery and its loading port have recently – finally – become the subject of public debate. They have been identified – albeit with considerable delay – as Mexico's worst polluters. Minatitlán befouls the air and the surrounding swamps; Coatzacoalcos has been contaminating the coastal waters for decades. In addition to everything else, Gulf fishing has already suffered considerably. Pollution has taken its toll on the marine population, in particular, the shrimp ("camarones") population. Fishing and shrimping, however, are the main occupations of the people who live along the coast. The government is now aware of this problem and has pledged to take action.

Campo La Venta

From here, Highway 180 continues on for 235 km (146 miles) through swampy coastal terrain to the state capital of Villahermosa. Sixty-five kilometres (40 miles) east of Minatitlán (at which point the highway no longer hugs the coast) are the ruins of **Campo La Venta, the ceremonial centre of the Olmecs** and the main archaeological site pertaining to this culture. It is located 4 km

(2.5 miles) off the main highway in the direction of the coast and is accessible via a paved road. It is because of this site that the culture of the Gulf coast Olmecs is also referred to as the La Venta culture (see map on page 80). As in other centres of this civilization, the only recognizable traces of architecture are earthen "platforms". The four colossal heads and the stone pavement of the "sacred grove" have been moved to museums. The paving stones and one of the heads are now in an authentic setting in Villahermosa's La Venta Park Museum.

Villahermosa

"Villahermosa" means "pretty town", but the name is sorely misleading. The capital of the state of Tabasco is situated along the dirty-brown Grijalva River in a region of stifling heat and humidity. Although it was founded in 1598, nothing from its colonial past is visible today.

It is a modern city of approximately 200,000 inhabitants which, as a centre of the oil industry, has recently become a centre of migration. The Mexicans say that the entire state of Tabasco floats on an oil bubble – and they could very well be right. Oil was struck at practically all the exploration sites near Villahermosa, and the oil boom – with all its positive and negative side effects – followed. The city's prices have risen sharply as a result of the presence of high-earning oil workers whose buying power far exceeds that of the city's other wage earners. This has caused a great deal of anger and the government has been called upon to do something. The question is, what?

Visitors to Villahermosa should take in the **Tabasco Museum** with its exhibits of artefacts found in the state. Monumental sculptures, stelae, "altars" and colossal heads are on display in **La Venta Park,** where the sacred grove of La Venta is now located. The park is situated in a swampy area across from the old airport, so when you visit it, take along some mosquito protection (indispensable in the late afternoon).

For many travellers, Villahermosa is the starting point for trips to the ruins of **Comalcalco** and **Palenque,** the northwesternmost centres of Maya culture. Palenque, in particular, is a site not to be missed!

(Thieme)

The South

Where the geographic south of Mexico begins cannot be exactly determined: indeed, many differing opinions exist as to where this region's northern boundary lies. Less controversy exists as to where the south ends: on the Caribbean coast and at the frontiers of the countries of Belize and Guatemala.

More appropriate here is a definition of the south as a cultural area as indicated by the overwhelming presence of Maya ruins. Seen this way, the south encompasses the northernmost part of the state of Chiapas, the archaeological site of Camalcalco in the state of Tabasco, and the states of Campeche, Yucatán and Quintana Roo. Oaxaca state, the Chiapas Highlands and the jungle region bordering the Usumacinta River will be described in the chapter on the southwest. This explanation is necessary, as regional divisions like these cannot be rationalized through mere lines on a map, but must be valid in human-geographical terms instead.

Palenque

The most important archaeological site in the north of the Maya region is, without a doubt, Palenque, which is within easy reach of Villahermosa. Travellers who are in a hurry can take one of the charter flights by sports plane which any travel agent or hotel in the city will be happy to arrange. Otherwise, the trip can be made by car or bus, in which case a visit to this site represents a day's outing from Villahermosa. There is also the option of staying overnight in Palenque at one of the tourist hotels which have gone up in the last few years.

The 120 km (74 miles) between Villahermosa and Palenque on Highway 186 can be driven in about one and a half hours. This road, however, is heavily used, as it continues on to Campeche and Mérida and is the main traffic route to Chetumal.

After having travelled for 100 km (60 miles) through marshy countryside, past endless tracts of pastureland and herds of horses and cattle, exit Highway 186 to the right and continue south. After about 15 km (9 miles) on this road, you will suddenly find yourself heading towards the mountains – the foothills of the Chiapas Highlands. Behind the village of Palenque, the road begins to twist and turn uphill. Here, it enters the mountain forest, characterized by giant, liana-draped trees, typical of the rainforest, and dense under-

Stucco head from the tomb of the high priest, Palenque

growth. It is in these surroundings that the Maya city of Palenque is located – situated on a mountain saddle in a commanding position above the wide plain.

"Amidst destruction and decay, we looked back into the past", wrote John Lloyd Stephens when he beheld these ruins buried under jungle vegetation for the first time. He and his genial artist Catherwood are credited with the rediscovery of this jewel of Maya architecture. This is not quite correct, however, as these ruins had already been mentioned several times during the course of the 18th century. Stephens was merely the first to publicize the discovery (in 1841 in his "Incidents of Travel in Central America, Mexico, Chiapas and Yucatán") and Catherwood's drawings made them famous. After that, the site was visited again and again – by Teobert Mahler, Alfred Maudsley and Leopold Batres, as well as by Eduard Seler and Sylvanus G. Morley – in short, by all the illustrious figures in the young field of Mexican studies in the 19th and 20th centuries. Somewhat surprisingly, excavations and restoration work (in the case of Maya ruins, the one is hardly possible without the other) have been carried out only since the 1940's. Palenque's present state of appearance dates from the late 1960's.

Palenque's central terrace with its main buildings grouped around the **palace** is accessible to visitors. All of these buildings have now been reconstructed, and they are painstakingly kept free of the tropical vegetation which – if left to grow freely – would once again become firmly established in every nook and cranny and eventually destroy the entire complex. The sprawling palace is dominated by a reconstructed observation tower which might have served as an observatory.

Via an open stairway you can reach the entrance gallery of the palace from where a hidden door leads to its northern section. A ceremonial courtyard surrounded by galleries stretches out to the left.

Behind this is a second large courtyard which obviously served as the palace's main place of worship: the sides of the staircases are adorned with larger-than-life reliefs depicting a procession of priests, and the stairway opposite is covered with glyphs. It was probably from this spot that the priests advanced in solemn procession towards the altars of worship. Galleries surround this courtyard as well and a chapel containing three chambers is located at its southern end. As you continue south, you pass through a number of vaulted rooms and connecting galleries which may have served as living quarters or fulfilled some other non-religious function. This section of the palace also contains underground chambers on two levels, whereby the upper level is clearly of more recent construction than the lower one. It is supposed that these chambers also served as living quarters, as some of them contain "hooks" which might have been used to hang hammocks. The experts are still unsure as to how to designate this palace: was it a priestly residence or was it only occasionally inhabited by guards or other personnel?

The columns, pilasters, walls and curb roofs of the palace were once covered with colourful stucco reliefs, but moisture, vegetation and the fires laid by the early excavators to combat the vegetation have destroyed almost every trace of them. What remains – the famous stucco masks from the burial chamber and the glyph-covered columns made of plaster – are now displayed in the small museum near the excavation site.

Of Palenque's many temples, seven have been excavated and restored. Three of them form part of the so-called "north group" on the edge of the terrace. Of the four most important temples, three stand on a separate terrace, an "acropolis" on the other side of the Otolum, a creek which runs through the complex.

These three, the **Temple of the Sun,** the **Temple of the Foliated Cross** and the **Temple of the Count,** were all built in the same architectural style during the Late Classic phase around A. D. 800. Their exteriors are characterized by steep platforms and high, honeycombed "crests" atop the roof. In the interiors, there are double galleries with corbelled vaults and sanctuaries against the back walls. In the Temple of the Sun, a cult relief in the form of a probable solar symbol surrounded by the magnificent portraits of two priests has been preserved. In the Temple of the Count and the Temple of the Foliated Cross, only secondary reliefs have been preserved, but these (in particular the ones in the Temple of the Foliated Cross) represent the most magnificent, almost individually lifelike portraits of priests created anywhere in the Maya region. (The cult reliefs from the Temple of the Foliated Cross can now be found in the Museum of Anthropology in Mexico City.)

The most famous and spectacular structure here is certainly the

Temple of the Inscriptions situated on the side of a hill to the right of the entryway to the terrace. Its platform – an imposing 22 metres (72 feet) high – is surmounted by the temple proper, which can be reached via a steep staircase. From the uppermost step, one has a panoramic view of the entire site. In the rear gallery of the temple there are limestone slabs with extensive, but as yet undecipherable, glyphs. It is after these that the temple was named. The date glyphs indicate that it was built in the late 7th century, i. e. in the Late Classic period.

A sensational discovery was made here purely by chance in 1952, when a floor slab, which was being examined, was lifted to reveal a staircase leading down into the interior of the structure. Halfway down, the staircase turns and then turns again until it comes to a burial chamber almost back at the level of the floor. When it was discovered, this tomb of a high priest was totally intact, i. e., it hat not been plundered by grave robbers. The sarcophagus was covered by an 8-tonne slab of limestone displaying a remarkable relief: a man half-sitting, half-lying on a sort of altar before a "cross of leaves": under him, the mask of the Sun God is visible. Perhaps it is the portrayal of a human sacrifice, as the excavator Alberto Ruz surmised. In no way is it an "astronaut at the control panel of his rocket" as Erich von Däniken has so ridiculously suggested. The tomb contained the body of the priest or prince, bedecked with precious ornaments of jadestone and wearing a jadestone mask. While the jewels can be admired today in Mexico City, the sarcophagus has been left in its place.

Like all of the other ceremonial centres throughout the Maya region, Palenque was abandoned around the year A. D. 900. The priests and princes disappeared, and with them went the artists and crafsmen whom they employed. The city went to ruin, was overrun by vegetation and was never inhabited again.

Agua Azul

The **waterfalls** of Agua Azul can be reached from Palenque in about 40 minutes via the winding road which leads to Ococingo. They are situated in a small valley that has been made into a national park and has a camp site and a restaurant. Surrounded by mangrove trees and aerial roots, you can swim in the crystal-clear waters near the falls.

From Palenque, you have several options for continuing your journey: you can either go south to San Cristóbal de las Casas and the Guatemalan border, or northeast towards Chetumal on the frontier of Belize (formerly British Honduras), or north to Campeche and Mérida.

Comalcalco

Comalcalco, located 60 km (37 miles) northwest of Villahermosa, is the westernmost Maya site known thus far. While it dates from the Classic period, it was probably built under the influence of Palenque, some 150 km (93 miles) away "as the crow flies". This was the main ceremonial centre of the coastal Maya or Chontal, as they call themselves. The architecture of the site resembles that of Palenque in terms of layout and detail. For example, two princely tombs found here were apparently modelled after the Tomb of the High Priest at Palenque.

Because there was no quarry near the Chontal's coastal homeland, these people used fired clay bricks in construction – a peculiarity in Mayan architecture which can only be seen here on such a large scale. The ceremonial structures cover an area of one square kilometre (½ square mile) and were cleverly positioned in this region constantly threatened by floods. By constructing the main buildings upon natural hills, the people avoided the tedious process of building up mounds.

The centre of the site is formed by a 200 metre (650 ft) long ceremonial courtyard surrounded by three separate architectural complexes. The most important of these is the **"Great Acropolis"** which consists of a palace and several temples situated upon a large platform. While these buildings have been examined and reconstructed, those on the eastern end of the courtyard have not yet been excavated.

The Great Acropolis, which rises up about 35 metres (115 feet), is dominated by the façade of the "palace", an 80 metre (260 ft) wide gallery which is comprised of two vaulted chambers one behind the other. Of the buildings on the southern end of the courtyard, one deserves special mention: when Danish anthropologist Franz Blom inspected Temple XX in 1925, he discovered in its interior a burial chamber with corbelled vaults. The tomb had been plundered, but what continue to be of interest today are the stucco decorations in the tomb and on parts of the northern acropolis. While the burial chamber was obviously modelled after the one in Palenque, it is not of the same high quality. Not until the excavation of Comalcalco reaches a more advanced stage will we be able to understand the function – and measure the true significance – of this, the westernmost Maya site.

Campeche

The drive from Palenque to Campeche takes you over 360 km (223 miles) of good road. Highway 261 reaches the Gulf coast near Champoton and follows it from there to Campeche, capital of the state of the same name. The Yucatán Peninsula is divided up between the states of Campeche, Yucatán and Quintana Roo, meaning that the geographic designation "Yucatán" ist not identical to the political one.

Campeche is a small, pleasant port town. Portions of the Spanish fortifications have been preserved and they now contain a museum in which locally-found antiquities are displayed.

A new El Presidente Hotel located directly on the beach promenade makes Campeche a suitable point of departure for trips into the interior.

Edzna

Sixty-five kilometres (40 miles) inland from Campeche lies the most important Maya ruin in the southwest of the peninsula – Edzna. This 6 square km (2-square-mile) large site was discovered in 1927, after which its centre and the nearby temples were excavated and reconstructed. Surrounding these main temples, however, lie thousands of stone structures, smaller terraces and houses which are still waiting to be studied. The excavations show that this city existed throughout the entire epoch of Maya civilization: its earliest buildings can be dated back to the year A. D. 200; others date from the Late Classic period up to the downfall of Maya civilization around the year A. D. 900.

What makes Edzna so interesting is the **flawless water supply and storage system** which was unearthed here. This system, which testifies to the technical know-how of its creators, was made up of reservoirs, cisterns and mile-long irrigation lines which guaranteed the constant availability of water and opened up vast tracts of land for cultivation.

In the swampy depression in which Edzna lies, the question of water supply is a question of survival. Here it was solved in a classic manner, and one which made permanent settlement possible.

The ceremonial centre occupies a sprawling plaza whose sides measure 170 x 100 metres (560 x 330 feet). Some of the buildings (the Platform of the Knives, the "western building" and the "southern temple") have not yet been excavated but are clearly recognizable under the vegetation. The **"great acropolis"** has been reconstructed: a large, artificial platform measuring 150 x 150 metres (500 x 500 feet) which was erected to serve as a foundation for the various temples on top. A steep stairway made of limestone blocks leads up to those smaller temples, all of which are in a more or less good state of preservation.

The largest and most important temple – and obviously the city's main religious structure – is the **Temple of the Five Storeys.** A stairway of differing widths leads from terrace to terrace and up to the temple which is situated about 30 metres (100 feet) above. Hewn stones with glyphic texts are embedded into the lower steps; as yet undecipherable, they could contain information about the history of the building, and at the same time, about the history of the city.

This building was constructed in a combination of the Puuc and Rio Bec architectural styles. A unique feature of this temple are the many corridors which lead into the interior from each level of the platform: perhaps these were priest's quarters and the ceremonial chambers were located in the temple proper. A "picota", an idol typical of the Yucatán-Maya style, stands on the plaza before the temple pyramid. This stone column, similiar to the many found in Uxmal, may have been a phallic symbol.

Those who have time may like to stroll about the site and take a look at the unexcavated portions of Edzna, whose "great acropolis" is certainly one of the most remarkable structures in the northern Maya zone.

Uxmal

From Edzna, continue north on Highway 261 and you will reach Uxmal within one hour. This ceremonial centre of the Mayas in Yucatán is one of the largest archaeological zones in the entire country.

Uxmal is only one of several archaeological sites in the Puuc region of southwestern Yucatán, the region after which the site's architectural style is named. The Puuc style is part of the Mayan baroque which also includes the Chenes and Rio Bec styles found in regions further south. Although Uxmal is the most impressive of the Puuc sites, the others – Kabáh, Labná, Sayil and Xlampak, all located not far from Uxmal (see page 321) – are also worth seeing. During the administration of the previous president, López Portillo, the last three sites were made accessible to tourists through the construction of a paved road.

All these sites have one negative feature in common: they have never been properly excavated! The buildings were cleared of vegetation, reconstructed, and a fence and a ticket booth were built. Conclusive information about the age of these sites is lacking because the layers of construction beneath the surface were never investigated. The earliest datings – which were arrived at more by chance than through scientific investigation – place the site in the 7th century A. D. The theory of the "old" and "new" Maya realms, which was accepted until only recently, probably grew out of this lack of in-depth scientific investigation. Recent excavations sponsored by New Orleans' Tulane University and carried out under the direction of W. Pendergast at Dzibilchaltun have proven these premature conclusions wrong. Pre-Classic layers have been uncovered there, showing that that site – within 100 km (63 miles) of Uxmal – is as old as those in the Petén, the nurturing ground of the Mayan civilization.

Perhaps similar discoveries will one day be made at Uxmal, but the question is: Will proper excavations ever be carried out? In addition to all else, this would certainly pose a financial problem as the site would have to be closed to the public for the duration of the campaign. In all fairness, and in defence of the Mexicans, it must be said that with the vast amount of sites waiting to be excavated, they do not know where to start shovelling first.

Uxmal's main points of interest are its ceremonial complexes – the **Pyramid of the Magician** (also called Pyramid of the Dwarf), the **Quadrangle of the Nuns,** and the **Palace of Governors** – all impressive examples of monumental architecture which are unmatched in the entire area of Maya settlement. Due to its decorations, the Quadrangle of the Nuns poses an interesting case. The complex consists of an almost rectangular courtyard, accessible from outside only through a narrow, vaulted tunnel. All four sides are flanked with façades facing inward which contain entrances leading into double chambers with the usual corbelled vaults: whereby one chamber always lies directly behind the other. It is the façades, however, facing the large ceremonial courtyard, which are so unique.

The focal point of this complex is the raised building on the northern end of the plaza, accessible via a broad stairway which contains a small temple. The frieze on the façades is underlaid with a rhomboid design and standing kaziks are portrayed over the entrances. Over the middle entrance, a throne composed of two jaguars is depicted, situated in front of a richly decorated house. Interestingly enough, such a throne is actually located at this site – it stands in the square in front of the Palace of Governors. The façade of the building on the western end of the plaza is decorated in the same way, and the question is: Are these portraits of people who actually lived?

This question should be asked, particularly in light of the local legends of the "dwarf" and the "old woman". One of the persons portrayed on the western façades is the "turtle man" – but this figure could later have been misinterpreted to be that of a dwarf.

The façade of the eastern building displays a rigid geometric design. Above the entrances, the face of the maize god is uniquely sculpted in a mosaic of maize kernels: the nose is an ear of maize.

Over the entrances in the southern façade, the one which contains the entry tunnel, huts, just like the ones built by Yucatán peasants today, are depicted: round adobe structures with high hip roofs made of sisal. It may be assumed that this galleried courtyard was used for cult dances or audiences.

From the Quadrangle of the Nuns, turn south and proceed through a small ball court to the **House of the Turtles**, a rectangular structure with a heavy roof and chambers on all four sides. Its name comes from the turtles depicted on the frieze which encircles the roof. Probably this reptile was venerated in Uxmal as a god or as the symbol of a god.

Behind the House of the Turtles, the platform which supports the Palace of Governors rises up some 15 metres (50 feet). This palace, the name of which is as unsuitable as the names of all the other complexes here, is a sprawling structure which can be entered via a stairway. The jaguar throne already mentioned stands on the plaza before the palace, along with a stela in the form of a column which might be another phallic symbol. This palace also contains a double row of inner chambers, each pair accessible via its own door. The usual question as to whether these chambers served as living quarters will probably never be answered conclusively. The façade which contains the entrance is surmounted by a heavy roof decorated with a frieze displaying the geometric designs typical of the Puuc style.

Behind and adjacent to the palace platform lies the **Southern Complex,** the largest yet to be found in Uxmal. It consists of three temples situated side by side on an immense platform preceded by a large courtyard. Unfortunately, this complex has never been excavated and restored – here and there, vines and bushes have been pulled away and walls have been exposed. A "cresteria", which has been known since Spanish times as the "colombario" or dovecote, rises up from out of the bushes. The vaulted gallery which it surmounted has collapsed and disappeared under vegetation.

In the southwestern section of the site lies the **Pyramid of the Old Woman,** which has only been partly cleared of vegetation and is therefore difficult to climb. Further architectural complexes are situated in the north and the northwest; namely, the Northern Group, the Platform of the Monuments and the Burial Complex where a number of graves have been uncovered. As these structures have not yet been fully excavated, only those with a special interest should undertake to visit them.

Kabáh

A few miles south of Uxmal on the road to Campeche lies Kabáh, another extensive Classic Maya settlement. Here, as elsewhere in the Maya region, only one of many complexes has been excavated and reconstructed.

Kabáh's main attraction is the **Codz-Pop**, which is part of a larger ceremonial complex with courtyards and palaces. This rectangular structure, which resembles but is smaller than the Palace of Governors at Uxmal, is located atop a platform accessible via a steep stairway. Its remarkable feature is not its architecture, but its façade, which is virtually covered with depictions of the mask of the Rain God, Chac, in mosaic (the long, trunk-like nose of the god has been broken off almost all over).

The mask of the Rain God is one of the main decorative elements of the Puuc style and of Mayan architectural sculpture in general. Here, however, the exuberance of the baroque Maya style was carried to extremes... and imagine that the façade and its decorations were once colourfully painted! Next to the Codz-Pop there is a complex of palaces and plazas similar to the Quadrangle of the Nuns at Uxmal, although somewhat less monumental in its dimensions.

On the other side of the road, a short path leads westward to a gate with decorative sculpture that is, unfortunately, no longer visible. Only after further excavations will we be able to say something about its function and significance. It should not, in any case, be misinterpreted as a town gate or arch of triumph as has so often occurred. Like a similar gate in Labná, it may have been the ornamental portal of a ceremonial courtyard.

What is particularly impressive about the Puuc style of Yucatán is the way in which its wealth of ideas and variety of decorative styles are implemented within the confines of a limited number of basic architectural forms.

Xlampak, Sayil and Labná

Between Kabáh and Uxmal, the newly-finished, paved road travels east, making it easier to visit the sites of Xlampak, Sayil and Labná. This entire region is strewn with Maya structures, most of which are in poor condition, overgrown with vegetation, and difficult for the untrained eye to recognize. The **temple of Xlampak,** however, is in surprisingly good condition and has now been excavated and restored. It is a rectangular structure with galleries of double chambers on all four sides. Nothing is known about its purpose, and only further excavations will be able to give us some answers.

The next site is Sayil, where one finds a well-preserved **palace complex** of impressive dimensions: two platforms surmounted by "palaces" containing the usual double chambers which have been reconstructed from remaining pieces. The elaborate half columns and pilasters on the façade are particularly interesting – obviously this decoration was first worked in wood and then transposed onto stone. A tall stairway divides the building in half: one can assume that it led to a sanctuary, but archaeologists have not yet been able to reconstruct it.

While Labná is the site of a very similar palace complex, its main attraction is the **monumental gate** which was found here in good condition. The stone mosaics which had once adorned the façade were found scattered in a wide radius about the gate. They have since been collected and painstakingly reset.

The gate with its vaulted entryway and numerous corbels displays the same features as the palace in Sayil. The projecting pilasters imitate a woodworking style which must have been used in early Mayan architecture: when stone replaced wood, the style was merely transferred to the new medium.

(Thieme)

Mérida

Mérida, the capital of the state of Yucatán (abbreviated Yuc.), is located 60 km (37 miles) from Uxmal. Besides being an administrative centre, this city is the hub of a vast agricultural region, and home to a number of important educational institutions. Among these are the University of Yucatán and the Instituto Technológico Regional de Mérida. In addition to the old fibre mills for the production of henequen (at present an ailing industry), Mérida also houses a developing

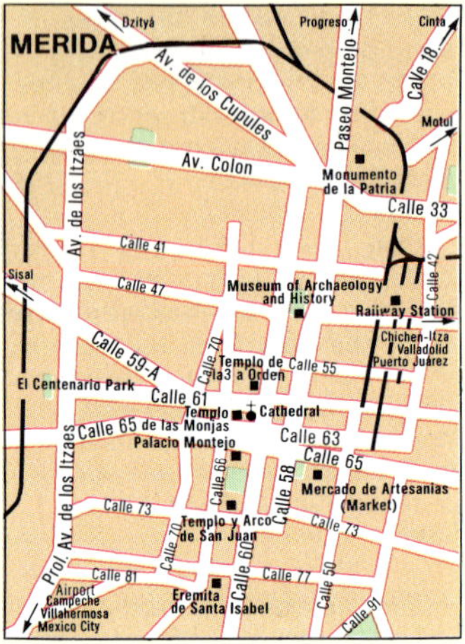

food processing industry which is to serve the surrounding region. This part of the country is relatively far away from the main centres of production in Mexico's central highlands.

Due to its charming atmosphere and its suitability as a point of departure for visits to Yucatán's famed archaeological sites, Mérida is also an important tourist destination with a number of good-to-excellent hotels and restaurants. Its international airport lies on the crossroads of air traffic lines between Mexico and Cuba, the west coast of South America and the western and central states of the U. S. Although it is the main metropolis on the Yucatán Peninsula, as well as one of southeastern Mexico's largest cities, its population of approximately 300,000 is relatively small.

Due to the topography of the region in which it is located, Mérida was able – in the course of time – to expand freely in all directions. Like many other Mexican cities, it has an orderly, checkerboard layout. Originally a city of a certain provincial charm, it has, in the past fifteen years, undergone a transformation to become a lively, modern metropolitan centre. Among other developments, an extensive industrial zone is going up on its periphery.

Mérida lies to the north of Campeche on the Yucatán Peninsula at the site of the former Maya city of Tiho. It was founded in 1542 by Francisco de Montejo, Jr., who later (in 1546) conquered the rest of the peninsula. By doing so, he realized the often-failed goal of his father, Francisco de Montejo, Sr. It was on January 23rd 1542 when the last ruler of the city of Tiho surrendered to the conquistador. The Mayan temple pyramids were razed and the rubble was used to level the site upon which the Spanish town of Estremadura (present-day Mérida) was erected.

Shortly after the importation of the first Negro slaves from Africa in 1648, a yellow fever epidemic broke out. Many of the inhabitants of the still small town lost their lives.

Because of its remote location – on the far edge of the great territory of Mexico, so to speak, Mérida remained largely unaffected by the sweeping political movements of the early 19th century. Although the desire to be independent was undoubtedly as strong here as anywhere else, this isolated region did not even take part in the Mexican War of Independence (1811–1821).

1874 saw the beginning of a Maya revolt in the region, backed by British merchants from the neighbouring Honduras (now Belize) who supplied the rebels with arms. The armed conflict lasted until 1901 when Mexican Federal troops finally succeeded in breaking the power of the insurgents and arresting their leaders. Since the end of the 19th century, the ups and downs in the production of henequen have been crucial to the development of the city and the region. As of the 1940's, the area's economy has been boosted by the interest of tourists from North America and further abroad.

Most of Mérida's streets are not named, but numbered: those running east to west have odd numbers, those running north to south have even numbers. Plaza Mayor and the cathedral of Mérida at the intersection of Calles 61 and 58 are more or less at the centre of the town. This centre lies within a zone bordered by Calle 66 (66th Street) to the west, Calle 50 to the east, Calle 53 to the north and Calle 65 to the south. Calle 65 is the arterial which runs east to Chichén Itzá and to Puerto Juárez and Cancún, two port and resort towns on Yucatán's east coast.

Mérida's most important buildings are located in the zone surrounding **Plaza Mayor.** The **cathedral,** built between 1561 and 1568 by Pedro de Aulestia and Miguel de Aguero, has a baroque façade. The interior contains a portrayal of the surrender of the Mayan prince Tutul Xiú to the conquistador Francisco Montejo. Also worth seeing is a wooden Indian statue, the so-called Cristo de Ampollas (Christ of the Blisters), which hangs in a small chapel, the Capilla de Cristo de Ampollas. Unfortunately, this statue was somewhat damaged in a fire which destroyed the small church of Ichmul in Yucatán where it was originally displayed.

The former **archbishop's residence** is separated from the cathedral by the Pasaje de la Revolución. The building, which included a seminary in an annex, was secularized in 1915. South of Plaza Mayor lies the **Palacio Montejo,** which was begun in 1549. Its façade, richly decorated in the plateresque style, features depictions of conquistadors armed with halberds and standing on the allegorically portrayed heads of wild, bearded men. There are also portraits and busts of Francisco de Montejo Sr., his wife and their daughter, Catalina de Montejo. This beautiful home – which is open to the public – is still in the possession of the descendents of the conquistador Francisco de Montejo.

Exactly opposite the cathedral stands the **Palacio Municipal** (town hall), a building with two galleries, one on top of the other, and a bell tower which dates from the 16th century. The square is flanked to the south by the **Palace of the Governor** (Palacio del Gobernador) of Yucatán, which was built in 1892 to replace an older administration building. The **Convento de la Mejorada,** which can be reached via Calle 59 going east, was built by the Franciscans at the end of the 17th century. With the exception of a church building dating from 1640, the convent is now used for residential purposes.

The earlier city limits are marked by two "city gates", the **Arco de los Dragones** (Arch of the Dragons) and the **Arco de la Puente** (Arch of the Bridge) which can be reached via Calles 61 and 63 going east.

Other interesting buildings include the **Teatro Peon Contreras,** built between 1900 and 1908 by Italian architects in the neoclassic style, and the building which houses the **University of Yucatán,** which was reconstructed after 1938 in Spanish-Moorish style. The interior of the building contains traces of an earlier structure, a Jesuit seminary that was built in 1618 and remained the property of the Jesuits until 1767. Especially near the entrance you can see traces of the classic baroque style.

The **Museum of Archaeology,** which is situated about 3 km (2 miles) north (towards Progreso) of the centre of Mérida, contains objects from distant archaeological sites (including Teotihuacán and Monte Albán) as well as from various sites in Yucatán (Chichén Itzá, etc.).

One of Mérida's special attractions is certainly its **market**, located about 1,000 metres (½ mile) south of the cathedral on Calle 56. Market day is everyday, but Sundays are the most interesting. Here, you can find "artesanía" articles, especially those made from the sisal fibre, henequen (hammocks and woven articles such as tote bags); and embroidered clothing such as skirts and blouses (called "huipiles"). This market is also an ordinary fruit and vegetable market where farmers from the surrounding countryside, dressed in traditional garb, gather to sell their produce.

(Schmidt)

Izamal

From Mérida, Highway 180 takes you west to Mexico's Caribbean coast. Since the development of the beaches here – and especially since the development of Cancún as an international beach resort under President Echeverría – this road, now heavily travelled, has become a racetrack of sorts. Along the way to Cancún, you will pass Chichén Itzá, the most thoroughly studied and carefully reconstructed of Yucatán's ancient sites.

If you are not in a hurry, you may like to add a 30 km (19-mile) detour to the 160 km (100 miles) to Chichén Itzá and visit Izamal. One of the twelve temple pyramids which once stood here was the largest in Yucatán. The importance the Spaniards attached to this site is evidenced by the fact that they constructed an immense monastery at it. Izamal was **a centre for the veneration of the Sun God,** whose cult was obviously to be superimposed by Christian elements. Up until now, this site has been neglected by archaeologists – extensive restoration could easily make it as attractive as Chichén Itzá.

Chichén Itzá

"On the Edge of the Itzá Well" is the literal translation of this name, which dates from the city's second great period of growth following the Toltec conquest of the Yucatán Peninsula.

Chichén Itzá's initial phase of settlement and construction occurred within the Classic and Late Classic periods of Mayan culture. The so-called Church Complex, located near the observatory, dates from this phase. A steep, massive temple pyramid with an annexed courtyard flanked by galleries displays the characteristic details of the Maya decorative style of this region: the carved columns and pilasters, the use of the mask of Chac in decorations, and the ornamented steps and friezes. When compared with those at Uxmal and Kabáh, these decorations are clearly less refined; even the work of stonecutting was not carried out with the same precision and care. This is generally seen as a characteristic of a later subperiod of the Late Classic phase.

Such an assumption can be mistaken, however, as detailed research at other sites has proven. Archaeological sites differ not only as a result of being built at a time when a particular style was prevalent, or because they were built with a specific purpose in mind (the quality of a structure depended very much on this), but also as a result of the number and kind of craftsmen employed. This is particularly important in the case of Late Classic Mayan art, demands made of architects and other craftsmen having greatly increased. At Chichen Itza, there are considerable differences in the quality of buildings which were apparently built contemporarily (the same phenomena can be observed in other places in the northern Maya region). The two structures described in the following paragraphs are good examples of this. The church is much less refined in its construction than the House of the

Mysterious Inscriptions, yet they date from the same period and stand only metres apart!

The **Church** (so named by the Spanish) is a rather strange structure which is difficult to fathom: a heavy, massive roof covers a house which consists of one vaulted room. On the lintel spanning the only entrance, traces of a mechanism with which to lock the door from the inside were found, suggesting that the room could have been occupied, although this hardly seems possible considering the nature of this structure. A portion of the gallery which surrounds the adjoining courtyard could also have been inhabited. The roof is decorated with interesting limestone reliefs depicting aquatic animals and enchained human figures.

In the bushes 50 metres (165 feet) away lies another structure which dates from the Late Classic phase: the **House of the Mysterious Inscription** as its Indian name goes. It is a "palace" of the usual kind: a double row of chambers with corbelled vaults surrounds a massive courtyard. Once again, the question may be raised as to whether or not such a building was inhabited. Its name comes from a relief on the first chamber on its front side showing a priest surrounded by a column of glyphs the meaning of which is undecipherable – the "mysterious inscription".

The main attractions of Chichén Itzá are the structures which date from its second phase, the age of the Maya-Toltecs. This phase followed the invasion of the Toltecs from the central plateau and is closely linked with the name of their most illustrious leader, **Ceacatl Topilztin,** also known as Quetzalcoátl. There is hardly an event in ancient Mexican history which is as well-documented as this one: Mayan as well as Aztec sources give similar and clear accounts. This is due to the fact that the Aztecs, especially, were fascinated by the mystic power of the name Ceacatl: he was one with their god Quetzalcoátl. They awaited his return and consequently mistook Cortés, who appeared "out of the east over the sea" with his rabble of soldiers, for the returning god. Aztec chronology places the beginning of the renowned leader's reign in the year A. D. 977, and his death in the year A. D. 999. According to Mayan chronology, Kukulkan, as they called Quetzalcoátl, reigned from A. D. 967 to 987. When one makes allowances for slight discrepancies and for the difficulty in translating Aztec and Mayan dates into the Gregorian calendar system, the concurrence is striking.

In both the Mayan and the Aztec accounts, Kukulkan/Quetzalcoátl left Yucatán "the same way he came" and returned to his home in the central highlands. Researchers have been able to retrace his steps in general terms on the basis of written and illustrated documents. Followed by a portion of the Toltec population, he travelled from central Mexico to the Gulf coast and boarded ship, possibly in the area of Tampico. Near Champotón on the Gulf of Campeche, he disembarked, and together with his Toltec followers and other peoples who had joined them, he travelled overland to present-day Yucatán state. Armed conflicts on land and sea are described in the accounts, but the defence against the intruders could not have been well organized. After the loss of their elite, the Maya lacked political and military leadership. As their names were soon to show, the Mayan upper class quickly became "toltequized".

Kukulkan founded Mayapan and turned Chichén Itzá into a religious centre. During his reign, other peoples, whose upper classes were already quite toltequized, migrated into the region – perhaps they had even been summoned there. So it was that he set up the Cocom family as rulers in Mayapan and that, with his acceptance, the Tutul Xiú established themselves in Uxmal. It seems, however, that he "settled down" in Yucatán only to disappear again into the highlands. It also seems that he endeavoured to establish Toltec religious concepts and societal forms in Maya land, something which, according to Maya accounts, met with resistance and disapproval. One source laments the moral decline which became evident after the introduction of the cult of the Plumed Serpent and describes the new lords as "debauchees". Erotic practices seem to have been connected with the new cult – practices which obviously aroused the objections of the Mayas.

Under Kukulkan and his successors, a real renaissance in art and architecture took place and Chichén Itzá experienced a second golden age. The new Toltec cult centre was erected just 150 metres (490 feet) from the **cenote,** a deep natural well that had been an object of fascination since prehistoric times. The water source that first attracted human settlers to the area later became the focal point of worship. Divers have explored this cenote and brought to the surface a multitude of devotional and sacrificial objects which had been thrown in over the ages.

This new cult centre of the Toltec lords consisted of two gigantic complexes, the temple platform of Kukulkan (also called **El Castillo**) and the **Temple of the Warriors.** The latter is a copy of the Temple of the Morning Star at Tula. Both structures were built over pyramids – still intact today – which date from the period of the reign of Kukulkan himself. In the case of the Castillo, even the altars within the earlier structure are intact, offering us perfectly preserved specimens of otherwise forgotten Toltec sculpture. The temple within the Castillo is open to visitors but the old Temple of the Warriors is closed due to the fragility of the fresco paintings there. El Castillo is on a platform with a base measuring 60 x 60 metres (200 x 200 feet), which rises up over nine levels to a height of 42 metres (140 feet). The number of the levels is no accident: it corresponds to a number system used in the Maya calendar. The number of steps which lead to the summit of the platform likewise has deeper significance: on all four sides of the pyramid, identical staircases, each with exactly 91 steps, lead up to the top. Altogether, there are 364 steps. Add to that the upper platform upon which the temple stands and you arrive at the figure 365 – the number of days in the solar year.

The raised temple of this second phase of construction was a new form which did not yet exist in Tula and which became an element of Maya-Toltec structures in Yucatán only after the 11th century: a hall with entrances on all four sides and lacking an obvious front. The more conservative Temple of the Warriors was built strictly along the lines of its model in Tula – it has only one staircase and the temple at the top matches the one atop the Temple of the Morning Star down to the details of its decoration. The great hall is supported by columns which bear reliefs depicting Toltec warriors. The principle of the atlantes is represented by the figures which support the altar and columns shaped like serpent bodies decorate the portal. On the platform before the temple stands a chacmool figure, generally interpreted to represent a messenger of the gods. These figures are typical of the sculptural style of the Toltecs.

The third of Chichén Itzá's large complexes is the **ball court,** the largest complex of this sort that has ever been found anywhere. Two phases of construction have been identified here: the older one, which dates from the time of Kukulkan's reign, is represented by a small temple that was incorporated into the exterior of the later complex. Inside, there are some interesting reliefs depicting a procession of Toltec warriors.

The great ball court dates from the second phase of construction. Built in the familiar double-T form, its 50 metre (160-foot)-long playing surface is closed in on both ends by galleries. It has vertical side walls, one of which is surmounted by a temple. Interior walls are painted with frescos which clearly depict scenes from the Toltec conquest of the region. Unfortunately, it must be kept closed to the public to protect the frescos from further decomposition. The rings through which the ball probably had to be thrown are placed very high in this ball court – one of several positions possible.

The **observatory,** called "El Caracol" (the snail), is another example of architecture unique in all of Mexico. The name, "the snail", stems from the spiral staircase in the interior of the round tower. This structure appears to belong to Chichén Itzá's later architectural phase, although the second, upper platform seems to have been only an extension of an early plaform which is still recognizable. In the upper wall crown of the tower, the remains of windows can be seen, the dimensions of which had been exactly measured. It has been shown that the angle of inclination of the sides and lintels of the windows were aligned with astral bodies – the planet Venus and the moon – thus proving irrefutably that this building served as an observatory.

Crumbled foundations and other rubble which could have belonged to living quarters for the astronomers – if such quarters existed – can be found scattered around the Caracol. In any case, it must be assumed that the tower was continuously occupied, as the sky was observed day and night.

Chichén Itzá can be recommended as an overnight stop for individual travellers as well as groups. The tourist facilities have been expanded and improved in the last few years and there is now an abundance of inns and hotels of every price category in the village and around the archaeological site. The best and also the most conveniently located for a visit to the ruins are the Hacienda and the Villa Arqueológica.

Chichén Itzá also has an airport which can accommodate not only small aircraft, but the larger propeller planes as well. These fly regularly from Mérida to Cancún and Puerto Juárez.

Dzibilchaltun

This archaeological zone lies just 10 km (6 miles) north of Mérida on the road which leads to the port town of Progreso. A visit to this site is recommended only for those with a special interest in it, for the number of intact or reconstructed buildings is sorely limited. The scientific value of this site stands in marked contrast to its value as a tourist attraction, however: this is one of the few ancient centres in Yucatán which has been seriously excavated and studied, and the findings are exemplary for the entire northern zone of Mayan settlement. Furthermore, it is clear that this was one of the largest Maya settlements in the region: an area encompassing 50 sq. km (20 sq. miles) containing traces of habitation has been identified.

Mayapan

What has been said about Dzibilchaltun applies to this site as well: its pre-eminence as an ancient Maya centre does not correspond to its value as a tourist attraction today. Consequently, those who visit it will not find it overrun with people. Mayapan was probably founded by Kukulkan himself and then passed on to the Cocom ruling dynasty. It is one of the youngest urban settlements of ancient Yucatán and displays an important feature characteristic of the later period in which it was built: it is surrounded by a 9 km (5.5 mile) long wall which traces an oval around an area measuring 4 sq. km (1.5 square miles). Its Maya name, "Ychpa", means "within the walls".

The city within the walls was densely populated; some 4,000 platform and house foundations have been identified. Its ceremonial and palace precinct was relatively small – the change in function of Maya cities as of the 13th century is clearly visible here. While in older Maya centres the ceremonial buildings far outnumbered the dwellings, here, the situation is reversed: Mayapan's buildings were primarily secular ones. Its population in the 13th and 14th centuries is estimated to have been between 15,000 and 20,000, whereby an added, unknown number of people are thought to have settled outside the walls as well.

The centre of the city is marked by a temple pyramid called **El Castillo,** probably in imitation of the one at Chichén Itzá. This structure was clearly designed after its great forerunner, but in its execution and workmanship it is markedly inferior. The Castillo, like all other official buildings in the city centre, is characterized by crudely laid stones and a crooked construction. Rough-hewn rock was merely stuck together with lime mortar and covered over with thick layers of plaster. It is clear that with workmanship like this, this building was never destined to hold up well, and indeed, it now presents an unsightly picture to visitors who look at it today.

Tulum

Although this site dates from the same period as Mayapan and its architecture is of the same poor quality, it is nevertheless interesting to visit as it is the only Maya settlement which was constructed by the sea. Its three landward sides are closed in by a massive wall which is even more obviously defensive than the one at Mayapan: it is thicker, it rises up to a height of 6 metres (20 feet) in parts, and battlements and casemates extend along its inside. It can be said that the city was specifically designed to deal with states of siege.

Tulum has become a favourite destination for excursionists from the newly developed resorts at Cancún and on the island of Cozumel. From Cancún, 120 km (74 miles) to the south, it can be reached via Highway 307. Excursions, which usually include the **lagoon of Xel-há** located north of Tulum, can be booked through the hotels in the resorts. Here, as well, you can see remains of buildings which date from the later years of Maya-Toltec culture (the Cocom phase). The lagoon, with its crystal-clear waters and limestone formations along its banks, is a dazzling sight to see.

From the highway, a small paved road runs directly to the city's surrounding wall where the entrance to the site is located. Upon entering you will see the main buildings along the coast at its opposite end.

The largest temple here – known as the **Castillo** – is modelled after its late Maya-Toltec (Cocom) namesakes down to the crude masonry which is recognizable under the thick layers of plaster. In front and to the left of this temple stands a relatively well-preserved structure, the **Temple of the Falling God,** named after a strange figure modelled in plaster in the upper frieze: a human being with jaguar features who hangs, head, shoulders and hands forward, from the temple's pediment. This figure, which appears in southern Mayan architecture as of the Late Classic period, must represent a god, but a more exact interpretation is impossible due to a lack of information.

The **Temple of the Frescos** is an elongate, galleried structure on the front of which can be seen remains of its original painting. It must be assumed that the plaster covering all these buildings was once brightly coloured, as this city was compared to Seville by the first Spaniards who sailed past years before the Conquest. From a distance, the ancient city of Tulum must have presented a magnificent sight.

Opposite the harbour in the corner of the north wall, two smaller buildings have managed to withstand the ravages of time: the **Temple of the Wind God,** located right by the sea, and a **well house.** In this northwestern corner of the city, the wall and the casemates as well are in better condition than elsewhere in Tulum.

A visit to this site is highly recommended on account of its unique seaside setting and the scenic beauty of its surroundings.

Cobá

Although this vast archaeological zone has been subjected to only minimal excavation, it is already quite popular with tourists, being just 50 km (30 miles) from Tulum and reachable via a paved road. The zone covers an area of approximately 60 sq. km (23 sq. miles) and was once one of the most densely populated zones in this region. According to the descendents of the ancient Maya, this site was connected with the cult of the "Falling God", the God of Honey. Cobá was a centre for the production of honey and cocoa and it seems that it was also a **commercial centre** of the first order during the Classic Maya period. Satellite photos have shown that the various sections of this sprawling settlement were connected to one another by a dense system of causeways. Cobá may be described as an early example of conurbation, with individual urban units that could hardly be told apart.

There can be no doubt that this settlement sprung up here because of the large number of funnel-shaped, water-filled sinkholes (cenotes) in the vicinity, which were able to provide a large population with water. Today we can assume that there were some 60,000 such wells here during the Classic period.

Near that part of Cobá which is accessible to visitors, a hotel has gone up recently that is highly recommended for those who would like to visit this site. It would be foolish to try to see everything here in a few hours – at least a full day is needed for a survey of the architecture in the "developed" sector of this vast area alone.

In the centre of this sector, which can now be easily visited on foot, stands the **Cobá Group,** dominated by a 45 metre (150 foot) high temple platform surmounted by a temple whose upper frieze contains an image of the "Falling God". From this vantage point, you can get a good look at the rest of the site: dozens of unexcavated pyramids are recognizable under the dense vegetation. Between them, the causeways – not visible from above – are flanked by hundreds of plazas, courtyards and ceremonial squares.

From this central point, networks of roads radiated out in all directions, hundreds of miles of which have been identified by means of aerial and infrared photography.

Chetumal and Rio Bec

Highway 307 takes you the 210 km (130 miles) to the port town of Chetumal on the border with Belize. This town is highly suitable as a base for trips to the archaeological sites in the vicinity as it contains a number of comfortable hotels.

A vast region of virgin forest extends west and south from Chetumal as far as the Guatemalan border and beyond, where it takes on the character of a tropical rainforest. Here, an unknown number of ruins of Classic Maya centres – some already discovered, others still awaiting discovery – lie hidden under the thick forest carpet. The decorative style of the structures in the region is highly interesting – it is called Rio Bec style after a site which was rediscovered in the 1950's: Rio Bec. It takes considerable effort to get to this site and a visit demands a full, long day.

From Chetumal, travel west on Highway 186 for about 160 km (100 miles), at which point you will have to turn off onto the dirt road which heads south. This road, which extends for some 40 km (25 miles), is negotiable only with a jeep or other four-wheel drive vehicle. You'll have to ask for directions to the ruins of Rio Bec at the filling station in Xpujil, where suitable vehicles are on hand and driver-guides can be hired. It is not safe to try to find the site by yourself, as you could easily get lost in the tangle of the jungle. Here, in this unpopulated region, you can't expect to find help in an emergency.

Rio Bec, which has never been excavated or explored in depth, offers a striking study of the destruction that can be caused by jungle vegetation: vines and trees grow as high as the roofs of the raised temples. The true extent of the city is still unknown, but the size and style of the temples tells us that it must have been an exceptionally large settlement. The typical features of the region's architectural style are clearly in evidence. The showiness of Mayan architecture, which can be witnessed throughout Maya land, was brought to new, almost grotesque heights here. The showiness of the actual structures was repeated in their sculptural decoration; in other words, the façades of temple pyramids were decorated with reliefs of temple pyramids.

Xpujil and Chicanná

For those who would rather not go through the trouble of getting to Rio Bec, there is an easier way to see temple decoration of the kind found there. Near the village of Xpujil, just on the road which leads to the ruins, there is a steep, towering temple platform decorated with a copy of itself. This building has been excavated and cleared of vegetation, so the remarkable reliefs are easily recognizable. The remaining ruins in the area have not yet been explored.

The same holds true for neighbouring Chicanná, an extensive site near Highway 186 between Xpujil and Chetumal. Two further, easy-to-reach but barely explored sites near this road are **Becan and Hormiguero.**

Kohunlich

Kohunlich, which is located near Chetumal and is accessible via a paved road leading off from the highway, is the only complex of ruins in this region which has been carefully excavated and studied. These ruins were first discovered and described in 1912, but the work of excavating them was not begun until 1969, and in 1976 the project was terminated for the time being. The object of study was the city's central zone, and the archaeologists who worked here still have no clear picture of exactly how large the entire site really is. Just under 200 buildings have been found in the area measuring 2 sq. km (¾ of a square mile) which has been explored; just short of a dozen of these buildings make up the ceremonial centre of the city.

The so-called **Acropolis** is a plaza which was obviously oriented towards the four compass points and was used for the erection of stelae. This part of the complex is in relatively poor condition and offers little to the average visitor. The ball court resembles those at other Maya sites: what is interesting, however, is the fact that stone balls the size of volley balls were found on the playing surface. It is not known whether these were the balls themselves. If the latter is so, a different sort of ball game must have been played here than the one already known about.

The most important building in the ceremonial centre is the **Temple of Masks,** a platform which displays little evidence of the regional Rio Bec style, but sooner resembles structures found at Uaxactún in the Petén and the lower structures of the North Acropolis at Tikal. For the construction of these temple platforms, a natural hill was levelled off to form the base of the artificial platform which supported the mammoth structure.

The staircase, with many steps leading up to the highest platform, is lined with enormous masks which represent the face of the Rain God. Unfortunately, the destruction caused by grave robbers – particularly in this complex – was so great that the various stages of construction can no longer be reconstructed. This makes the task of dating very difficult indeed. A comparison with the more easily datable architecture of the Petén has shown, however, that these masks date from the early Classic phase of Mayan culture – meaning that the Temple of Masks is a very archaic piece of architecture. *(Thieme)*

The Southwest

It is as difficult to demarcate the southwest of Mexico as it is any other region of the country. The same arbitrary criteria as have been used throughout the regional section to facilitate description must come into play here too. For our purposes we shall therefore take southwest Mexico to mean the states of Chiapas and Oaxaca. Northern Chiapas (the part of the state which borders on Tabasco and Campeche) is not included in this section, however. As far as Chiapas goes, the area in question consists of the highlands (between the capital of the state, Tuxtla Gutiérrez, San Cristóbal de las Casas and the Guatemalan border) as well as the stretch of tropical rainforest along the Rio Usumacinta (the river which constitutes the border with Guatemala here).

The important Maya sites of Bonampak and Yaxchilán will also be described.

Oaxaca de Juárez

With its tropical, mountain climate and incredibly varied landscape, the state of Oaxaca (abbreviated to Oax.) is considered to be one of Mexico's most beautiful. Oaxaca de Juárez is the capital of the state.

Today, some 180,000 people live in this attractive and friendly city, which is the centre of administration and the most important market town in the valley of Oaxaca. The timber industry has established itself in the higher-lying areas around Oaxaca. Marble and onyx are quarried here as well, and the mining of metallic ores (silver, gold) also takes place, although the latter is not a particularly profitable concern.

A certain amount of manufacturing is also in evidence in Oaxaca. These industries are based, above all, on the production of consumer goods and the processing of foodstuffs. Home industries such as weaving and pottery play an important role in the economy of the state, easily bearing comparison to that of larger industries.

Oaxaca is also an important centre of the tourist industry. Tourism has developed as a result of the city's pleasing appearance, its wealth of impressive colonial architecture and its proximity to some outstanding archaeological sites. The visitor will find that Oaxaca has quite a number of "good, solid" hotels – most of fairly long standing – restaurants and facilities for tent and trailer holidays.

Oaxaca's position on the northern edge of a high-lying valley at the foot of hills (some of which surpass the alpine foothills in terms of altitude) in an otherwise level region has left its mark upon the city. The limits of the main part of the town are marked in the west and south-west by the Rio Atoyac (the upper course of the mighty Rio Balsas) and in the east by a smaller river, the Rio Donaji. It is only in recent years that scattered settlements have spread across the Rio Donaji and up the slopes of the surrounding hills.

These restrictions placed on the town by its setting have meant that Oaxaca has, on the whole, retained the appearance of an historical city. There are impressive old patio houses of one or more storeys, plazas and courtyards resplendent with trees and flowers and the regular, chequerboard layout of streets so typical of Spanish colonial towns in Mexico.

The Valley of Oaxaca has long been an area of human settlement. The best-known of the early settlers were, without a doubt, the Mixtecs and Zapotecs. Extensive archaeological finds have been made at sites such as Monte Albán, Mitla, Yagul, etc., providing clear evidence of the lifestyles and beliefs of these two civilizations.

The beginnings of the town of Oaxaca are usually said to have been laid in 1485, when the Aztec emperor in power at the time, Ahuitzotl, established a military colony there. The task of the soldiers sent to this outpost (it was given the name Huaxcayac, which means "on the nose of the Huajes") was to keep a watch on the activities of the Zapotecs in the region.

In the 1520's (there is some disagreement about the exact date), the settlement was conquered by the Spaniards. Once in Spanish hands, it was given the name Segura de la Frontera (frontier fortification); shortly afterwards, the name was changed to Antequera.

Antequera was officially granted its civic charter in 1532, and fifty years later it was built up as a town proper. In 1782 the Oaxacan Corregimiento was awarded the rank of an "intendencia". The town became the metropolis of a region stretching from the Sierra Madre Occidental to the Pacific. It was the seat of a bishop and the centre of trade and Spanish colonial administration. It was at this time that the town really came to life: a great many buildings sprang up and the population experienced prosperity such as they had never known before. That the town thrived in this way was mainly a result of the export to Spain of cochineal dye.

In the course of the war of independence, Morelos besieged the town of Oaxaca, staying there several months. After the republic was declared, a decree was issued to the effect that the town was to be known officially as Oaxaca de Juárez. This was to honour Benito Juárez, the national leader whose birthplace is in the vicinity. (Porfirio Díaz, the president who ruled Mexico much as a dictator for almost thirty years, also came from Oaxaca.) But it was not only such

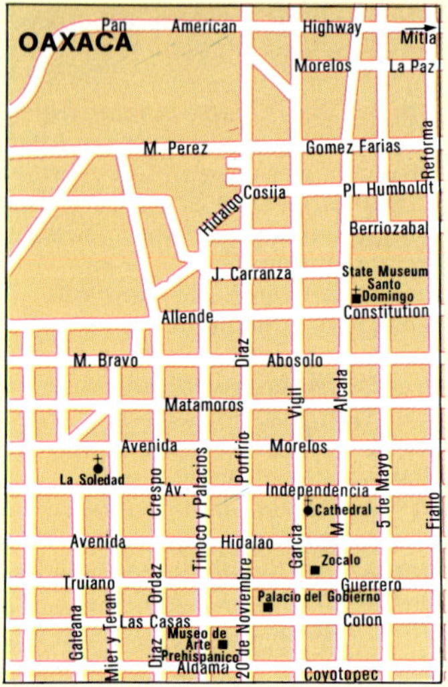

prominent figures who were active politically in this region. The people of Oaxaca also fought bravely in the Mexican revolution and the struggles of the civil war.

The present-day situation in the state of Oaxaca is dictated by problems within the agricultural sector (where traditional methods still predominate) and by the rapid growth of the population. Limited amounts of arable land, high levels of aridity in other areas, and large-scale destruction of land suitable for agriculture by over-exploitation have all contributed to make Oaxaca one of the states with the highest rates of migration to the industrial towns and cities of central Mexico. The daily growth of Mexico City's population is clear evidence of such a migration of the rural population.

Most of Oaxaca's places of interest are concentrated in a fairly small area of the old town. The cathedral and vicinity form the real heart of the town. The cathedral stands at the junction of two of Oaxaca's main streets – the Av. Independencia (runs in an east-west direction) and the Av. C. M. Bustamente. The most interesting buildings and other sights are situated in the area between the following streets: Mier y Teran and Unión in the west, Quetzalcoátl and Berriozabál in the north, Melchor Ocampo and Juárez in the east, and Las Casas and Colón in the south.

The **Zócalo,** which is situated at the junction of Hidalgo and Bustamente directly south of the cathedral, forms the centre of activity in the city. Lined with cafés and always buzzing with activity, this zócalo is considered to be one of Mexico's finest. The **cathedral** of Oaxaca is an impressive building with a baroque façade embellished with bas-reliefs and statues. Construction work began as early as 1544, but it wasn't until the first half of the 18th century that the building was completed. It resembles a basilica with a nave and two side-aisles.

The **Palacio del Gobierno** (del Estado de Oaxaca) stands south of the Zócalo. A Neo-classic building, it dates from the 19th century and is now the seat of Oaxaca's state government. Directly opposite, at the corner of Flores Magón and Guerrero, stands the small church of La Companía. It was built in the

17th century by the Jesuits and has a baroque façade.

Oaxaca's huge public **market** is also located not far from the Palacio del Gobierno, at the corner of Flores Magón and Colón. The many stalls spill out of the main market place and onto surrounding streets. Saturday is the most important day of the week as far as the market is concerned.

Besides those articles we would usually expect to find on a market (fruit and vegetables, hardware, ropes and other supplies for the farming community of the state), you'll find a wonderful range of "artesanía". It is first and foremost the Indians from the surrounding villages who bring such wares to market. Their traditional arts and crafts – pottery and, above all, woven goods – make shopping at the market a delightful experience.

But apart from this, a visit to the market should be considered a "must" for anyone visiting Oaxaca. Just to walk around and see the people of nearby areas in their traditional dress, and so learn something of their way of life, is an experience in itself.

Another "must" is to eat something! A visit to the market would be incomplete without trying some of the delicious, unusual and reasonably-priced snacks available at numerous stalls scattered around the market place.

Moving westwards along the Av. Independencia from the cathedral we come to the church of San Felipe. The church was built in the 17th century and has a baroque façade. Inside, the valuable altar dates from the 18th century. It is carved and gilded.

Further west stands the church of **Nuestra Señora de la Soledad** (Our Lady of Solitude), one of the most impressive buildings in Oaxaca. A flight of wide, limestone steps leads into the courtyard, whence one enters the church itself. Built between 1682 and 1690, the baroque façade of the church is generously embellished with gorgeous relief work. The most imposing aspect of the interior is the shrine of the "Virgen de la Soledad". The Madonna is wearing a unique black velvet robe decorated with semiprecious stones. Maria de la Soledad is the patron saint of Oaxaca.

Other churches in Oaxaca include San Francisco, San Augustín and San Juan de Dios. Although these churches cannot be compared with a magnificent building like Nuestra Señora de la Soledad, if they stood in a town with fewer impressive buildings, each would be sure to receive its fair share of attention. They all date from the 17th and 18th centuries.

Leaving the centre of town in a northerly direction along the 20 de Noviembre, at the crossroads with Morelos Street you find the **Tamayo Museum of Prehispanic Art** (Museo Rufino Tamayo). The museum is housed in a large, Spanish colonial-style building with a wide patio. The famous artist Rufino Tamayo built up a fine private collection of terra-cotta figures stemming from many of Mexico's pre-Hispanic civilizations (some of the articles were found at Monte Albán, for example). He later presented these works to the state of Oaxaca. The collection is not particularly large, but the quality of the individual pieces is truly remarkable.

Again heading northwards, but this time along the Calle 5 de Mayo, we arrive at what is probably Oaxaca's most important "sight", the church of Santo Domingo. Before reaching the church, however, be sure to enjoy a leisurely walk along the fascinating 5 de Mayo. Large, colonial-style buildings line both sides of the road. Their elaborately decorative façades, mainly worked in greenish, "cantera" stone, are clearly the work of master stonemasons. Walls and supporting columns are solidly-built. The intention of the architects and builders was obviously to keep the interiors pleasantly cool in spite of high temperatures outside, but it's also clear that they were aware of the danger of earthquakes in the Valley of Oaxaca. Between 1603 and 1931, fourteen severe earthquakes were recorded in the area – of these, the quakes of 1727 and 1787 were the most destructive.

The **church of Santo Domingo** was built in the second half of the 16th, and early part of the 17th century. It was originally part of a much larger monastery complex. Many of the buildings which made up the latter have now been secularized, and house the State Museum, the Museo del Estado de Oaxaca.

The baroque façade of the church is a massive construction flanked by two 35 m (115 ft) high towers. Despite the enormous proportions of the building, the overall impression one has is of fine detail and a harmonious whole. The church was built in the form of a Latin cross. The interior is resplendent with stuccowork and polychrome murals and is surely one of the masterpieces of Mexican baroque – indeed, some would say of baroque anywhere.

At the entrance to the church there is a piece of stucco relief with an interesting motiv. The relief depicts the genealogical tree of Domingo de Guzman, the Spanish priest who founded the Dominican order of preaching friars. It was the Dominicans who built the church of Santo Domingo. The work of the relief took around three years to complete (1662–1665); the figure of the Virgin Mary was a later addition.

The gilded high altar is the first thing that meets the eye as one enters the church. The paintings and statues which decorate the altar date from the 17th and 18th centuries. The large dome over the intersection of nave and transept features striking geometric designs, paintings and sculptures. Saint Dominic, Saint Francis of Assissi and Saint Thomas Aquinas are among the saints who are depicted.

Unfortunately, the fourteen side altars suffered a great deal when the church was transformed into a stable in 1862. They have now been restored, however, and represent an impressive variety of (architectural) styles.

Built onto the church betwwen 1724 and 1731, the Chapel of the Rosary (Capilla del Rosario) is also shaped like a Latin cross. The dome of the chapel is decorated with painted stuccowork, but the highlight of the interior is without doubt the altar with its richly-gilded statue of the Virgen del Rosario.

Leaving the chapel one enters the cloister of the monastery where the remains of early murals can still be admired.

The rest of the buildings which made up the former monastery nowadays house the State Museum, the **Museo del Estado de Oaxaca.**

The ground floor contains the ethnographic section of the museum. Among the exhibits from the Oaxacan area, there are masks which would formally have been worn (primarily by leading people in a particular village) on the occasion of village "fiestas" and dances, and for celebrations as part of the yearly cycle of cultivation and harvesting.

The upper storey of the museum is devoted to exhibits dating back to pre-colonial times in Mexico, and in particular to items found in the area around Oaxaca. The treasures brought to the museum from the legendary tomb No. 7 at Monte Albán are especially noteworthy. Over 500 examples of Mixtec art (jewellery, etc.) were found in this one tomb alone: it was discovered by Mexican archaeologists in 1932.

There is a small exhibition of religious art in the same building. Guided tours of the museum take place at regular intervals.

While in Oaxaca, it's also well worth making one's way to the outskirts of town and up to the Monumento a la Bandera, the monument to the flag. The monument stands on a hill northwest of town, along State Highway No. 190. It can be reached on foot from Oaxaca, but some might prefer to take a taxi for the trip uphill. From this spot there is a fine view of the whole of the old quarter of town as well as of the western and southern suburbs.

There are a number of "fiestas" and other special events to be enjoyed while staying in Oaxaca.

The so-called "Lunes del Cerro" and the "Guelaguetza" are held on consecutive Mondays at the end of July. Festivities take place on a hill, the Cerro del Fortin de Zaragoza, outside town. The "Guelaguetza", an Indian tradition, is a festival of dances from the seven regions of the state.

Other important dates on the Oaxacan calendar of festivities include: 4th August (Santo Domingo); 31st August (St. Ramón); 22nd–24th October (San Rafael), celebrated in the church of San Juan de Dios; and 16th–18th December ("Virgen de la Soledad").

Christmas celebrations are the highlight of the festive year all over Mexico, and Oaxaca is no exception. "Posadas", processions which take place every night or so from 16th December until Christmas Eve, commemorate the Holy Family's search for lodging. On 23rd December, the "Noche de los Rabanos" (Night of the Radishes!) takes place. This is a kind of competition in which competitors try their skill at carving representations of prominent figures in public life out of giant radishes!

(Schmidt)

Monte Albán

Monte Albán lies just 10 km (6 miles) southwest of the centre of Oaxaca. The drive from town to the site takes around half an hour as the road zigzags its way up the mountain. A public bus makes the journey several times a day.

The **largest ceremonial centre of Zapotec civilization,** Monte Albán (the name means "white hill") is situated on an artificially levelled-off plateau which dominates the

Example of gold jewellery found in Tomb No. 7, Monte Albán

whole valley. The plateau is some 1,830 metres (6,000 feet) above sea level and a good 300 metres (984 feet) above the modern city of Oaxaca. Because of this vantage point, Monte Albán is often referred to as a "fortress". It is clear, however, that the centre never served as a fortification.

The buildings of the cult site stand on a spacious, elongated plaza (the **Great Square,** 200 metres/ 656 feet in length). At the narrow ends of the plaza the buildings extend quite a way from the plaza itself; the extent of the buildings along the longer sides was dictated by the extent of the plateau. The back walls of these structures are flush with the steep slope down to the valley.

The visitor enters the site between the ball court and the eastern side of the north platform. There is a particularly beautiful example of a Zapote tree at this spot. It is now protected by law.

The **north platform** is reached via a long, steep flight of steps. At the summit there is an entrance gallery with immense supporting columns. This gallery leads into a sunken courtyard with an "altar". The shrine stands in a second gallery behind the altar.

Such sunken inner courtyards, characteristic of the architecture of Teotihuacán, are to be found in two further constructions on the plaza at Monte Albán. There are two similar temple pyramids with forecourts on the west side. It is between these two pyramids that the **"Danzantes" complex** is located. The Danzantes (dancers) are one of Monte Albán's most interesting elements. Unusual in very many ways, it is nigh on impossible to find parallels anywhere.

The complex stands on a platform at a height of around 9 metres (almost 30 ft) and consists of a number of chambers grouped around a small courtyard. Several tombs were discovered here, one with a cruciform layout similar to the tombs uncovered at Mitla.

The Danzantes complex clearly belongs to Monte Albán's "younger" buildings, dating from the time when the site had been almost completely abandoned, the time when the Zapotecs were constructing their shrines in the valley below.

The final structure was the result of enlargement upon smaller, existing structures. The exact chronology of the construction has not as yet been conclusively established.

Relief blocks were incorporated into the façade of the building. These appear to have been removed from some previous position to be used here anew – they belong to the very oldest sections of Monte Albán. It is in these reliefs that the Danzantes, the dancers, are depicted.

The "dancers" are grotesque or deformed humans represented in vigorous movement – as if in dance. The disproportionately wide heads of the figures are indicative of the influence of Olmec style. Some of the figures have deformations of the face or genital area. It is not clear what these figures mean or whom they portray. Archaeologists have only been able to ascertain that they are examples of one of the oldest forms of Zapotecan art, a form which obviously received significant stimulus from the Olmecs.

The **south platform** has not yet been fully excavated. An immense creation, the platform rises some 25 m (82 ft) above the plaza.

The group of buildings in the east were built very close together. Consisting mainly of small temple platforms, the group ends in the north with a ball court. The function of one of the buildings, a "palace", has not as yet been clearly established. There are no indications, for example, that the building was ever inhabited. Several chambers are grouped around a sunken inner courtyard. An interesting aspect of the palace is the entrance. This is not axial, but was set to one side, generally a characteristic feature of secular architecture.

From the rear wall of the palace, the view of the valley and the city of Oaxaca is truly magnificent.

A further group of buildings stands in the middle of the plaza. These buildings were built in such a way that their main axes correspond with the four cardinal points. The central platform is accessible from both east and west via wide flights of steps. The steps leading up to the platforms built onto the north and south faces of this central platform face northwards and southwards respectively. The function of the buildings which stood on the summit of the platform remains a mystery. They may well have been temples but a possible connection with a structure further south makes another interpretation feasible. This other structure, known as monticule J, is clearly an observatory. Its main axis lies at an angle exactly 45° east of north, i. e. due northeast; in the interior, there is a tunnel which deviates exactly 17° from due north, this time in a westerly direction. Such precise alignments could well have been used for the purposes of observation of celestial bodies.

Leaving the main ceremonial centre – at best by climbing the terrace of the north platform, crossing its large sunken courtyard and leaving it at the far end – the visitor can continue on into the burial grounds. These are found north of the plaza in an area which was – unlike the rest of the site – not levelled-off. The holy mountain was used as a place of burial once the main religious ceremonies had been transferred to sites down in the valley, and the mountain itself had been abandoned as a place of worship.

The kind of tombs found at Monte Albán took the place of the cave burials previously used by the Zapotecs. Some such tombs were even laid out underneath city palaces; others featured a superstructure, a "house" built above the actual burial chamber but never, of course, inhabited. Such dwelling places for the dead are known to many cultures, and are in keeping with the belief that the deceased are still present in the community and continue to play a part in the lives of the living.

A total of 150 tombs were discovered at Monte Albán. All except one had been plundered at some point in their history. The one exception is the famous Tomb No. 7. The precious objects found in this tomb can be seen today in the State Museum in Oaxaca (in the Santo Domingo Monastery) and are a "must" on any itinerary.

Zaachila-yoo and Cuilapan

The name Zaachila-yoo means place of rule. The ruins of this, the last capital of the Zapotecs, are 18 km (11 miles) south of Oaxaca on State Highway 175. Zaachila was still a seat of government when the Spaniards arrived in Mexico.

There is only a limited number of excavated and reconstructed buildings. The most important structures are **two cruciform tombs,** apparently royal tombs from the period of Mixtec supremacy in Zaachila-yoo.

Not far away from Zaachila-yoo, in the village of Cuilapan, stand the ruins of a monastery dating back to colonial times. The Dominican Order began construction of this extensive monastery complex in 1548. Had it been completed, it would have been the largest monastery in all of New Spain. The basilica is the most impressive of the buildings here. Its façades, inner arcades and corner towers are all in a good state of repair.

With the exception of Monte Albán, the most important centres of Zapotec civilization are located along the highway leading southeast from Oaxaca to Tehuantepec. Leaving Oaxaca on State Highway 190 (which forms part of the Pan-American Highway here), the village of **El Tule** is reached after some 10 km (6 miles). A gigantic cypress tree (or as the Indians call it, "ahuehuete") stands in the village. This is said to be **the oldest tree in all of Mexico.** The height and circumference of its trunk are both around 38 metres (125 ft), and botanists estimate its age to be between 2,000 and 2,500 years.

After another 10 km (6 miles) or so, one arrives at the small town of **Macuilxoxitl.** Recent excavations by Ignacio Bernal have brought to light the same Olmec horizon as is represented in Monte Albán.

Teotitlán del Valle, a centre of Zapotecan sun worship, is situated east of Macuilxoxitl in the direction of the hills. Most of the antique ruins lie buried beneath the present-day village, however, and so have not been excavated as yet. While in Teotitlán del Valle, try to fit in a visit to one of the many factories where sarapes are manufactured. Although they are now produced and sold all over Mexico, it's especially interesting to see the weaving of these large reddish-brown, woollen blankets in a region where it is a traditional craft.

Dainzu and Yagul

Another archaeological site lies just a few kilometres farther along the road, still heading southwards. Dainzu is a little off to the west, but is clearly visible from the road. Excavated as recently as in the seventies, this site was found to consist of a ceremonial centre with temple platform and palace. Its origins can be traced back to the Olmec phase.

Yagul, another site of pre-Hispanic ruins, is east of the main road opposite Dainzu. A visit to this well-excavated and reconstructed site is definitely to be recommended. Evidence provided by finds made here indicates that Yagul was inhabited as early as the period known as Monte Albán I (700–300 B.C.) but didn't experience its heyday until Monte Albán IV, the period which marked the beginning of classic Zapotecan culture. A ball court and two large courtyard complexes have been reconstructed here. Everything points to the fact that the courtyard complexes were secular buildings.

Mitla

After Monte Albán, the most important centre of Zapotec culture was Mitla, also a product of the later period after Monte Albán had already been abandoned and the Zapotecs had moved their centres into the valley. While Zaachila-yoo was the place of secular rule, Mitla was the place of spiritual rule. This is where the Uija-tao, spiritual leader and high priest of the Zapotecs, lived in solitude and strictest seclusion. Politically, he was equal to the king and represented a counter balance to his worldly power.

Five separate building complexes have been identified here, and at least one of them, the **Hall of Columns,** was described by the Spanish chronicler Burgoa. In his account, fact and fantasy blend together in the usual way; nevertheless, it is clear that this building must have been the palace of the Uija-tao. In 1895, the architect Holmes turned his attention to this complex and began its reconstruction. He calculated that the walls of the structure were composed of over 100,000 limestone tiles set in mosaic – a meticulously executed decoration which was reserved for buildings of the utmost importance.

A large sunken courtyard precedes the stairway which leads up to the gallery situated before the palace. The roof of this gallery is supported by columns. The entrance, which is not aligned with the building's axis, opens up onto a hall lined with chambers. The walls of these chambers and of the hall itself are covered with limestone mosaics set in decorative geometric designs: cruciform and rhomboid patterns alternate with "running dogs". Due to the geometric decorations, these rooms are called the

Patios of the Greeks and the Zapotecs have been dubbed "the Greeks of America" – a rather ridiculous comparison. According to Burgoa's account, the Uija-tao not only lived here, but he exercised his office from here as well. He never left the palace; even the king had to come in person to seek his counsel.

In front of this residential wing of the complex lies another hall which, although situated diagonally to this structure, is obviously connected to it. The hall is lined with galleries which do not fulfil any recognizable purpose beyond a decorative one. These were once highly elaborate "house tombs" used for the burial of Zapotec high priests. Here as well, two cross-shaped tombs were found under the galleries – these were obviously collective graves for priests who were buried here one after the other, each one provided with rich grave furnishings. When discovered, these graves had already been plundered and Burgoa's account tells us nothing about them.

A further complex here was used as a "quarry" for the construction of a church, but from the portion which was not torn down but was instead incorporated into the church construction, we can see that it was a galleried hall with intact chambers on three sides. Remains of fresco paintings can be seen here which are thought to represent mythological scenes. Unfortunately, nothing is known about their context.

Tehuantepec

From here, the Pan-American Highway winds its way for another 230 km (143 miles) down through the Oaxacan highlands to the tropical zone along the coast of the Gulf of Tehuantepec, an inlet of the Pacific Ocean. Here on the Gulf there is a giant saltworks for the production of sea salt – once the main source of income for the small town of Tehuantepec. Now, however, another, more profitable industry has set up here: a Pemex refinery – one of the cleanest and most modern in the country – complete with its own shipping port.

Chiapas

The feeling of "not being in Mexico" can easily come over you in Chiapas – even easier than in the Yucatán. The population here is ethnically and culturally attached to that of Guatemala – as the state itself is attached to the country to its east and south. It is not traditionally or naturally a part of Mexico; indeed, the Mexicanization of Chiapas – like that of the Yucatán – was a strenuous and often painful process. It was not until after 1868, the year that saw the end of the War of the Castes (a partly political, partly religious war which broke out in the south in 1839) that the decision was made in favour of Mexico. The deeper-seated reason for the difficulties, however, lay in the fact that the frontiers of the state did not correspond to the frontiers of the area of settlement of the region's native peoples. They had their own interests... and they saw them through as well. Just as the Spanish colonial administration before it, the weak federal government in far-away Mexico City was unable to stand ground.

The territory of the Zoques extended far into the states of Tabasco and Oaxaca; that of the Tzotzil extended to Huetenango in Guatemala. Historic animosities complicated the situation: the Zoques had been loyal to the Aztecs, to whom they paid tribute in the form of valuables – including the highly coveted feathers of the quetzal bird. This loyalty was later transferred to Spanish conquistadores, whom they helped battle the Chiapanecs, a people they saw as a kind of traditional enemy.

Tuxtla Gutiérrez

The capital of the state of Chiapas is Tuxtla Gutiérrez, a relatively new town without a grand past, whose population today is just under 100,000. With an average elevation of 1,200 metres (4,000 feet), it has a pleasantly warm climate and tropical vegetation. Worth visiting is the new, spaciously built **State Museum of Chiapas:** the exhibits of objects found in this region present a cross-section of the cultures whose influence has been felt here at different times in history.

A scenic point of interest in the vicinity is the **Cañón del Sumidero,** a deep canyon formed by the Rio Chiapa located 20 km (about 12 miles) from Tuxtla Gutiérrez. From a natural terrace, you can look down 750 metres (2,500 feet) into the jungle-covered depths of the canyon.

San Cristobal de las Casas

From here, return to the Panamericana, cross the Rio Chiapa and continue east towards the Chiapas Highlands which are clearly visible ahead. After Chiapa de Corzo, the highway begins its serpentine route through these mountains and on to San Cristobal de las Casas, one and a half hours (90 km/56 miles) away. At an elevation of 2,100 metres (7,000 feet), the town enjoys mild, warm temperatures which can drop considerably at night – even in the summer. San Cristobal (population 50,000) is the **Indian capital of the south:** it serves as market place and administrative centre for the region which extends to the Guatemalan border at Ciudad Cuauhtémoc or the Usumacinta River in the lowlands. The fact that this region is home to the Tzotzil people can be seen quite clearly in the streets of San Cristobal. Two main groups are distinguishable by their traditional dress: the Chamulas and the Zinancantecs. They come in large numbers to the San Cristobal market from their villages in the vicinity.

San Cristobal de las Casas was founded by Diego de Mazariego in 1528, immediately following the conquest of the region by the Spaniards. The city was initially given the name Ciudad Real or "Royal City". This Mazariego was certainly one of the worst characters to have floated ashore with the rest of the flotsam and jetsam of the Spanish conquest. After breaking with Cortés, he headed south to seek his fortune at all costs. Once in the territory of the highland Mayas, however, he met with a great deal of unexpected resistance: the Tzotzil people evidently had a rather clear picture of what lay ahead and understandably had little desire to be forced into slavery or murdered. Indeed, Mazariego killed off all the people who refused to be enslaved and acquired a reputation as a slave hunter and slaughterer of Indians – a reputation, incidentally, which carried as far as Spain. The sadistic methods he and his rabble employed were also known about.

This was the subject taken up by Fray Bartolomé de las Casas, a priest who had taken part in one of Columbus' later voyages (1502) and who had been fighting for the cause of Indian rights since the beginning of the Conquest. In the colonies, where he held many different offices, as well as in Spain, where he had access to Charles V, he pleaded his case intelligently and vociferously and denounced the atrocities which were being perpetrated in the colonies in the name of God and the Spanish crown. He was responsible for the institution of legislation meant to guarantee humane treatment for the Indians, but needless to say, these laws were never taken seriously. De las Casas made enemies – very powerful ones, in fact, such as the doctor Sepulveda, who was the chief intercessor for the conquistadores at court. The priest triumphed over Sepulveda on all intellectual battlefields, however, and the doctor's writings were even confiscated by the Inquisition. Nevertheless, this did but little to help the Indians. The greed of all those involved was too great, and the Spanish crown let financial interests have the upper hand even though it was aware of the deeply immoral, unchristian and criminal acts being committed in the colonies.

In 1544, after having turned down the office of Bishop of Cuzco, de las Casas became Bishop of Ciudad Real. Here, this great man continued fighting for the Indians until, embittered, he retired to a monastery near Madrid in 1557 where he died in 1566 at the age of 92. A monument was raised to him in the form of an entire city – "his" city, Ciudad Real – which was later renamed after him. The church in which he served is still in good condition today.

The greatest attraction for visitors to San Cristobal de las Casas, however, is its **market,** which is open daily except Sundays, It is not so much the assortment of goods offered for sale, but the assortment of people found inside and outside its doors that makes this covered market so fascinating. You, the stranger, will find yourself observed by people of the various Tzotzil tribes (all distinguishable by their dress) with a mixture of suspicion, disapproval and indifference.

From San Cristobal de las Casas, you can make half-day excursions to **Chamula** (10 km/6 miles) and **Zinancantan** (12 km/7.5 miles). These villages should only be visited, though, in the company of a guide who is known to their inhabitants. Upon arrival, you should first visit the office of the "presidente" which will have to issue you a visitor's permit and permission to take pictures. Here, you will also be informed of general rules and regulations, and these should be strictly adhered to! The villagers are becoming more and more allergic to touists and problems can easily arise where there is a camera in sight.

San Cristobal is also an ideal starting point for day-long excursions to Bonampak and Yaxchilan, both of which have landing strips which can accomodate sports planes.

Bonampak

"Place of the Painted Walls" was the name given belatedly to Bonampak after the American Healey discovered, in 1946, the frescos which made it famous. The ruins had actually been found a few months earlier by Carlos Frey, an American who lived among the Lacandons of Ocosingo and therefore had contact with those living in the Lacandon Forest. A small clan of Lacandons from that area traditionally made pilgrimages to a ruin which they considered sacred to the old gods. Out of friendship, Chan Bor, the high priest of the clan, took Frey along on one of these pilgrimages, and thus the location of the site became known.

Bonampak lies 170 km (106 miles) "as the crow flies" from San Cristobal and can be reached in about 40 minutes. Planes fly only in fair weather because of the danger posed by the mountainous terrain. Overland, Bonampak can be reached only under the greatest of difficulties. The site, which has not yet been completely excavated, is situated amidst the wild and romantic entanglement of the tropical rainforest; the climate is hot and damp. It is a rather small centre – not to be compared with the enormous complex of Yaxchilán on the Usumacinta River only 60 km (37 miles) away.

This cult centre features very little free-standing temple architecture; rather, it consists of a plaza measuring about 70 x 120 metres (230 x 400 feet), the surface of which was once covered with lime plaster. This plaza, which is flanked on two sides by unexcavated structures, was used for the erection of stelae: sadly only a few poorly preserved specimens of these remain. The actual ceremonial complex is situated in terraces on a natural hill which can be ascended via a stairway measuring 120 metres (400 feet) across. Atop the terrace stand two chambered temples; the famous frescos cover the walls of three adjacent chambers in the one on the right. Unfortunately, they were improperly cleaned after their discovery, and are now in a miserable state as a result of dampness and mildew. Attempts at restoring the frescos to their former brilliance and perfection have failed: it must be assumed that these paintings from the Classic Maya period have now been lost forever. Today, if you look closely (through the grating which has been put up), you can see only a few blurred figures. Fortunately, on the other hand, good colour photographs were taken in time, from which a life-sized model of the chambers containing the frescos was made which now stands in the garden of the Museum of Anthropology in Mexico City. Only by looking at this model is it possible to recognize and understand the context of these magnificent, high-quality frescos, which depict an almost dramatic series of events.

In the first chamber, we see a convocation of dignitaries in rich attire surrounding a ruler or high priest sitting upon a throne. They are obviously assembled to discuss the preparations for the events depicted in the following frescos.

The second chamber shows a wild battle scene in which the members of the two warring parties are clearly distinguishable by their attire: the victorious warriors from Bonampak are noticeably better dressed than their enemies. Prisonors have also been taken, some of whom are being tortured and killed (as sacrifices?).

The third chamber on the right side of the structure obviously shows a victory celebration complete with singers and dancers.

An exact study of the levels of construction has never been undertaken in Bonampak, but the visible buildings have been dated between A. D. 700 and the period of Mayan decline after A. D. 900.

Yaxchilán

While little interest exists in the further excavation and study of Bonampak, neighbouring Yaxchilán presents a completely different case. For years now this immense archaeological site in the central Maya zone has been the object of a large-scale excavation campaign organized by the INAH.

As was often the case, the discovery of these ruins in the impenetrable vegetation of the Lacandon Forest was an accident. In 1881, the surveyor Edwin Rockstroh reported that he had discovered architectural remains submerged under jungle growth. Intrigued by this information, Teobert Mahler came here to make drawings, ground plans and even photographs. It was not until the 1930's, however, when Sylvanus G. Morley turned his attention to these ruins, that they were finally explored in depth. Yaxchilán was discovered to be **the most extensive Maya site on Mexican territory** and certainly equal in importance to the great sites of the Petén.

It was soon noticed that in Yaxchilán there were strikingly many inscriptions on buildings and stelae. It was suspected – and has since been confirmed – that these might have historic content. The glyph expert T. Proskouriakoff of the Carnegie Institute has succeeded in deciphering parts of the inscriptions: they contain information about historic events, geneologies and rulers, all in combination with dates. From these glyphs we have learned that Yaxchilán experienced its heyday and period of greatest political strength in the 8th century. The names of the most important rulers have been deciphered as "Shield Jaguar", "Bird Jaguar" and "Bat Jaguar". The dates have been borne out by studies of the various styles of architectural sculpture and of the layers of ceramics found. Like all Maya cities, this one slowly declined: right at the heels of its golden age came its period of decline. The city finally fell around the year A. D. 900.

The area of the city that has been explored thus far extends along the Usumacinta River and southwest into the jungle for about 600–700 metres (a third of a mile). As in other Maya cities situated in similar surroundings, building complexes here are located on artificial terraces connected to each other by roadway embankments. The terminology is standard: building complexes are known as acropolises and the embankments are called causeways.

The building complexes that extend along the river bank seem to have fulfilled secular functions. Here, there are a number of adjacent platforms and small buildings closed in by two ball courts. At the western end of the site stands a building the function of which remains a mystery. This complex is known as **The Labyrinth** on account of its intricate system of stairways, chambers and terraces. Perhaps it could be interpreted as a municipal building, the seat of the temple administration.

Three hundred metres (1,000 feet) inland from this point is the **Western Acropolis,** a well-preserved temple complex the excavation and restoration of which have not yet been completed. The most striking features uncovered thus far are the lintels made of finest-quality limestone and decorated extensively with glyphs and depictions of human and mythical beings.

Deep in the jungle stands the **Southern Acropolis,** an immense and lofty temple complex which was probably not in regular use but was reserved for special ceremonial occasions.

At the geographic centre of the site stands what is probably the most important, magnificent and richly decorated building here: Structure 33, also known as the **Palace of the Kings** – a misleading name as the building's architectural style is clearly that of a temple. This monumental structure, the base of which measures 22 metres (73 feet) across, stands on a levelled-off hilltop. The stairway extends up past three platforms to the three entrances which lead into a narrow, seven-chambered room with corbelled vaults. The sides and lintels of the doors are decorated with date glyphs, inscriptions and depictions of mythological creatures in relief. The temple's most striking feature is its crown or "cresteria" – with a height of 7 metres (23 feet), it is just as tall as the temple façade. With a total height of 14 metres (46 feet), this structure rises above the canopy of trees and presents an overwhelming sight when viewed from the river. The temple roof is decorated with over 100 niches which, as countless remains have shown, once contained spherical sculptured figures. This decoration is repeated in the cresteria, which contains eight rows of window-like perforations creating the effect of finely-worked and highly ornamental filigree. The cresteria frames a large niche which rises up the entire height of 7 metres (23 feet). The figure it once held is now kept in the temple interior to protect it: it is an enthroned human figure which probably represents the god Hachakyum, who is frequently mentioned in texts appertaining to the statue. The head of this statue, along with the impressive headdress it bore, is missing – a fact which has special significance for the Lacandons who come to Yaxchilán year after year to honour the gods. They believe that if the head and the body of the statue are reunited, the world will come to an end, and they are convinced that this will one day come to pass. Then jaguars will descend from the heavens and destroy mankind.... *(Thieme)*

Useful Information

Currency

The standard monetary unit of Mexico is the peso ($). This is divided into 100 centavos. The peso sign is often confused with the US$ sign. If in any doubt, ask before making your purchase. You may also find certain prices given in m. n., which means "moneda nacional".

For the present rate of exchange, see separate, fold-out map. Due to constant fluctuations in the value of the peso, it is always best to enquire immediately before your departure.

Currency Control

At the moment there is no limit on the amount of currency – Mexican or foreign – which may be brought into or taken out of the country.

There are limitations, however, on how many dollars you may buy back when leaving the country, so don't buy more pesos than you will realistically need.

Traveller's Cheques, etc.

On the whole, your best bet is probably to take along U. S. dollars, either as cash or in the form of traveller's cheques. Banks, bureaux de change and larger hotels will, of course, be willing to change other foreign currencies, but you'll find that you often receive a better rate of exchange for the dollar. Although the peso is the only legal tender in Mexico, the dollar has in some ways assumed the function of a second currency – a clear indication of the important role played by Mexico's northern neighbour both in tourism and in the Mexican economy in general.

Whichever currency you have with you, it's definitely advisable to go to a bank or official exchange office to buy pesos since they always offer better rates than hotels, etc.

As always, tourists should be aware of the dangers involved in carrying too much ready cash on their person. Traveller's cheques or credit cards are a far safer and better bet. Traveller's cheques can sometimes be used to purchase goods – providing, of course, that identity can be proven.

Those wishing to frequent smaller guest houses and "cantinas" should bear in mind, however, that a credit card will not hold much weight there – nor will traveller's cheques be of much use.

While on the subject of ready cash, the most important Mexican coin is without doubt the 20-centavo coin, the "veinte". You'll need this everywhere – among other things, for coin-operated telephones and parking meters.

You should have no problem changing traveller's cheques issued by any international bank – as always, American banks (Chase Manhattan, Bank of America, etc.) are probably the best proposition.

The leading international credit cards (American Express, Diners Club, Eurocard/Master Charge, Visa, Carte Blanche, etc.) will be accepted by all larger hotels, businesses and restaurants, airlines and car hire firms and up-market bars.

Entry Formalities

In recent years, and as one of a series of moves to encourage tourism, the Mexican government has simplified the requirements made of visitors to the country.

Most people now need only a valid passport and tourist card to enter "Méjico". The tourist card can be obtained (on production of a valid passport) from a Mexican consulate, a Mexican Government Tourist Office, any airline which flies to Mexico or any tour operator serving Mexico.

The tourist card is issued free of charge. It is made out in duplicate and both copies must be stamped by the border police on your arrival in Mexico. The officials retain one copy of the document; you keep hold of the other until you leave Mexico.

Tourist cards are valid for a maximum of 180 days. As a rule they are issued for the desired length of stay in Mexico. If you intend to stay for the full six months, make sure that this is specified on the form as you may find that it's bothersome and time-consuming to apply for an extension once in Mexico.

Technically speaking, US citizens do not need a passport to visit Mexico. Besides their tourist card they need only proof of citizenship – often easiest with a passport, but a birth certificate or voter's registration card would suffice. Foreign nationals permanently resident in the U. S. should inquire at a Mexican Consulate or Government Tourist Office about entry requirements.

U. S. and Canadian citizens do not need a tourist card for border visits lasting less than 72 hours.

Motoring into Mexico

Anyone crossing the U. S.-Mexican border in a private vehicle must obtain a car permit from the Mexican authorities. This will be issued upon presentation of the vehicle's registration card and proof of ownership or authorization. Vehicle and permit holder must leave the country at the same time; the permit is then returned to the Mexican authorities. If for any reason the permit holder has to fly home, the vehicle must be left in the custody of the Mexican Federal Vehicle Registry.

U. S. and Canadian insurance is not valid in Mexico; short-term insurance policies are available at most border crossing points (all compensation is paid in Mexican pesos).

Vaccinations, etc.

Vaccination certificates are no longer required for a holiday in Mexico.

Malaria prophylactics are recommended, however, especially if you intend to spend a longer period of time in the humid swamps of Tabasco or Veracruz.

Typhus prophylactics are also recommended for extended stays in rural areas. Do keep in mind that one must allow a week between courses of tablets and should therefore begin the course of treatment well ahead of one's departure date – usually around three weeks beforehand. Ask your own doctor or enquire at the Department of Health.

Cases of infectious hepatitis still crop up. Again, ask your doctor about possible precautionary measures.

Health Precautions

Change of diet, change of altitude, too much of the good things in life... there are many things which can lead to an upset stomach and even diarrhoea. It would be wrong to make light of something which could easily ruin your vacation, but on the other hand, worrying too much about what you eat and drink will probably make you even more susceptible to stomach upsets. There are a few simple precautions you can take, however.

Don't drink unpurified water. Hotels usually purify the water as a matter of course – this will be labelled "agua purificada". Otherwise you will find that bottled water is readily available.

If buying from street vendors it's as well to keep to bottled drinks and to enjoy them without ice cubes.

Medical Care

It's definitely a good idea to take along a few basic medical supplies, including perhaps something for the dreaded diarrhoea. Anyone who takes a medicament on a regular basis should of course bring along sufficient supplies for the duration of the holiday. Mexico's pharmacies, "farmacias", are well-stocked with modern medicines. Most medicaments (including antibiotics but excluding tranquilizers) are available over the counter.

Larger hotels, and especially those with a high proportion of international guests, will definitely have the name and address of a doctor who regularly treats foreign visitors in case of emergency. Most of these doctors will speak at least a little English.

You'd be well-advised to take out some form of health insurance for the duration of your stay in Mexico.

Language

Spanish is Mexico's national language. In the tourist centres, however, you'll find that English is spoken fairly widely.

In Mexico City there are special tourist police who speak English well and are there to help any tourists who have "gone astray". They wear badges in Mexico's national colours and are therefore easy to recognize.

Electricity Supply

110–125 volts, alternating current. Plugs in Mexico are the same as those found in the United States.

In better hotels, adaptors can usually be hired (for a nominal fee); in more rural areas, they are not so easy to come by.

Opening Hours

Shops usually open at 9 am. Many close for a "siesta" from 1 or 2 pm until 4 pm. The business day then ends at around 7.30 pm.
Banks are open Mondays to Fridays from 9 am until 1.30 pm.
Public Offices are open from around 9 am to 2 pm, and from 4 pm to 6 pm. ("Important" people rarely appear before 10 or 11 am!)
Post Offices are open Mondays to Fridays from 9 am to 7 pm, on Saturdays from 9 am to 5 pm.

Telephone

Local phone calls in Mexico are very reasonably priced, the standard charge being 20 centavos (for public phone boxes you'll need 20-centavo coins).

Long-distance calls can only be made from post office, private or hotel phones.

International calls via satellite are, as a rule, put through quickly and without difficulty but are heavily taxed and therefore very expensive.

Clothing

The kind of clothes you should take along with you depends upon which area of Mexico you will be visiting, as well as upon the time of year you choose to travel.

As a general rule, light cotton and other natural fibres are suitable all year round in Yucatán and the Pacific resorts (in the summer months, an umbrella or light raincoat is a useful addition). In the central highlands (including Mexico City) and the north, warmer, woollen clothes are a must, especially if travelling in the winter months.

Generally-speaking, the same rules of dress apply in Mexico as at home. And, as always, the golden rule is to try to fit in with local customs as much as possible.

Beach resorts are geared to tourism, so more freedom and phantasy in the choice of clothing is possible here. Once away from the beaches and hotel swimming-pools, however, one should dress more conservatively. Ladies do not generally walk around in shorts on the streets. Nude and topless bathing are not the Mexican way to enjoy the sun.

Good, comfortable shoes are an absolute must when visiting archaeological sites. The same goes for museums, where visitors can easily clock up quite a few miles!

Good sunglasses and some kind of headgear will afford protection from the hot Mexican sun.

Tipping

The power of the "propina"... Tipping can make the impossible possible, and can speed up the possible considerably!

In the service sector, wages (and therefore costs) are based upon the assumption that those employed will receive tips from customers. Tips should therefore be seen as part of their earned income and not merely as a gesture on the part of the satisfied customer.

It's difficult to arrive at fixed rates. Waiters usually receive approximately 15% of the total bill, taxi drivers between 10 and 15% depending upon the fare (unless, that is, you agreed upon a final price before setting off). As a rule, chambermaids receive the equivalent of US$ 3 per week per person, porters between 50 cents and US$ 1 per large piece of luggage.

Photography

Every tourist is allowed to bring one camera and one film camera for his personal use into the country. In addition, 12 films per camera are excluded from duty.

You'd be well-advised to bring a good supply of spare film with you. Not only are prices of film in Mexico considerably higher than at home, but you may also find that, while standard sizes of film are fairly widely available, more specialized requirements cannot be met.

There are certain restrictions governing photography in museums, public buildings, archaeological sites and monuments. For the tourist this means that, in order to take photographs with a tripod and flash, or to film with a 16 mm movie camera, he has to obtain a special permit. Apply to:
Instituto Nacional de Antropologia e Historia
Cordoba 45
Mexico D.F.
Tel. 511-08-44

Time Zones
Most of Mexico is in the North American Central Standard Time zone, which is six hours behind Greenwich Mean Time. Along the west coast, from a point just north of Puerta Vallarta northwards to the state of Sinalco, and in the southern half of Baja California, Mountain Standard Time is observed (seven hours behind G. M. T.). The northern half of Baja California is in the Pacific Standard Time zone (eight hours behind G. M. T.). There is no system of daylight saving in the summer months in Mexico.

Safeguarding Personal Property
In Mexico's larger towns and cities, and above all in Mexico City, you unfortunately have to reckon with the same kind of theft and petty criminality now found worldwide. In Mexico City there are organized groups of youths who live by picking pockets and snatching handbags. As one might expect, apparently affluent tourists have become quite a lucrative target for such bands.

The risk of being robbed is particularly high in public transport. Women have proven to be at greater risk than men. Wearing eye-catching jewellery, obviously expensive watches, etc. makes a person an obvious target and should be avoided. Only carry as much ready cash as you need at a particular time, and keep this in a money belt if possible. Larger sums of money, cheques, passport, plane tickets, jewellery, etc. are best kept in the hotel safe. Do not leave them lying around in hotel rooms while you are out.

Customs
Tourists may take the following duty-free into Mexico: 50 cigars or 250 g pipe tobacco or 200 cigarettes; 2 bottles of spirits; all items for personal use during their stay.

A camera and a video or movie camera (and 12 films) may be taken into Mexico. They must be declared on arrival, however, and produced on departure if required. Duty must be paid on electronic equipment.

Generally-speaking, customs checks are waived for tourists except for spot checks, or when the authorities suspect contraband.

Tourists are not allowed to bring arms, drugs, pornographic material, plants or foodstuffs of any kind (including chocolate and tinned foods) into the country.

It is illegal to take arms, drugs and antiques out of Mexico.
Please note:

In accordance with the "Convention on International Trade in Endangered Species of Wild Fauna and Flora" **(CITES),** you should make a point of not buying souvenirs, the production of which involves the use of wild animals or wild flowers.

In Mexico's case this applies to tortoiseshell, black coral, various kinds of shells, certain species of butterfly and snail, stuffed baby crocodiles, cat skins, shells of turtles or tortoises, live or dead tortoises, live or dead boas and iguanas (lizard skins!), live or dead parrots (often offered to tourists as nestlings), bird spiders and cacti. Cacti should never be dug up without special permission.

Please do refrain from buying souvenirs of this kind. In doing so you will be making an important contribution to the preservation of endangered animals and plants (and you may well save yourself a lot of unnecessary expense and bother at customs at home – many countries ban the import of such items).

As well as the statutory personal exemption for U. S. citizens returning home from a vacation, a Generalized System of Preferences (GSP) exists whereby many articles (including arts and crafts, jewellery, certain kinds of leather goods) can be imported duty-free over and above the normal personal exemption.

Getting Out and About

Taxis

In Mexico's larger cities there are a number of different kinds of taxis with varying tarifs. The cheapest of them is the "pesero", a group taxi which sticks to fixed routes and charges a fixed fare. A wave suffices to hail one of these, and they generally continue to stop for passengers until they are full.

Regular taxis can either be flagged down or picked up at a taxi stand. These taxis are called "sitios". Although most of them have a meter, not much attention can be paid to it as fares are continually being adjusted to keep up with the inflation rate and rising gasoline prices. Current fares are published, however, and can be seen upon request. As a rule it is a good idea to ask about the fare or to fix a price before setting off.

Radio taxis, which can be ordered from your hotel, are more expensive than taxis which are hailed on the street.

"Hotel taxis", limousines not identified as taxis, can be found in front of the larger hotels. These are the most expensive, but also the most reliable, type of taxi. Their drivers speak English and one can be absolutely sure that they are trustworthy (as a final precaution, the hotel's porter makes a note of their arrival and departure). These taxis can be rented by the hour, the half-day, or the day in order to make excursions, and their drivers are often able to act as guides as well. Frequently, fixed prices for such excursions are posted in the hotel: in any case, it is a good idea to discuss the trip's cost with the driver beforehand. Obviously, the limousines are a particularly suitable means of transport for women travelling alone or for tourists who have no knowledge of Mexico and can't speak a word of Spanish.

Car Hire

Cars can be rented in all of the larger cities and at airports. An international credit card must be produced, as well as a valid driver's licence. An international driver's licence is recommendable, but not necessary.

In view of the speed at which rates change to keep up with inflation, there is no point in listing prices current at the time of publication.

A few things to bear in mind should you rent a car: Make sure the car is in good condition and that any damage to its body has been accurately recorded. Find out if the car can be dropped off at no additional cost at another branch of the same company. Don't forget to take out insurance! It is unwise to pick up hitchhikers in Mexico, or to drive at night: in case of a breakdown after dark it is unlikely that anyone will stop to help you.

If you are intending to rent a car in Mexico, it is worth enquiring about special tourist rates, such as the Avis "Mexico Package Ride".

Bus

In Mexico the bus is the most popular means of travel, both for long and short distances. Hundreds of national as well as local bus lines provide the country with an exemplary transportation network. Virtually no road is too narrow, no village too remote to be serviced by a bus of one kind or another.

Of interest to the tourist are the long-distance connections – well-equipped buses that leave hourly from most big cities in the direction of all major centres.

Every place has at least one bus station. The capital city has four, now located on the outskirts in an attempt to minimize the chaos caused by the frequent arrivals and departures. Each of these is named (logically) after the direction in which buses departing from it drive:

Central Camionera del Norte (North Station), Av. de los Cien Metros;

Central Camionera del Sur (South Station), Av. Taxquena;

Central Camionera del Oriente (East Station), Av. Zaragoza;

Central Camionera Poniente (West Station), Av. Sur (Colonia Tacubaya).

Buses heading towards Yucatán leave from the East Station (C. C. del Oriente).

The stretch from the U. S. border to Mexico City is well-serviced by lines such as Chihuahuenses, Omnibuses de México, and Continental Trailways. Bookings on any of these can be made either in the U. S. or in Mexico. Buses on the routes from border towns direct to the capital have two drivers and generally stop only briefly every couple of hours. Several classes of service are available: the better the class, the faster the bus. Tourists are probably best off in the "primera clase" or "de lujo", which offers not only the newest, most powerful buses, but also stewardess service and refreshments.

Although the constant devaluation of the peso along with a general increase in prices has sent bus fares spiralling upwards, bus travel continues to be relatively economical.

In the cities, at least, the buses leave at frequent, regular intervals and no reservation is necessary. It is advisable, however, to be at the